FROM THE
BEGINNING
ONWARDS

BY

JOHN ROBINSON

VOLUME I

1935 – 1979

love and
Hilary
+

This story is for my grandchildren
Charlotte, Lucy, William, Sam, Kimberley, Harry, Amber

and dedicated to all those who have shared my
Extraordinary Journey

my loving companion
Margie

and
Fellow Travellers

Alan
Allan
AnnaA
AnnaC
Ben
Damon
David
Enzo
Fabio
Georgina
Jimmy
Jean
Mario
Mike
Pat
Peter
Richard
Robert
Ron
Ronnie
Roy
Tim

my sons

Tim - Peter - Mark

and with
loving memory
of

Bill and Nan
Nana

III

First published 2005 by
Edition Limitée,
Geneva,
Switzerland

Volume I   ISBN   0-9549833-0-0
Volume II   ISBN   0-9549833-1-9
Volume III   ISBN   0-9549833-2-7

Typeset in 12pt Garamond.
Typesetting and origination by
Edition Limitée, Geneva.
Printed and bound in England by
J.H. Haynes & Co. Ltd, Sparkford
www.haynes.co.uk

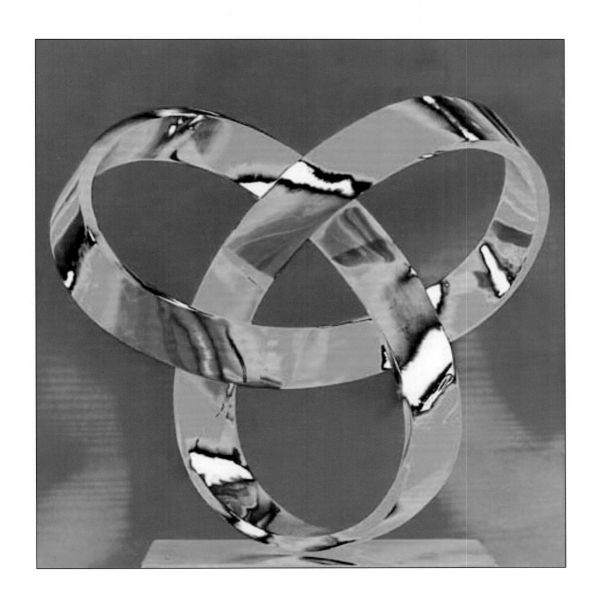

IMMORTALITY

V

CONTENTS

Volume I

INTRODUCTION p 3 – 4, Roses 3, Title 4

SUMMARY p 5 – 12,
School 5, Fabio 5, *Hula Hula* 5, Merchant Navy 6, Farm 6, Sculpting 7, England 8, Mancini 8, Wakeford 9, Crowther 10, Plazzotta 10, Freeland Gallery 11, Brown 11, Damon 11, RIII 11, Benbassat 11, *Blue Madonna* 12, Hippocrates 12

FIRST DECADE p 13 – 58

Memories 13, WS Grandfather, Churchill 19, Evacuation to Australia 24, London 36, Farnborough Air Show 41, Chute Standen farm 43, Sandroyd School 53

SECOND DECADE p 59 – 124

Rugby School 59, Fabio Barraclough 63, France 65, Rugby School Reunion 66, Madeira 71, Anne-Françoise 76, Port Napier 77, Arrival 81, Roseworthy 86, Rosalyn 89, Professor Hedley Marston 90, Kimberley 98, Police 100, Lommel 106, GoGo 114

THIRD DECADE p 125 – 202

New Zealand 122, Ninety Mile Desert 126, Chute 129, Margie 134, Wedding 147, Tim 160, Peter 165, Mark 173, Boys 175, Father dies 181, Hoyle 135, Clay 188, Hot Day 193

FOURTH DECADE p 203 – 450

England 195, Jimmy Smart 199, Marwood Hill 207, Mancini 211, *Françoise Gilot* 215, Paris 220, Roy Wakeford 228, Chelsea Flower Show 231, Plazzotta 235, *Hammer Thrower* 240, Fred Kobler 245, Sir Maurie Mawby 247, Joseph Hirshhorn 248, Greece 251, Knossos 261, Mycenae 267, Delphi 270, Corfu 273, *Acrobats* 275, *Banbury* 280, Crash 282, Araganui 291, Agecroft 293, Royal Academy 295, Damon 297, Lindsay Fox 299, Lassie 302, *Children* 306, Erica 317, Lilly 321, Michael Ball 322, Danaide 324, *Shorthorn Bull* 329, Niagara Falls 330, Webers 330, Hobe Sound 333, USSA 339, Peg Newman 342, Grand Traverse 345, Sailing 353, Shedo 356, Demark 357, Hoshi 360, Surry 373, Rubber Duck 363, Golden Jubilee 365, *Queen Mother* 366, *Elizabeth II* 369, *Bonds of Friendship* 373, Italy 377, *Papageno* 378, *Flying Horse* 380, Fascination 382, Enzo 385, Etruscans 389, Paestum 393, Rome 394, Renaissance 396, *North Cadbury Church* 398, Michelangelo 402, Florence 405, Venice 410, Aubusson 416, *Universe* 420, Wells Cathedral 425

Volume II

FIFTH DECADE p 451 – 618

Beaver Galleries 451, Canberra 454, Lausanne 461, Sweden 462, Honeywell 466, *Transcend* 469, Petra 471, Kuwait 481, Ayers Rock and Olgas 482, Freeland 489, Henry Moore 489, Joanna Harding 492, Opening 493, Anna Coyle 494, Mensing 496, Ronnie Brown 498, R III 499, Aspen 502, Mapuche 505, Matisse 508, Coyote Trail 516, Peter's Lion 522, Harvard 535, Webb 536, MeiLi 537, Mount Agnes 541, Spiders 548, Base camp 551, Quizzical 554, Swimming Pool 556, Ascent 557, Borya 559, Spaceman 563, Strange paintings 564, King George 565, Sadex Swans 567, *Symbolic Sculptures Book* 573

SIXTH DECADE p 619 – 704

De Laszlo Expedition 619, McCubbins 619, Green Ants 622, Medals 625, Grahame Walsh 629, Robert and Charles 631, Hann River 632, Moon 636, Cathedral 643, Bradshaws 644, Indian File 646, Bradshaw 649, Drysdale 651, Borya 656, Paradise Pools 661, Bigge Island 665, Dancers 671, The Book 676, Paris 678, Flynn 684, Isaac Newton 689, Coxeter 690, Aspen Intuition 692, Gates 697, Martin Rees 699, The Globe 701

SEVENTH DECADE p 705 – 904

Diving 705, Seals 706, Cayman Brac 707, Madinina 709, Pyrenees Niaux 711, Trois Freres 717, Le Portel 721, Lascaux 723, Easter Island 727, Atacama 727, Mapuche 729, Rapa Nui 731, Kon Tiki 734, Double Canoes 739, Moai 740, Festival 742, Anakena 744, Orongo 748, Rano Raraku 752, Marathon 757, Chronology 765, Imagine 767, Brazil 771, Santa Catarina 771, Santinho 774, Campeche Island 776, *Adam and Eve* 789, Arvoredo Island 791, Coral Island 794, Wild Children 797, Samarkand 799, Registan 801, Bokara 803, Samanid 810, Tashkent 814, China 815, Beijing 816, Forbidden City 821, Jane Yang 823, Xian 825, Warriors 826, Qin Shihuang 829, The Forest Stele 831, Chungking 833, Hangchow 837, Shanghai 839, Harvard 843, Chauvet Cave 845, 1st Day 848, Altar 860, Holy of Holies 864, 2nd Day 868, Story teller 871, *Computer Paintings* 873

Volume III

SEVENTH DECADE p 903 – 1222

Brancusi 903, Avenue of Heroes 906, Creed Ride 911, Aspen Institute 913, Bozeman 916, Emerald Ranch 917, RIII Thebes 927, Pyramids 930, Sphinx 934, King's Chamber 916, Museum 940, Saqqara 942, Sunset 945, Dendera 947, King's Valley 952, Nefertari 956, Tomb Plan 958, Kheruef 962, Ramesseum 966, Memnon 968, Karnak 972, White Chapel 973, Hypostyle 975, Sailing 977, Tuc 979, Bison 982, Sahara 987, Dabous Giraffe 993, Mould 995, Moonlight 1003, Tenere 1007, Arakua 1012, Madonna 1018, Cast 1019, Egypt with Damon 1023, Red Pyramid 1027, Fefi 1030, Lion 1032, Karnak 1035, Dendera 1040, King's Valley 1045, Nefertari 1049, Birthday Party 1053, Grand Canyon 1055, Stromatalites 1061, Little Colorado 1064, Anasazi 1066, Lava Rapids 1073, Cancer 1078, Sonnenschein 1078, New York City 1080, Frick 1086, Boston 1091, Twin Towers 1092, Tufts University 1092, Cape Cod 1095, Whales 1100, Airport 1103, Madrid 1105, Chauvet II 1113, *Madonna* 1137, Pietrasanta 1138, Eyes 1139, Prague 1141, Michelangelo 1143, Donatello 1145, Durer 1146, Agecroft 1147, Celts 1149, Stonehenge 1149, Avebury 1152, Silbury 1154, Horses 1159, Giant 1160, Sardinia Corsica 1161, Carnac 1166, Jersey 1168, Ireland 1170, Scotland 1177, Cornwall 1188, Malta 1191, Hypogeum 1197, *Hokusai Wave* 1213

EPILOGUE p 1223 – 1302

Crow's Nest 1224, Shells 1228, Dusty Blue 1231, Nautilus 1237, Slime Mould 1239, mtDNA 1243, Epicurus 1245, Nanobes 1247, Math Magic 1248, Utopia 1251, Monet 1256, Villefranche 1257, Pont du Gard 1258, Cordoba 1259, Granada 1261, Bayeux 1262, Oslo 1263, Silk 1268, She 1270, Dogs 1274, Holcombe 1275, Birds 1278, Agecroft 1284, Fossils 1289, Pikaia 1294, Toba 1295, Salt Mines 1299

GATHERING FLOWERS p 1302 – 1324

Jung 1302, Van der Post 1312, Quotations 1316, Martin Rees 1326, Lucian Samosata 1328

Index of Thumbnail Photographs at close of each Volume

What did you feel like when you turned 70?

As though I had just run a 100 yard sprint!

What do you plan to do now?

Collapse on the grass and try to get my breath back!

QUALIS AB INCEPTO

FROM THE BEGINNING ONWARDS

BY

JOHN ROBINSON

1935 – 2005

1

INTRODUCTION

The idea of recording my life's adventures for our grandchildren had been suggested by Granny Margie many times, but was always rejected by me on the grounds that it would take a very long time, involve a lot of hard work and be of little interest to anyone. The first two predictions have turned out to be true, and the third will probably follow suit! However, push came to shove one Christmas when Peter, our middle son, admired the beautiful yellow roses I had bought for Margie to mark our wedding anniversary.

A very long time ago in Melbourne, I telephoned Margie's home. My call was answered by her mother who told me that the girl had a poisoned leg and was very upset about it because she had been confined to bed. She then said, "Why not come over in an hour and cheer her up." When walking to the Beggs' house I happened to pass some yellow roses growing through a fence, and being tidy-minded, quickly pruned a few blooms with my penknife!

Yellow Roses

Margie was thrilled with the roses, told me that yellow was her favourite colour and thanked me for buying them for her. Of course this made me feel guilty so I had to confess they were stolen! That sounds a bit like a Jane Austen novel, but ever since that day I have given her a bunch of yellow roses on our wedding anniversary, December the First.

Once persuaded to write my story it soon became obvious that the only way to cope with all the separate tales would be to gather them into ten-year periods, so instead of chapters the text has been divided into *Seven Decades*. The third volume contains an *Epilogue*, in which I try to sum up 'what I have learnt during my life', and closes with a collection of quotes, made by famous people, that I have called *Gathering Flowers*. If you are wise you will turn to these straight away and skip the rest, as they are much more interesting!

As I am bad at remembering when things happened, each *Decade* will be a mix of memories written down as they come to mind, one memory leading to the next, just as throughout my life, one chance encounter has led to another. On looking back over my life, I am forced to agree with Epicurus who wrote: *Life is a fortuitous combination of events*. It has certainly been true in my case!

I was lucky enough to be blessed at birth with some imagination and the ability to use my hands to interpret this gift, but, it was pure 'chance' that led to my becoming a sculptor, and since then 'chance' has played a central role at every twist of the 'fortuitous combination of events' that has shaped my life.

As the number of pages grew, the story took on its own identity and needed a title. I asked my talented niece, Georgina, for the meaning of our family motto, *Qualis ab Incepto*. She said it was a quote from Horace's *Ars Poetica* that translated as, *From the Beginning Onwards*. I thought this was the perfect title for a book about 'Fortuitous Happenings'!

Writing this story turned out to be like sculpting a child. With sculpture you first block out the figure in clay and then spend ages working on the surface, until you decide you can go no further. Writing this story has been a similar experience, because after the text was blocked out, it has taken ages to correct, The main problem has been the discovery that I am illiterate! Fortunately Georgina, Anna Anthony, her mother, Mrs Green, and Margie, have spent hours correcting the text, for which I shall be eternally grateful, as you, the reader, will no doubt be as well! Making these corrections has been an enormous job and without their help I would have given up and burnt the text long ago. If you find mistakes, or the odd typo, I do apologise, but as Cromwell said to the artist painting his portrait, "I am afraid you will have to take it as you find it, warts and all."

Having written a story, what do you do with it? Sir Thomas More discussed this same problem with Peter Gilles after finishing *Utopia* and wrote:

To tell you the truth I still haven't made up my mind whether I shall publish it at all. Tastes differ so widely, and some people are so humourless, so uncharitable, that one would probably do far better to relax and enjoy life than worry oneself to death trying to entertain a public... Besides, some readers are so ungrateful that, even if they enjoy a book immensely, they don't feel any affection for the author. They're like rude guests who after a splendid dinner go home stuffed with food, without saying a word of thanks.

He closes his letter with this request: *Please go on liking me as much as ever – because I like you even more than ever.*

On the eve of our 46th Wedding Anniversary in 2004 the paper was ordered and I managed to cut a finger on the edge of a sample sheet, so sealed the deal with blood! The third book of the trilogy will be delivered to the printers on May 4th 2005, my 70th birthday and released to the invisible public on October 20th, Margie's 70th birthday!

Hopefully, those who read this story of the life Margie and I have shared together will find some amusement, but 'please' remember Sir Thomas More's words and 'go on liking us as much as ever'!

SUMMARY

If I had enjoyed my schooling, paid more attention to my lessons and gone to university, surely my destiny would have been to work behind a desk either in England or Australia! Life at Rugby after WWII was a pretty Spartan affair. If we left water in the dormitory basins it would freeze overnight, and with food rationing of one egg a week and 'guaranteed-no-meat' sausages, we were always hungry. However, this was not the reason for my unhappiness. The main problem was the sheer boredom of school life when compared to holidays.

The one bright spot at Rugby was the Art School. It was my first experience of actually having a 'hands-on' opportunity of practising art. The lessons took place in an enormous studio above the school library. We had three art masters: the Big Chief, who never talked to us, his assistant Fabio Barraclough, and a Junior Master. There was no instruction in art history at all, which in retrospect staggers me.

I was really enjoying myself in the painting classes until the day our task was to design and illustrate a book cover. As the lessons were double ones, I had plenty of time to try two covers. Along came the Junior Master and said, "I see you're one of those people with too much imagination," a remark that still causes me pain. The teacher's sarcasm had the effect of completely putting me off the one subject I was enjoying! Fabio Barraclough must have noticed this and asked me to join his sculpting group in the tiny studio he had under the stairs in the basement. The room was about 15-foot square and smelt pleasantly of wood and linseed oil. He gave me a chisel and mallet, a block of wood and asked, "What would you like to carve?"

'Hula Hula Girl'

Rugby was strictly a 'boys only' school in those days, resembling a male prison as girls were kept well out of reach. Being a red-blooded 15-year-old and starved of any contact with the opposite sex, when Fabio asked me what I would like to carve, my reply had to be, "A Hula Hula girl in a grass skirt." Learning to carve the wood was a fabulous experience and remains the happiest memory of all my days at school.

Fabio became a friend and the finished sculpture won me my only prize while at Rugby. I shall never be able to thank him enough for taking me under his wing. Many years later, when I was a farmer in Australia, the *Hula Hula Girl* became the catalyst of my starting to sculpt again. Now she overlooks me from the window sill of my study while typing.

Except for geography and geometry all the other subjects bored me rigid and, longing to escape, I asked my father if it would be possible to leave after passing my O Levels. He agreed and with luck I managed this, so left at the age of 16, my one regret being parted from Fabio's carving studio.

As I was too young to do my Army National Service, my father suggested joining the Merchant Navy as a deckhand to work my way around the world. I boarded a cargo ship named *Port Napier* as a Supernumerary, with the pay of one shilling a month and keep. The ship set sail for Australia from the London docks on a wet January day in 1951.

To my surprise, when we arrived in Adelaide, my father was there to meet me! He suggested that I should leave the ship when it reached Melbourne, our next port of call, visit my cousins who lived on a sheep station on the Murray River, and then rejoin the ship in Sydney for the trip home. My brother Mike and I, like many other children during WWII, were evacuated from England to escape the London bombings, and sent to Australia to live with my cousins. Visiting a place, that had such fond memories, seemed a fantastic idea, and on reaching the property it felt like I had come 'home'. I decided to make farming in Australia my career!

On telling my father about my wish he agreed, on the condition that I attend Roseworthy Agriculture College in South Australia. Fate decreed that I only managed to stay at the College for part of the three-year course, so I left to become a jackeroo (farm apprentice). The next five years were spent working my way around Australia learning about the land and hard work. They were wonderful carefree years spent in a young man's Paradise.

Then began the serious business of earning a living and becoming independent! After five years of roaming the Australian Outback, working on sheep and cattle stations, it was time to settle down. By chance I found a semi-developed block of land in the Ninety Mile Desert of South Australia that cost ten shillings an acre, and asked my father to lend me the money to develop it.

I built a house, fell in love, got married, and with Margie's help, worked the property. Over the next ten years the sheep numbers grew to 2,000 and our sons to three, Tim, Peter and Mark. When the property was developed my workload lessened enabling me to have some spare time at weekends.

My mother had sent my *Hula Hula Girl* carving out to Australia. The sculpture sat on the bookshelf in our sitting room and was the catalyst that took me back into sculpting, because on looking at the wooden figure it made me want to carve again. One day I happened to pass an art shop in Melbourne that had an offer of 'clay for sale at half price', so I bought a bag and took it back to the farm. It wasn't carving, but could be the next best thing!

I began by modelling figurines and when the clay was dry, finished them off by carving them with my penknife. This led to modelling relief heads of our own sons, casting them in plaster and colouring with bronze paint. Next came busts of willing victims like my mother when she visited us.

Sculpting my mother's head in the shearing shed with Peter watching

Life on the farm was unbelievably kind to us. Our children were healthy, the sun shone and the air was fresh. We were free and we could make just enough money to live on from growing wool. We lived amongst beauty and we had fabulous friends. The one drawback to the Ninety Mile Desert was that it was a long way from schools and we had three little boys who needed educating. It was time to sell up and move on.

That summer was a scorcher, with the temperature reaching 115 degrees in the shade. One day I came into the house to escape the heat and found it as hot inside as outside! We decided to sell the farm and move nearer to a city and schools, but before looking for another farm, go to England for two years and rent a furnished house in the country so I could sculpt and show our sons where I had grown up. Regrettably my father had died by this time, but my mother lived in London and it would be marvellous for her to get to know her grandchildren and for me to get to know her again.

I wrote to my mother and told her about our decision and waited for a reply. Her letter arrived and was read with some surprise. *Do you remember my giving you a set of woodcarving chisels when you were twelve? It was because a fortune-teller had told me that my youngest son would be a sculptor.* I don't believe in fortune-tellers, but it certainly helped that my mother did!

I flew to England and was lucky to find a lovely house in North Devon to rent. The house even had a barn beside it to use as a studio. We arrived in England in 1969 at the beginning of January, 12 months after we had decided to make the change. We left a boiling-hot summer to arrive in a snow-covered winter, something the boys had never seen. Life was idyllic and the house was bliss to live in. Our landlord, Jimmy Smart, was one of the kindest men we had ever met, the locals were incredibly friendly, and there was a village school. The countryside was beautiful and Margie found superb beaches for children's picnic teas after school while I worked in the barn.

'Tim', my first life-size sculpture in England

I bought some clay from the nearby pottery, asked our eldest son, Tim, to pose for me playing marbles and started my first sculpture. By luck I was given the name of a master plasterer, Mr Manzini. On my finishing the figure he drove down from London and took a waste mould of the sculpture. He in turn introduced me to a man who did cold-resin-bronze casting, (which is a cheap way of producing bronze-looking sculptures), so my sculpture was cast. I was thrilled and, although a complete amateur, felt like a real sculptor!

Fired by the whole adventure, the first sculpture was followed by more children sculptures, then a mother teaching her son to walk, who was followed by a figure of a kneeling mother holding her daughter up in the air. This last became my first sale as our landlord bought it for the island he had created in the lake of the gardens. It is still there and you can buy a picture postcard of it!

During my trips to the resin-bronze foundry near London to collect a sculpture, I got to know Roy Wakeford, the man who had done all my casting. Roy's craftsmanship and the care he put into the finished work 'had to be seen to be believed'. He was not happy with his employment and wanted to start his own business using his garage as a workshop. We got on very well so I agreed he could do all my work, which turned out to be one of the best decisions I have ever made.

'Mother and Children' was the first sale

Without Roy, my sculpting days would have soon ended. Instead, over the next 25 years he took every waste mould and cast every positive-plaster of all my sculptures. According to Roy's records he cast 100 different children. On top of that he did several athletic figures, one of which was 16 foot high, and all cast in his one-car garage!

Having committed myself to Roy, it became imperative to find a market. I went to London to meet Derek Crowther of Syon Lodge after seeing an advertisement in the *Illustrated London News*. The Chelsea Flower Show was due and Derek said that he would take the sculptures 'on sale or return' and show them on his stand. Much to our joint surprise they all sold and he took repeat orders! Now, not only did Roy have to cast the original sculpture in resin bronze, he had to make editions of nine of each of them. How he coped I shall never know!

Our first two years in England had come to an end. We asked our landlord if we could remain another year to see if my new career would stay the course. He agreed, but said that at the end of the third year he wanted to sell the house. We had discovered we were too far from London, so decided to buy a cottage in Somerset near King's School, Bruton. We settled into our new home and have remained there for 35 years. Fortunately an old barn came with the cottage and so I had a studio.

One other stroke of luck played a very important part in the establishment of my new career. After doing several sculptures, I had to obtain an opinion from a real sculptor as to whether or not to continue. After all I was a 35-year-old father with a wife and three sons! Were the sculptures any good and would they continue to sell and provide an income?

I had seen some of Enzo Plazzotta's bronzes advertised in an art magazine and greatly envied the skill of the sculptor. I wrote to him enclosing some photographs of my own work, asking if we could meet, and if he would give me some advice. Luckily he agreed and for the first time in my life I entered a real art studio with northern light, turning stands, even a changing room for models! I was overawed by the sight of the stunning wax figures that he was working on.

Enzo gave me a cup of coffee and while he looked at my photographs I asked, "Should I continue to try and earn a living as a sculptor?" He asked in return, "Do you want to do anything else other than be a sculptor?" "No." He looked me straight in the eye, "Then why are you asking me? Go and do it."

Enzo became a great friend. He took me to Italy and introduced me to the Fonderia Mariana, who later cast all the Symbolic Sculpture bronzes of the *Universe Series*. He lent me his studio in Pietrasanta and taught me to model in wax. I shall never be able to thank him enough for the encouragement he gave me and convincing me to believe in my own intuition. Another Fabio!

At the time of Enzo's death in 1975 I had begun my Symbolic Sculptures. By now all my Figurative Sculptures were being cast in real bronze and the Harrods Fine Arts Gallery had become my main outlet, even showing my sculptures in their windows! Roy was still handling all my plasterwork, but the Figurative bronzes were now cast in England and Symbolic ones in Italy.

Neither Harrods nor any other gallery were interested in my Symbolic work. "Stick to what we can sell," Harrods advised. Well, you can't live like that if you are full of ideas you want to try. But how to solve the problem?

When my mother died she left me her flat in London so we decided to sell it and invest the money in our own gallery. I talked the idea over with Joanna, the manager of the Harrods Gallery, and asked her if she would consider working for me as gallery manager. She agreed and found some spectacular premises off Piccadilly on Albemarle Street. Using my mother's maiden name, Freeland, the Freeland Gallery was born.

The gallery displayed the bronze children in the front window, and the Symbolic Sculptures inside. We only kept the gallery for two years for during that time three men visited it and completely changed my life. The gallery was no longer needed, because I had found my Patrons.

Damon de Laszlo is the grandson of the famous portrait painter Philip de Laszlo. He and his wife Sandra had seen my *Leapfrog Children* in the Summer Exhibition at the Royal Academy of Arts and asked me to sculpt their three children. This commission led to our becoming great friends with Damon and Sam. When we opened the Freeland Gallery I was able to introduce them to the Symbolic Sculptures and they now own a large collection!

When Robert A Hefner III walked past the gallery window he saw the Symbolic Sculptures in the background, walked in and asked Joanna if he could meet me, saying that he was leaving the next day for the States. The story of how we breakfasted together in his hotel before he left for the airport will have to wait. Robert is passionate about art and is the owner of a superb collection of contemporary Chinese paintings. At our first meeting he bought two heroic Symbolic Sculpture pieces for his Aspen home in Colorado where he now also has a large collection of my work. Robert and Damon have become my closest friends and we have shared many adventures together over the past 40 years. Our partnership touches nearly every page of my life's story.

My third friend is Professor Ronnie Brown. When we met he was Dean of the School of Mathematics of the University of Wales, Bangor. Ronnie was on his way to give a lecture at the Royal Institution, next door to Freeland, when he saw the Symbolic Sculptures and recognised them as models of mathematical knots. Because of Ronnie, the Symbolic Sculptures became known to universities around the world, many of them wanting sculpture and have received them through the generosity of my patrons.

Robert and Damon have donated Symbolic Sculptures to Aspen Centre for Physics, Aspen Institute, Field Institute Toronto, Cambridge Institute of Astronomy, Universities of Macquarie Sydney, Wales Bangor, Harvard, Montana State, Durham, Oxford and Cambridge's Isaac Newton Institute.

Enzo Plazzotta introduced me to Mario Benbassat in Geneva. Mario created Edition Limitée which published a book on my Symbolic Sculptures with 90 colour plates. Edition Limitée has donated sculptures to the Universities of Cambridge, Oxford, Wales, Barcelona and Zaragoza in Spain and Mario personally financed the writing of this story.

In the 16th century the Florentine art critic, Sperone Speroni defined *Civilisation as the creation of wealth and the patronage of the Arts*. How incredibly true that statement is. Just look at the world's artistic treasures; buildings, paintings, music and poetry all depend on patrons. Without the support of my patrons there would be no Symbolic Sculptures!

My Figurative Sculptures gave way to the Symbolic Sculptures over a period of years. To me it has been a natural progression of the analysis of my innermost feelings about the *Values of Life*. Recently I read a statement by my hero, Brancusi, concerning the searching-element involved in sculpture. *Simplicity is not an end in art, but one arrives at simplicity in spite of oneself, in approaching the real sense of things.*

This story is about the need to create sculptures for myself. Being able to share them with others is a secondary joy. For me the Symbolic Sculptures are the individual steps of my search for answers to the question of 'purpose'. It has been the most exciting adventure that anyone could imagine and I count myself among the luckiest of men who have ever lived.

As my life comes to a close, again chance played a part by introducing me into the world of cast glass. Later I shall tell the story of how

Michelangelo's *Pitti Tondo* was turned into the *Blue Madonna* and how it has come to rest in the new Roman Catholic cathedral in Los Angeles.

I know how insignificant my own work is when compared to the great masters of the past, but what fun I have had in trying. What a barren world this would be without ART! The beauty of the Neolithic cave paintings; the glories of the Renaissance; the Dutch and English Masters; the French Impressionists; not forgetting the master skills of the Orient. Art is Man's finest achievement.

Ars Longa, Vita Brevis : *Art is long, Life is short* : Hippocrates

Some might construe this autobiography (remember it is written for our grandchildren) as an ego trip, but be assured I have no hidden ambition to be successful in the eyes of others! I have led the life of a *Robinson Crusoe*, but am a very ordinary *Alexander Selkirk*! It would not worry me in the slightest if all my sculptures, or this book, vanished, as they are merely the product of my selfishly indulging in the opportunity to exercise my imagination. This is the story of someone passionate about using his hands as his imagination dictates, be it farming, sculpting, painting and now writing. Competition and ambition find no place in my world, because, as all artists will agree, no financial reward can equal personal gratification. The world has nothing better to offer.

I have been extremely lucky always to be self-employed and able to navigate my way across the troubled waters of life under the banner of independence. I have been fortunate not to have to compete with anyone.

My morning walk with our spaniel, Holly, takes me to one of the best views in the world, looking out across the Vale of Camelot. In the distance glitter the red roof tiles of our village and I can see the trees Margie and I planted 30 years ago in our garden, their tops dancing in the wind.

If, having read this shortened version of my story, you are brave enough to continue, I am sure you will understand why I am so content!

Bon Voyage.

FIRST DECADE

MEMORIES

I was meant to be a girl! My mother told me that having produced Pat and Michael, she longed for a daughter. After having her second son the doctor advised her that if she waited for five years, her body chemistry would change and the next baby would be female.

My mother, 'Nan'

13

The doctor was wrong! I was born near Marble Arch in London at my parents' home in Cambridge Square on May 6th 1935, according to my nanny. However, that is not the date on my Birth Certificate! My father registered me as having been born on May 4th, so that has become my official birthday and the day the family celebrate. Having two birthdays every year has not made any significant difference to my life.

My father, 'Bill', with 'Little John Citizen'

My mother was so disappointed at producing another boy that as soon as she was allowed out of bed, my parents sailed for France, presumably to recover from the shock by having a flutter at the tables in Le Touquet casino. Her absence made no difference to my up-bringing because after birth I was handed over to Nana and only brought down for inspection at afternoon tea.

I was christened John after 'Little John Citizen', a character drawn by the cartoonist, Strube. Until demanding to be called *John*, I answered to *Strube* for the first eight years of my life. The only thing of any importance that seems to have happened to me while living at Cambridge Square was that the local Rabbi was called in to perform a circumcision on the kitchen table.

According to Nana once my mother had recovered from the shock of another male, she decided to dress me extravagantly and I became the best-dressed little boy on the 'nanny pram parade' in Hyde Park. Photographs show me as being remarkably well turned out at the tender age of two!

'Nan' and 'John', aged two

15

Always having considering myself to be a late starter I have no memories until the age of four. My first recollection is of snow at our home in Wiltshire that my parents had bought when my father was taken seriously ill with tuberculosis. What a shock it must be for children when they first see snow! One day everything is green, and the next it's white. To awake to snow in the garden still gives me a wonderful surprise.

A winter scene near 'Chute Standen' in Wiltshire

At the beginning of 1936 my father had to have a lung collapsed. In those days the cure for tuberculosis was long months of recuperation in a sanatorium in the Swiss Alps. The alternative was to buy a house in the south of England, which my parents did, having decided that moving the whole family to Switzerland was impossible. This is how I came to grow up in the beautiful countryside of Wiltshire on a small 250-acre farm called Chute Standen with 12 Jersey cows that produced the milk my father was ordered to drink. There was a draft horse, an orange-coloured tractor, an enormous thatched barn and a blacksmith across the road. In fact everything that makes a small boy's life bliss. Farming became my father's weekend hobby and the cows his pride and joy.

Chute Standen is halfway between the villages of Upper Chute and Lower Chute. My mother moved the family into what was always called the Big House and built a conservatory on to the side of the sitting room for my father so he could breathe the fresh clean air of the English countryside. He recovered in two years and returned to the Zinc Corporation as Managing Director, a firm founded by his Melbourne-born father, William Sydney Robinson, known always as WS. Nana MacKay had joined our family when my elder brother, Patrick, was born three years before Mike, and stayed on for my arrival eight years later. From the moment of arrival my every whimper was attended to by an adoring substitute mother, Nana.

'John', aged three and already listening to the passage of time

The 'Big House' with the new conservatory for my father on the left

At the outbreak of the war the Big House was taken over by the Land Army and the family moved down to the Farm House at the end of the front drive. Previously my father had leased the house to his great friend, Sydney Emanuel, wife Vera and their son Tim. Uncle Syd enlisted in the army and Vera moved back to London with Tim, so we moved into the Farm House.

Vera had a son from her first marriage named Val, who was training as a Fleet Air Arm pilot in 1939. During one of his flights he buzzed the Big House to drop a message in his cigarette case to a Land Army girl he had taken a fancy to. Very high beech trees surrounded the house and I happened to be playing in the shade of one of them when Val flew over trying to make contact with the girl.

He misjudged the height of my tree and clipped the top, removing a chunk of his tail in the process, which fell to the ground beside me! Some years later Margie jokingly pointed out to Val that he had very nearly nipped my life in the bud! He was kind enough to apologise, saying that he remembered the event very clearly, because he thought that he had also prematurely ended his own! His mistake had been to look back to see if the girl had retrieved his cigarette case rather than looking forward at the treetops. He luckily crashed in a ploughed field next to a gun battery so was able to get the men to carry the bits of tail, with branches still imbedded, into the woods and hide them in case he was court-martialled. He recalled that he had walked away from the crash unscathed and had gone out dancing with the girl that evening!

Tim Emanuel was a year younger than me. Living so close we often played together and my second memory was of his toys. I had lead soldiers, but Tim had lead Eskimos! He also had a board covered with pretend snow that included an igloo, husky dogs, and a sledge. Part of the board was covered with blue water where an Eskimo paddled a kayak. To remember it so vividly must mean I was very envious of such a grand display!

My grandfather, known universally as WS, played a very important role in the early lives of brother Michael and me, as he insisted that we two should be moved to Australia for the duration of the war. At the time of the outbreak of hostilities between England and Germany WS was principal adviser to both the British and Australian Governments for the supply, production and distribution of strategic metals vital for the armament of all the Allied Forces and a close friend of Winston Churchill. In 1935 WS wrote a book about war with Germany being inevitable! Because of the threat of a Nazi invasion WS advised my parents to get their children out of Britain and back to Australia.

In the winter of 1939 the Russians had signed a Non-Aggression Pact with the Nazis in Berlin. In 1940 the Germans entered Paris and France collapsed, causing the evacuation at the end of May of the 300,000 British soldiers from Dunkirk with the aid of everything that floated, from dinghy to destroyer. With the capture of the French airfields the Germans were able to bomb London and by the middle of 1940 had killed 22,000 civilians.

The cross-Channel invasion of Britain by Nazi Germany was a real threat. The island was totally unprepared for the onslaught as nearly all the British heavy armament had been left on the beaches of Dunkirk. We were saved from an invasion by the 'Heroes of the Battle of Britain' who successfully defended our skies in their Spitfires during the first half of

September of 1940. Providentially, Hitler followed Napoleon's fatal choice and invaded Russia.

In 1941 Hitler invaded Russia and captured most of the Red Army who had been ordered not to fire on their allies. Stalin awoke from a twelve-day coma and his revenge came when the Russians took Berlin, but not before 20 million of them had been slaughtered by the Germans. Because of the fascist ambitions of Germany and Japan, 65 million lives were lost in WWII, equivalent to the present population of Great Britain. Most people today don't realise that to rid Europe of the Nazis, 10,000 Allied soldiers gave their lives for Democracy on D-Day, the name given to the first day of the Allied landings on the beaches of Normandy. *10,000 young men in one day*!

These were fateful times for Britain and if it had not been for Churchill's courage and leadership, our Democratic Freedoms would have disappeared. *The Lights had gone out all over Europe*. However, none of this had yet happened at the beginning of 1940 when Mike and I, aged ten and five, set sail with Nana from Liverpool, bound for Australia via America.

WS had an awesome reputation. I don't remember him when we were staying at the seaside cliff cottage at Portsea during the war, because he was constantly travelling around the world. Most of my knowledge about my grandfather comes from his autobiography called *If I Remember Rightly*. The book is fascinating and covers from his childhood, to the founding of the Zinc Corporation, which later amalgamated with Rio Tinto to become RTZ when my father succeeded WS as chairman. In a tribute paid to him on his death he was named as a Founding Father of Australia's immense mining industry. He never made any personal gain from his knowledge of the companies he created as he refused to hold shares in them. He lived off his salary and died broke. At the end of the war he refused to accept his war salary from the Government.

WS

WS got on very well with Winston and when the war was over he gave him a pair of black Australian swans for his home in England. Winston, in return, gave him two boxer dogs, appropriately called Winston and Brendan, after Brendan Bracken, one of Churchill's close advisers.

Churchill also wanted to give him a title in recognition for his service to the British Commonwealth. WS, being a socialist, didn't want anything to do with titles, so refused the offer by saying he liked getting *The Age* newspaper straight from the Press with his initials written on the top!

The Age arrived every morning because, like his father Anthony Bennett, WS had been Financial Editor of that newspaper. Instead of a title Winston gave him a rare 1568 Treacle Bible to commemorate his service to the British Commonwealth. WS donated the Bible to his old Melbourne school, Scotch College, where it is kept on display in the Chapel.

In presenting this ancient copy of the Holy Bible to Scotch College we should like to inscribe the name of a son of your School, William Sydney Robinson.

In the six relentless years of war that preceded the victory of 1945 the services manifold of William Sydney Robinson to the British Commonwealth were beyond computation.

There is no token more fitting to commemorate the work of this man of unquenchable faith than the book of Scriptures.

Winston S. Churchill

1949

Bernard Baruch wrote: *WS Robinson was one of the very few men I met in my life who had elements of real greatness.*

WS's first job was on a fruit farm working for one of his five older brothers. Although he was Dux of Victoria's Agricultural College, once he was working on the land he changed his mind, and instead became a journalist at *The Age*.

He specialised in mining and one of the things he reported on was the silver mine that was operated by BHP at Broken Hill, in the outback of New South Wales. On a visit to the mine in 1905 he saw the enormous heaps of slag that had been extracted from the open-cut to expose the silver vein and realised it was full of lead and zinc, two metals that were in great demand.

His older brother Lionel had returned to London to deal in Australian mining shares on the Stock Exchange. WS gave up his job and joined his brother, founded the Zinc Corporation and floated it on the market. The treating of the slag was so successful that ZC leased the mining rights at one end of the open-cut, and North Broken Hill Company leased the other.

These two companies joined forces and built the Port Pirie smelter and went on to make Broken Hill what it is today. The city honoured my grandfather and father by naming their university *WS and LB Robinson*.

'Little Bill', grandmother 'Charlotte' and 'Peg'

When WS moved to England he took his wife Charlotte and their two children, Bill, then aged three, and Peg his elder sister. Young Bill was actually christened Lyell Bryant, but was always known as Little Bill or LB. WS commenced a life of travelling back and forth by sea between London, Melbourne and the United States of America.

'Peg' and 'Bill' with their donkey cart

In those days the only way to travel was by steamship. He would arrive, spend a couple of months working, and then sail again. He had a personal valet named Albert who travelled with him. The voyages would have been opulent as he always went First Class, socialism not applying to travel! After the war WS set Albert up in a barbershop near the ZC office so he could have his morning shave when in London! Albert used to cut my hair in the holidays!

This lifestyle may have suited WS, but not so my grandmother Charlotte who found living in a strange country very difficult. In fact the situation became so bad in the end it led to a separation, which must have been very distressing for Little Bill and his sister Peg. Charlotte died in 1927.

WS's mother was Harriet Barton, the sister of Edmund Barton, Australia's First Federal Premier, who was also a blood relation of Helen Raine, Margie's mother, which means that Margie and I share some genes!

WS second wife was an English girl named Gertrude from Wimbledon, London. It was not until after WS died that Margie and I really got to know Gertrude as a person. One day we were amazed to receive a letter asking if she could come and stay with us on the farm. She had been very generous and given each of WS's grandchildren some money, which we spent on building a

10,000-gallon stock tank next to the house as a swimming pool that became a lifesaver for the children in the hot Australian summers.

Gertrude

During Gertrude's visit we discovered she had a wonderful sense of humour. She told us incredible stories about her teenage life when she and her best friend, who had the unbelievable name of Lala de Bath, visited India to stay with a Maharaja who took them tiger shooting. The girls each had their own tent with a sitting room, a bedroom and a bath with hot water to wash the dust off after a hard day on an elephant's back!

She also told us about the time that WS was courting her. He liked to take her out on evening picnics in Windsor Park. WS would collect Gertrude after work and drive down to Windsor Park for summer evening picnics. While she and the chauffeur set up the table, laid out the silver and opened the champagne on one side of the car, WS would retire to the other side and have Albert give him a close shave with a cut-throat razor! We just rolled about laughing when we heard her stories of the 1920s. What amazing times!

WS's first car was a Daimler. It was the first car ever made in which the chauffeur was under cover rather than exposed to the elements. In those days a car's bodywork was tailor-made to the buyer's specifications and WS, being a socialist, insisted that he and the driver rode in the same roof, although of course there was a glass window between them to keep conversations private! Within a week of its being delivered he had a letter from Buckingham Palace asking if he would mind if the Queen copied him and had a similar car built!

WS was passionate about new technology. In 1903 he had his first ride in a chain driven car, a whole two miles! He wrote in his autobiography: *I was highly excited by the experience…and enthusiastically delivered the news to my father. Not so the 'Governor' who said, "Don't waste your time and money, my boy, over those contraptions; they cost a thousand pounds—you can buy a horse and buggy for £90."*

He then ordered a Rolls Royce on condition it had a starter motor! RR agreed to do this if WS paid the cost of the blue prints, a total of £2 12s 6d, as they thought the idea would never catch on because everyone who owned an RR had a chauffeur who could swing the starting-handle! As soon as they completed the job they wished to break the contract, to which WS agreed on condition they paid for the blue prints themselves, which they did! The amazing thing is that WS never held a 'diving licence', preferring to be driven!

WS had given Gertrude a small Constable painting that came into our possession in a roundabout way when she died. The Constable was highly valued and no one wanted it, so the solicitors decided to ship the painting to London for sale at a famous auction house. The experts declared that it was not by Constable, but agreed to sell the painting at a value of £50. I wrote to the solicitors and said that we would like to buy it for that amount and they agreed. I went to collect the painting and was told that they had mislaid it, but would pay me £50, the value they had put on the painting. I would not accept this and claimed that they should instead pay £500, the value the painting was insured for, saying I would write to the solicitors handling Gertrude's Estate and explain what had happened. Several days later a letter arrived from the auction house saying that they had found the painting!

'Nana', 'Mike' ten and 'John' five in 1940 before sailing

But going back to our departure from England in 1940. Pat was 13 at the time and my mother refused to let him leave, saying that as he was such a good shot, already bringing home game from hunting around the farm, if the Germans did attack, his place was here to shoot them!

And so it was decided that the two youngest sons, with our dear little Nana, should go to live with WS and Gertrude at their seaside home near Portsea, a little fishing village some 60 miles out of Melbourne.

We were booked to sail from Liverpool to New York and so began the first of many trips that I have been fortunate enough to make to Australia. I remember nothing of the journey up to Liverpool or saying goodbye to my parents, but I do remember the horrible Customs official! My lead soldiers were carried around in a little cardboard suitcase and before boarding the ship they took them away from me saying that the lead was needed for bullets to kill the Nazis. As bullets were needed I don't hold a grudge, but since that time I have been very wary of all Customs men.

Nothing is remembered of the Atlantic crossing. My next memory was of looking down from the top of the Empire State Building in New York and seeing the railway lines of Penn Station, presumably having been told that we were going to take a train from there to cross Canada.

Captain Marvel

The train journey from New York to Montreal and across to Vancouver must have taken at least five days. Mike was ten years old and loved reading, but my being only five, and the Customs man having purloined all my toys in

Liverpool, and my not being able to read, must have been a problem. The answer was a pile of *Captain Marvel* comics from the station bookstall.

My only memory of the train trip across Canada was stopping on the Great Plains when we got out to walk up and down the platform. Can you imagine my surprise on being introduced to the Chief of the Blackfoot tribe, wearing a knee-length white-feathered Indian headdress. It was a breathtaking experience for a five-year-old!

Nothing is recalled of the Pacific Crossing but I remember crossing the Sydney Harbour Bridge. WS asked the driver why we were going so slowly and I recall the chauffeur's reply, "I thought the children would enjoy seeing the bridge." This is my first memory of the spoken word.

In the pre-war period it was the fashion to dress boys in kilts. WS had discovered that the Gunn clan, founded in 1237 by Olaf the Black, King of Man and Lord of the Isles, included a Robinson branch, so he had a kilt made for LB, and my mother did the same for Pat and Michael. This photograph shows my two brothers wearing kilts with me between them looking angelic in white rompers, aged two, which makes Mike seven and Pat ten.

'Michael' and 'Pat' in kilts

When we arrived in Melbourne we moved into a flat in Clivedon Mansions. The only memory of the flat was triggered by a photograph of myself dressed in the kilt. No doubt the kilt I am wearing in the photograph taken in 1941, aged seven, was a hand-me-down from Mike.

Looking at the photograph brings back very painful memories of a children's party and Nana dressed me up for the occasion. The look on my face shows me feeling happy and totally unaware of what an awful day it was going to be; the sort of day that every child remembers with squirming anguish. We arrived at the party and all the girls laughed at me wearing a skirt! To make matters worse I was obviously bigger than Mike as it looks like a mini skirt!

Wearing the kilt! August 1941

In my defence Nana talked about Scottish soldiers, but my psyche was obviously severely damaged that day and still bares the scars! Perhaps this horrible experience is the cause of my lasting dislike of all parties.

One of my great joys of those early days in Melbourne was the journey we made every day to Melbourne Grammar School in a green and yellow tram. The same trams are still running today! The big thrill was that we had our own book of tickets from which the conductor used to tear one out every trip.

Unfortunately those exciting rides came to an end as it was decided that Melbourne was much too dangerous a place for a school because the Japanese might bomb the city, even though the distance from Singapore made that quite impossible. Consequently the junior school was moved up to the clubhouse of a golf course near Healesville in the Dandenong Ranges.

I am afraid I didn't learn very much at MGS. On arriving back in England three years later, aged eight, I was still reading *Captain Marvel* comics and could hardly write my name! When being asked to sign my name on my ration book at the Chute Post Office I left the first D out of Edward, which when pointed out to me caused considerable embarrassment. One of my Healesville memories is of playing with plasticine and modelling a submarine!

My cousin Annie, who later taught me to ride a horse, tells a story of her young brother Gavin and me playing at Convoys in the gigantic front hall of their homestead called Torrumbarry near Echuca, a town on the Murray River. The rugs on the floor were land and the wooden floors between them the sea. Aunt Peg, my father's sister, had married Harry Baillieu and they had four children, Barbara, Annie, Peter and Gavin. When Annie passed us she heard me tell Gavin, "My submarine has sunk the ship carrying the children." This is a pretty scary story as a German U-boat did sink a ship loaded with children travelling from England to Canada, causing all evacuation to cease immediately.

My first clear memory of using my hands to build an object happened at Healesville. The object was a model aeroplane made from balsa wood covered with tissue paper. I had been given the kit for my birthday and as a treat had been invited into the Matron's sitting room to assemble it. The Matron was my own nanny who had presumably been given the job of Matron to keep an eye on Mike and me when we had been sent up to Healesville.

I can remember her sitting room very well as it had a wood fire and was warm and snug, something the rest of the school wasn't. My birthday being in May meant it fell in the middle of the Australian winter and it was very cold. The model kit came with paste glue that had to be mixed with water and then left to set for ten minutes. After cutting out the sections, I mixed the glue and immediately set to work. The result of not waiting ruined the glue, so it didn't stick! To make up for this disappointment Nana gave me sixpence to buy something at the village shop. I must have been desperate for vitamins that day, because I spent the whole sixpence on a raw carrot!

Jack

28

The Healesville Animal Sanctuary was at the end of the First Hole of the Golf Course, so we were able to walk down and through a gate into the sanctuary. It was a magic place with kangaroo and emu running free.

The great attraction was Jack the Platypus, not because of the animal himself, but because of his greedy appetite and the money we made from feeding him. Jack ate three and a half jam tins of worms every day as well as ten egg yolks. The keepers always welcomed the live supply provided by us boys and paid sixpence for a tin of worms. Jack lived for 17 years, dying in 1954, and was the father of Corie, the first platypus hatched in captivity. He had poison spurs on his hind legs, which could make a man very ill so had to be handled wearing gloves. He was twenty-four inches long, six of which were tail, and so famous he is mentioned in the *Australian Encyclopaedia*!

The headmaster at Healesville used the harshest form of punishment I have ever come across. At Sandroyd Preparatory School the headmaster regularly beat us on the backside with a cane. At Rugby School we received the same treatment either from a master or a senior boy. But at Healesville we were beaten across the *fingers* with a cane. We had to hold out our right hand, palm up, and he would whack us across the fingers in front of the whole school during Assembly. The bruise would last for a week!

My cousin, Gavin, was just older than me and obviously an afterthought like myself as his siblings, Peter, Barbara and Annie, were already teenagers. Thinking back to those days it must have been very lonely for Mike as Gavin and I were nearly the same age. Mike was much younger than his older cousins, so must have spent most of his time on his own. I don't think being in Australia during the war was not a happy experience for my brother.

Torrumbarry was a large station in the Riverina where Uncle Harry bred Dorset Horn sheep. The homestead was beautiful and a very elegant building. The house was one storey high and built around a large square grass lawn, with one side being the main house, another the kitchen wing and the third the children's cottage. The fourth side was a covered walkway joining the children's cottage to the kitchen wing. It had the feel of a *Gone with the Wind* plantation home as it had a Palladium portico over the front door. Except for Aunt Peg's roses the gardens were mainly grass, but in the middle of the front lawn was a huge Botany Bay fig tree. Beyond the garden hundreds of giant gum trees surrounded a vast billabong where we could swim. It was an adventure playground for us, apart from the need to keep an eye out for the odd poisonous snake.

All the stock care was done on horseback and as the station hands were away fighting the war, Annie and her brother Peter did much of the work. One day Annie decided it was time I learned to ride, so saddled up a large mare saying that it was known to be the gentlest animal that had ever lived!

As her own horse was rather frisky, Annie soon got bored of towing me along behind her on a lead rein. By the time we got into the gum-tree forest she decided she had taught me to ride, unhitched the rein and trotted off ahead down the track leaving my mount to amble along behind at a steady walk. The next thing that happened was the saddle slipped right round under the horse's belly, leaving me hanging upside down with my head bumping along the ground. Annie had forgotten to tighten the girth! The mare lived up to her reputation and immediately stopped dead in her tracks. When Annie heard my cry, she came back, tightened the girth and lifted me back up on top again, assuring me that the horse was all right!

My next cousinly lesson came on the raft moored out in the middle of the billabong. Peter decided that it was time he taught Mike and me to swim. The water was deep; warm on top, however, a foot down absolutely freezing. It also had very long slimy weeds growing in it, the type that really gives you the creeps if your feet touch them. Peter decided the best way to teach us was to attach a rope around our waists and throw us into the water. He then walked round and round the raft as we dog-paddled madly to keep above the cold water and our feet out of the reeds. He definitely taught us to swim, but he also gave me a lifelong fear of seaweed.

The cliff cottage that 'WS' built for us at 'Kilmarie', Portsea

We spent some of our holidays at Portsea with Nana living in a little wooden cottage that WS had built for us beside his old white weatherboard house called Kilmarie. Shelley Beach was straight below us down the cliff path. It was a paradise for children; our playground and swimming pool.

'Shelley Beach', Portsea

Aged six at Portsea

In 1943 the tide of war had turned and my mother wanted us home. I can imagine the discussions that must have gone on about whether this was a wise thing to do when the German U-boats were very active in the Atlantic and still sinking cargo ships. However, it was decided that if we travelled on a fast Banana boat on its own rather than in a convoy, we had more than a pretty fair chance of making it back to England!

Dis. 1.

CERTIFICATE OF DISCHARGE

FOR A SEAMAN DISCHARGED BEFORE A SUPERINTENDENT OR A CONSULAR OFFICER.

ISSUED BY THE BOARD OF TRADE.

No. **44**

Name of Ship and Official Number, Port of Registry and Gross Tonnage.	Horse Power.	Description of Voyage or Employment.	
M.V. "PORT WYNDHAM" LONDON. OFF. No. 163561 5234 TONS NETT. 1566 N.P.H.		Foreign	

Name of Seaman.	Year of Birth.	Place of Birth.
John. Robinson	1935	England.

Rank or Rating.	No. of R.N.R. Commission or Certif.	No. of Cert. (if any).
Carpenters Junior assistant	Nil	Nil

Date of Engagement.	Place of Engagement.	Copy of Report of Character.*	
		For Ability.	For General Conduct.
Sydney 4th Oct. 1943	Sydney		
Date of Discharge.	Place of Discharge.	V.G.	V.G.
Liverpool	4th Dec. 1943		

I certify that the above particulars are correct and that the above named Seaman was discharged accordingly.

Dated this 4th day of Dec 1943

AUTHENTICATED BY

BARNUCLE BILL ......MASTER.

FATHER NEPTUNE

Signature of Superintendent or Consular Officer.

* If the Seaman does not require a Certificate of his character, enter "Endorsement not required" in the spaces provided for the copy of the Report.

Signature of Seaman J ROBINSON.

I was eight and a half years old on October 4th 1943 when we set off from Sydney on *Port Wyndham* (5,234 tons) on an Australian spring day and arrived in England on December 4th in the middle of winter. Of course these dates are not carried in my head! My Certificate of Discharge shows me as a *Carpenters Junior assistant* and the Master's name was *Barnucle Bill*. The certificate was witnessed by *Father Neptune*!

My Character Report reads *V.G.* both for *Ability* and *For General Conduct*. The *Very Good* means that this is without doubt the best report I ever had. I signed the document so it seems that MGS had taught me to form letters by then as I could just write my name! My wages were one shilling per month for two months and one day, with an added War Risk of one shilling a month, two days' Leave Pay of two shillings and Subsistence of two shillings. A grand total of eight shillings, but the same amount was deducted for Slops! To wipe out any blemish from my youth, I must point out that 'slops' is a Naval term meaning 'sailors' clothing and bedding issued from the ship's store'.

ACCOUNT OF WAGES. F.

Issued by the Board of Trade, In pursuance of 57 & 58 Vict. ch. 60.

Name of Ship and Official Number	Description of Voyage or Employment	Refr. No. in Agreement
Mr. V. Port Wyndham 163561.	Foreign	0.

Name of Seaman	Date and Port of Engagement	Date of Discharge	Rate of Wages
J. E. Robinson	Sydney 4 Oct 1943	4 Dec 1943	1/= monthly

Earnings	Amount	Deductions	Amount
Wages at £ 1/= per month, for 2 Months 1 days	2	* Reduction of Wages on disrating by £ per month for months days	
*Increase of wage on promotion by £ per month for months days.		Advance on joining ...	
Overtime Hours at		Allotments	
		Fines	
		Forfeitures	
WAR RISK & DIFF. 1/=	2 0	Cash	
DAYS LEAVE PAY 2.	2 0	Tobacco	
		Slops	- 8 0
" SUBSISTENCE 2.	2 0	Channel Money ...	
		Insurance Weeks	
		Health & Pensions ...	
Deductions as per Contra ...	8 0	Unemployment ...	
Balance due ... £	NIL .	Total Deductions ...£	8 0

Dated at the Port of Liverpool.

this 4th day of Dec 1943. 19

Barnacle Bill The Sailor. {Signature of Master.}

'Slops', eight shillings!

When Nana took us ashore in Auckland Mike bought a wristwatch for himself. The wristwatch became a bad memory as he very kindly allowed me to wear it, but as his wrist was bigger than mine, it slipped off when I leant over the rail and fell into the sea, which was not a popular move!

My popularity waned even further when he bought a tiny tortoise at the market in Fiji. The tortoise swam in the lavatory, being the only salt water available, and of course one day I flushed the poor creature out to sea. This didn't make me feel nearly as bad as losing the watch! My purchase in Fiji was a model of an outrigger canoe, which gave me endless hours of fun in the bath.

My other great joy was Chippy, the ship's carpenter. He was a most friendly man who allowed me to follow him around like a puppy while he went about his duties all over the ship. Chippy had a daughter and in his spare time was making a wooden scooter for her as a Christmas present. I used to look at the red scooter with longing!

Nana gave me a New Zealand copper halfpenny coin. On one side of the coin is stamped a Tiki, a small bug-eyed creature worshipped by the Maori people. Chippy taught me how to cut around the Tiki with a hacksaw and smooth the edges with a file. I left a little bump at the top and he drilled a hole in it for a string. As I was very proud of my creation it was worn with pride around my neck for years. It was my first sculpture!

On returning to England in 1968 to look for a house to rent, one of the things I did with my mother was to visit my old home at Chute, and of course we called in to see Dorothy, the maid who had looked after our family during the war years. When my parents sold the Farm House and moved to London, they gave Bottle Cottage in Lower Chute to Dorothy as a 'thank you' for all her years of service. It was marvellous to see her again and before leaving she told me that she had something for me. I couldn't believe it when she gave me the Tiki still hanging on its original piece of string.

Dorothy and my mother outside Bottle Cottage

Dorothy was a wonderful person, short, round and always smiling, who liked Gordon's Gin! My mother used to leave a couple of inches in the decanter for her when we left to go to London on Tuesday morning. When we came back on Friday the decanter was always empty, sparkling clean and ready for the new bottle that was standing beside it.

Only once did Dorothy ever show any sign of having overdone the gin. One day she came into the dining room carrying our dinner on a tray. The poor woman didn't quite reach the sideboard and put the tray down in mid-air. There was an almighty crash, followed by a stunned silence, a pause, and then "Oh Madam, I do love you," before rushing out of the room.

Our ship passed through the Panama Canal, which was great entertainment for us boys, before heading out into the blue waters of the Caribbean. Next stop was England, but first we had to cross the Atlantic.

Mounted on the stern of the ship was an enormous gun that was our protection against submarines. When we left the tropics the weather got steadily worse and the seas became very rough. On one of the calmer days the gun cover was removed so the crew could practise firing it. We watched the sailors as they turned handles swinging the gun from side to side and up and down. After doing this for a while they threw an empty 44-gallon oil drum over the side as a target. It slowly fell astern and when some way off the crew opened fire. Great spouts of water flew up where the shells hit the sea but they didn't hit the drum, although they might have hit a submarine, that is if we were still afloat and hadn't already been torpedoed!

We had done some casual lifeboat drill when we left Sydney, but with the advent of gun-practice and being in the Atlantic, the drill took on quite a different meaning. It was fortunate that we didn't have to take to the boats as we two boys had eaten all the Horlicks tablets out of the emergency rations! We had found that we could climb up into the boats and crawl under the tarpaulins. The tablets were very chewy and quite delicious and, yes, I have felt guilty ever since about eating them.

The only other thing clearly remembered about the voyage across the Atlantic, was Nana's bananas. Our fast refrigeration boat was built to bring fruit and meat to England from the Colonies. These ships were faster than the German submarines and this was the reason that we were alone on the ocean and not part of a convoy of slower ships escorted by Destroyers.

Before leaving Panama City, Nana purchased a hand of bananas and asked the Captain if he would put them in the freezer. About a week before we reached England the Captain informed Nana that the bananas were not going to last the trip. Nana hated waste so she shared the bananas with the crew rather than see them thrown overboard. I don't remember eating a lot of bananas at the time, but just maybe it was the seed of my now eating one a day!

During the war we all had Ration Books that contained coupons for everything under the sun. Children's Green books entitled them to one banana a month. This was my monthly treat as it used to be mashed up with sugar and cream from our Jersey cows. What a taste!

After two months at sea the ship arrived at Swansea on the south coast of Wales on December 4th 1943, in time for Christmas at Chute Standen. The ritual in our house was that we met in my mother's bedroom before breakfast to open our presents that were laid out in little piles. My mother sat up in bed with her breakfast tray, something she had always done since her brothers and sister had left home. Being eight years younger than her nearest brother she had been brought up as an only child, and her mother, who never got up until eleven o'clock, had considered it easier to have breakfast brought to the child in bed rather than have the servants set the table for one small person!

The reason for remembering the first of these Christmas rituals was because, when all the presents had been opened, my mother asked if I had any gifts to give. I didn't, thinking Christmas was like my birthday, where only I received presents! I have never forgotten the feeling of terrible shame and maybe this is why I have always preferred to give than receive. Actually I did have a present for Pat, but had completely forgotten about it. It was a wooden paper knife with a green-eyed Tiki on the handle that Nana had helped me buy in New Zealand.

Nana had not only been my mother during the three years spent in Australia, but also my constant companion since the day of my birth and had looked after me for eight long years.

I recall nothing of the train ride up to London from Swansea, but I vividly remember our arrival in London. The moment that we were all standing on the platform was the 'first time' I was aware of my mother. I was a very shy little boy and consequently refused to move from behind Nana and be kissed by a stranger. Mike had left as a ten-year-old and was now nearly a teenager, so obviously had memories, but I had left as a nursery-raised five-year-old. Looking at our own grandchildren of the same age, makes it easy to appreciate just how young I was when we all left England and what a terrible parting it must have been for my mother.

At the end of 1943 the war was still raging in Europe and the Far East, as the Germans and Japanese had not yet been defeated. London was still being attacked and on my first night in London there was a flying-bomb raid. After our arrival Nana went to join her elder sister who was a nurse and lived in a bedsit in Putney. I don't remember any leave-taking with my surrogate mother and suspect it was all done very quietly. Suddenly I was alone with strangers, but I guess it was even harder for Nana. I once went to stay with the sisters in their one-room flat, but the visit was not a success and left me with unpleasant memories, which included the fact that everyone in the three-storey building shared one lavatory!

My parents' London home was a company flat, number 21A, in Grosvenor House Hotel on Park Lane, and looked out over Hyde Park. It consisted of a very big sitting room that was joined to the front door by a long wide passage. Off the passage were a double and single bedroom, separated by a bathroom. My parents slept in the double room, me in the single, and my two brothers shared a room down the corridor. I was already in bed when the flying-bomb raid started, but on being woken clearly remember my father saying he was going to take Pat and Mike down to the shelter in the hotel cellars. My mother refused to go, saying it was safer in the flat than in the cellar. She had a point as the V2 rockets were designed to penetrate to the cellar, blow up and collapse the building, whereas the doodlebugs, (flying bombs), were designed to glide into the street and set all the houses on fire. You had more chance of surviving in the cellar if it was a flying bomb, but less if a V2, which made it a difficult choice!

My mother took me into her bed when my father left. Lying in the dark we could hear the guns firing in Hyde Park and the flashes from the explosions lit up the room like lightning. Lying together in the dark with my mother was the beginning of our bonding. She probably stayed awake for a long time holding me, but I soon dropped off to sleep and was still in her bed on waking in the morning. From that moment on I felt very close to my mother. Over the next years we became great friends and remained so right to the end of her life.

The following day we left my father in London and went down to the Farm House that was to be my home for the next eight years. Chute Standen was deep in the heart of the English countryside and a long way from the doodlebugs and V2s.

My father used to come down from the London office for the weekends. As chairman of the Zinc Corporation, one of his responsibilities was the aluminium-smelters outside Bristol. His twin jobs of being in London and Bristol meant he was allowed a petrol ration for an office car and as the farm was halfway between the two cities, he was usually able to spend the weekend with us. By then I was really enjoying having parents and the farm was a wonder-world for me to wander around at will. It was still a pre-war world where the farmhands lifted their caps to the master's children!

'Chute Farm House', the centre top window was my bedroom

Our farmlands ran down to the village of Lower Chute about half a mile away. One of my joys was to walk down with my mother to the little post office and buy sweets with my ration coupons. On the way we passed the thatched Hatchet Inn, which looks exactly the same today as it did then. As it is about halfway home Margie and I love stopping there for lunch when driving back to Somerset from London. Returning to Chute always brings back happy memories of my growing-up years on the farm.

Nothing seems to have altered in this backwater haven of peace and tranquillity, even though it is only 60 miles from Piccadilly Circus. We love taking our overseas visitors there as the taproom has not changed for centuries. When holding a pint of ale with your back to the log fire burning in the great inglenook you step back into the past. The pub also reminds me of when Mike and I were arrested by the local policeman for smoking a cigarette in the road outside the premises. We were marched back home and handed over to my mother for a lecture!

The 'Hatchet' Inn

However, I should not have counted my chickens before they were hatched! My world of bliss was completely shattered after Christmas when my mother had to return to driving a canteen, her war work being serving cups of tea and selling cigarettes to the troops who manned the ack-ack guns in the surrounding countryside. Because of this Mike and I were sent off to boarding school, Mike to join Pat at Rugby, and me to Sandroyd, a preparatory school. It was unbelievably terrible to be sent away again!

'Nan' with her mobile canteen

Many funny stories were told about my mother's days as a canteen driver. The vehicle was our own saloon car converted into a wooden box. My mother and her friend, Ursula, would drive to the local army store and have it filled with goods for the crews manning the guns that were dotted all over the county. She said that she knew more soldiers by their first name than any general did. She loved the work, especially as to begin with she had been made to work in an ammunition factory, which apparently is a filthy job.

Ack-ack gunner crews

'Nan and Ursula' on active service!

The car was often breaking down so when an issue of *Punch* came out with a joke about canteens of course she cut it out and had it framed. I still have the original cartoon, so can't resist including it here as a memorial to my mother and Ursula's active service during WWII.

The world was agog over the breaking of the Sound Barrier by the new jet-engine fighter planes, so my mother took me to see the *Victory Day* Farnborough Air Show. The posters advertised that the Sound Barrier would be broken above the airfield for us all to hear. It was a perfect day with not a cloud in the sky.

At last the moment came that we had all been waiting for. The loud speaker announced that John Derry, in a twin fuselage De Havilland DH 110, was waiting above us ready to break the Sound Barrier. Moments later a single-fuselage fighter thundered past us flown by Nevil Duke, and the announcer said he would break the barrier after Derry.

You could have heard a pin drop as we waited. Then came the double *boom boom* and we could see the aeroplane plunging down towards us. The fighter flattened out as it reached the runway and started its run past us just 50 feet off the ground. As it came level to where we were standing the plane suddenly disintegrated with a terrible explosion, flying into hundreds of pieces right before our eyes.

We were all struck dumb, and then suddenly there were screams as parts of the plane bounced towards the crowd. Luckily no bits made the distance, but this didn't stop the crowd panicking. Fire engines roared past us heading for the torn wreckage that had travelled quite a long way down the runway before coming to rest.

The announcer asked us all to stay where we were so we all sat down on the grass and waited. About ten minutes later he announced that Nevil Duke would now break the Sound Barrier as a tribute to his friend who had just died. Within seconds we again heard the double *boom boom* and then the fighter roared past us and did a victory roll as it passed over the wreckage of the smouldering fighter. Nothing in my life has touched me like that moment and I hope never will again.

Many years later Robert Hefner rang me and asked me to join him at the Explorer Club's annual dinner in New York. The only way of getting there in time was to fly over on Concorde. I had always thought it would be fun to do this just once, so agreed to go.

It was an incredible journey, although, when waiting to use the loo I heard a man report on leaving that the lining of the ceiling had just fallen in on him! Perhaps the plane was due for retirement after all. For an aeroplane to fly at a speed of 1,200 mph, equivalent to one mile every three seconds, only 60 years after the Wright brothers first flew an aeroplane at Kitty Hawk in 1903, must make the Concorde one of Man's greatest technological achievements, equal to 'Walking on the Moon'.

The most memorable part of that trip was when the Captain announced that in a few minutes we would hear a thud and feel a slight shudder, but we were not to worry as we would be passing through the Sound Barrier. Of course the memory of John Derry's death, and Nevil Duke's bravery, came back to me when I felt the shudder. I had gone through the Sound Barrier and felt that in some way it was a tribute to our pilots in the war.

'Harvesting the wheat into sheaves', Tunnicliffe

There are two medical memories from my childhood days on the farm. The first happened when I was ten years old. One morning I couldn't be woken, so my mother called our local doctor. After he had examined me he told her I probably had Poliomyelitis, a notifiable disease requiring immediate transfer to a hospital. However, the doctor said that in his experience if I was moved I would wake up paralysed, so suggested leaving me to sleep. He promised to return the following day to see if there was any change.

Apparently I slept for two days and on waking complained of being very hungry. My mother rang the doctor and then put me into a hot bath, while Dorothy made some warm broth and toast. When the doctor arrived he found me sitting up in bed, eating my meal, and talking like Rip Van Winkle. I don't know if it was polio or not, but when I meet someone who was unfortunate enough to have been afflicted by this dreaded disease, I wonder if, but for the wise doctor, the same thing could have happened to me.

My other medical happening was waking up one night in London with a violent stomach-ache. This led to another hot bath on the advice of the doctor, while waiting for an ambulance. I was whisked away to a Nursing Home where a surgeon immediately removed my appendix. My reward was a five-inch long scar to boast about, which is something, as nowadays all you get is a half-inch keyhole cut that is hardly worth showing to anyone! Thank goodness the operation was then possible, as one of my mother's brothers died of peritonitis before the war. The worst thing about the event was having the plaster ripped off my stomach!

To recuperate from the operation I was packed off to the Grand Hotel in Brighton for a week with my 20-year-old cousin, Annie, the one who had taught me to ride a horse when aged six. We had a wonderful time until my mother came down to take us back to the farm. She was furious with Annie because the poor girl had taken me roller-skating instead of pushing me along the front in a wheelchair. Today exercising as soon as possible is recommended, but in those days it was a bit like childbirth. When Margie had the boys, she was kept in bed for ten days after giving birth!

Apart from these two events my memories of growing up on the farm are all golden. In those days the wheat was still harvested in sheaves and then stooked in little tents by the farmhands and their wives. I was taught to drive our orange-coloured tractor between the stooks so the farmhands could toss the sheaves up onto the trailer with pitchforks to a man who would stack them. I would then drive over to a corner of the field where old Sylvan Cook was building a stack. He was famous for estimating the size of stack needed for the harvest so that the last sheaf would neatly fill the gap in the top.

'Mr Brackston on the Threshing Machine', Tunnicliffe

When the stack was finished it always seemed to be just as the sun was going down, which was the signal for my father to arrive with a barrel of beer to celebrate the harvest-home. The farmhands and their wives would sit around on the stubble until dusk, gossiping as they helped themselves from the barrel sticking out of the back of the van. What happy days!

Some weeks later the threshing machine would arrive pulled by a giant steam-engine. The excitement of seeing the funnel belching out smoke as it came up the sunken lane would send me off to meet it on my bicycle. The machine would be positioned by the stack and then the engine moved around so the belt could drive the threshing drum. The belt was some 40 feet long and gave out a resounding slap with a regular click as the belt joint passed over the colossal flywheel.

Mr Brackston was always on top feeding the sheaves into the hopper. He must have been very hot as he wore the traditional flat cap, collarless shirt fastened with a gold stud and a waistcoat, across which you could see the silver chain of his watch stretched between the little fob pockets. He was the official timekeeper for *Smoko*, pulling out his watch and announcing when to stop the engine for tea. One awful day his watch chain snapped and he dropped the timepiece down into the drum. He was heartbroken! When my father heard of the accident he gave Mr Brackston his old gold fob-watch from his Cambridge days so he was able to continue to call out *Smoko*.

The entire farm was mine to explore. The woods were carpeted in primroses, bluebells and white windflowers. One wood was a hazel stand reserved for the hurdle makers, who would come and weave fantastic portable fence panels. They lived in an old gypsy caravan and cooked on an open camp fire so there was always a smell of smoke drifting through the woods.

There is nothing like an English bluebell wood

We had twelve beautiful Jersey cows on the farm, which my mother called *Flushing Flos*. They were milked by hand and produced the most amazingly tasty milk, cream and golden butter, which our cook made in a churn. The milkmaid was named Olive and she smelt of cows. The farm was run by the three Hamilton brothers, Jack, Leno and Bert. Jack was the oldest and the manager; Leno was in charge of the ploughing and taught me to drive the tractor; while Bert looked after the garden and vegetables.

'Milking by hand', Tunnicliffe

We had one draft horse and across the road from the barns was the Smithy, which was my favourite place to go, especially on rainy days. Mr Green didn't seem to mind my being there, or at least he never said he did, and sometimes he would even let me work the forge bellows. The hearth was full of blazing red coals and even now the smell of burning coke brings back memories of the sound of hammering, flying sparks and the pungent smell of sizzling horn as Mr Green burnt the red-hot shoe onto the horse's hoof. When he was satisfied about the fit he would plunge the shoe into a cooling tank to quench it, causing the water to boil and belch forth steam. My fascination of watching men in foundries must have begun at that time. Working with men like these is one of the joys of being a sculptor.

Mr Green was a vast man and Mrs Green tiny. He had arms like fence posts and an enormous belly that was covered with a stained brown leather apron. Once a week he would take Mrs Green shopping in their tiny black

Baby Austin Seven. His weight would make the car so lopsided that it looked as though it was going down the road sideways. Mr Green was also the wicketkeeper for our farm's cricket team. He was famous for not wearing gloves to catch the ball, preferring to receive it on his stomach then clasp it with his hands. One cricket match was very memorable. Our farm team was playing the Upper Chute team and my brother Pat gained lasting fame as a fast bowler by taking nine wickets! I was dragooned into being Eleventh Man that day for our side and was out second ball!

Because the farm owned a pheasant shoot we employed a gamekeeper. Pat was an excellent shot, but I never found the desire to kill birds. In those days the wheat stubble hid large coveys of beautiful red-legged partridges, and I was always horrified to see the guns blast them to smithereens, although I must confess I love eating them!

The three villages that made up the Chutes had a bus service that took the shoppers into market once a week in a very old charabanc. Always on hearing the song, *Didn't we have a lovely time when we went to Bangor*, I think of old Mr Milson who owned and drove the village bus. He was quite mad and in the summer would only wear pyjamas, even into market. One famous and gloriously sunny day he collected all the ladies and then announced that the weather was far too good to waste shopping, so he had decided to take them all to the seaside, and he did! There was a terrible row and the police threatened to take his licence away, although they knew they couldn't as there was then no national bus service, and to stop the bus running would have caused an even worse row!

Every summer my mother would arrange an adventure holiday away from the farm. My older brothers seemed to come and go at different times, as did various cousins and sons of friends, but for some reason we never had any girls with us! As we were not allowed abroad we would go to Wales, Scotland or Northern Ireland. The only holiday that my father was able to join us on was in Wales. I remember it because he was actually persuaded to bathe in the freezing sea, but only once! My mother taught me to play tennis that summer. She served underarm and was able to apply an incredible amount of spin to the ball, making it almost impossible to return.

Our best British holidays were on the Isles of Scilly, off Land's End. The first one was spent at a small hotel and there must have been at least six of us present, five males and my mother. My future stepbrother Henry was there on leave from the Navy and he taught me to play *God Save the King* on an old upright piano for the sole purpose of driving all the other hotel guests from the lounge, leaving it just for our use!

On a bad day the ferry crossing to the Isles from Penzance is one of the roughest sea voyages in the world. On our first holiday we arrived at Penzance to find the ship could not sail because of a storm. We had nowhere to stay so my mother went to the police and they found lodgings for us. It was a terrible night spent fully clothed in damp sheets. The ship sailed next morning, although the sea was still very rough. It was on this trip that I discovered my immunity to seasickness, as every single passenger was ill except myself!

The second year we went to the Scilly Isles was thrilling as my mother discovered she knew one of the Naval Commanders based on the main island of St Mary's. He would collect us in his Sea Rescue launch and ferry us at high speed across to an uninhabited island. He would leave us for the day on a deserted beach to swim and picnic before collecting us in the afternoon on his way home from his patrol. The landlord of our B&B was a lobster fisherman, so we ate like kings. He used to meet the French boats at sea and exchange his crayfish for their lobsters. Thank goodness the French preferred crayfish so we could have lots of delicious lobster claws!

My mother taught us boys to play Gin Rummy to keep us amused between adventures. She thought she was rather good at cards and usually she would win, but this particular summer, when we were playing outside in the sun, we always beat her. In the end we had to admit that we were cheating as we could see her cards reflected in her dark glasses. She was absolutely furious at first, but eventually saw the funny side!

The Farm House front lawn

They were wonderful years that we spent growing up in the Farm House. When we arrived back from Australia my parents still owned the Big House and Bert ran the huge vegetable gardens. All through the war Bert had kept all the people who worked on the farm in fresh vegetables and still had a surplus to give away to other villager families. Everyone pulled together in the war.

A high wall surrounded the vegetable garden with locked gates, but Mike discovered a place to climb over so we could steal the ripe fruit, which caused an awful row. In a Victorian glasshouse, that smelt like a tropical jungle because it was heated by a coal-burning furnace, Bert grew the best Muscat grapes and baby Tom Thumb tomatoes I have ever tasted. But the best of all the fruit were the deliciously-tasting Golden Victoria plums that melted in the mouth. I have never found a plum to match them.

The strawberry beds provided a feast for the house, but as we had never liked them, even with Jersey cream and sugar, they were not stolen, much to Bert's relief. Slugs were a problem around the beds, but he kept them at bay with a barrier of barley whiskers, an old-fashioned trick.

Bert and his boy helper were hard workers. I remember watching them mowing the large croquet lawn in front of the Farm House with a hand mower, the boy in front pulling with a harness while Bert pushed from behind, wearing a waistcoat and gold stud in his collarless buttoned-up shirt!

Things were still very primitive compared to today. I remember watching one of our men drilling a field with grass seed from a box balanced across a wheelbarrow, the wheel driving the mechanism. The poor man must have covered miles and miles pushing the heavy contraption through the mud. The fields around the house were thick with cowslips that we used to pick and take to the flat in London. They have all disappeared now because of the use of fertiliser, as have the butterflies that used to be in swarms. Margie has planted a few cowslips at Agecroft for me and they bring back very happy memories.

When my parents bought Chute Standen they soon found out why it had been so cheap; the water supply disappeared in the summer because the house well dried up. This led to my father having a very expensive 600-foot hole drilled down to the Green Sands beneath the chalk. The pump was driven by a magnificent diesel engine that had an enormous flywheel. It was a family joke that the well had cost more than the whole farm!

The resulting water was so soft that when WS came to England he used to ask my father to bring it up to London in gin bottles so he could use it for shaving, the town water being so hard in those days. The City was a very dirty place with coal fires burning in every house creating appalling smog in the winter months, causing men to wear shirts with detachable collars that they changed twice a day. My father told me that before the war he always carried a torch in the car because the London night fogs could suddenly blanket the city while they were dining out with friends. To get home my mother would drive the car and he would walk ahead with one foot in the gutter and the other on the pavement, shining the torch backwards for her to follow.

My parents loved going to musicals and saw all the new American shows like *Oklahoma*, *Annie Get your Gun*, *South Pacific* and *Kiss Me Kate*, the last being my father's favourite. If on holiday I would be included in the theatre outings and loved them. We used to eat out a lot, so I got to know the restaurants and grills of London. Quaglinos Grill was especially popular and it was there I was taught to dance the Samba and eat a crêpe suzette, set on fire at the table!

When petrol rationing eased my parents had a weekend routine. My father would come down to the farm by train on Friday afternoon and return to the City on Sunday evening. My mother would drive up to town in her little Lancia car on Tuesday morning and stay until Friday morning.

There was also an evening routine when we were at Chute for the weekend. My father always said that if he was going to have a bath and change for dinner at six o'clock, he might as well be comfortable and wear a Black Tie. My mother always wore a long evening dress. When I turned 13, Dorothy would lay out a dinner jacket on my bed ready to put on after my bath! At seven o'clock my parents would meet by the fire for a dry martini in front of the Laura Knight portrait of Lady Kelly and wait for dinner to be announced by Dorothy. I was allowed a small glass of sherry!

There was a routine after dinner as well, as my mother insisted that we play some kind of game together. Sometimes it would be Liar Dice or Shove Halfpenny, but mainly it was cards. The best game for five people is Hearts, which is a kind of Bridge where you pass your three worst cards on to your neighbour. The game would usually take an hour and then, being the youngest, I would go to bed while the adults sat around chatting over a nightcap. Often my mother would have a liqueur while playing cards and of course allowed me to have a sip. Her favourite was crème de menthe with ice as she said it helped her digestion!

WS and the Laura Knight

The Laura Knight painting became an icon of my days at Chute Standen and I can't remember any other painting in the house. On returning to England I was delighted to find that she still had it hanging in the sitting room of her tiny flat in Cadogan Square. On walking into the room it was like meeting an old friend again. It is the most three-dimensional painting I have ever seen. She must have noticed my love of the painting as one evening she asked me to take it down and then wrote my name on the back, saying that she would like me to have it when she died. Originally the painting came to her as a *thank you* from her sister, Habby, and Uncle Joe for looking after their four daughters when they had chicken pox. My mother made the most of that episode and used the girls' comb on her own three boys, so there were seven cases in the house at the same time. This was before the war when we were living in the Big House with plenty of help, but even so, the nursery wing must have been like a hospital!

After inheriting the painting we hung it at Agecroft. One day a friend told us that Laura Knight was all the rage at the moment and the painting was worth thousands of pounds. We had a fit at the sum he mentioned as it was the value of our house! For a year we would take it down and hide it under the bed whenever we went away, but as this still left the worry of fire, we decided to sell it. We asked the friend to arrange a sale on the condition that the auction house had three photographic copies made on canvas paper. He did this and we had each mounted in an old gilt frame so they looked like the original painting! One we gave to Tim, another to Peter and the third we keep at Agecroft for Mark. Every day the painting gives me enormous pleasure when I walk past it. The fake painting also makes me laugh, because our guests, who have no idea that it is a photograph, greatly admire it and envy us!

We went to the auction and nearly died when it fetched twice the estimate! Both Tim and Peter needed houses at the time so they really benefited from their grandmother's nursing seven children with chicken pox!

'Laura Knight's' portrait of 'Lady Kelly'

The first holiday adventure abroad was to ski at Wengen in Switzerland. In those days we still used long wooden skis and boots with leather bindings, similar to the ones my parents used in 1930.

The most memorable thing about that holiday was my falling in love with a girl named Sally, who was staying in the same hotel with her father. We used to share a toboggan on the sleigh ride down to Lauterbrunnen, which, for me, a 12-year-old, was a wonderful excuse to hug her for 30 minutes as we shot round corners at breakneck speed! My first attempt at learning to ski will never be forgotten because I ran into a tree, which has left me with a sore right knee as a constant reminder to this day!

Nan and Bill in St Moritz in 1930

With hundreds of things to do on the farm, holidays were always full of fun. No wonder I hated being driven back to Sandroyd and later being taken to the railway station to catch the train to Rugby. The stations in those days looked exactly as Monet painted them, full of engines belching out smoke as they moaned and sighed, while waiting to depart. Giant steam-engines may be glamorous, but for me they still represent long months of boredom at school before returning to my own halcyon world on the farm for the holidays.

School was a part of my life, so some of the things that happened during the eight years spent at Sandroyd and Rugby should be recalled. Although I might have given the impression that those times were awful, in fact it wasn't all bad. There were happy times and although not much was learnt from the set academic lessons, an awful lot was learnt about life, and that surely is the main point of education, or at least I think so. I was also introduced to the joy of sculpting, thanks to kind Mr Barraclough, and that was worth all the tedium, because eventually it led to my having the most wonderful life imaginable.

My dear parents, 'Bill and Nan', Portsea 1959

'Gare Saint-Lazare', Claude Monet, 1877

Sandroyd was chosen as my preparatory school because my elder brother Pat had been a star pupil there. At the outbreak of the war the Government requisitioned many large private country houses and converted some of them into boarding schools. Sandroyd was evacuated from London to such a house near Tollard Royal that was quite near to Chute Standen and so was the obvious choice for me.

My mother drove me to the school on a cold wet January day to start my new life as Number 61. Ever since being numbered for the first time various authorities have been trying to label me in some form or another. For some extraordinary reason I have always thought of 61 as my lucky number and chosen it in raffles, although it has never won me a prize! Maybe one day it will, and one can't change horses in midstream at my age.

The day my mother took me to boarding school, aged eight, I was wearing my first pale-grey flannel suit with long pants and feeling pretty smart. Being expected to grow it was of course too big for me! As clothes were rationed and required coupons, they had to last a long time.

Actually it lasted at least two years, and still fitted when I was aged ten. This is remembered very well because my parents took me to Copenhagen in the *Dove*, the company's four-seater aeroplane, and on our way we became lost over Holland's Zuider Zee. In those days there were no commercial flights so the Zinc Corporation had its own aeroplane. My father was on a business trip to meet a man who sold bone calcium, which the Bristol aluminium smelters used. We had taken off on a nice sunny day but ran into bad weather over the English Channel. The only way then to find out one's location was to pick up a landmark so we had descended below the cloud, which meant the flight got very bumpy. All this happened only minutes after being given a tomato juice to drink and through my lack of concentration and not holding on tightly, the liquid jumped into my lap when we hit a bump and made an awful mess. My father was very cross about this, but probably because he was extremely worried about our safety. We found out where we were and eventually arrived safely in Copenhagen and the hotel cleaned my suit.

The trip was very memorable as the wife of the businessman we were visiting was a leading actress and stunningly beautiful, according to my mother. We had dinner with the couple and the wife signed a photograph for me, which I kept for years. The business was not a success as my father found out that the calcium came from India and was suspiciously like human bone!

As we drove to the school I was feeling very apprehensive, as this would be the first time I had been left alone in the world without a friend. All my life there have been occasions where I have experienced a feeling of my being out of place and being different, and my arrival at the school was just such an example as all the other boys were dressed in grey herringbone coats and knee-length knickerbockers. A confrontation must have taken place between my mother and the headmaster, as my mother explained to me when she said goodbye that there was no way she was going to waste clothing coupons on such a ridiculous outfit. So my school days began with my being the only one improperly dressed amongst a hundred boys. It was a great start!

They soon discovered that I was also illiterate for although I had been at school for two years in Australia my reading and writing abilities were way behind all the other eight-year-old pupils. Moreover my contemporaries were learning French and Latin, neither language used by *Captain Marvel*. A crash course was needed and thank goodness there must have been a brilliant teacher because by the end of my first term she had me up to scratch with the reading and writing and moved back into my correct class.

The race to catch up with Latin, however, was always a non-starter. My first Latin lesson was a total mystery to the extent that as England was still at war I thought that the teacher was trying to teach us some kind of Secret Code the Germans wouldn't understand. My introduction to the Dead Language will never be forgotten, or the freezing cold converted horse-stable classroom where it took place. The lesson started with the master asking us to repeat after him the verb 'I love': *Amo, Amas, Amat*. Believing he said, "A Mole, A Mouse, A Rat," that is what I shouted out. A roar of laughter filled the room so from that day on my mind was completely closed to Latin.

French was not quite as bad and I still retain enough of the language to understand a menu and book a double room with a bath. Luckily all my friends in France have perfect English. It really would benefit World Peace if we all spoke one language. A couple of years ago Professor Ronnie Brown was commissioned by the University of Lisbon to compile a CD-Rom on mathematics, which he illustrated with some of my Symbolic Sculptures. We were both asked to the official launch of the CD-Rom which had been distributed to every school in Portugal where English is an obligatory language for all students. One step forward to peace!

Listening to Italian is a pleasure, although I can't understand a word of what is being said. To be surrounded by chatting Italians in a restaurant is a bit like having a picnic beside a babbling brook.

My one piece of good fortune at Sandroyd was that the teaching of mathematics didn't start until students turned eight years old. I was slightly behind the class, but was soon able to catch up as they were only doing adding, subtracting, division and multiplication. When algebra and geometry were introduced, guess who came top of the class, much to everyone's amazement! I was overjoyed to receive the prize that has remained the only academic award I have ever won. The leather-bound volume is still on my shelf, although it has never been read. Fancy giving a ten-year-old a book about road building and transport in medieval England!

Also team games such as football and cricket were new to me. The only sporting activity at school in Australia had been walking down to the animal sanctuary. I had been taught to swim by my cousins, but as Sandroyd had no pool that didn't gain me any Brownie points.

My cousins had taught me to ride a horse and as there were some ponies, long afternoon rides through the woods that surrounded the school I did enjoy. The ponies were not very well trained and all liked to race for home, so of course one day I was thrown off and landed on my head as we charged into the cobbled stable yard. In those days no one wore hard hats and, as the fall had left me stunned, I was confined to a sick room for two days.

The timing could not have been worse as my incarceration coincided with the one day of the term when mothers were allowed to take their sons out for lunch. It was the only time in my life that I have really felt depressed, and remember very clearly the feeling of utter despair.

We didn't wash much at Sandroyd. Football was played twice a week and after the game we all went to the Tosh to wash, a function that took place in a cottage which had once been the laundry to the big house. The Tosh consisted of two large rectangular pools side by side full of tepid water, each about 18 inches deep. In the first you were meant to soap up and remove the dirt and in the second rinse off. This was all right if your game was the first to finish but if you were unlucky to be last, it was awful.

As my games always seemed to finish last, by the time we got into the first pool the water was muddy and the second pool was cold! On top of all that, our towels were always damp as the only way of drying them was to put them through the old laundry's wooden roller before hanging them back on your peg. Of course in the winter they never dried completely even though they wouldn't be used again for another three days!

The only memorable thing of pleasure about the bathhouse was the fuchsia that grew around the front door. The flowers were a brilliant red and if you picked one and sucked the nectar from the base, you got a beautiful sweet taste. Those fuchsias were my first awareness of flowers. The one treat during those awful school days was the handing-out once a week of a battered tin that contained five boiled sweets. Sucking a drop of nectar from a fuchsia was definitely an added bonus if you had a sweet tooth.

There were no fire escapes as it had never been intended that the house should sleep 100 boys. The solution was a Dead Man's Winch in the window of each dormitory. The idea was that you slipped a harness around your chest under your arms and then launched yourself out into space in the belief that you would be gently lowered to the ground some twenty feet below. The only practice we had of how to use them was to stand below the window and watch a demonstration once a year by a master!

The Germans were defeated during term-time so the school planned a celebration for VE Day consisting of no lessons and a giant bonfire for us ten-year-olds to dance around in the evening. It was a good excuse to clean up the woods around the school, as we spent the whole day bringing in fallen sticks!

Because petrol rationing was still in force it was difficult for parents to come and see their children, although as the school only allowed the boys to leave the grounds once per term for lunch, this was no big deal. Some boys went the whole term without leaving the school or seeing their parents.

At Sandroyd we all called each other by our surnames and being the only Robinson it was not a problem having such a common name. On arriving at Rugby I entered as Robinson Octus. It took four years to work my way up to Minor and I never did reach the exalted rank of Major.

I had one close friend at Sandroyd and his name was John Barstow. When my mother came to take me out for the one allowed meal Barstow would come with us. His father had been wounded in the Great War, a bullet passing right through his head behind his eyes leaving him blind, although, with the aid of Braille, he had become a successful solicitor in Hampstead.

On arriving in London in 1969 and searching the London telephone book, I found a Barstow living in Hampstead. A woman answered the number and on asking to speak to John she told me that she was his mother and that John had been drowned in a sailing accident when he was 20. It was the saddest news that I have ever heard. John was my one happy memory of those terrible days at Sandroyd School.

The school had a Scout Troop and we were members of the Curlew Patrol. That is really my only memory except that knots came easily to me but not to Barstow, so hours were spent teaching him, as he was quite hopeless.

Once the school was hit by an outbreak of influenza and most of the boys were confined to bed for a week. Twice a day we would be brought a big earthenware jar full of boiling hot water mixed with Friar's Balsam and made to sit, with towels over our heads, inhaling the fumes for half an hour. During the rest of the day we were meant to continue our studies as we lay coughing, but as soon as the door was closed we would of course just talk.

My prize possession as a schoolboy was a wonderful penknife that Uncle Fredrick Bowring had given me. It had a mother-of-pearl handle and contained two blades, a screwdriver, a can opener, a corkscrew, a spike for getting stones out of horses' hooves and a saw. It was the forerunner of every Swiss Army knife that has ever been. It was beautiful and the blades were very sharp.

Unfortunately I shut the big blade on the back of the index finger of my left hand, cutting myself so badly that the scar is still visible 60 years later. On going to the matron to have it dressed she confiscated my knife! The injustice of this action absolutely horrified me and to make matters worse the knife was never returned. My main use for the knife had been to carve the hulls of sailing galleons out of the bark of a giant cedar that grew in the school grounds, so my sculpting career was abruptly nipped in the bud by the confiscation!

Before we boys left Sandroyd the Headmaster, Mr Ozane, called each of us into his study one at a time and gave us a lecture on the Facts of Life. It is hard to imagine anything worse for the poor man than having to repeat this task to some ten boys, year after year. The lecture ended with an instruction about it being sinful to look at pictures of naked women. It was pretty hard trying to keep a straight face!

Another reason not to forget Mr Ozane was because of being constantly sent to his study for *Six of the Best* that were delivered with a Charlie Chaplin bamboo walking stick. The blue stripe bruises across the bottom would last for a week and were admired by the rest of the boys in the Tosh when proudly displayed by the victim. Caning hurts for a moment and then leaves a rather pleasant tingling sensation in the buttocks!

It was certainly ineffectual as it never stopped us repeating our misdemeanours. I was once beaten for using a water pistol in class, which, like the knife, was also confiscated and never returned. This didn't upset me nearly as much as losing the knife.

Everyone had to be a member of the choir. The headmaster would conduct the singing practice in the dining room accompanied by a teacher on the piano. There was always a rush to get in the back row. One day something happened and the back row lost control. Mr Ozane was in a particularly bad mood that day and suddenly exploded, "Robinson, wipe that asinine grin off your face and get out of here. And don't ever come to choir practice again."

The food was awful, which was not surprising as rationing was still in force. It must have been a nightmare to feed all hundred of us. One day we had tapioca pudding for dessert. The slimy white balls went round and round in my mouth and couldn't be swallowed. Because food was so scarce it was a rule that we had to eat everything on our plates. When Mr Ozane saw that everyone had finished but me, he told me to go and stand against the wall and stay there until the plateful was finished. Dutifully following his instructions, watched by everyone, I took a mouthful, swallowed and was violently sick, bringing up not only the tapioca but also the rest of my meal!

Inevitably the dreaded day came when those who were leaving to go on to a Public School had to sit a Common Entrance Examination. I was dreading this knowing I would fail in Latin. Up to then I had managed to scrape through with the aid of a barter system that existed with my fellow students. Those who were good at maths would pass notes to those who weren't and vice versa with Latin. When exam day arrived we sat at desks that were positioned so far apart it was impossible to pass notes!

Eventually the marks were returned and my Latin score was abysmal. However, Rugby accepted me on condition that I did some extra Latin during the holidays. Barstow was accepted into Winchester on the same conditions but with mathematics. Both of us were relieved, but shuddered at the thought of our holiday being ruined by having to stay indoors with a tutor.

Mr Ozane suggested to my parents that they should employ my Latin master Mr Cookey-Yarborough for the holidays. When my parents told me about this, I couldn't believe it. The master was a crusty old bachelor whom I didn't like and besides it would do no good.

At our first lesson he quickly understood that it would be impossible to bring my Latin up to scratch when, through my tears, I explained to him that I had been having help from other boys for years and knew next to nothing of the language. With that he set me to do a couple of hours of elementary grammar each morning and went off shooting rabbits with my brother, Pat, leaving me free to read an adventure book.

By this time I had turned into a bookworm as my mother had discovered a series of adventure stories that recorded the exploits of two American brothers who were my age. The boys were detectives who helped the police capture foreign spies, contraband smugglers and gem thieves. There must have been at least 15 books in the series and my mother used to produce a new book as soon as one was finished. The boys had access to motorboats and it was very exciting stuff that set my imagination running wild.

Only one of the stories has actually stuck in my mind and I must record it because there is a quite amazing coincidence about it. The brothers were on a holiday on the south coast of England with their parents at a place that had little bays set into white chalk cliffs, a bit like Lulworth Cove in Dorset, which they explored in their motorboat.

One day, when the smugglers were chasing them, they had to hide in a cave and in the process of finding a way out they discovered an ancient sculpture of a bull. Fifty years after reading this story I was taken up an underground river in a tiny bathtub-boat into a French cave. After crawling for some time along a tunnel we arrived in front of a clay bull and cow that had been sculpted 15,000 years ago!

So ended my days at Sandroyd School. Resigning myself to another five years of prison at Rugby, I was quite prepared for this knowing it would be broken by wonderful holidays.

SECOND DECADE

RUGBY SCHOOL

I was two years into my Second Decade when I moved from Sandroyd to Rugby and I had no expectations of my time at school getting any more acceptable. In fact, going from the top of one heap to the bottom of another, I expected things to get worse, which would have turned out to be true but for Fabio Barraclough. Anyone who tells you that their school days were the best time of their lives must either have had miserable holidays or led a very boring life since leaving.

By 1948 the Japanese had surrendered and the world was at peace, although the Cold War was beginning to hot up and soon the Russian blockade of Berlin would have to be broken by a giant Air Lift. My father was now both Chairman and Managing Director of the Zinc Corporation, which required him to live half the year in Australia. For me this meant that my mother and I spent even more time together during the school holidays.

My first trip to Rugby and introduction to the housemaster of Michell House was again with my mother and by car. Pat had been a very successful student at Rugby and had won a mathematics scholarship to Trinity Hall Cambridge where he obtained a Double First. Hopefully they didn't expect me to do the same!

Michell House

This time at least I looked like all the other new boys so felt less conspicuous than when I had arrived at Sandroyd. The required dress was a sensible pair of grey flannel trousers and a Harris Tweed sports jacket, black tie and House cap. The Michell cap was a brown and white striped affair that looked like a chocolate cake filled with thick layers of cream. Most of the studies held two boys and had been allocated in alphabetical order.

Rugby it was universally recognised that I was hopeless at both Latin and French so was allowed to do extra geography and art instead. My masters had seen the light.

My study mate was a boy called Shaw. We didn't have anything in common but got on well enough for the first year. At the end of the year we were allowed to choose our own study mate but I was slow off the mark and didn't get around to doing anything about this until too late. My only true friend was Colin Naylor and he had already agreed to share with another boy. Consequently as the odd man out I was told that I had to share with David Rawson, a boy from the year above my own. Like many other chance happenings in my life this turned out to be a blessing and by far the best thing that could ever have happened to me.

Rawson, being a year older, made my days at Rugby bearable. Sharing with someone from the previous intake dragged me up a notch that resulted in my being given privileges before any of my own year. However, the main advantage was that Rawson and I talked the same language. After one term at

Rawson was streetwise and taught me how to survive in what was to me a very hostile environment. He was not quite my height, stocky and non-athletic, which was another thing we had in common. However, he was a supremely gifted musician, played the cello beautifully and at the end of term concert he would give a solo performance in front of the whole school. His music ability excused him from all sorts of odious tasks as he would just say, "Sorry, I have cello practice," and simply disappear.

Rawson smoked a pipe. This was of course illegal and meant that even on the coldest days we would have our study window wide open if he felt the urge to light up. Because I was sharing with Rawson it meant we had a choice of studies before my own year and the advantage of this was that some studies were better suited to not being overlooked by Prefects. Rawson also knew which were the best ones for anti-smoke detection. I never took to smoking a pipe as it burnt my mouth, but occasionally while he was puffing away I would have a cigarette. How no one complained about the smell of the tobacco smoke is quite beyond me, but maybe it was because our housemaster also smoked a pipe and everyone thought the smell came from his study next door!

Rugby had a Boys' Army. Although the war with Japan was over, the Korean one looked possible, so the masters took the School Corps very seriously. Everybody was given a soldier's uniform, boots and a rifle, which we were shown how to clean but not to fire! Once a week we would have a parade and be taught to obey the orders yelled at us by a fierce Sergeant as we marched up and down backstreets. In the summer a General would come and inspect us after which we would be split into Blue and Red squads for manoeuvres, which meant slogging through muddy fields and hiding from each other in ditches. On one of these occasions Naylor and I had to lug a very heavy bren-gun around, so for fun, during a quiet moment of boredom, we set up a roadblock on a public highway. This turned out to be disastrous as the first car we flagged down was driven by the headmaster of Rugby School! Luckily he didn't report us, supposedly because he thought we had been instructed to do so!

The only time I saw the housemaster was for a caning or when he came up to the playing fields to watch rugby matches. He had a little terrier that I shall never forget as one day on our way home after the game, when he stopped to ask how we had got on, the dog lifted his leg and filled my boot!

Food was in short supply. We always had porridge for breakfast and, occasionally for a treat, one 'guaranteed-no-meat' sausage. Lunch was more substantial and always included mashed potato, while supper was bread and butter or occasionally a half slice of fried bread thinly spread with fish paste. Halfway through the morning between lessons we would return to our respective houses to change books for the next two lessons. This was when we each collected a slice of bread covered with salted beef dripping, which was simply delicious. The House matron had to supervise the bread and dripping dole-out so no one could steal two slices! Her room was also where, in the evening, we listened to *Dick Barton – Special Agent*. I can't remember what Dick, Snowy and Jock got up to, but I do remember the theme music very clearly and whenever I hear it I am immediately reminded of salted beef dripping on bread. It actually must have been a very healthy diet for although it was meagre I can't remember ever being hungry during my years at Rugby.

We slept in dormitories, the largest of which had about 30 beds each divided from the other by partitions. Down the centre of the room there was a row of basins, one for each person, and if you happened to leave water in the basin it would freeze on exceptionally cold nights.

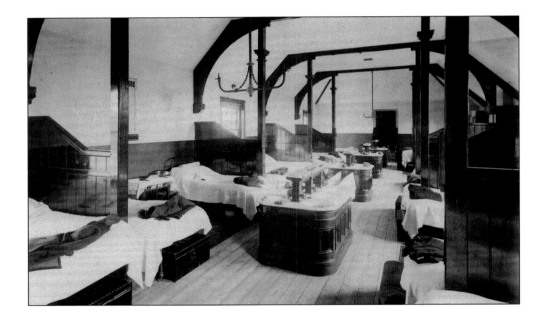

The icy cold big dormitory

In the winter the classrooms were bitterly cold as the central heating system burnt coal, which was then in short supply so the heating was seldom turned on. In contrast to the cold winters I remember the summers as being gloriously hot.

The school had a wonderful Sanatorium that had only just been completed at the outbreak of war, so was very modern. It was here that we had to go to *cough* so the doctor could feel if we had a hernia or have our feet inspected and painted purple if there was an outbreak of athlete's foot. The only time I was admitted to the San was when I was knocked off a bicycle by a car and they thought I might have concussion. My overnight stay was a blessing as it got me out of potato picking, something that happened every year

60

when the local farmers needed extra hands to bring in the harvest. Potato picking is a back-breaking job and to be avoided at all cost.

We all had bicycles as the playing fields were miles away from the school. A shop in the town stocked a vast array of second-hand bikes where we could buy one when we arrived at the school and sell it back when we left. As there were 600 boys in the school there were a lot of bikes around. In those days gears were very rare and progress depended on straight pedal power. This became very obvious each year on the one day of the summer term when we were allowed to bicycle beyond school bounds.

Rugby is not far from Stratford-on-Avon so on this one particular day several of us would set off early in the morning and on arrival hire a punt and have a picnic on the Avon. We used to collect sandwiches from the kitchen after breakfast and start pedalling. It took over an hour to reach the Avon and was hard work but well worth the effort. Those hot summer outings were some of the happiest days of my time at school.

When you first arrived at Rugby everyone was enrolled into the Big Choir whether you could sing or not and of course over the years many of us were asked to leave. The first and only year I was a member we were taught the chorus from Wagner's opera *Tannhäuser*, which was my first real introduction to real classical music.

Rugby School

▲ ▲ ▲ ▲

Memorial Chapel, Pepper Pot, Classrooms, School House

Every morning we had to attend a service in the enormous Victorian chapel that was called the *Pepper Pot*. It is an extremely ugly building made more so by being beside a beautiful Memorial Chapel built to commemorate the Old Boys who lost their lives in the Great War. The most impressive thing about the Pepper Pot was its colossal organ, which made an amazing sound.

Religious instruction was a build-up to our being confirmed. We all went along with this and became devout Christians although I never did manage to learn the Creed off by heart. It turned out that to be confirmed you had to have been christened and have a certificate to prove it! Rawson's parents had never got around to doing this so one day we had a bizarre ceremony in the Memorial Chapel to witness Rawson being named David. The only sermon I remember was the one when the chaplain mounted the pulpit and announced that his text was taken from the top of a milk bottle!

Petrol rationing still made getting around very difficult but my mother always found enough to come down and stay at the Grand Hotel once a term. The highlight of her visit was Sunday lunch to which she would also invite Rawson and Naylor. Although the hotel didn't pretend to live up to its name it did serve a far larger meal than our normal fare. My mother also believed in giving us a glass of cider with our lunch, which was a great treat.

Colin Naylor was in the same year and form and we used to play squash together when we weren't chosen for one of the House teams. One Christmas he asked me to his home in Yorkshire for a party his parents were giving for him and his two brothers. It was the first time that I had ever stayed with a friend away from home and I loved the experience. Colin was the only person I kept in touch with after leaving school and many years later when we passed through Yorkshire with our three boys, we stayed with him, his super wife, Bev, and their three daughters.

We were forbidden to go to the cinema in the town, but Colin and I did and the risk of getting caught added to the excitement of the film. I don't suppose the ticket sales girl gave a hoot about us being from the school but buying the tickets was always a nerve-racking business.

Really I got more and more rebellious as my boredom intensified and my hatred of being at school grew. Before each meal we had to stand until a Latin Grace had been said. The housemaster usually did this but if he was away then the head boy would. One evening we stood for five minutes waiting for someone to say something so we could eat. In desperation I suddenly blurted out, "For what we are about to receive may we be truly thankful." There was the usual uproar as 60 students all sat down at once mixed with the clatter of plates and talk. My friends looked at me in utter amazement. I don't know what drove me to do such a thing and I spent the rest of the meal wondering what would happen to me as a consequence. Could I be caned for saying Grace? As it turned out nothing happened, not even a rebuke.

The art class was the one bright spot in my life at Rugby and the day Fabio Barraclough introduced me to sculpting really was the best thing that ever happened to me in my school days. The seed that he planted took 20 years to germinate but has grown into the joy of my life.

Fabio and I became friends and the finished *Hula Hula Girl* won me my only prize while at Rugby and meant I had a capital C (*Copy*) after my name in the school roll-call booklet we all were given at the start of ever year. A prize for algebra at Sandroyd and one for sculpture at Rugby were the full extent of my scholastic achievements, but if I were to choose any two subjects to win prizes at, I would wish it to be those.

On seeing the sculpture my father claimed that no one could get into that position but then they say that none of the Sistine Chapel figures can *actually* stand up! Unfortunately it was the only sculpture my father lived to see, which is the biggest regret in my life. I shall never be able to thank Fabio enough for taking me under his wing and inviting me to his house where I worked in his attic studio before having tea and cake with him and his wife.

Apart from art, geography and geometry, all the other subjects I was forced to take continued to bore me rigid and I couldn't wait to get out of the place, so I asked my father if I could leave if I passed all my O levels. With a lot of luck I did manage to pass everything and left aged 16½. My one regret was being parted from Art. On my return to England 17 years later I was able to track Fabio down at his home outside Madrid where he now lived growing grapes and advising art collectors, while still keeping his hand in with mallet and chisel. Because he sometimes comes to London I was able to meet up with him and thank him for saving my life. He hadn't changed a bit from how I remembered him all those years ago.

Hula Hula Girl

Three of my friends were also leaving at the end of the summer term; Batty was off to Calcutta to join a firm, Hinton was going into his family's grocery business and Dyde was heading for Medical School. One day while chatting, the four of us decided that it would be fun to go camping on the French Mediterranean coast! I don't know how we all managed to persuade our parents that it was a good idea, but we did. We met in London at my parents' flat a week after we left school. When the day came we all arrived on time and set off for the railway station.

I can't remember anything about the trip down, which is surprising as I am sure we were all very excited. I guess it was Dover, Calais, Paris, change stations, and then south. I have no idea why we were heading towards Barcelona although I do have a vague memory of studying an atlas, which presumably showed railway tracks heading west from Marseilles. I am sure the choice of heading towards the under-populated area just north of the French-Spanish border and staying away from expensive places like Nice, had something to do with the decision. As none of us spoke any Spanish we decided to get off the train at the last town before the border, which happened to be Port-Vendres. We hoped our money would go further in this out-of-the-way place, which was important as we were still only allowed to take £50 each.

The plan was that we would arrive and walk east along the coast until we found a nice cove and just settle down on a sandy beach. We each carried a small canvas bag full of summer clothes and bathers, but no proper camping gear such as a tent. We hoped that we would be able to exist on fruit and have just one hot meal a day in a café.

I remember the day we arrived at Port-Vendres was hot and that the coast road out of town was uphill. By the time we had walked a few miles we were exhausted and our spirits had sunk very low. We struggled on until we found a café and fell inside and begged the woman behind the counter for a glass of cold water, which she gave us and then asked where we were going. On explaining our quest for a camping spot by the sea she suggested that we go no further as below the café was her boatshed that we were welcome to use and she would give us supper every evening. Madame was an angel in disguise, but also a smart businesswoman, or should that be the other way round! Why let four boys with money go elsewhere? The boat shed, café and the sea were all utter perfection. We had certainly landed on our feet and just in time, as we were all absolutely knackered.

We settled in for our week of doing nothing but swimming and lazing around in the sun. The boatshed afforded shade during the day and the nights were warm enough to sleep out under the stars. The water was azure blue, deep and crystal clear. The seabed was covered with sea urchins that we soon learnt to avoid, as the spines proved to be painful and poisonous, but otherwise the spot could not have been better even though it had pebbles rather than sand.

Madame fed us every evening and sold us fruit for breakfast and bread and wine for lunch. She also told us of the carnival that was about to happen on the coming Saturday. The next town down the road was called Collioure and it was the home of the only bullfight in the whole of France. She told us that because it was in France, and because the French were not barbarians, the bulls were not killed so the odds of being hurt were all against the Matador. We could catch a bus from the café and buy tickets at the entrance of the bullring.

When the day arrived we caught the bus into town and as all the other passengers were going to the bullfight the party was already in full swing when we climbed on board. Bottles were passed around during the trip and by the time we arrived we were well into the spirit of the carnival. We bought tickets for the shady side and took our seats. What an afternoon and what a noise! The arena was small and packed with cheering people so the sound was deafening. The bulls looked ferocious but had tennis balls glued to the tips of their horns. The horses were well padded and instead of spearing the bull's neck the Picador had to stick a rosette at the tip of his lance onto a pad roped to the bull's shoulders. The Matador, after playing the bull to a standstill, had to lift a rosette from between the bull's horns with his sword. It was all good clean fun and one of the most hilarious afternoons I have ever spent. Having seen the French bullfight I am more certain than ever that I don't want to go to a Spanish one.

Our holiday ended and it was time to leave. We sadly said goodbye to Madame and walked back to the railway station to catch the evening train to Paris. We got on board and, presenting a united front to the poor conductor, the four of us took over the whole of an old-fashioned eight-seater compartment refusing to let anyone else enter, saying that all the seats were taken. During the night two of us stretched out on the lower sofa seats, while the other two climbed into the luggage racks.

Early the next morning we heard a commotion in the corridor that turned out to be an argument between the conductor and a very rough-looking Irish sailor from Liverpool. Neither understood what the other was saying so our best linguist offered to sort out the problem. The sailor was unshaven, smelly and spoke a dialect that we could hardly understand ourselves so the poor conductor had no hope. We learnt that he had been kicked off his ship for fighting, given a one-way ticket to Paris and told to go to the British Embassy. According to him he had been given no money for food and hadn't eaten for days. As we drew into Paris we counted up what little money we had left and gave him enough for a meal at the station café. Nowadays I would probably suspect that he was lying, had his wages in his pocket and thought that four baby-faced English schoolboys would be good for a meal!

We had a whole day to spend in Paris before catching the night boat train back to London. We walked the Champs-Élysées, ate patisseries, drank coffee for lunch and to fill in the rainy afternoon we went to a cinema. So ended one of the most memorable holidays I have ever had. It was my first experience of organising something for myself and coping with the outside world on my own. Before this trip I had always been with my mother in good hotels with hot water and delicious meals. It was the perfect preparation for my next big adventures of being a Merchant Seaman on *Port Napier* and then a jackeroo in Australia. Right then I had no idea about my Australian future, but knew that I was about to step out into the world and I just couldn't wait to get going. I felt as though I was throwing off all my dull old clothes and exchanging them for bright new ones. Life was good!

I think of my years at Sandroyd and Rugby as just filling in time waiting for this moment. I am positive that I would have learnt a lot more from a private tutor. I didn't conform to the required pattern and therefore was outside the interest of the masters.

In those days Rugby was a mass of male teenagers jammed in together with not a girl in sight. The school made one brave attempt while I was there to normalise the situation by holding a dance for all those over sixteen. It took place in the gym during my last summer term. The needed girls were brought in from the local Grammar School and none of us had anything in common. They might as well have been from Tahiti as from Rugby! It would certainly have been more exciting if they had been.

65

In the last week before departing for good, all the Leavers were instructed to attend a mass lecture. The headmaster arrived and introduced the Town's Health Inspector who talked for ten minutes about Social Diseases. He actually said, "If you do catch a sexually transmitted disease and have to go to a doctor don't say you caught it off a lavatory seat. You might as well say you caught it off a train ticket."

Rugby was summed up for me by the event that took place on our last day before catching the train. As it was a glorious sunny morning four of us decided to go for a swim before breakfast in the school's Olympic-size pool that was surrounded by a high wall.

We arrived at the pool to find the gates locked, but could hear sounds of laughter and splashing coming from inside the walls so others had obviously decided that a swim before breakfast was just the thing to do before catching the train. We climbed the gates and had a wonderful half an hour before climbing back over the wall to find a master taking down names. We couldn't believe that he would report us, having told him that we were Leavers, but at breakfast our names were called out and we were ordered to report to the housemaster. In the study he told us that he didn't consider us to be Leavers until we stepped on to the train and therefore he would have to cane us, which he proceeded to do, each receiving six strokes! When I arrived in London I told my mother about the unfair treatment but she only found it very funny! It was certainly a dramatic way of bringing down the curtain on the final act of my formal education.

I couldn't believe it when I received a letter from one of my year's intake into Michell House announcing that he was planning a 50-year *Reunion Dinner*. I rang Colin and asked him if he was going. He was extremely doubtful about meeting a lot of people whom he had nothing in common with, but I eventually talked him into coming by pointing out that it would be fun to see how much we had all changed. I arranged for us to share a room for the night and go to the dinner together.

We arrived and found all but one of our year were present. Tony Dyde, who had become a heart surgeon, pointed out that statistically at least one tenth of our age group should have died so we were performing above average! The dinner was good and the chatter was constant, although a bit like a purposeless cocktail party. No one had changed that much in looks, which surprised me. What did astound me was that most of them had retired and spent their time playing golf, which seemed an awful waste of an education.

To end off the evening we lined up for a typical Michell House team photograph. I couldn't help but laugh inside wondering what my friends would say if they knew it was the only Team Photo I had ever been in!

The climax of the evening came with the organiser asking us all to stand and sing the Rugby School song. Of course Colin and I didn't know the words and never had, but everyone else did, which rather impressed me. I came away from the dinner knowing that life had been very kind to me and not at all regretting that I didn't know the words to the School song.

Several years after the dinner I was rung by Colin's brother, John, and with great sadness heard that my old friend had died from cancer. John told me that fortunately it had been a quick release, but I felt Colin had been dealt some pretty awful cards by Life having also lost his wife, Bev, to cancer when she was very young. Alone he brought up their three daughters while making a great success of his women's fashion business, becoming fluent in French and as the Commanding Officer of the Yorkshire Territorial Army.

The extraordinary thing was that John and Colin's voices sounded so identical on the telephone that I had the weird feeling I was actually talking to Colin. Our conversation brought back only happy memories of what was a very difficult time in my life.

Year Reunion
'Colin' fourth from left top row, me left bottom row

After 30 years of badgering by Margie to take her to Rugby and show her around, I eventually gave in; besides we were passing the town on our way back from Durham University where I had been advising the Institute of Computational Cosmology on the placement of three sculptures. It was lunchtime so I suggested that we have a meal at the Grand Hotel for old times' sake, parked the car near Michell House and walk down the High Street to the hotel. We arrived at the clock tower that was surrounded by smelly fast-food stalls and looked across to the Grand Hotel. It had gone, replaced by a noisy shopping mall.

Walking back we found the Three Horse Shoes still existed in what used to be called the Shambles because it had been the home of the town's butchers who used to throw the blood from the slaughtered animals out into the muddy street, but not in my days! Perhaps the brick pedestrian way was an improvement after all. The main gate of the school was open so we entered through the arch into the old quadrangle. What memories came flooding back! I must have walked across this Quad a million times. I pointed out a classroom door behind which someone had tried to teach me Calculus.

We walked past the entrance to the Debating Hall that had been the main schoolroom when Rugby was founded in Queen Elizabeth I's reign and out into New Quad that is surrounded by a prison block of classrooms and the 'Pepper Pot' chapel. Fortunately the chapel doors were locked. Out on the playing fields I showed Margie the plaque that commemorated Webb Ellis, who, *with a glorious disregard of the rules of soccer, first picked up the ball and ran with it.* At first the game was played with up to 100 boys taking part, all the boarders from School House on one side against the town dayboys on the other!

Here we had paraded in our ill-fitting army uniforms and learnt to march to orders. It did all look wonderful on the sunny day we were lucky enough to be enjoying. Out onto the road and past the Art School and then left down past Tudor House to the swimming pool where I had been caught on the last day at school. An aeroplane hangar with no character has replaced the beautiful open-air pool and the wall we had had to climb had been removed. Back down past the athletic grounds where I won a race but was deemed to be too slow to qualify and out onto the road to the B&B which my mother had used if the Grand Hotel was full. At last I found an improvement! The B&B was now a girls' boarding house; Rugby has turned coed. If only we had had girls in my day, life would have been so much more pleasant.

We walked back towards the school for the grand finale, Michell House. I pointed out the study window that Rawson and I had to keep open when he was smoking his pipe. Above were the dormitory windows behind which I slept and dreamt of freedom. We walked up the driveway to the Michell House back door. How many times had I walked that path? I looked through the door and saw an improvement as the brown passage had been painted cream. A boy offered to let us in through the door that can only now be opened by punching in a code for security, but I declined. "No, I was here a long time ago and don't think I wish to repeat the experience." He agreed that I might have a point.

The school now has a museum that we were allowed to enter for free when I said I was an OR. I bought a postcard of the playing field and Pepper Pot and hurried back to the car. We had to drive past the Art School to get out of town and as we did so I saw that the door was open. I asked Margie if she would like to see Fabio's sculpture studio where I had first held a hammer and a chisel and struck my first blow at a block of wood.

We entered, walked past the library on the left and down the stairs on the right that led to the basement and Fabio's studio, only to find it had been turned into a uni-sex washroom! Disappointed, but in need of relief, we made use of the facilities and left to drive home.

MADEIRA

In 2002 Margie and I went to Madeira for a week to escape a grey English February. One day we walked across town to Reid's Hotel and as we sipped a cold beer on the balcony overlooking the harbour of Funchal I told her about my other holidays on the island some 50 years before. Madeira was discovered by the Portuguese in 1418. It is a volcanic island about 150 miles out in the Atlantic with a 6,000-foot high summit, is 35 miles long and 15 wide. It is steep sided and boasts of not having a single sandy beach. Off to the north is a smaller island called Porto Santo that does have a five-mile-long beach of golden sand and a legend! Porto Santo claims that Christopher Columbus once lived there with his wife Filipa Moniz, the daughter of Bartolomeu Perestrelo who was the first Commander of the island. If Genoa-born Columbus did reach Porto Santo, I am not surprised that he thought the world was round as there is a lot of sea between Madeira and Italy!

I was 15 years old when I first saw Funchal's harbour. Apart from the mushrooming of huge hotels around the bay the scene has hardly changed. The hillside is still carpeted with little bright red terracotta tiled houses painted a traditional pale yellow with spinach-green window shutters, interspersed with bougainvillea. The town cascades down the side of the mountain into the harbour like a waterfall of scrambled egg.

The scene in front of me brought back many happy memories, but gone were the coal barges that floated like giant black sausages beyond the great stone wall that protects the harbour. Two small islands capped by 15th-century forts joined to the mainland by a wall form a well-protected harbour.

On the evening of our arrival we could see a three-masted brigantine berthed at the wharf. Thousands of these ships must have visited the island in the days of sail, as it was the watering port for the merchant ships on their way to the Caribbean, Brazil, Argentina, South Africa and Australia. The island's main source of income then had been fresh water, vegetables, fruit, sugar cane, wood and a place to repair storm damage. When I was 15 years old the Castle Line steamship company was still running between London and Cape Town.

It was the grape that made Madeira really famous. To begin with the local juice was not very good, but it was then discovered that the technique used with Port wine also worked well for Madeira. The secret of success was to put the wine into old oak brandy casks and ship it to India and back as ballast in a sailing ship. The rolling and pitching of the ship as it sailed the oceans kept the wine moving in the casks and that, along with being heated and chilled as it crossed the Equator and rounded the Cape of Good Hope, turned the contents of the barrel into the beautiful Madeira wine that was so much loved by the English.

When the British warship *Northumberland* called at Madeira to water on its way to St Helena in 1815 Napoleon was given a cask of wine. When he died in 1840 the cask was returned to the island unopened, so in 1950 it was broached and a bottle given to Churchill who drank it with great satisfaction, or so I read. By then the wine must have been at least 140 years old!

The export of sugar, bananas and wine made the islanders prosperous and the population grew. When I first went to Madeira in 1950 nothing much had changed for a century and the English still ran the place. As nearly all the wine was shipped to London a large number of British came to work on the island and as was typical of the colonial days, they soon established an English Club to cater for their social life.

When steam replaced sail the island became a coaling station and this was the reason for the black barges moored out in the bay. Cargo ships loaded with tons of coal would arrive from Wales and fill them up and when a steamship docked, a barge would be towed alongside so its coalbunkers could be replenished. More and more people got to know about the island from visiting it on their way to South Africa and because of the island's very favourable year-round climate they began to break their voyage for a holiday. It was not long before Mr Reid decided that it would be a good investment to build a luxury hotel for the wealthy travellers. Today the island is dependent on tourism. Madeira now has a land airport and is only a three-hour flight from Britain, which keeps the hotels full of tourists. We were told that there is such a demand for hotel staff they have to be brought in from Ukraine!

For our visit in 2002 we had been recommended by my teenage friend, Jimmy Welch, a native of Madeira, to stay at the Hotel Quinta Bela Sao Taigo. After settling in we went for a walk along the new promenade that has been built around the harbour. It was a wonderful feeling to be back once again on the island that had given me so much as a boy.

The replica of the 'Santa Maria'

One of the benefits of our hotel was that we could look out over the harbour and watch a replica of Columbus's *Santa Maria* sail by. The juxtaposition of the tiny wooden three-masted galleon chugging sedately past the giant tourist cruiser berthed at the quay was one of the most bizarre things we had ever seen.

One evening we walked down to inspect the *Santa Maria* at close quarters. Margie thought the tiny galleon looked like a floating walnut shell. When the ship cleared the harbour wall we watched the white canvas being unfurled and were amazed to think that such a ship had sailed to America and back. One of the fun things about living in Agecroft is that the house is 500 years old so was built around the time of Columbus's voyage!

My first visit to Reid's was when the island was just beginning to recover from WWII. As the two of us were on our own my mother decided that she would take me back to her old teenage haunt for the summer holidays. My two elder brothers had been drafted into the forces to do their National Service and my father was away in Australia on business.

School holidays were not long enough to include a week's trip out and back by boat, so we took to the sky and used the new Sunderland Flying Boat service from Southampton. It was a wonderful adventure and one I shall never forget. Our journey started very early in the morning just before sunrise. We were ferried out by launch to the giant silver seaplane, climbed on board and were shown to our seats in the belly of the whale. The water level was only just below the tiny portholes. The engines started up and we taxied across the bay watching the water streaming back from the float under the wing.

Sunderland Flying Boat

The roar from the engines got louder and louder making the whale groan. As we gathered speed the rushing water blocked out the world. The plane broke free of the ink-black sea and rose into the first hint of dawn on the horizon. As we climbed, the temperature dropped rapidly so we wrapped ourselves up in the blankets provided while swallowing hard, for the plane wasn't pressurised.

After a six-hour flight we arrived over Lisbon and started our approach to the River Tagus. Slowly we sank towards the water and when we touched down the whole world turned muddy yellow. It was a relief to climb out into the launch and be taken to the terminal, where we could walk and stretch our legs while the seaplane was refuelled for the two-hour flight to Madeira. Landing in the Funchal harbour was totally different as this time it was crystal-clear seawater that went swishing by.

That was 52 years ago and now, looking down from the Reid's balcony, memories of when I was a shy 15-year-old teenager came flooding back and I started to tell Margie about my summer of happiness.

Starting in 1920 my grandmother, Nell Freeland, used to go to Madeira every year with her monkey, Jacko, to avoid the English winter. She left England at the end of October and rented Quinta Vista Allegro, (Villa with the Beautiful View), that now looks onto the back of a giant hotel. She stayed there passing the time gambling at the Casino until her eldest son telegraphed to say that the first cuckoo had been reported in *The Times*, around the beginning of April. My mother said the house was very damp and the only heating came from burning charcoal in three-foot-wide brass dishes that used up all the oxygen and caused everyone to fall asleep at the dining table!

Because my mother was an afterthought and 18 years younger than her elder sister, she was brought up at home as an only child until Granny Nell could leave her in an English boarding school. For some odd reason the school chosen was a Roman Catholic convent and my mother said she had loathed every moment of her time there, as she was the only Anglican. The thing she most hated was laying the table at mealtime. Because the Great War had only just ended food was still rationed and one of the items in short supply was sugar. Each girl was only allowed one lump at teatime so the exact number of lumps necessary for each table were put into a bowl every evening. One day, when my mother was feeling exceptionally rebellious, and it was her turn to lay table, she decided to show her resentment by eating all the lumps allocated to her table. When the empty bowl was discovered my mother was dragged off to the Mother Superior who immediately expelled her.

My mother was delighted and as far as I can make out that was the end of her education, although at the age of 18 she and a friend were sent to the Sorbonne in Paris to learn French. That hadn't worked, as her French, like mine, was only adequate to read menus, which was not surprising, as she and her friend never attended lectures. Their chaperone had the wonderful name of Miss Gabitas and according to my mother she spent most of the time ill in bed. The two girls would set off each morning pretending that they were going to the university, but instead they went window-shopping, unless it was raining, when they took shelter in a museum.

'Nan with Jacko' in Madeira

Immediately after her expulsion she was loaded onto the next ship bound for Madeira by her married sister, Habby, and so began one of the happiest times of her life, judging by her oft-repeated stories. My mother would hark back to those days and tell me about how she and George, the father of my friend Jimmy Welch, had won the tennis tournament at the English Club, as well as how they had performed on the dance floor doing the Charleston. Jimmy and I worked out that his father must have been about 25 and my mother a highly spirited 18-year-old. What a dashing young couple they must have made, a sporty young blade with a dance-mad girl on his arm. According to my mother they had a ball!

Adam Blandy, the son of another of my mother's companions of the past, used to come down to Reid's in the morning to swim with Jimmy and me. The hotel's raft was moored fifty yards out from the rocks and acted as a private island for us boys. The water was crystal clear, about twenty feet deep, and you could see the bottom as clear as day, but we were never able to reach it.

Sometimes my mother used to borrow the hotel dinghy and row out to the coal barges in the bay with me swimming along behind. As we got further out the bottom would disappear and I felt as though I was suspended in space surrounded by a ball of sunrays that reached down into the black depths. I remember worrying about being swallowed by a whale, as in those days we often saw whales spouting as they swam past the island. Madeira had been a commercial whaling station until the great beasts vanished at the end of the 19th century. A taxi driver told us that the last whale sighting was in 1985, nearly 20-years-ago!

One day my mother decided that we would send Jimmy home in a bullock sledge and that we would go with him. These sledges used to compete with the horse-drawn carriages for passengers between Reid's and the cathedral down in Funchal. The bullock driver must have been surprised when we asked him to take us all the way up to Jimmy's beautiful home of Quinta Palmeira, a journey that would take well over an hour. We thought it was great fun, but Jimmy's father was not amused when we arrived in front of his house drawn by two lovely white oxen.

After lunch Reid's became as silent as a morgue as everyone retired for a siesta. Ever since those days I have been a great fan of siestas when on holiday. Shutting the eyes for ten minutes after lunch on a hot sunny afternoon is one of the great pleasures of life. The glory of Reid's was that after the siesta they served tea and patisseries on a trolley from which we were allowed to choose two cakes each. This ritual started at half past four and it was important to be there on time to get the first choice. I have never come across such succulent cakes anywhere else in the world, especially the *mille-feuille*, or is that just a greedy childhood memory?

Also staying at Reid's that first summer was the de Stoop family, consisting of four children and their mother. Ann-Françoise was the eldest and seventeen, followed by Ivan, then Martine and lastly a younger brother. Being a close family they always moved around in a group, swimming or playing table tennis under the trees.

In those days I was very shy, especially with girls. One day when I was sitting with my mother Ann-Françoise came over and asked me to join the family and play table tennis. I remember saying, "No thank you very much," in a shy English way, only, much to my surprise, to hear my mother say, "Yes, he would love to and thank you very much for asking him," while at the same time giving me a sharp kick under the table.

So began my second relationship with a girl if you count hugging Sally on the toboggan aged 12. Ann-Françoise was one of the kindest and nicest people I have ever met. She invited me into her family and made me feel one with them when we played games, swam, or walked around the hotel gardens. Never having had a sister I knew absolutely nothing about girls so to have Ann-Françoise as a friend was an amazing experience.

One evening Madame de Stoop organised a teenage dinner party and Ann-Françoise invited me to join them. After dinner we walked in the gardens under the full moon and for the first time in my life I became aware of the magic mixture of moonlight and a girl. The gardens are criss-crossed with paths, one of which led out to the headland on which the hotel is built. On this first visit to Madeira my mother's sister, Habby, and her husband were also staying in the hotel and one night Uncle Joe took me down to the headland to see a flowering cactus that blooms for one night a year when the moon is full. The magnificent flower was about six inches across and a mass of soft yellowish white stamen. Next morning when I went to look at the flower it had wilted into a heap of brown mush.

The Moon Flower was on the point of Reid's gardens

Leaning out over the terrace railings I showed Margie the balcony room the two sisters had shared looking out over the garden. After the de Stoop dinner and the unforgettable walk in the moonlight, the girls retired to bed as they were due to leave on the flying boat next day. I was much too excited to think of going to sleep so went back into the garden. I was extremely sorry my new friend was leaving and already missing her company. Of course I ended up in the shadows beneath the girl's balcony where I unashamedly began singing

Some enchanted evening from the musical South Pacific! When I told Margie this she nearly fell over the railing laughing, but that night my singing had the desired effect and the two giggling sisters came to the balcony and told me to go away or they would get into trouble.

As Ann-Françoise seemed to have enjoyed the friendship as much as I had we kept in touch by letter over the winter months. When the next summer holidays came around and my mother suggested that we should go to Madeira again, I immediately wrote and asked Ann-Françoise if she and her family would be there. She wrote back and told me that they unfortunately were not, but asked if I would like to come and stay with them for a week on the way home at their farm outside Lisbon. I was delighted and luckily my mother also thought it was a good idea.

My second summer in Madeira was quite different. I remember playing a lot of tennis with several island boys and being included in their mixed parties, but not having Ann-Françoise there meant it was not nearly as much fun and I couldn't wait to leave for Lisbon. When it was time to go little did I think that within six months I would be sailing past Madeira aboard *Port Napier* as a deckhand on my way round the world via Australia, my English school days over and a lifetime of adventure ahead of me.

The day of departure from the island finally arrived and three hours later we settled into the yellow waters of the Tagus where Ann-Françoise met me. I was so excited I didn't even wait to wave goodbye when the plane took off. The de Stoop family lived on a beautiful estancia surrounded by olive trees a little way out of Lisbon.

Ann-Françoise and I immediately picked up our friendship and I vividly remember our going to the cinema one night. When she suggested it I was really excited as I thought we would be alone, as she had a driving licence. As we were about to leave I was very surprised when a little old lady, dressed in black, climbed into the back seat of the car. It was her old nanny acting as a chaperone! Fortunately the old lady could not speak English so at least our conversation was private, but sitting in the dark with her beside us was pretty daunting as we couldn't even hold hands!

One hot afternoon after the siesta Ann-Françoise and I went for a walk. I was leaving the next day and this would be our last time alone. We strolled down a dusty farm track and came to an old ruined windmill. The roof had fallen in and all that remained was the circular wall with an opening that had once been a door. We went inside to explore and while there we shared our one and only kiss. It was only a light brush of the lips but it was the very first time I had kissed a girl. Thinking about it now I suppose Ann-Françoise must have intended it to happen or we would not have been standing in a ruined windmill, quite out of sight from prying eyes and chaperones. She must have chosen the spot for which I can only thank her as the kiss was a milestone in my life. Male horses might pull the chariot but female hands hold the reins!

Ann-Françoise and I wrote to each other over the next six months during which time I passed my exams and persuaded my parents that it would be better for everyone if I left school. Ann-Françoise, who was an extremely clever student, had arrived in London to study at a college. My mother had seen her several times during my last school term and when holiday time came she suggested that I should ask two of my friends to a theatre party in London and take Ann-Françoise as my partner. The evening arrived and I collected Ann-Françoise looking very sophisticated with her hair up and wearing a long dress as in those days the men wore black tie to the theatre. I can't recall anything else about the evening except dropping her off at her lodgings and there being *no goodnight kiss*. I guess we had both outgrown those two summers of happiness. For me it turned out to be Australia and for Ann-Françoise it was married life in Luxembourg.

In 1998 I was looking through a magazine in the dentist's waiting room and happened to see an article praising a book about Portuguese architecture written by Martine de Stoop, a name that of course immediately caught my attention. I wondered could this be Ann-Françoise's little sister?

I wrote a letter and addressed it to the publishers asking for it to be forwarded. Weeks later I received a letter telling me that, no, it was not the Martine that I had known, but the wife of Ann-Françoise's younger brother who had married a girl with the same name. The letter also gave me an address in Luxembourg. I wrote off again and soon received an answer from my friend of long ago, telling me that she was happily married to a lawyer with children and grandchildren. When I asked her if she would like to meet again if Margie and I ever passed through Belgium, she bravely agreed.

The following year when we drove down to Italy I decided to go via Luxembourg and call on her. The plan fell into place and we arrived one evening to stay the night with her and her older brother Ivan, who happened to be staying with her. We took them both out to dinner and talked about the past but sadly it was not a success as all we had in common was the past.

All along the Funchal breakwater in 2002 I saw 16-year-old students locked together in passionate embraces. How things have changed over the 50 years since my first kiss when we had to be chaperoned to the cinema!

When I left school my father asked me what I planned to do for the next six months before being conscripted into the armed forces to serve my two years of National Service, something everyone had to do when they turned seventeen in the years after the war. I had absolutely no idea how to answer the question, because I had not given any thought to my future or how I would earn my living. In the back of my mind I had a picture of sons following in their fathers' footsteps, as my friends planned to do. In those days there was no such thing as a Careers Master at schools.

One evening my father suggested that I should work my way around the world in a cargo boat via Australia, which sounded like a fantastic idea to me and I leapt at the suggestion. The trip would only take four months so I would be back in time for my call-up.

The next time we were in London my mother took me to Gieves and bought an 'off the shelf' seaman's uniform and an officer's cap with a Merchant Navy badge. When I got home and tried on the clothes I thought I looked pretty smart and the future very rosy.

One wet afternoon I put on the uniform and my mother drove me down to Tilbury Docks. We found the *Port Napier* and it looked extremely bleak, painted as grey as the day. I asked the chauffeur to drop me some way from the ship so I could walk alone to the gangway. I said goodbye to my mother and watched the car drive away. Suddenly the world didn't seem quite so rosy after all!

'Port Napier'

I climbed the gangway as though I was walking the plank and wondered if I hadn't jumped out of the frying pan into the fire. Perhaps I should have stayed another year at Rugby after all. I thought, *in for a penny, in for a pound*, and walked up the gangway to be met by a very friendly young officer, who seemed to know all about me and was waiting for my arrival. He took me straight down to a cabin.

The cabin could not have been nicer and I found out later that it was meant for the third mate, but because the ship was sailing without one the cabin had been assigned to me. My friendly officer told me to unpack and settle in and that he would be back in three hours and take me to supper in the saloon to meet the captain and the other cadets with whom I would be working during the voyage.

We sailed within a couple of hours of my coming on board by which time it was pitch dark outside. I have no recollection of meeting the captain or the cadets that evening. My next memory was of the mist-shrouded White Cliffs of Dover as they slipped by the following morning, while watched from the deck as I leant on the rail feeling decidedly miserable. If I had realised then that I would not see England again for 17 years I guess I would have been even more miserable, but thankfully what you don't know you don't worry about.

Work is a great cure for the blues and the bosun was just the man for the job. The first week on board I was employed with other deckhands to scrub salt from the paintwork with very cold fresh water, which left our hands numb. If during this job we found areas of paint lifting we chipped it off with a hammer. This was a rather satisfying job and warmed us up so we tried to find as much paint to chip as possible. As we steamed south the weather improved and the sun came out, making life on deck extremely pleasant.

The cadets spent at least four hours of every day learning navigation and all the other things a Naval officer is required to know. I was excused these lessons, which is why I spent so much time chipping paint!

The 'Cadet Officers' and gloomy 'John'

The cadets and I had our own table in the dining saloon while the captain and officers ate with the six fare-paying passengers. These privileged people used the upper lifeboat deck for exercise and as we headed slowly south we put out deckchairs so they could sit rugged up in the sun. My most important job during the whole voyage was to paint the little white circles on the deck for Shove Golf, a game played with a broom handle and wooden discs instead of golf clubs and balls. When it became hot we erected a canvas swimming pool and filled it with seawater in readiness for crossing the Equator and the inauguration of the passengers into the services of Father Neptune by the bosun and the carpenter. On Sundays we had the day off and were allowed to swim in the pool.

My work actually boiled down to helping the bosun and Chippy. Both men were extremely friendly and ran the ship as far as I was concerned. I became their *Go-for*. One day the bosun asked me to go up to the Bridge and ask for the 'key to the keelson'. The officer on duty told me to ask the wireless operator and he in turn sent me to someone else. This meant my running this way and that for an hour before the captain told me to tell the bosun to behave. The keelson turned out to be the spine of the ship and it certainly didn't have a key!

The bosun taught me how to splice a rope and I became quite good at it, spending many hours helping him with hessian ropes while he tackled the steel cables. He was so skilled that watching him was like watching someone knitting a wool jumper with heavy steel cables. Being able to splice rope has come in very handy all through my life.

Our first port of call was Cape Town where I remember feeling very important as I was given my first officer-type job and allowed to wear my white Naval cap. I was told to sit on the edge of the hold and count the boxes of frozen cod as they came on board, each one carried up the gangway on the shoulder of a native stevedore. I had to count the boxes as they passed me before they were put on a shoot and slid out of sight to be stacked into the freezers by more natives down below.

It was a beautiful sunny day and I couldn't get over the fact that all the natives wore thick army overcoats. The mystery was cleared up when we unloaded the cod in Adelaide and found that quite a few boxes were empty, so I guess the missing fish ended up in the pockets of the greatcoats!

My other exciting job in Cape Town was to go to the post office and collect the crew's mail. This entailed a long walk into town and my first footfall in Africa. It was also my introduction to being amongst a mass of black people as in those days there were very few to be seen in Britain.

Chippy was in charge of the dunnage that held the crates in place in the cargo holds, this being before the days of containers. We used to climb around down in the holds between the crates making sure that none of them had broken loose and had caused damage by crushing other crates. This was a very frightening job as we were surrounded by the creaking and groaning of the shifting cargo caused by the rolling ship.

When we were crossing the Indian Ocean we hit some extremely rough storms. I shall always remember one particular day when we were steaming well below latitude 40° south, close to the Raging Fifties, as it was then that the funnel caught on fire and we had to heave to while the flames were extinguished. While we wallowed in a very angry sea I watched the enormous wave crests race past us level with the lifeboat deck. It was one of the most frightening displays of raw nature I have ever seen as the huge waves had to be seen to be believed. Since that day I have always had unbounded admiration for sailors like Captain Cook as no words can adequately describe the fury of the southern oceans in a gale.

The mess in the holds caused by this event was frightful and the broken dunnage beyond repair. When Chippy and I went down to look in through the bulkhead at all the smashed timbers he decided that it would be suicide to go in to rectify the mess, so we didn't. The insurance companies were not going to be very happy.

Years later I read the diary of my great grandfather, Anthony Bennett Robinson's, first voyage in 1850 to Melbourne in a sailing ship. He also ran into very heavy weather in the Indian Ocean, which nearly caused the timber ship to sink as they were carrying bricks that began to swell when the sea broke through the hatch covers. It must have been an extremely risky passage in the days of the First Settlers. I read one very tragic story from the early history of Melbourne when after a six-month voyage a sailing ship ran aground and sank at the entrance of Port Philip Bay, only a few miles from its destination. The ship was carrying migrant families and everyone was drowned.

'SS Great Britain' in the ice heading for Australia

Anthony Bennett survived two trips out and one back so he was lucky. In an entry in his diary he wrote, *I managed to send a letter home on 'SS Great Britain' before it left Melbourne*, the second of Brunel's steel steamships, built in 1845 and now lying in a Bristol dry dock.

Anthony Bennett was born in 1805 and christened in Holcombe Church in Somerset only a few miles from where we now live, a fact that amazes me. When he settled in Melbourne he worked his way up to become the Financial Editor of *The Age* newspaper.

'Anthony Bennett Robinson' and 'WS' at 'The Age' offices

One of the jobs the bosun used me for was cleaning the outside of the Bridge windows. To reach them meant my climbing a very long ladder while he held onto the foot, struggling to keep it upright! Up at the top I hung on with one hand and scrubbed away at the glass with newspaper with the other. It was a scary job as the ship was rolling and I was very pleased when I had finished.

When the ship arrived in Adelaide we unloaded the frozen cod and three brand-new Jaguars, the most luxurious car to be built in England since the war. The holds of ships in those days were roofed over with heavy timber planks that were stacked onto a net by the ship's crane and then lifted out of the way. Unfortunately one corner of the net was not made fast, so as it was lifted the planks broke free and slid out, one by one, onto the top of the new cars below. The damage was unbelievable and it was lucky no one below was killed. It was definitely not going to be a good voyage for the insurers!

Much to my surprise, just after this accident happened, I was called up to the Bridge to report to the captain. What had I done wrong? I had been sharply told off by him a week before for whistling as I cleaned his portholes. He told me that I was out of tune and besides sailors considered it to be bad luck to whistle for the wind, so I should stop immediately.

I went up to the Bridge and the captain told me that he had received a message requesting shore leave for me to go and see my father. I couldn't believe my ears but immediately went and put on a clean shirt and ran down the gangplank where a taxi took me to the Adelaide address I had been given. It was wonderful to see my father so unexpectedly and we had a very happy lunch with me doing most of the talking. We had only a few hours as the ship was due to sail that evening, but in that time he suggested that I should disembark at Melbourne and stay for a month before catching the ship back to London from Sydney. I thought this was a great idea as I was thoroughly sick of the sea by then and happily agreed.

When the *Port Napier* arrived in Melbourne I asked my father if I could take the three cadets out for a meal and to the theatre as a 'thank you' for all their kindness to me during the voyage. The captain agreed to give them leave and we had a great evening as my father sent his chauffeur, Jim Ellis, to collect us from the docks and drive us around. I can't remember what the show was or where we ate but it was a very happy and fun party.

This was my first meeting with Jim and the beginning of our long friendship. He returned us to the ship where I found the bosun and Chippy waiting for me, both men more than a little under the weather and insisting on my having a drink with them. They were drinking rum and very soon I was completely fuzzy headed. Chippy asked me if I would give him my officer's cap as a souvenir, which I couldn't refuse, even though I was very sorry to give it up as I would need it for the voyage home.

The two men got very philosophical as they became steadily drunker and I got steadily sicker. They told me that they both intended to come back in the next life as a rich woman's pet dog, because they had had enough of being at sea and wanted to spend their next life sitting on a lady's lap! They eventually left me lying in the scuppers where I spent the rest of the night being sick. Jim came in the morning to collect me and my thumping brain. I have never had such a headache and it took many years before I could face drinking rum again.

In those days when he was in Melbourne my father made his home at Menzies Hotel. Jim took me there and I had a body-mending hot bath before being sent off to buy some summer clothes. The following day my father was flying to Broken Hill and he wanted me to go with him.

We set off in the morning in the Silver City aeroplane, the same small *Dove* that I had been in when we were lost over Holland and had spilt the tomato juice. The trip took several hours as Broken Hill is in the top north-east corner of NSW.

It was my first experience of being in the Australian Outback and I loved it, finding the smell, heat and space all very exhilarating. My father arranged for a tour underground and I found going down the shafts and walking the drives of the lead and zinc mines very exciting. We didn't have time to explore out into the Bush, but when we took off again for Port Pirie I saw more of the barren open sun-parched country that is so typical of the Outback.

We landed at the smelter plant in Port Pirie, north of Adelaide at the head of Spencer Gulf, and it was then that my father suggested that I take the overland train to Kalgoorlie to see the gold mines. He also suggested that, as I would then be in Western Australia, I should go on down to Perth and meet Willie Williamson, who was joint owner with WS of a wheat farm called 'Wanneranooka' 300 miles north of Perth near 'Three Springs'. I could spend a week with him and then return to Melbourne on the train before catching the ship home from Sydney.

The train trip across the Nullarbor Plain was an eye-opener to a boy who was fresh from the green English countryside. East to west the Nullarbor is 350 miles wide and 150 miles from the north to the southern edge, where it falls into the sea over a 300-foot high cliff. There are no rivers on the limestone plateau as the annual ten-inch rainfall immediately disappears underground, which is why, as the name applies, there are 'no trees'. The train track runs for 300 miles in a dead straight line without a bend over dead flat country. I had not experienced anything like that before in my life and found the two days of unchanging scenery absolutely fascinating.

I think the carriages must have been at least 100 years old and as I was travelling steerage and the seats were wood covered with brown leather, it was exceedingly uncomfortable. We rattled along at a very leisurely pace, stopping every now and then to fill up the old steam engine with water. I suppose the ticket included refreshments but I don't recall eating anything. I do remember only having enough money to buy ten Black and White cigarettes and that they were disgusting.

A canvas water bag hung at the end of the carriage with a tin cup on a chain so no one would pinch it. It was necessary to quench my thirst all through the day, as the heat was stifling, even though all the windows were open. This actually added another problem to the journey as the air was full of red dust that settled in a thick layer over everything. You could write your name on the leather seats by the time we reached Kalgoorlie and all the passengers looked like Red Indians.

Very early in the morning we pulled in to the station where I was met by Frank Espie Sr, the Manager of Great Western Mine. He took me to his bungalow for a much-needed shower that I stayed under for hours. When I was clean his wife gave me breakfast and then handed me some overalls, a pair of heavy steel-capped boots and a hard helmet as Frank had organised a trip underground for me.

A budding miner in Kalgoorlie

The most memorable thing about that trip underground was when I walked out of a tunnel into one of the largest caverns one could ever imagine. It was vast. I was standing on a balcony looking down on dinky-toy tractors loading ore into miniature trains. Looking up I could see the rock roof miles above. It was like a movie set for a James Bond film as lights shone this way and that illuminating different areas where I could see tiny men working. This vast chamber had been excavated to extract gold.

There was another shaft nearby called Iron Duke. Both this name and Great Western became very familiar to me as WS and Willie Williamson had named their racehorses after the two shafts. I believe one year Iron Duke won the Melbourne Cup or something equally prestigious.

Frank collected me when I returned to the surface and took me back to the bungalow for another shower. He was the proud owner of a brand-new Holden saloon, the first General Motors car made in Australia. He also owned a Jack Russell dog that used to stand on the back seat with his paws resting on the top of the front one. His head was directly by my right ear and his breath smelt awful. I shall never forget the next moment as suddenly the dog vomited down my neck! Another shower was needed and thank goodness I had been wearing someone else's overalls! Frank was only worried about his new car!

I took the train to Perth, arriving in the late evening and caught a taxi to the Esplanade Hotel. I was met by Willie who announced that we were off at first light to drive 300 miles north to 'Three Springs'.

The drive north was another eye-opener, as the road seemed to go on forever. Willie was very friendly and explained about the type of farming country we were passing through along the way. It was all very different to Chute Standen in Wiltshire as there was not a single blade of green grass to be seen anywhere. And was it hot! We had the windows open to catch some breeze but as it was mid-summer the air seemed to be coming from the open door of a furnace.

I had a wonderful few days at 'Wanneranooka'. Mrs Williamson was very kind and cooked red-hot curries for Willie, a taste he had acquired when he was manager of a silver mine in Burma that WS had been associated with, which is how they had met and became friends. Willie had been forced out of Burma by the Japanese invasion in WWII, escaping to Australia.

At the end of the week I returned to Perth on a very old bus. The car trip might have seemed to take forever, but compared to the bus it had been lightning fast. In those days there were no loos on buses, so the one stop we were allowed was something of a relief, as well as being my introduction to Bush facilities!

When I went to the railway station I was not looking forward to boarding the dusty old train one bit, so imagine my surprise and delight when I started to walk down the platform beside a giant snake of gleaming silver metal. A few days after my arrival in Perth the new Trans Australian Express had been inaugurated and I was about to travel on it. Each passenger had a little compartment to himself with an armchair that turned into a bed. Opposite the chair were a basin and a loo. You could even drink the water out of the tap, although I missed the swaying canvas bag with its chained cup as I had never seen anything like that before. There was a restaurant car where I had a beautiful dinner followed by a sumptuous breakfast the following morning before pulling into Adelaide. The whole journey had taken only one night instead of the two days on the way over. What a change, although the view from the rear observation car of the 300-mile long dead-straight track hadn't changed one jot.

I arrived back in Melbourne to be met by my father and was all set to join the ship again for the voyage home from Sydney. Over dinner that night he asked how I had liked Australia and, as I enthused, he asked, "Why don't you stay here?" I replied, "What about my National Service?" My father answered, "Well if you're not there you won't have to do it." Having heard what an awful time my brother Mike had had in the army in Germany I had no desire to suffer as he had. *Right*, I thought, *you like it here, why not stay?* So I did. Believe it or not in those days people from Britain didn't even have to have a passport to disembark in Australia. Looking back you could say I *jumped ship*.

If I was to become a farmer my father thought it would be a very good idea if I went to an agricultural college. As the academic term didn't start for a few months he suggested that I went to work on my aunt's property Torrumbarry before going to work for some friends near Ladysmith in NSW. This would take me up to Christmas, when my mother was due in Melbourne for the holidays.

It all seemed very simple and in hindsight I am sure the whole thing was planned right from the moment it was suggested that I should work my way around the world on a cargo boat. It had been a clever parental plot to get me to Australia, and the sort of trick I learnt to play when I became a father and started to worry about what our three boys were going to do with their lives. All I can say is I am extremely thankful to my parents for hatching the plan, as I can't bear to think of all the wonderful adventures I would have missed out on if I hadn't stayed Down Under.

I went to both Torrumbarry and Ladysmith and loved both places. By that time I was completely hooked by 'life on the land' and couldn't think of any alternative as a job. I fully intended to become a sheep farmer, although little did I know what was around the corner in the form of Roseworthy Agriculture College. All I could think about was spending the Christmas holidays with my parents at a hotel on Port Philip Bay.

When my father suggested that I should go to an agricultural college he asked WS for his advice as to how to go about getting me a place in the Victorian one where he had been a student, but this proved to be impossible as there was a long waiting list. Fortunately WS found out from his friend Professor Hedley Marston that there was a place available at the South Australian college near the town of Gawler just north of Adelaide, so it was decided that that was where I should go.

My mother and I flew over to Adelaide and were met at the airport by Hedley in an enormous maroon-coloured American car. The trip to Roseworthy luckily only took about half an hour as the day was stinking hot and the car was extremely fumy. I was full of foreboding, which grew steadily worse when we pulled into an avenue of giant date palms that led to a large red stone building that looked uncommonly similar to Michell House. I had landed back at Rugby!

I learnt later that after leaving me at Roseworthy my mother cried all the way back to the airport. Well, I remember wanting to cry myself when I thought about the next three years I would have to spend at Roseworthy!

Roseworthy Agriculture College

As it happened my time at college turned out to be an amazing experience and one I would not have missed for anything in the world. I was not yet 18 and about to start a new adventure. The lessons learnt on the ship as I worked my passage to Australia stood me in good stead, as I now realised that I had been brought up with a silver spoon in my mouth, but in fact I was a 'nobody'. The ship life had taught me one of the axioms I have followed all my life, *Keep your nose above the water and your head below the bullets.* I immediately realised that this would be a very good policy to follow at Roseworthy. The fact that Fate had other plans was not to be foreseen.

I was put into a three-bedded dormitory, one bed of which was used by Austen De Caux and another by Peter Dunn. They became my firm friends and we had a great deal of fun together. De Caux's parents owned a sheep station in the semi-desert near Broken Hill. Life there was rough and Austen was a tough nuggety character who liked to bomb around on his old army motorbike. Years later I learnt the tragic news from Peter Dunn that Austen had died from cancer not long after finishing his three years at Roseworthy.

Peter came from a wheat farm on the Eyre Peninsula, which borders the Nullarbor Desert. What a mixture! Two tough Australian characters from the Outback and one privately-educated Pommy schoolboy raised in the Home Counties and the West End of London! These two companions turned my time at Roseworthy College into an unforgettable experience.

Peter Dunn became the Parliamentary Representative of the Eyre Peninsula and was eventually elected Leader of the House of Legislation for South Australia. Years after Roseworthy, he and his wife Heather came to England on official Government business and visited us at Agecroft. I was recovering from a back operation and so had to greet him in my pyjamas, but it was as though we had only just parted, rather than over 40 years ago; but that is what friendship is all about.

In 1952 the college was an old-fashioned farm that still used draft horses to pull carts. Lessons included learning to milk cows, which meant getting up at four thirty in the morning in the pitch dark and wandering around with a torch looking for the brutes out in a paddock, while freezing to death. The college had a winemaking course, but I never tasted the product. When the grapes were harvested they were dumped in a big concrete holding trough and left overnight. In the morning before pressing them they had to chase the possums off the grapes!

I had been at the college for about a month when my father arrived in Adelaide on business, and drove up to see me in a little Ford Prefect car that my brother Mike had used when he was working up at the Broken Hill mines. Mike had crashed it, but it had been repaired and my father gave it to me. I couldn't believe my luck at having my own car. However, there was a problem, I didn't have a licence! Thank goodness in those days it was easy to get a licence in South Australia as you were only required to take a written test on How to Drive! You learnt to drive on your own after you got the licence. I had taken lessons from my mother in England, so luckily did know the basics.

My father had been introduced to Sir Keith and Lady Angas who lived quite close to the college on a beautiful property called Lindsay Park, near the little town of Angaston. They had very kindly asked us both to stay for the night and we drove over to meet these two dear people who agreed to act as my guardians while I was at the college. I drove my father back to Adelaide in the Ford Prefect and then returned to college with my beautiful new battleship-grey baby. The joy of the car was that it gave me and my new friends the freedom of the open road and ability to escape occasionally from the college.

The farm work was mixed with school lessons so it was just like the environment that I had fought so hard to escape from in England. However, our trips to Adelaide for parties became more and more frequent as Peter and Austen had many young female friends from their school days. Life soon took on a whole new aspect!

I often spent the weekend at Lindsay Park with the Angas family and their daughter, Sarah, who was a few years older than me. It was like a second home, the family became my friends, and their house an oasis for me to escape to. Riding a horse in the hills around the farm with Sarah through some of the prettiest country in Australia was an absolute joy.

The Roseworthy swimming pool was an earth dam full of the most disgusting brown slimy water you can imagine. The college had a water polo team that used to play against other colleges in Adelaide. Thinking it to be a form of escape I volunteered for the team, but only once, as our opponents held us under when the referee was not looking and pulled our trunks off from behind when swimming for the ball. Competitive sports!

I have never much liked competitive sport and was brought up by my mother to believe that the point of playing tennis, golf, ping-pong or cards was to have fun, not to win. It was certainly not my idea of fun to be half drowned in water stinking of chlorine or in liquid mud.

My dislike of competitive sport became very apparent to me at Rugby. Everybody in the school had to enter at least one event at the school's annual athletic competition and pay one shilling for doing so! As I enjoyed the long-distance runs that we were sent on when it was too wet to play games I put my name down for the 1,500 metre heats. When we were halfway through the race and I was running second, I suddenly realised that I could go much faster, so passed the leader and won the race. I confess to being rather pleased with myself when I went up to the master who was recording the names for the next heats. I gave my name and was told that I had not qualified, even though I had won as I was outside the time limit! I went away in disgust and have never competed since in any athletic sport. I do love watching the Olympics, golf tournaments and of course, Wimbledon, but stick to being an armchair participant!

The little Ford Prefect was a joy and was the beginning of my love affair with Ford cars. I must have owned at least eight Ford cars since that first one, all second-hand. We could get five people in at a squeeze for trips into the Gawler cinema. Gawler was a small town in those days and owed its existence to being a railway junction. Lines went north to the wheat country and east into the vineyards of the Borossa Valley. The main street was the Sturt Highway that ran all the way from Adelaide to Sydney via Mildura.

Gawler became a necessary haunt for me after buying some toothpaste at the chemist's one day. The girl behind the counter was a beautiful black-haired doe-like creature, an Audrey Hepburn look-alike, and absolutely enchanting in her white uniform. I was instantly smitten and found that I was in desperate need of a lot of articles from the chemist's. Her name was Rosalyn and she didn't seem to mind serving me, so before I ran out of money I asked her if she would like to come to the local cinema one evening. Luckily she agreed and so began my third romance.

The college dance was coming up and I asked her if she would like to come as my partner. The dance became the best event of the college year as far as I was concerned as Rosalyn was quite the most beautiful girl there and I enjoyed basking in her aura. Not only was she pretty, but she had a good sense of humour and was great fun to be with.

Rosalyn became such a part of the gang that I took her to Lindsay Park one day to meet the Angas family. They received us all with what appeared to be open arms, but I learnt later from my mother that Lady A had written to her saying that she did not approve of my girlfriend and that the association should be curtailed immediately! Rosalyn's father worked on the railway line, his job being to hammer spikes into sleepers. He was a nice gentle giant of a man and when I used to call to collect Rosalyn from her home he and his wife were always friendly and welcoming. They were good salt-of-the-earth Aussies and the type of people I have always preferred to be with.

One day I fell ill, waking up with very sore testicles. Thinking back to the lecture at Rugby about VD and catching a disease from lavatory seats, I knew it wasn't that. I obviously had something else wrong with me so I drove into the hospital and saw the doctor who told me that I needed a course of penicillin, and, much to my relief, that there was nothing wrong that a few days in hospital would not fix. He gave me an injection straight away and told me to go back to college to collect a toothbrush.

Whether it was the injection, or the dirt road out to the college, or I was driving too fast, I don't know, but as I reached the last corner before arriving back at the college gates, a dog ran out in front of me and in trying to avoid it I lost control of the car. The outcome was that I found myself in the back seat and upside down. I climbed out and walked back to the college, rang the local garage and asked them to come and sort the problem out. Thoroughly disgusted with myself, I called a taxi that took me back to hospital to get well.

I was in hospital for about a week, but luckily discharged in time to be Rosalyn's escort at her Coming Out Dance in the Gawler Town Hall. In those days these country town dances were very important affairs especially to 18-year-old girls, who wore white wedding dresses and long white gloves for their presentation to the town's Mayor. It was to be the biggest night of Rosalyn's life and I knew that she had been looking forward to the event, had made her own dress, and been practising her curtsy for weeks. She had chosen me as her escort and I was to wear a dinner jacket and black bow tie. In fact I was looking forward to the affair as much as she was.

The week before Rosalyn's big night two of our First Year were punished for a minor infringement of some stupid college rule. The students of each year's intake elected two colleagues to represent them and one of ours was way too big for his boots. He called a meeting and proposed that we should ask the master involved to let our two mates off, and that if the master didn't agree to our demands, we should walk out of the lesson and go on strike. Hard to believe but absolutely true!

Well, of course the master didn't let our mates off, so we walked out and the Principal of the college cancelled all leave for a fortnight, a period that covered Rosalyn's 'Coming Out Dance'. Come the night I slipped out of the college with a small bag containing the dinner jacket I had hired for the evening. I changed at Rosalyn's home and drove to the ball in the Prefect, hoping that there would be no one present from the college.

Rosalyn looked like a bride that evening and was the belle of the ball. There were about ten girls being presented to the Mayor and when the time we were all marshalled into a crocodile at the entrance of the Hall. The band started up and we walked forward as couples so the girls could be presented. Thank goodness we were the last in line so I had time to see what I was meant to do when we got to the rostrum. Rosalyn curtsied to the Mayor and then we all danced around the floor to the applause of the crowd. As we passed the clapping crowd I saw the master whom we had walked out on when we had walked out on strike!

It was well into Sunday when I eventually got back to the college having changed into day clothes on the way. Surely the master wouldn't report me after seeing that I was a partner to one of the girls at the most important event of her life. I was wrong again! It was another leaving Rugby and getting beaten after visiting the swimming pool situation. He must have rushed home and reported me immediately because at breakfast I was told the Principal wished to see me in his office at once. I finished my breakfast while working out what I would say. I realised that I was in deep trouble and that the punishment would probably be the cancellation of all leave for the rest of the year; something I just could not tolerate. After nine months the college atmosphere was boring me to tears and there were still two more years to go. Could I stand that? Perhaps this was the best chance I would ever have of getting out of the place with my honour intact, so I decided that I would resign.

Having come to this conclusion I marched off to the Principal's study, knocked and was called in. "Good morning, Mr McCullock, I have come to resign from the college. I don't think this place is suited to me." He looked at me and said, "Good, that means I won't have to expel you." It was lucky I had resigned as obviously the intended punishment was to be worse than I thought it would be. *Expulsion*! I had visions of having the buttons stripped from my uniform and sword broken over the knee of the General and being drummed out of the Regiment in front of my fellow officers!

I went upstairs and packed my bag and said goodbye to Peter and Austen and drove away from the college, literally shaking the dust from the soles of my feet. When I think back on all the adventures I had over the next two years that I should have spent in college, undoubtedly it was quite the best thing that I have ever done. I drove away feeling free and also missed the exams that I probably would have failed!

Of course there would be repercussions and I would have to face the music, but I believed that I had done the honourable thing by Rosalyn and had no regrets whatsoever. In my eyes I had behaved like an Officer and a Gentleman, although I did wonder if anyone else would agree with me.

The first person I went to see was Rosalyn. She was of course very upset and blamed herself, but I explained to her that wasn't the case. I told her I was going to have to disappear for a while and had come to say 'goodbye'. Both of us shed tears, but as she was the prettiest girl in town I was quite sure that there would be plenty of Roseworthy students buying more toothpaste than they needed as soon as the news spread that I had left the scene. I heard years later that she married but the relationship hadn't worked out. I hope now she is leading a happy life as she was a really beautiful person, fun to be with, and every time I see Audrey Hepburn in a film, I think of her. She was a fawn. I never saw Rosalyn again after saying goodbye that morning, but I remember her oh so very well.

My next stop was Lindsay Park as an explanation was due to Sir Keith and Lady A as my guardians. I told them the whole story and they both agreed that I had done the right thing going to the ball as Rosalyn's escort. The dear people said that I was welcome to stay with them until the end of the year as it was the haymaking season and they needed an extra pair of hands to bring in the bales and stack them. I really had to work hard for my bread and butter, but loved every moment and learnt a lot.

But, to return to the man who got me into Roseworthy: Professor Hedley Marston. What a wonderful man and what a character! On my trips to Adelaide I would often go and see him at his office at the University of Adelaide. He was Head of the Commonwealth Scientific Institute Research Organisation, or the CSRIO. He was a brilliant scientist, a Fellow of the Royal Society, specialising in nutrients connected with animal health, especially sheep. He was the inventor of the Cobalt Bullet that stops fibre breaks in wool. Years later, when I was a farmer in the Ninety Mile Desert, I had to shove his bullets down the sheep's throats so he was constantly in my mind when I was doing what was an extremely unpleasant job.

Hedley's office was like an Aladdin's Cave. It was large, like the owner, and his desk was huge, completely covered with stacks of papers. On a wall between two windows was an amazing black and white mural depicting African dancers that he was painting. It was like a giant woodcut. Behind his office was a laboratory and in pens outside were his pet sheep, which always greeted him with welcoming bleats. Whatever went in, came out, or was cut off, was collected and weighed by Hedley.

Professor Hedley Marston

Sometimes Hedley used to invite me to his home for dinner. His house was wall to wall with books. It was a typical one-storey old-fashioned Victorian colonial house with a central corridor running away from the front door with small rooms off it. Either side of the corridor along the floor were stacks of books four feet high. The sitting-room walls were covered with books, as was the study and the dining room and, I am sure, the bedroom as well.

Hedley was a big man, but his wife was tiny and hardly ever spoke. He, on the other hand, never stopped talking, had an infectious giggle and loved telling stories. He had an enormous egg-shaped head and his body was a similar shape. After finishing the meal Hedley used to take me into his study and tell me tales, and what tales they were!

He told me that he was an orphan and had grown up in a boys' institute where he had received a brilliant education. As he did so well at school he was able to sit for the entrance exam for the university when he was very young. He had won a scholarship and met an elderly Professor named Archibald Watson who adopted him as his son. Watson guided Hedley's studies at the university and when he had finished his courses, achieving Distinctions in every subject, took him on as his personal assistant. Towards the end of Watson's life, when he was in his eighties, he taught Hedley to speak a Polynesian dialect saying that it would improve his mind. Once Hedley was fluent, he then taught him to write the language using the Greek alphabet, which the younger man gladly went along with to please his mentor. As it turned out, there was a reason for learning to read and write this secret language, because when Watson died at the age of 91 he left his personal diaries to Hedley, written, in, guess what, *Polynesian Greek*! Hedley couldn't show me the diaries of this obviously brilliant and gifted scientist-cum-linguist because they were locked away in a bank vault, but he told me some of the stories and I am positive that they were true.

Australian Encyclopaedia. Archibald Watson was born on July 27th 1849, the son of a sea captain who became a land settler on the upper Murray River. He was educated at Scotch College, Melbourne, and then spent some time in the Pacific Islands as a trader. He was persuaded to follow a scientific career by the noted botanist F von Mueller whom he met in New Guinea. He obtained a medical degree at both the Universities of Göttingen and Paris and became a Fellow of the Royal College of Surgeons in England. In 1885 he was appointed the first Professor of Medicine at the new University of Adelaide and occupied the chair for 34 years. He retired to live on Thursday Island in the Torres Strait at the very tip of Queensland, dying on July 30th 1940, aged 91.

The main cash crops in Queensland in the second half of the 1800s were sugar cane and cotton. Harvesting these two crops requires a lot of labour, which is why the infamous slave trade triangle came into existence between Bristol, Africa, West Indies and the southern states of America. The same manpower shortage was experienced in Queensland and to solve the problem *Blackbirding* came into being. Blackbirding was the name given to traders who kidnapped natives from the South Sea Islands and brought them back to sell to the Australian plantation owners. The first 67 slaves to be sold made £7 a head and were imported into Queensland in 1863 by the captain of the *Black Dog*. The trade was not made illegal until 1904 by which time over 50,000 natives had been blackbirded, a little talked-about black page of Australian history.

Archibald Watson apparently was an adventurer in his early twenties who wanted to go to sea like his father. It is possible that he knew something about the blackbird trade as he spent some time in the Pacific Islands as a trader, could speak the language and retired to live on Thursday Island. Considering his later illustrious career in Adelaide I am not surprised that he would want to keep his diary secret and what better way than to write them in Polynesian dialect using the Greek alphabet.

Hedley never mentioned blackbirding and only told me the stories that concerned the mines, because of my family's connection to Broken Hill. One in particular was a fascinating tale and I should record it because it is quite amazing. The diaries were kept in Watson's old sea chest and I believe Hedley destroyed before he died in the Sixties.

The background to the story follows the discovery by the famous explorer, Charles Sturt, of the Barrier Range in the north-west of NSW in 1844. The range is traversed by numerous white quartz reefs, which are associated with gold deposits. These features gave rise to a fruitless gold rush in 1867 that ended in tragedy as no gold was found.

It was not until 1883 that a boundary rider on Mt Gipps Station named Charles Rasp pegged out a 40-acre mining claim that he mistakenly believed to be tin on a *broken hill*, a great iron stone outcrop. He and the manager of the station sank a 100-foot deep shaft and struck a silver vein. The ore samples they sent to Adelaide for assay proved to have 18,000 ounces of silver to the ton. They founded Broken Hill Proprietary in 1885 and by 1952 the value of mineral output from the mines was £335,000,000.

Hedley's story began when bachelor Charlie Rasp became a rich man. His discovery meant that he had to go to Adelaide on business and it was on one of these trips that he met a beautiful 17-year-old German waitress called Agnes who worked in a bakery, (not a chemist like I had!). He fell head over heals in love with the girl the moment he set eyes on her and proposed marriage immediately. But there was a problem; the girl was already engaged to another young man.

Charlie was in despair but, being a resourceful man, he decided that the only thing to do was to get rid of his rival. As murder was out of the question, the solution to the problem was to buy him off! Cash was scarce, but perhaps he could tempt the rival to disappear from the scene if he gave him shares in his new BHP company. He met his rival and they settled on Charlie getting the girl in exchange for some of his shares.

Charlie broke the news to the girl of the departure of her fiancé and then comforted her broken heart, promising to take care of her if she agreed to marry him. They lived a happy life together in great comfort above the city in the Adelaide Hills for 15 years before the hard life in the Outback, which had included digging a 100-foot deep shaft in hard iron stone, took its toll. He died in 1907 leaving Mrs Rasp a very rich widow.

When Agnes had recovered from her loss she decided to visit the land of her parents as she had heard many stories about Germany in her youth and she longed to see the country of their birth. She travelled by sea to Europe reaching Germany in 1913. When she arrived she decided that she would like to marry again but also that she would like to have a title. Agnes let slip at a girls' tea party that it was her intention to marry, and before you could say 'Jack Robinson', she was being courted by an elderly Count, a retired officer in the Imperial German Army. She accepted his proposal and a wedding date was set. The Count then confessed that he was very short of cash and had to settle some debts before the wedding could take place. Agnes was no fool so said she would settle his debts on the day of the wedding.

On the morning of the ceremony she and the Count went to the bank where she transferred a large sum of money into his account before going to get dressed for the ceremony that would take place later in the day. She arrived at the church and walked up the aisle to be met at the altar by the officer in full military dress uniform. With great ceremony he stepped forward, saluted, drew his revolver and shot his brains out!

Hedley said that Watson's diary went on to tell that Agnes was made of pretty stern stuff and without flinching, *flicked the grey matter from her dress*, and asked if there were any other takers! An army officer stepped forward, also introduced himself as a Count and Agnes left the church as his wife, having insisted on the wedding taking place before settling the new Count's debts. The groom had agreed to this arrangement as long as he was not expected to return to Adelaide with her, which suited the bride as she also wanted to stay.

Fate still had one cruel trick to play on the poor unfortunate baker's waitress. The Great War began the week after Agnes was married so she spent the duration of the war in Germany under house arrest while the Count went back to the army and was killed in the fighting.

After the war Countess Agnes returned to Australia, took up her life again in her old home in the Adelaide Hills and became a recluse, only seeing a very few close friends, one of whom was her doctor, Archibald Watson, who used to take Hedley with him when he went to see her. When she died Watson attended to the Estate as the executor of her will. He went to the bank to check the financial situation and found to his surprise that the account was virtually empty. He returned to the house and with the aid of the servants started to lift the carpets in her bedroom where they found thousands of high denomination notes and hundreds of BHP share certificates. She must also to have slept badly as her mattress was stuffed with money! Countess Agnes had lost her faith in people during her years in Germany.

So ended one of Hedley's stories. I am sure you can imagine my fascination on listening to such a tale when only just 18 years old. Hedley was a marvellous storyteller and I have the fondest memories of the great man. William Dobell did a fabulous portrait of him, which is in the Adelaide Art Gallery. Dobell also painted my grandfather, but WS was so horrified by the portrait he had it locked away in a bank where it stayed until he died!

I met Hedley only once more after my departure from Roseworthy and that was when he and WS drove up from Adelaide to visit me in the Ninety Mile Desert. Margie and I had only just been married and we were very nervous about having two such great men visit us for lunch. Hedley returned to Adelaide after the meal, but at least Margie had a chance of meeting him. I showed WS around the property. I remember complaining to him that the fertiliser came in three bushel bags weighing 186 lbs each and were very heavy to carry. He laughed, telling me not to be a weakling as when he was my age they used four bushel bags! Nowadays nothing can packed in bags over 50 lbs so I wonder what he would have to say about that! After the tour he had a long siesta and we then put him on the train for Melbourne before Margie and I went off to dance all night at a shearing-shed party with our friends.

Hedley opened my mind to Adaptation. I was thinking about this the other day on my walk before breakfast through the glorious countryside of Somerset. I recalled the giant elm trees that used to grow in every hedgerow 35 years ago when we first came to live here. Standing up to 75 feet high and a good 4 feet in diameter they were spaced out along the lanes at intervals of about 20 yards or so, all over the countryside. Now there isn't one left. The mighty have been brought low by a microscopic virus carried by a beetle. The Dutch Elm disease shows just how fragile our environment is and how vulnerable to change. All life has to *Adapt*.

After helping bring in the hay at Lindsay Park, I said goodbye to the Angas family. It was time to leave South Australia and I set off to drive the 900 miles to Melbourne in my trusty Ford Prefect. We crossed the Mount Lofty Range and headed towards Bordertown where I intended to stay the night. Before reaching the town there is a wide plain of barren scrubland that stretches for miles and miles. It was right in the middle of this stretch of nothingness that the Prefect decided to die on me.

It had been a boiling hot December afternoon and the needle of the Prefect's temperature gauge had reached the red line and had stayed there while climbing over the Mt Lofty Range. I had decided to push on, freewheeling down the hills, in the hope of limping into the next town. In those days there were no filling stations along the highway. The day might have been very hot but the night was absolutely freezing. I didn't want to leave the car with all my worldly possessions in it, including a rifle, so I decided to sleep the night in the back seat and get towed into town next morning. I don't think I have ever been so cold in my life and it was a truly miserable night. Luckily I had some drinking water and the Angas family had given me a box of chocolates for Christmas, so I didn't go hungry.

Next morning I flagged down a truck and he kindly towed me into Tailem Bend, the next town. I found a garage but as it was Saturday there was no hope of getting spare parts until Monday. I had just enough money to send a telegram to my father asking him to wire me £50 to cover fixing the engine and pay for a room at the local pub. Tailem Bend really was at the end of the world at that time and a more terrible place to be stuck in with or without money you can not imagine. My father telegraphed the money on Monday so the engine was fixed the following day and I was able to leave. For years afterwards, whenever I drove through Tailem Bend on our way to and from Adelaide, I would get the shudders thinking about that weekend.

However, my troubles were not over yet. On arriving in Melbourne I got a rocket from my father for not telephoning to let him know I was all right. My parents had got it into their minds that I had had an accident. I have never forgotten the lesson of how important it is not to leave people guessing. As he firmly pointed out, one can always reverse the telephone charges!

My father had asked his great friend, Syd Emanuel, who owned a vast cattle station in Kimberley in the north-west corner of Western Australia, if I could work there for a year to gain experience. Not only had Uncle Syd agreed to my going to his three million acre station that carried 55,000 breeding cows, but he also gave me an introduction to the owner of a sheep station called Liveringa, where I might possibly find work. I had to wait three months before departing for the North because the Monsoon season happens at Christmas and there would be no point in leaving for Kimberley until the end of March, as the place would be under water.

To fill in the time I enrolled for an electrical welding course because if I were to become a farmer I would need to know how to fix things. I really enjoyed the course and found that I could run a smooth weld.

I also enrolled for flying lessons. I had been for a flight in a Tiger Moth biplane and had become enthralled by the thought of learning to fly. The flight had been from Coffs Harbour into a cattle station near Thora that belonged to a friend of my father, Sam Horden. I had flown in a small plane north from Sydney to Coffs Harbour and then transferred to the Tiger Moth for the last leg over the mountains. I couldn't believe my eyes when the pilot walked me out to the little plane with an open cockpit. The pilot gave me a leather helmet and goggles, strapped me in, plugged in the speaking tube and told me not to touch anything. He then climbed in and a mechanic swung the propeller. Once, twice, *contact*, and then a third time when the engine burst into life. We taxied out and roared off down the runway. The pilot shouted in my ears, "You okay?" I shouted back, "Couldn't be better." I felt like the Red Baron in the Great War! The wind whistled over my head and the joystick wiggled about between my legs. I had never been so exhilarated.

My favourite book as a child had been *Pilot Small* and here I was as my childhood hero. The feelings one experiences in an open plane are so entirely different to those felt in an enclosed one that they cannot be compared. To begin with the land below was mainly neat little squares of banana plantations, but soon their order gave way to mountain ranges and miles of forest. We were flying no more than 1,000 feet above the terrain, so I could see everything as clear as day.

'The Little Aeroplane' by 'Lois Lenski'

"We'll be there in ten minutes," came the pilot's voice from the speaking tube. Blast, it was all going to end too soon! "Can we do some acrobatics like looping the loop?" I shouted back down the tube. "No, not with your case in the back. I'll do a stall turn when we are over the field," he replied. What was a *stall turn*, I wondered? The pilot had climbed steadily since my request and we were now about 3,000 feet above the ground. "Okay, here we go," came the

96

voice in my ears. We went into a dive to gain speed and then pulling out started going straight up. Just as we were about to stall he flipped the biplane over on the end of its wing and we were nose down and hurtling towards the earth again. What a thrill! We landed and the manager of the station drove out to meet us. I thanked the pilot for the best experience that I had ever had. What a memory! Writing about it left me quite breathless.

The reason for my flight was not just to amuse me but to collect a car for Sam and drive it back down to Sydney. My childhood friend, Tim Emanuel, arrived from another cattle station and the two of us set off to drive south. When we reached Sydney we were asked to a party where I met a girl, but that is another story.

My memory of the stall turn was the reason I decided to learn to fly while waiting for the Monsoon to end. I found out that I could get lessons at the small grassed Moorabbin Airfield just outside Melbourne so I drove out and enrolled in the course. I never flew solo as I just could not get the knack of landing the damn thing. I loved flying in the Tiger Moth, taking off, stall turning, looping, side slipping; all came to me with relative ease, but I just could not judge the three-point landing and always bounced several times before coming to a halt. Always flying with an instructor meant that I was completely free from any worries about crashing, as when I made a mistake he would take over and straighten up before I took control again. It was a complete joy, but I found out that I was not a natural pilot.

My time was up and I had to leave. I am not sorry I didn't get the knack of flying as my life might have taken a completely different course. I was really hooked and dreamt of becoming a full-time pilot. When I think of the wonderful life I have had, thank goodness I didn't. Years later I was taken up in a hang-glider while skiing in France. I thought that I would be flying like a bird in complete silence. Gliding turned out to be a great disappointment as the noise of the rushing wind completely ruined the sense of freedom I had hoped for. I realised then that most birds lead a very noisy life, apart perhaps from owls and buzzards!

However, I still dream about flying Tiger Moths so have organised for my grandson Sam to go for a flight on his 13th birthday. I can't wait to see his face as he climbs on board and lands again. Boys will be boys!

I have only once kept a diary in my life and that was during my time in Kimberley, and the extraordinary thing is that over the 50 years that have passed since that time it has remained in my possession. Keeping the diary on this one occasion was probably something to do with the stories Hedley had told me from Archibald Watson's diaries only months before I went north. Sadly my diary makes very dull reading compared to those tales, but when I read it recently it did make my Kimberley days come alive for me again. The diary also played a part in my life many years later when I became interested in the Bradshaw paintings of Kimberley.

My entries capture my reaction to meeting Aborigines for the first time and working with black people. It was not until WWII when the American army was billeted in England that most Britishers came in contact with black people. My first mass contact with a coloured race had been with the Zulu stevedores in Cape Town, when the ship had docked to load cargo on my voyage from England to Australia. The diary shows how my feelings about the Aborigines changed from fear to a paternal friendship.

I read that I arrived in Perth on April 6th 1955 and stayed at the old Esplanade Hotel. What a superb old-fashioned Victorian hotel it was in those days! I am sure it has long since been pulled down; if so, what a shame! I was only in Perth long enough to meet the owner of Liveringa Station, Mr Forest, who I hoped would employ me. The interview must have gone well enough as he agreed to give me a job for a few months. I flew north the following day and arrived in Derby to be met by Robert Rowell, the town's shipping agent.

Robert was very kind to me and let me sleep the night on his veranda as there was no way of getting out to the station until the following day. Liveringa was the first of two stations I was to work on during my time in Kimberley. It was a giant sheep station on the north bank of the Fitzroy River, about halfway from Derby to Fitzroy Crossing. Uncle Syd's cattle station was located on the south bank further up stream and opposite Fitzroy Crossing.

When I arrived at Liveringa I was met by the manager, Mr Kim Rose. That night he asked the four jackeroos working on the station to dinner. He was a perfectionist and we all had to wear white shirts, shorts and long white socks so we looked like officers in the Royal Navy. The homestead was of a simple open design situated on top of a steep rocky outcrop where it could capture every bit of breeze during the sweltering monsoon. From the veranda that ran around the house there was a wonderful view out over the flood plains of the Fitzroy River and I remember the sunset that evening was very spectacular. However, this luxury was not to last as the next day I was driven to an out-station called Paradise to work for Robin Campbell.

My diary tells me that Liveringa and Paradise were comprised of 700,000 acres, and carried 44,000 sheep that annually cut 900 bales of wool. Also there were 700 miles of fences and 70 windmills. On my first day I was one of a group that mustered 3,200 sheep on horseback from a 15,000-acre paddock called Duchess. Numbers are very big in Kimberley!

The diary goes on to say that the mosquitoes were also numerous and that I was eaten alive during the night, and that frogs were everywhere, even in the lavatory bowl. I also did a lot of riding to muster sheep and a lot of driving natives around in a truck, helping to put up and take down temporary sheep yards. I read that we marked thousands of lambs by cutting off their tails and that it was the Aborigine women who used to catch them for us while we worked with the knives. That entry brings back memories of lots of laughter, rude jokes and ample bosoms popping out of shirts made from old flour sacks.

The Paradise homestead was very basic and totally misnamed. I remember concrete floors and fly-wire netted walls populated with gecko lizards that ran around gobbling up mosquitoes. The dining area was a separate building attached to a cookhouse manned by more laughing Aborigine women.

As the road from Derby to Fitzroy Crossing passed the homestead we had quite a few visitors who stayed overnight. One of these was the Fitzroy policeman, Buster Thorpe, who told us that he was about to make a 700-mile ride over the Leopold Ranges. I said that it sounded a very exciting trip and he kindly invited me to join him. I put the invitation away in the back of my mind, just in case there was a chance of taking him up on it.

I stayed at Paradise for five weeks helping with the shearing and then got a lift back to Derby to meet Uncle Syd who had arrived from England. I often wonder what has happened to the hundreds of people I have met throughout my life. Robin Campbell was only a couple of years older than me, but had an enormous job that he did extremely well. I would be fascinated to know how his life had panned out.

'GoGo' station, 'Perth to Darwin 2,000 m'

I met Uncle Syd in Derby and we flew up to GoGo Station in a very old Dakota aeroplane that took mail and supplies around the stations. It was fascinating to look down on the country that I had been riding over for the last five weeks. We flew along the course of the great Fitzroy River and the country looked quite green from the air, although I now knew that it was mainly rubbish weeds of no value as fodder for the animals. The over-stocking with sheep and cattle of the alluvial flood plains of the river since the first graziers arrived in 1881 had eaten out most of the nutritious native grasses.

On May 25th I met Buster Thorpe again in the Fitzroy Hotel. He said that he was still willing to take me along on his epic ride, which was to be the last mounted police patrol over the Leopold Range because the following year it was planned to bulldoze a road north from Fitzroy Crossing to Gibb River Station. I really wanted to go so summoned up courage and asked Uncle Syd if it would be possible to borrow four mules and an Aborigine tracker for the trip. Two of the mules would be for riding and two for our gear. The tracker was needed to help Bohemia Jack, the police tracker, handle the mules. Uncle Syd was very generous and provided me with the four mules and Jacky Bill.

My mule above 'Fitzroy River', 1955

So began one of the great experiences of my life, one that turned out to have many extraordinary ramifications. If I hadn't made the trip, so many astonishing things just would not have happened. The trip lasted exactly a month and the diary is packed with details which are far too boring to record here, but when I arrived back in Melbourne for Christmas my father made me sit down and write the following précis:

THIRTY DAYS IN THE WILDERNESS

On June 7th I set out with Buster Thorpe on a historic trip, the last mounted police patrol to ride the Leopold Range. The following year the constable was to patrol his 14,000 square mile beat from the seat of a jeep rather than a mule.

With us we had two black boys, Bohemia Jack and Jacky Bill. Bohemia Jack had been with the police for about 30 years and was credited with two murderers' scalps, while Jacky Bill was a GoGo boy. We had not gone far before the GoGo boy was re-named Billy, as two Jacks proved confusing.

Our mode of transport was on mules. We had twelve in the 'plant', six for riding and six for the packs. Also we had two horses. Mules without horses will split and wander at night, whereas with horses they will stay bunched together while grazing, making it easy to round them up in the morning.

PC Buster Thorpe

On the first day we crossed the bare flood plains of the Fitzroy River up to Brooking Gorge. We camped early and packed up before turning in so as to be sure of an early start in the morning. However, two of the GoGo mules I had been lent thought otherwise. In the morning we tracked them back the ten miles to Fitzroy Crossing. They were on their way home!

Bohemia Jack told me that once a Fitzroy mule was lent to a drover going to Wyndham. When he arrived there he forgot to short hobble the animal in his hurry to get to the pub for a beer and the mule turned up back in Fitzroy five weeks later after travelling 600 miles on its own! After hearing this story I always made sure my mule was short hobbled!

That afternoon we climbed through Brooking Gorge and crossed the Oscar Range arriving at Leopold Station homestead at sunset. The Oscar rock is a sharp limestone that made the mules' feet sore. The most impressive thing about the Oscar is that the 50-foot high outcrop is actually an ancient fossilised coral reef.

On arrival the manager's children at Leopold Homestead made us play tennis even though it was nearly dark, and at first light we were dragged out of bed to play again! We spent the day shoeing the front feet of the mules and went to bed early as the next day we had 40 miles to cover to Fairfield, an out-station of Leopold. It rained during the night, so we were lucky to have a roof over our heads.

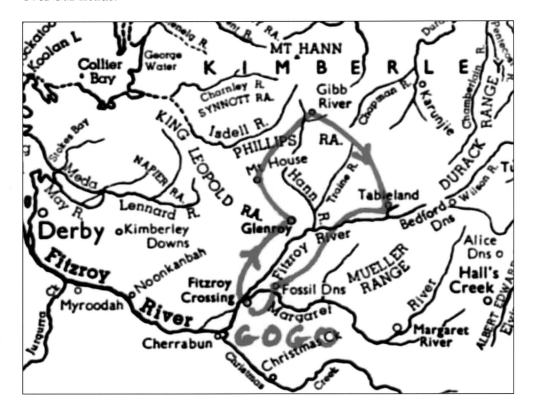

Fitzroy Crossing to Gibb River, Kimberley

The morning brought a stroke of luck. Paddy, the manager, decided to deliver stores to Fairfield, so we threw all our gear onto his truck and left the boys to bring the mules along on their own. We bounced along the rough track over the black-soil plains covered with eight-foot high rank Mitchell grass. Following the Napier Range we arrived at Fairfield safe and sound after a very quick trip, instead of riding for nine hours!

We spent the day with Bill Rathenbury who was building a house for Paddy. Bill had the place very well organised. He didn't have to look for the eggs the hens laid as there was only one place they did lay – on his pillow! He led a very lonely life and, as he was a rum drinker, had a tough time because Paddy had him on short rations. Unfortunately, he got his ration that day.

On the 12th we set out at sunup and passed through McSheady Gap. We had no trouble with the pack mules that morning as they had settled down at last. When we had set out from Fitzroy Crossing two packs were thrown off in the first ten minutes. We passed through McSheady Gap and entered the Leopold Range proper. The gap is characteristic of the whole mountainous region, high vertical red cliffs called Jump Ups reaching in height anything up to a thousand feet. We followed the plain along the cliffs for about ten miles and then up a creek and through a gap into an area called Richenda. After a couple of hours we reached the Bricon Creek and camped on a waterhole.

Camping on a waterhole

Next day we set off again having rested the mules and two horses, following Bricon Creek along for some way and then cut across the range to Black Mountain. We had a good view of the country from the top of the Jump Up we had to pass over to get onto the Black Mountain plain that was very green and covered with eight-foot high spear grass.

Surrounding the plain are red sandstone mountains that are a stark contrast to Black Mountain itself which stands dark and foreboding, a colossal heap of dark brown stones with no vegetation growing on it at all. We crossed the plain and rode down to the Richenda River. We followed along the banks of the river for about ten miles and camped the night on a rocky waterhole. The river was not flowing, but looking at the debris left high in the branches of trees along the banks we could see that an awful lot of water flooded down it in the wet.

Next day we continued along the river. We were glad to get going as that night the largest mosquito I have ever come across invaded us. We left Richenda River at the foot of Mt Broom. This massive tableland mountain is made of red sandstone and its sides go up vertically for at least 1,000 feet above the plain. All the mountains around this area look the same – massive and foreboding.

We climbed up a very steep 300-foot high Jump Up. The mules are really marvellous climbers and they pick their way over the loose stones and between the jumble of rocks with no trouble at all. The pack mules do a remarkable job carrying 300 lbs each. We travelled on until we came to the foot of Mt Millie Windie. We could see large black clouds on the horizon that evening and as it looked as though it was going to rain we piled all the packs and saddles in a row about twelve foot long and two foot high and over which we stretched a tarpaulin. As we finished it started to rain heavily and continued all night so the four of us were very glad to be under shelter.

We were up early in the morning and soon came to the first Jump Up. From the top we could see Mt Millie Windie with Mt Ord dominating it to the left. Inspector Ord was one of the first policemen in Kimberley and Bohemia Jack said that he was particularly tough on the blacks. We passed into Millie Windie Gap. An old bullock track once ran through the Gap, as all the stations north of the range got their supplies via this route in the olden days. When we had gone through the pass we climbed up yet another Jump Up and then up yet another. By this time the mules were getting very tired as we had been travelling all day and had climbed four very rough Jump Ups.

Aerial view of 'King Leopold Range' and 'Jump Ups'

We crossed this plateau and arrived at Jack's Bowl that is an extraordinary crater about a mile across with a nearly circular rim that falls almost vertically for 600 feet. The way down is a spur that is the only break in the cliff. We picked our way down this with reins in one hand and hanging on to the mule's tail with the other!

Running out of the bowl was a dry riverbed that cuts through a gorge of red sandstone. The walls are sheer and it is so narrow that the sun only shines in it for a couple of hours a day. From the gorge we came out into the Walsh and found a deep rock waterhole where we camped for two days to rest the mules. The hole abounded with bream and crocodiles. Buster fished all day but caught nothing. When we had rested up for a while we travelled on into Mt House Station. Mr and Mrs Doug Blythe welcomed us and we stayed for a day talking about the air beef industry they were trying to establish. The cattle were killed on the station and then flown to Darwin in an old Dakota war plane before being frozen and shipped to Singapore.

We were very glad to leave and get away from the smell of the slaughterhouse. We camped under the Phillip Range and crossed over it next day. On top of this plateau there is a forest of cypress pines. Jack showed us a tree where the bark had been stripped with a stone axe by the natives on Walkabout to tap the sap for glue to attach flint spearheads to wooden shafts.

We came down off the Phillip Range and had lunch at Muirs Camp that had been deserted for 50 years. A crystal clear creek runs past here with pandanas growing thick all along it. After lunch we pushed on into Mt Barnett Station. As the husband was away and Buster did not know the woman we camped a little further along the Barnett River.

We broke camp early and pushed off. We were meant to have lunch at Snake Creek about 20 miles further up the track, but when we got there we found the creek was dry so we had to go right through to Gibb River Station. This was about 40 miles and we did it in nine hours. Boy was I glad to get off my mule! On the way we crossed the dry Hann River that we were to cross again later near Glen Roy Station.

Mrs Russ with her children

Frank Russ, the manager of Gibb River, was out mustering but his half-caste wife and her five children gave us a great welcome. I greatly admire the wives of men in Kimberley for they live alone most of the time. Mrs Russ had a good garden with bananas and pineapples that she watered by bucket from a well. We rested up for a day, while Buster fixed the lighting plant and got the truck engine going again.

June 23rd 1955, a red-letter day

We rode out from Gibb River Station to find Dr Andreas Lommel and his wife, Katharina, who were studying native paintings for Munich's Natural History Museum. It took us an hour to ride out to the Lommels' camp and they were very surprised to see us come out of the Bush without any warning. One of the reasons that Buster was on patrol was to check what these two German scientists were doing, so he had put his police badge on his hat and strapped a revolver around his waist!

'Ngungunda' rock shelter where we met the Lommels

Buster introduced himself and then Andreas made us a cup of tea and explained how they were taking tracings of the paintings that would then be transferred to canvas by Katharina back at the station. She would then return to the site and copy the exact colours with oil paint. Andreas told us that if the natives wanted rain they would bash the bigheaded figures on the nose with a rock and we could see the damage for ourselves. It was fascinating listening to him explain all this to us, but I noticed that Jack and Billy stayed well away from the paintings, as they obviously didn't like the place.

Andreas explained that the paintings are of the gods and are done in the shelter of mushroom-shaped rocks to keep the rain off. They paint with a chewed stick for a brush using red or yellow ochre on a white chalk background. The Rain Gods have large heads and no mouths and are called Wandjinas. The Aborigines also paint a lot of big fat serpents.

106

'Katharina' copying the 'Wandjina' painting

The main painting was of a serpent encircling a little girl figure. Andreas told us that the Aborigines believe their souls come from a snake that lives in the waterhole and when the man wanted a child he would collect a little soul from the snake and gives it to his wife. When a child is born it belongs to the waterhole where the snake lives so this is the child's country. If possible he must die by the waterhole, so his soul will go back to the snake.

The main painting is a snake with a little girl

Around the site were several rock slabs that had been stood upright and Andreas said that these represented serpents coming out from the burrows.

Serpents coming out of the burrows

It was time to push on so we said goodbye and I think the Lommels were glad to see us leave. On the way back to the station Jack told us that the best way to make rain was to file clear crystal that he called Rain Stones. He warned us that we must not smash the stones or lightning would burn our houses, which is why the stones should only be gently filed to cause rain!

We left Gibb River Station and followed the Hann River for a while before climbing out of the valley up into another one. We went along Pussy Cat Creek till it ran into the Train River. We followed the Train down to Sidons' homestead that was built by one of the earliest settlers. This country is mostly sandy and grows only useless wheat grass. We branched off the Train and rode into the Tableland Homestead. We did not get a very good welcome here as the previous year Buster had charged the manager with receiving stolen horses and had taken 20 from him!

We pushed on down the Train till we got to Red Lake where we saw a native boundary. In the old days the natives had the country split up into hundreds of small areas, each one having its own language and laws. These areas were divided off from each other by boundaries marked with heaps of stones called Sneezing Heaps. If a native was caught hunting in someone else's country he was killed. The first white men in the Kimberley called the stone piles Sneezing Heaps because every time the natives went past them it sounded as though they sneezed. In fact they were forcing air out through their nostrils as a way of stopping the evil spirits in the heaps from entering their bodies.

At Red Lake, Buster caught a few small fish that he used as bait to catch a crocodile on a shark line for the boys. They cooked the creature in a bed of hot coals and then persuaded us to try some of the tail. It was quite disgusting and smelt of rotten fish.

'Bohemia Jack' with dinner

Jack told me that human beings were not considered 'good tucker' so natives did not eat their flesh! However, the kidney fat was always eaten by the man who did the killing, as he believed this gave him the strength of the dead victim and made him twice as strong.

From Red Lake we re-crossed the Hann River and arrived at Mornington Station. Here we spent a night with Frank Bridge who had two black wives looking after him and had a very good paw-paw garden. Next morning we set out again and followed Connor's Valley up to the Fitzroy River. The valley is very steep sided and the only way to get out is by following the gorge that the river has cut. We crossed over the ridge and proceeded to do a most frightening zigzag climb up the face of the cliff. The view from the track was terrific as we looked straight down into the river 300 feet below us crowded with crocodiles. We crawled along the all-too-narrow edge and I nearly died of fright when my mule stumbled. He went down on his two front knees but luckily recovered his footing, so from then on the scenery was forgotten. I would have jumped off if there had been room.

At the top we stopped and had a well-earned cigarette before I was told that the worst was yet to come, as we had to go down the other side. The boys were quite right – the worst was yet to come. We had to descend 500 feet in loose gravel at an angle of one in one. I swear my mule did not take more than two steps to complete the distance as we slid most of the way surrounded by a lot of rolling gravel.

From here on the rest of the trip was a bit dull. No Jump Ups or Slide Downs, just easy going. We followed the river down the west boundary of old Leopold Station then crossed over to Fossil Downs. We camped at Margaret Crossing, but only stayed until the full moon gave us enough light to ride the last ten miles into Fitzroy Crossing. So ended a 30-day 700-mile ride through the Leopold Range.

I wrote that account 50 years ago when I was 20 years old. What I didn't know then was that I was completely hooked by this wild and wonderful country, nearly empty of people and completely untouched by the modern world. The mule ride over the King Leopold Range with Buster was the beginning of my love affair with Kimberley. Since then I have been lucky enough to have had four opportunities to enjoy the beauty and mystery of this special place.

In 1981 I returned with my son, Peter, and some friends to climb Mt Agnes. I told Damon de Laszlo about this trip and he asked me to organise a trip for him and his family in 1989. After my telling Robert Hefner III about the amazing trip that Margie and I had done with Damon, he asked me to organise one for him and his son, Charles, in 1991. For this trip I suggested that we employ Grahame Walsh as a guide. I had met Grahame quite by chance in 1989 with Damon on Mt Elizabeth Station. I knew that he was an expert on Wandjina paintings as he had written a book about them that I had bought. Robert wanted to see Wandjinas and Grahame knew where hundreds were hidden.

Grahame agreed to be our guide and we had a superb trip with him. While sitting around the campfire one night Grahame mentioned the name Andreas Lommel and I told him that I had met him when I was 20 years old on Gibb River Station. He was very surprised and went on to tell me that he was still alive and living in Munich, so it was my turn to be stunned.

Grahame said that he would give anything to meet Andreas and Katharina as they had found some breathtaking Wandjina paintings and were the only people who knew their location. I made contact with Lommel on my return to England and when Grahame came to London I took him to Munich.

'Andreas and Katharina' both aged 80

110

The Lommels asked us around to their apartment to discuss the Wandjina paintings that he had found and his wife had copied. It was a great pleasure to meet them both again after so many years. They remembered the day Buster and I had ridden into their camp unannounced very clearly as they immediately saw that he was a policeman and wondered if they had broken some law by copying the paintings!

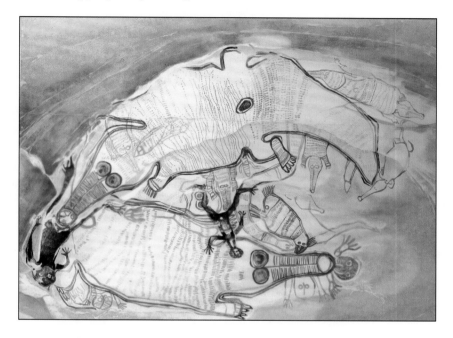

Katharina's Wandjina Crocodile painting, Sundron

Next day Andreas took Grahame and mysself to the Munich Natural History Museum to see the paintings that his wife had done on that trip that are truly amazing, some being ten foot long. It was very strange to see the painting that I had watched Katharina working on in 1955.

With Katharina's painting done in 1955

That evening I took Andreas and Katharina out to dinner to celebrate our reunion after a gap of 38 years. What a delightful couple and what an eventful life he had led! During dinner he regaled us with stories of his time with the Unambal Tribe in 1938 and his second trip in 1955 when Buster and I had invaded their privacy.

Andreas had first visited Kimberley in 1938 with the Frobenius Institute of Frankfurt. The Institute had mounted an expedition to study the primitive peoples of Kimberley and in particular the Unambal. The Aborigines of this area were still living in the Stone Age and had only just come into contact with White Man. While others of the Frobenius group collected artefacts, Lommel studied the natives.

Unambal Aborigines photographed by Lommel in 1938

Grahame Walsh has since published a book by Andreas documenting all the information he collected in 1938. The book includes some of his unique black and white photographs of Corroboree dances as well as a wealth of material on the social life of the tribe, which he told us had completely

112

disappeared by his second trip in 1955. He then went on to tell me about his WWII experiences which I think are quite amazing and should be recorded.

Andreas arrived back in Germany at the end of 1938 and was immediately conscripted into the army and transferred to Rommel's Afrika Korps that invaded Libya in 1941. He was at Tobruk when it was defended by the famous Australian Desert Rats and at the German defeat at El Alamein. He could see very clearly that this was the end of the Korps as the retreat had turned into a rout. Because the British had command of the air the convoys of fleeing trucks could only travel at night, being forced to hide in woods along the road during the day so they could avoid being attacked.

One day he decided he had had enough but as they were guarded by SS soldiers to stop desertion he pretended to have an upset stomach. After he had made several hurried trips in and out of the trees the guards got slack so on his last departure he just kept walking until he found a place to hide. He stayed there until the fighting passed before walking back to the road to wait for an English truck to appear.

When he had made sure that the trucks passing were British and not German he decided it was time to give himself up before an Arab found him and slit his throat for the reward. Eventually a lone truck happened to pull up near where he was hiding and the driver got out for a pee. Andreas grabbed the chance to give himself up and walked up to the soldier with his hands held high. The soldier swung round and put his arms up as well. It must have been a wonderful sight, both men surrendering at the same time! Lommel spoke English and was able to convince the Tommy that it was he who wanted to be taken prisoner and was able to climb on to the back of the truck.

Andreas was shipped back to a POW camp outside Cairo and because he spoke English he was put in charge of the camp school and told to give English lessons to the prisoners, which was a very agreeable job with a few privileges. The only problem was that the camp soon started to fill up with Nazi SS officers who immediately saw that Andreas had the best job in the camp so ordered him to enrol them also as teachers, which he definitely didn't want to do.

He got out of having to do this by inventing a fictitious test saying that the British would only take on teachers who understood Latin, which of course he could do himself. He told the Nazis that if they wanted to become teachers they would have to answer a written test in Latin that would be marked by an English officer. Of course none of the SS knew any Latin so he avoided having to take them on as teachers!

The Frobenius Institute in Frankfurt had survived the bombing of the last war and Andreas arranged for Grahame and me to visit it. The Institute is housed in a dark musty building full of books and papers on Rock Art from around the world. He also arranged for us to visit the warehouse of the Frankfurt National History Museum where one of the largest collections of Australian Aboriginal art in the world is stored. We walked through room after room full of decaying treasures. Our time was short so we were not able to study closely what was in the showcases, but we could see that much of the organic material was being eaten by insects, leaving things like bird feather headdresses in tatters. It was a very distressing sight.

Our interest was to see the Wandjina bark paintings. When we arrived at the door of a large room we just stood and looked, absolutely stunned. The room was full of hundreds and hundreds of bark paintings stacked against each other like Roman soldiers' shields. We could not believe our eyes. We were only able to look at the front few as they were jammed together so tightly we couldn't move them around. What a shame and what a loss there would be if there was a fire as the bark was tinder dry and crumbling!

After the war Andreas returned to Munich, married Katharina and was made Head of the Natural History Museum. He was a remarkable man and she a superb artist and two of the nicest people I have ever met. Katharina died at the end of 2004 and Andreas a couple of months later in 2005.

I wonder what has happened to PC Buster Thorpe. I shall never be able to thank him enough for allowing me to come with him on that epic ride in 1955. Back at GoGo I was sent out into the mustering camp to help round up fat cattle for market. I was then asked if I would like to take part in a 300-mile trek to the port of Derby down the stock route that runs along the banks of the Fitzroy River. How could I refuse?

I wrote an account of my days on GoGo and as a cattle drover so for fun will again include what I scribbled a lifetime ago.

GOGO

When I got back to GoGo I went straight into the Cherabun camp. GoGo consisted of three stations, the others being Margaret Downs and Christmas Creek, an area of three million acres!

The mustering camps usually consist of about 25 native boys and are run by a half-caste, with a few Aborigine women looked after the tucker. Although the food is rough it is excellent and I am sure is much better for you than all the rich food you eat from takeaways nowadays. Damper is baked every other day in an iron camp oven buried in red hot coals.

We took a week to muster the 400 bullocks needed for the Perth-bound boat. Every day we would set off at daybreak to sweep a strip of country with the boys split into three groups to do a pincer movement on the cattle, with the main party mustering the middle. We would meet at a pre-arranged waterhole where the cattle would be herded into one mob and watched by a couple of men, while the rest of us went into camp to have dinner and get fresh horses. This midday meal would usually be enjoyed at about ten o'clock.

Mounted on fresh camp horses, specially picked and trained for the job, we would start the draft so it would be finished before the day got really hot. Drafting when taken slowly is quite easy as the horses know exactly what they are meant to do and are eager workers. However, once the mob is stirred up things are liable to get very troublesome. Bullocks are continually breaking away and have to be brought back, which tires the horses unnecessarily and stirs up a cloud of dust as thick as a London fog. The prime bullocks are cut out to a small mob of cows and calves that help to quieten the bullocks. When all the prime bullocks have been mustered the cows and calves are separated and set free.

While all this is going on the Tailers have appeared with the herd of bullocks from yesterday's muster. They add the new bunch of steers and then disappear to a waterhole nearby where they camp during the heat of the day before taking the bullocks out to feed in the afternoon. As the sun disappears the Tailers return and bed the cattle down in a circle. The first watch takes over and for the rest of the night the cattle are patrolled by two riders walking round and round. When the mob reaches 400 head of fat bullocks they start the walk to Derby and then are shipped south by boat to Perth for slaughter for meat to be sold in Asia.

In the Cherabun camp I did a different watch each night but soon found out that the three o'clock watch was the best one because you got a continuous sleep, which is why it is known as the Boss's Watch. Also the cooks get up at that time, which means you can get a hot cup of coffee before going out on watch.

Cutting out a bullock

While watching the cattle you must sing or make a continuous and soothing noise. This is to tell them you are around and warn them not to try anything foolish. Cattle are nervy beasts and if they hear your horse stumble on a really dark night they are liable to stampede, but if they can hear you singing it reassures them there is no danger and they will stay lying down. The two riders walk their horses at the same speed and on opposite sides of the circle. Because of the singing you can also tell exactly where the other man is. The Aborigine stockmen sing native Corroboree songs which is a fantastic sound to listen to on a starlit night.

On the first night of being on watch I sang every conceivable song I could remember. Later on in the week I settled down to three or four but before long it became the same song right through the watch. After a lifetime of cattle watching I was told you sing the 'brand' song.

"XR7 is the Cherabun brand – the Cherabun brand is XR7"

The 400 bullocks that were going to Perth were taken in hand by a half-caste foreman and three Aborigine boys who were told to take them back to GoGo with me in tow. As soon as we left after lunch it started to pour with rain and continued to do so until we reached GoGo 24 hours later. Right at the height of the storm a herd of wild camels trotted by and as the one thing cattle don't like is the smell of camels, things very nearly got out of hand, but we managed to hold them together and eventually reached the Holding Yards wet through and miserable. After closing the gate on the cattle we hurried to the shed where our swags had been dumped. In the shed was a kerosene engine that drove the pump used to raise water from the nearby billabong for the cattle in the yard.

We had a blazing fire going in no time with the aid of some engine fuel we stole from a large drum that was on a six-foot high stand outside the shed. To get at the fuel we had to drop the drum which on hitting the ground nearly got away from us and went tumbling into the billabong, it was only just stopped by two boys standing up to their knees in the water!

Johnny, Clancy the Boss, his wife Queenie,
and Sandy, GoGo's head stockman

On returning to GoGo I joined Sandy Shaw's camp that was mustering the mob that I was going to help walk down to Derby. One of the reasons I was there was because I could write messages for Sandy that would be sent via an Aborigine stockman back to the station manager telling him how many cattle we had and where we were camped. We collected 410 steers in about a week and took them to a pre-arranged place where the drover boss, Clancy Doherty, was waiting. Sandy handed over the cattle and me for the 200-mile walk down to Derby that would take 30 days.

For the first few days I was bored to tears and missed the excitement of the muster camp. The pace of the feeding cattle ruled our lives as the order of the day was, *don't push 'em, take 'em easy.* Eventually I became like one of the cattle. Droving is the slowest way to get nowhere but once I settled in to it I began to enjoy the relaxed lifestyle and the whole experience. I actually got to know certain beasts and would talk to them! I had been given a wonderful grey horse that knew exactly what to do to the extent that I needn't really have been sitting on his back. My main job was to keep the flies out of his and my eyes with a leafy whisk.

We reached the boundary of Paradise Station and I rode over to the homestead to say hello to Robin Campbell whom I had worked with earlier in the year when he was shearing the 19,000 sheep he cared for.

The moustache didn't grow!

As a drover you spend up to 16 hours a day in the saddle. The food we ate while droving was very simple. The day's meals consisted of a lot of coffee made with muddy billabong water, unleavened bread called damper and boiled salt beef, while chewing on an apple-sized raw onion, which was our only vegetable. I actually got to really enjoy eating raw onion although I can't imagine what my breath smelt like. I avoided looking too closely at the chunks of salt beef that was stored under the chuck wagon on a canvas hammock, open to the flies!

Damper always reminds me of when I was a child and being told by my nanny not to drink my milk too fast, as it was liable to turn to a block of ice if I did. Damper does the same sort of thing, as if you don't chew it well it turns into concrete and then sits in the pit of your stomach for hours.

No droving trip is complete without a stampede so of course we had to have ours! It happened about ten o'clock on a clear night halfway to Derby. Bullocks are said to be one of the fastest animals in the world reaching up to

60 mph. Later I was told the mob passed within ten yards of my swag but I didn't see this as I am ashamed to confess I was under the cart. How I got out from my mosquito net and under cover in so short a time I don't know.

After the bullocks had passed by I came out and found that all the night horses had gone so there was no way I could help. I sat around till midnight and as nothing had happened went back to my swag. The boys arrived back at first light and after a count found that they had recovered all but ten. They also reported that they had smashed through five fences during the night!

Johnny, the head stockman, set off to track the ten missing bullocks with me tagging along to help bring them back if he found them. We must have travelled about 15 miles towards GoGo before Johnny said that they would end up back on the station and we should forget them. Next morning we pushed on and five days later we arrived at Yedda Plains, and on watch that night I was delighted to see the loom of Derby's lights, although we still had two days' riding before reaching the port.

The next obstacle in our way was a deep billabong called The Cutting. Johnny told me that on his last trip they had to make the mob swim across but it turned out that my horse was the only one who had to this time. As we were pushing the mob across, my trusty nag suddenly plunged into a deep hole and we both nearly disappeared, much to Johnny's amusement. Fortunately the horse found a firm footing before I remembered that I should have slid off and hung on to his tail. By staying in the saddle I did save my tobacco and my camera from getting wet. Later Johnny told me that man-eating saltwater crocodiles had been seen in the billabong!

Watering 410 cattle in a billabong

This dipping makes me think of billabong bathing which is a very tricky pastime. The problem about washing in a billabong is how to get from the water to dry land without getting completely filthy again while crossing the two-yard wide barrier of foot-deep mud along the bank. Actually it is impossible so washing in a cattle trough is much easier as long as you have a bucket.

After The Cutting we quickly covered the last few miles and soon arrived at the mouth of the yards that led into the mile-long jetty leading down to the ship that was sitting high and dry on the mud flats. The ships come in at high tide and then slowly settle into the mud on the 30-foot ebb tide of the Kimberley coast. We had reached our destination and the job was done.

Next morning at four o'clock they started loading the cattle and had all 400 on board in a couple of hours. They used live electric wires taped to sticks to hurry the cattle along as time is very short. By midday the tide had floated the ship off the mud and it immediately set sail. Having lived with the bullocks for 30 days I felt very sorry to see them heading off to be slaughtered.

I must say something about the town of Derby, which lies at the mouth of the Fitzroy River that flows into King Sound. HMS *Beagle* of Darwin fame explored the sound in 1839 and sent a row boat up the Fitzroy River for 22 miles. Derby has the longest jetty, broadest mud flats and highest population of mosquitoes of any town in the world. The bar is full of cigarette smoke so walking in it is like cutting cheese with a knife and I have never heard so many different language all being talked at the same time. To counterbalance the bar the police use a hollow giant Boab tree as a prison to lock up drunks! A doorway had been cut into the trunk and a grill gate bolted to the outside.

The original Derby police prison was a hollow Boab

The only other extraordinary thing that happened to me while I was working on GoGo was to see a Flying Saucer, that were all the rage in those days. It happened when I was driving back from Christmas Creek to GoGo with the manager on a pitch-black night brilliant with stars. There was no moon and it was freezing cold and there were a couple of Aborigines riding on the back tray of the truck.

119

We were bowling along the dirt track that snaked away in front of us in the headlights, heading north up a flat valley about half a mile wide and bordered on each side by Jump Ups. Suddenly from the East a reddish gold Rugby ball shot across the valley and disappeared over the horizon in the West. It was impossible to tell whether it was 100 yards or half a mile in front of us, but if it was half a mile away it must have been huge.

The extraordinary thing about the event was that as it crossed in front of us the engine cut out and the headlights went out. The manager jammed on the brakes and we came to a squealing halt. When the orange shape disappeared over the horizon the headlights came on again. We climbed down from the truck and all began to talk at the same time asking the same question. "What the hell was that?" We were all quite frightened.

The manager got back into the truck, turned the key in the ignition and the engine sprang into life so we set off again talking about the event. It was a completely new experience to the manager who had never seen anything like it in the 45 years he had been in Kimberley, often travelling at night.

Years later I went to a lecture given by the TV presenter, Sir Patrick Moore, at our boys' school in Somerset. The headmaster asked me in for a drink after the lecture to meet the man so I told him my Flying Saucer story. He only laughed and suggested that it must have been what scientists call Ball Lightning, which they knew existed but have no idea exactly what it was. He said it certainly wasn't a Flying Saucer full of little green men!

Sadly my days in the Kimberley came to an end when the Monsoon rains arrived so I made my way up to Wyndham to catch the plane to Darwin. The Wyndham Hotel was a slice out of Australia's pioneer era as it had not changed since then. There were two sleeping verandas, one for men and one for women. I don't know what the women slept on but the men's veranda was bare boards and you just picked a free spot to roll out your swag. The gent's bathroom had a wonderful notice on the door that read, *No spurs to be worn in the bathroom, they ruin the lino.* I still have one of my spurs and use it for opening beer bottles!

I flew from Darwin to Brisbane to be best man for my brother, Mike, at his wedding to Bernice Grahame. Both my mother and father were at the wedding so we had a great family reunion. Returning to a city had its compensations but by now I was really hooked by the outdoor life and soon longed to be back in the Bush.

Aunt Peg, my father's sister, who had provided a home for Mike and me when we had been shipped out to Australia in the war, had come to the wedding and during a conversation she suggested that I should jackeroo for some friends of hers named Dampier-Crossley in New Zealand. My father thought that this was a very good idea as perhaps I could also work in the Swift's meat works as he knew the American owners. So it was decided and letters were dispatched.

Fortunately in those days letters were not electronic and took weeks to travel around the world. It was not be possible for me to leave for New Zealand until after the Christmas holidays, which meant that I could spend some time with my parents whom I had not seen for a year. I agreed to this plan as I thought a month doing nothing would be a wonderful way of celebrating the end of my second decade!

Kimberley, 'Land of Long Shadows'

THIRD DECADE

NEW ZEALAND

My Third Decade started with one of the best holidays as my parents had rented a house called Sefton on the top of Mt Macedon above the summer heat of the plains and some way out of Melbourne. The house was surrounded by a private four-hole golf course, had a croquet lawn and a tennis court. It was the perfect spot for a family holiday. Beyond the lawns there was a forest of giant gum trees in which we could walk, look for, and find koalas.

Every weekend my parents would ask their friends to come and stay and, of course, the newly-weds, Mike and Bern. There was a billiard table so after dinner we could play snooker or cards and have a family game of Hearts as in the old days at Chute Standen in England. Magnificent food was prepared by our cook, Marianna, with my father's chauffeur, Jim, helping where needed.

The halcyon days of that wonderful summer came to an end when a letter arrived from Guy Dampier-Crossley in the South Island of New Zealand saying he would accept me as a jackeroo. Another arrived from the manager of the Swift meat packing company in the North Island agreeing to my working in the factory for a three-month period. It was time to return to work. Aeroplane tickets were purchased and I set off on a new adventure.

Guy and his wife, Bridget, met me at Christchurch Airport and we drove north to their farm on the Canterbury Plains. So began a glorious six months of fun working for one of the nicest couples I have ever met. They had a little boy called Christopher, who was looked after by a nanny most of the time. This meant that the parents were free to party during the weekends and oh boy, did the South Islanders know how to party.

Most of the houses in New Zealand are built of wood because of the earth tremors that continually shake the countryside. I shall never forget the first night I spent on the farm. I awoke to feel the bed shaking and hear the walls creaking. Immediately I was out of bed and on the lawn, barefooted and freezing cold. The house remained standing and I returned to bed when I saw that no one else was going to join me. Next morning I asked Guy if he had felt anything in the night and he told me that he hadn't, but that he had heard on the News that they had had a minor earth tremor. He assured me that I was not to worry, that the house had stood for over 100 years and that I had better get used to such events as they happened quite frequently! Within a week I would quite happily sleep through much worse earthquakes and not bat an eye.

During the week we worked hard on the sheep farm, looking after the stock or ploughing the fields for seeding in the coming spring. The weather was very English and sometimes a bit like Rugby because our boots would be covered by hoarfrost until ten in the morning. When it was time for the opening of the duck-shooting season Guy organised a party of guns to meet at six o'clock by the river before first light. I have never been so cold and was not in the least surprised when I saw that my gun barrel was white with ice crystals. The problem was that we had each brought a flask of whisky knowing that it would be needed to keep out the cold. When the sun came up and the duck flew, surprise surprise, not one was hit. The river that flowed through the valley was also home to the largest trout I have ever seen.

Guy owned the grazing rights on a mountain. The sheep used to be taken up when the snow had melted and left there to fend for themselves over the summer. This was fine until it was time to muster them again for by then they could have wandered anywhere over a vast stretch of alpine countryside. To muster the sheep the shepherds would climb several thousand feet with their dogs before sunrise to hunt the animals back down the valleys to a yard. The problem is that having been left to roam wild for so long the sheep were not very keen to give up their freedom. It is very hard walking in New Zealand's Southern Alps as many of the slopes are covered by loose scree. The shepherds carry long poles that they use as a balance when they are sliding down them like skiers. It is spectacular to watch and a real art, as if you fall you are liable to be engulfed in the landslide you have started during your descent. Fortunately Guy didn't participate in this activity and didn't ask me to either.

Occasionally on weekends we would go up into the mountain to shoot deer. Like the sheep they have the freedom of the mountains but, unlike their woolly companions, they can't be rounded up with dogs. They have multiplied to such an extent that they have been classified as vermin and professional shooters have a full-time job trying to keep their numbers down. I am afraid our shooting skills were quite inadequate to make any difference to the numbers, but we had a great time trying. We would walk up during the day and camp overnight in the huts used by the shepherds after having a delicious barbecue washed down by rather too much whisky and wine.

Guy and Bridget' at a shepherds hut in the mountains

Guy was a keen follower of the horses so occasionally we would all down tools and go to the races. It must sound as though we did no work at all, but that isn't true as Guy's philosophy was work hard and then play hard. He and Bridget treated me as one of the family and when they found out that I was about to turn 21 they asked all their friends to the farm and gave me a brilliant party. It was not until I had left the South Island that I learnt that in those days New Zealand was one of the largest whisky-consuming countries in the world per head of population. I shall always remember Guy and Bridget as one of the friendliest couples I have ever met and my time with them on their property as being full of happy laughter. I could not have had a more fantastic 21st birthday party as it was a night I shall remember for the rest of my life.

I suppose what had made the stay with the D-Cs even more memorable was what followed. It was time to move on up to the North Island and the Swift's meat packing factory. I sailed overnight on the ferry up to Wellington from Christchurch, boarded a train and after hours of slow travel arrived at a small town on the east coast. There was one street and one hotel and the factory. When I was shown my room in the hotel I literally groaned with horror. It was an icy cell with one iron bed, one chair, one table, no curtains, dull grey linoleum on the floor, walls painted a faded blue and my home for the next three months.

After dinner, that was served at six, I walked down the only street to see what I could find. Absolutely nothing! There was no pub, one shop and several houses all in darkness. There were a couple of streetlights but otherwise everything was black and looked completely deserted. I had arrived at the end of the Earth!

A message told me that I would be collected at eight o'clock the following morning by the man I would be working with. I was ready when a car arrived and an elderly man got out and introduced himself as the Farm Adviser to the meat packing factory. I was to travel around the countryside with him for the next few weeks on his visits to the local farmers. His job was to advise them on how they could improve their land with fertiliser, in order to provide the factory with better meat.

The most interesting thing about the job as we went from property to property was meeting the farmers and their wives. It was soon very obvious that they all needed help from my boss as most of them were not well educated and many of them lived very basic lives indeed. It was an eye-opener, especially having experienced the lifestyle that Guy and Bridget and their friends enjoyed. This was a real backwater, a forgotten world.

During the weekend there was absolutely nothing to do in the town, which didn't even have a cinema, the nearest one being too far away to reach even if there had been a bus service. I soon got tired of reading trashy novels and as I hadn't yet started my self-education phase of reading facts, I became terribly bored.

I was saved by a letter arriving from my godmother, Angela Govett, containing a cheque for my 21st birthday. I had noticed that the one shop in the street had a portable typewriter on its shelf. I decided to buy it with my cheque and teach myself how to type during the long lonely evenings. In those days typewriters were the old hammer type that used the QWERTY layout which was invented to stop the keys meshing together when they were striking the paper. We are still stuck with this format and probably will be for ever. I took my new acquisition up to my room and every evening I would try typing on it and I suspect that the click-click of my activity was the only sound in the whole town.

Time was passing very slowly and I was counting the days to my release when the manager asked me if I would mind giving his son-in-law a hand to split logs on his farm as he had been given a big order for battens and needed help to fulfil it in time. I jumped at the chance because it would mean getting out of the hotel and a change to the awful food that was served in the dining room every evening. I had met the manager's daughter, a round jolly character, and I knew she cooked excellent cakes as she had given us some one day when we called in for afternoon tea.

Her husband was a Tarzan and being an expert axe man had built the little wooden house they lived in. It was all very quaint and had a path that led down to an outhouse. Luckily there are no spiders in New Zealand, so at least I didn't have to check under the seat for lurking Red Backs before sitting down. In Australia, where they are prevalent, their sting can make one very ill indeed; such is the joy of country living. The farmer's wife turned out to be just as good at cooking gigantic meals of meat and two veg as cakes for tea, so taking all into account, things definitely were looking up.

Splitting battens was fun. My boss had felled several giant gums, so our first job was to cross-saw them into three-foot long barrel-shaped logs. As the trees were all at least four foot in diameter this was quite a job, but as the saw was razor sharp and I had an expert partner, I soon learnt go with saw and let it do the work. When we had cut up the tree into several logs we would drill a one-foot deep hole in the side with an inch auger. We then packed black gunpowder into the hole with a fuse and lit it before retiring. There followed a dull thump and the log split in half, which we would upend and then sledgehammer wedges into the top, slowly working our way around like slicing up a cake. The end product was a beautifully neat batten of wood that looked like a cricket bat. The farmers stapled the battens on to the fence wires as spreaders. I didn't know it then of course but learning to use gunpowder came in very handy when I had to start planting fence posts in solid rock the following year on my own farm. The only way to make the required hole was to use sticks of dynamite, which in those days you could buy at the local store!

When the batten job was completed I had to leave, as there was no more work. I was sorry to go as the meals had been superb, but fortunately I had been introduced to a young bachelor called David who owned a farm nearby. He needed help mustering so I took my leave of the meat packers and went to work for him for the last two weeks of my stay in New Zealand. David turned out to be great fun and after work we would set off to meet up with his bachelor friends who gathered at the local hot springs at the end of each day to recover from walking up and down the very steep hills mustering sheep. I had never been in a sulphur springs bathhouse before and, although I enjoyed the experience at the time, I don't think I ever want to repeat it. When you first walk into the communal bathhouses the smell of rotten eggs is overpowering.

It was time to return to Australia. I couldn't believe a whole year had gone by and that it was again time to relax over Christmas. I had learnt a great deal about sheep, how to blow things up with gunpowder and also how to type after a fashion, although I still have to look at the keyboard. Thank goodness for computers, spellchecker, and being able to make mistakes and correct them without having to start all over again on a clean sheet of paper, although if anyone reads my story they will notice that I still have a lot to learn about the English language!

I am glad I learnt on an old hammer machine as it is a bit like learning to drive a car with a gear shift rather than going straight to an automatic, if you know what I mean!

I believe the umbilical cord is cut twice in life for men. Once at birth and again when one's father dies. It is only after the death of a father that a son feels really on his own. No longer is there a *strength* to turn to for guidance.

I shall never forget the day my father died. He had been physically weakened when he had a lung collapsed after contracting tuberculosis at the age of only 35. He had recovered remarkably well and within two years went back at work, putting in long hours all through WWII guiding the vital aluminium industry that produced the raw materials necessary for the British to defend Great Britain, and with our US allies, defeat the Fascists.

During the war my father lived in Grosvenor House Hotel flat that overlooked Hyde Park. During the night he had to do duty as a night watchman on the roof, like the other guests of the hotel. The Germans used to drop thousands of incendiary bombs on London on their nightly raids. These would set roofs on fire and actually caused more damage than the big explosive bombs. Whole streets could be burnt out because there were never enough fire engines to cope.

The incendiary bomb looked like a roll of chocolate biscuits. The watchman had a broom handle with a claw on the end with which they could grab the bomb and plunge it into a bucket of water. The only thing my father ever mentioned about this experience on the hotel roof was his horror at the sight of London burning. When the searchlight beams found a German plane the whole of Hyde Park exploded with the ack-ack guns firing off tracer shells trying to shoot them down.

My mother always said that she had been very lucky as her three sons had been too young to serve in the forces during the war, unlike so many of her friends who had lost either a husband or a son and sometimes both. She was ten when the Great War started and her two older brothers had fought in France. As she was 18 years younger than her sister and the only one left at home her mother used to make her read the 'Reported Missing' announcements in *The Times* every day to see if her brothers had been killed in action. Having experienced that as a child, I am not surprised she felt so lucky about her own children in WWII. Both her brothers survived the Great War although Uncle Pat was so badly gassed in the trenches that he had to spend the rest of his life farming at high altitude in Rhodesia.

I heard of my father's death when I was a farmer in South Australia. My brother, Mike, rang to tell me that he had died in London from a sudden heart attack. I was desperately sorry to lose my father, but since his death I have always felt his presence beside me.

I am sure that it was then somewhere deep inside me that I started down the road that led me to becoming a sculptor. I also fear that possibly, if my father had lived another ten years, I would never have made that journey, as I needed to be flying solo. However, my one regret in life has been that I was unable to share with him the joy that sculpting has brought to me, as I was able to with my mother, although he did share the *Hula Hula Girl* with a big bosom and a grass skirt. When I brought her home my father asked, with a big smile on his face, "Can anyone actually get into that position?" When I look at her she always reminds me of his comment!

I have many fond memories of my father, although far too few because of being sent to Australia for three years aged five during WWII, then being packed off to boarding school on my return aged eight. As my father worked in the City and we lived in the country during the holidays we were literally ships passing in the night for most of my youth. As soon as the war was over he had to spend six months of each year in Australia rebuilding the mining industry, so I grew up not really knowing him at all.

I remember being very excited one Christmas when he came home from Australia, because he had gone to a shoe shop in Melbourne and bought several pairs for us boys using paper outlines of our feet. None of them fitted very well, but having a new pair of shoes was a great treat as they were hard to come by in England after the war and needed clothing coupons.

I didn't spend any time alone with my father until he bought the farm for me in the Ninety Mile Desert of South Australia. When I was growing up, there was an occasional holiday when he was able to join my mother and me, but they were few and far apart. Sometimes the family was together over the weekend, but it was seldom that there were five of us sitting around the dining-room table. When it happened, it was always fun and the conversation bursting with laughter. I was terribly fortunate to have such a very happy and harmonious family.

Pat was at Cambridge so his holidays didn't coincide with mine. Besides, he was eight years older and a 19-year-old university student doesn't want to talk to an 11-year-old Prep schoolboy. I used to think he was terrifyingly clever until I dropped my wristwatch and it stopped. He claimed that he could fix it and popped the back off. After a bit of fiddling he put the back on again and reported that it was mended. When I pointed out that there were still some bits left on the table, he blandly announced that they weren't necessary! Of course the watch didn't work and I decided that perhaps after all he wasn't quite so clever. He painted my portrait soon after that event which entailed sitting for hours when I wanted to be outside. Pat was a very good artist and when I moved into the house on my farm I commissioned him to do some watercolours of Chute Standen to hang on the walls.

Our relationship took a turn for the worse when I discovered some classical records. The gramophone was enormous and played the old type of records that were a foot in diameter. My mother had loved to dance in her youth, so most of the records were foxtrots by composers like Cole Porter and Irving Berlin. I often heard long stories from her about how she and my father used to go dancing at the Savoy to the music of Carol Gibbons and his band and tales of the Saturday night special at the Berkeley Hotel where, for a guinea a head, you could have dine and dance until dawn! She told me that once she danced with Irving Berlin on the *Queen Mary* when he was trying out a new tune during a voyage to New York!

We always had music in the house when my mother was around. She would come into the sitting room and ask me to put on some records. The machine took six discs so played for half an hour and my love of romantic melodies comes from that time. After dinner our family would play cards and I would stack the gramophone up with records, so we had background music throughout the evening. There were two piles of records with about 50 in each pile and the system was to work down through one pile and then start on the other. It would take a couple of weeks to get through both piles before starting all over again. Four particular tunes stick in my mind.

The first was titled, *Three little fishes and a mummy fish too*. The song is about fish that all lived happily in a pond until, *Stop said the mummy fish or you'll get lost, but the three little fish didn't want to be bossed, so they swam and they swam, right over the dam.* Another song went, *I was watching a man paint a fence, he painted it blue, like the blue of your eyes, like the blue of the skies, bluer than bluer than blue.* The third was a song called *Transatlantic Lullaby*. I have asked many dance band conductors if they knew the tune, but none ever has, which is a great shame, as it is the most beautiful melody I have ever heard and one I still hum.

The song, *Brother can you spare a dime*, made a lasting impression on me. Quite recently Margie and I were watching a New York ballet company on TV and one of the dances was choreographed to this song. Margie was astounded that after 50 years I could sing along word perfect. Our recording was by Bing Crosby and is utterly heartbreaking as it is about a returned soldier from the Great War during the 1930 Depression. It has the saddest lyrics that have ever been written and goes like this:

> Once in khaki suits gee we looked swell
> Full of that Yankee doodle dee dum.
> Half a million boots slogging through hell
> And I was the kid with the drum!
> Say don't you remember they called me Al,
> It was Al all the way.
> Say don't you remember, I'm your Pal,
> Brother, can you spare a dime?

One day I found some old giant records in a cupboard under the gramophone, so of course I had to play them. One of the records turned out to be Dame Nellie Melba singing *Land of Hope and Glory*. I loved it and thought that it was the best thing I had ever heard, so played it on every possible occasion. Pat didn't object to the music at first, but said he didn't want to hear it ten times a day. After several threats of dire consequences, eventually he couldn't stand it any more and broke it over my head! This hurt as it was made of very tough Bakelite. Thus ended my classical music interest until Margie and I bought a *Reader's Digest* album of popular classical symphonies when we were first married and we came to know about the music that we now love.

I have already written of how my parents adored going to musicals such as *Annie Get Your Gun*, *Oklahoma*, and *South Pacific*. When I was about 14 we went to one called *Irma La Douce* about artists living in Paris between the wars. One of the songs in the show made an enormous impression on me and the memory of it has stuck with me all my life. The theme phrase was, *If you want to have a wonderful life, be an artist*, sung and danced by a chorus of cancan girls and painters. I know that that sounds like 'being smart after the event', but I promise that it is true and I can hum the tune right now.

Being the youngest I was always made to have my bath before Mike. One summer evening I forgot to let the bathwater out so Mike grabbed me and locked me in the bathroom saying that he would not let me out until I had pulled out the plug. I thought this was rather an excessive threat for a minor crime, so I climbed out the bathroom window and down the drainpipe. He was furious to find me sitting by the fire when he came downstairs to explain that he was going to be late for dinner because I was still in the bathroom.

In fact I do believe that as a family we all got along very well and there were hardly any serious family rows. I suppose Pat and Mike did their own thing, while I amused myself around the farm and fell in love with being outside in the fresh air. This early way of life certainly led to my becoming a jackeroo in Australia, which in turn led to my father buying me the 1,600-acre block of semi-developed land in the Ninety Mile Desert near Keith, a small town on the border of Victoria and South Australia.

During the Christmas holidays after New Zealand my father was repeatedly heard to mutter things like, "When is the boy going to settle down?" I had been jackerooing around Australia having fun for five years, but I believe he knew that he didn't have much time left on earth and so would like to see me settled before too long. He had heard about a land development scheme from a business colleague and suggested that I should take a job with the man running it. As he would be allowed to write off some of the costs of developing virgin scrub against his income tax, it seemed to him a golden opportunity to stop my roaming and force me to settle.

He suggested that I worked for the land developer who had a property near Keith called Desert Downs and in my spare time I explored the country on a scooter. As a Director of the AMP he arranged for me to meet the manager of the company's Land Development Scheme, Noel Gowing, who kindly asked me to dinner one night. I drove over on my motor scooter and had a very pleasant meal, but oh was it cold returning home as the frosts at Keith were quite arctic. I got on well with Noel and I told him that I wished to settle in the area and was looking for a small block of land. Some days later Noel left a message for me suggesting that we should meet because he had a property to show me that he thought might be suitable.

On my day off I drove over to his office and he showed me where the property was on a map and said that the AMP had decided to sell the block and planned to advertise it in two weeks' time. He suggested that he should take me to see it straight away and if I liked the land he recommended that I should buy it, as it was in a very good area 25 miles south of Keith with nice neighbours. In addition the AMP would advance me a loan to purchase it if I was interested. It all sounded too good to be true!

We set off in his Land Rover to see the property. The block ran north-south along the west side of the Black Range in the Hundred of Willalooka. Most of the property was virgin scrub that ran along a range that was about 100 feet higher than the surrounding countryside. The 600 acres of flat land on the west side of the range had been seeded with pasture.

It was a beautiful block and I fell in love with it straight away. The pasture had never been stocked, so the grass and clover were thick on the ground. The area was studded with small gums that would provide plenty of shade for the stock in the summer. The ground was not nearly as sandy as I had found on other properties that I had visited and the dark green of the mallee scrub along the low range of hills gave the property a character that most of the country in the Ninety Mile Desert lacked. We went up onto the high ground for an overall look and when there I discovered a hidden valley and a clump of big old gum trees around a tiny water soak that had made their growth possible. The block was fenced so could carry stock immediately and Noel said that if we wished to purchase the land he would put down two wells for me as part of the deal, so stock water would not be a problem. The property had an air of romance about it and I wanted it.

What to do? I had only two weeks in which to ask my father if buying this block was in any way possible, but he was in England. I decided that the first thing to do was to talk to WS and ask his advice. I rang my friend, Jim, the chauffeur, and told him I would be taking the train to Melbourne that night and asked him if it would be possible to meet me and if I could borrow an office car to go out and see WS in the morning.

Faithful Jim was there to meet me when the train arrived in Melbourne at six o'clock in the morning and I drove out to WS's little horse farm at Keilor. As nothing was stirring in the house I waited in the car watching the back door. Eventually WS came out for his morning walk with Winston, the Boxer dog Churchill had given him.

After a surprised greeting I told him I needed his advice. He invited me to walk with him and I explained about the block of land and how I had fallen in love with it. I asked if he thought I was crazy or should I ring my father and ask him if it would be possible to buy it? By the time we got back to the house he advised me to call my father and tell him everything I had told him and, no, he didn't think I was crazy, as long as I didn't ask him for help as he was broke!

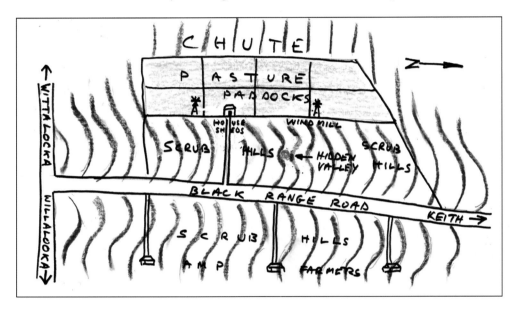

Map of 'Chute' and the 'Black Range Road' to Keith

I rang my father as advised and he told me to go ahead and get all the paperwork involving the sale sent to him in London. He also asked me to draw up a budget for the things that I would have to do before the property could carry any stock. This would include a tin shed to live in, two windmills with tanks, troughs and some sheep yards. He went on to say that I had better get myself a solicitor in Adelaide!

I rushed home and went to see Noel and told him what my father had said. He seemed genuinely pleased and wished me luck and promised to attend to the paperwork and have it forwarded to London. I resigned my job and took the train to Adelaide to see Sir Keith Angas, who had acted as my guardian when I was at Roseworthy, and asked him if he could recommend a solicitor. He very kindly introduced me to his own solicitor and also his accountant. Talk about growing up in a hurry! One week ago I had been a carefree jackeroo and now I was a property owner trapped in the world of solicitors, accountants, budgets and bank loans!

My father had also told me to buy a VW car. I went to see the dealers and came away with a beautiful steely-blue Beetle, which I drove back to Keith.

I found lodgings with Michael and Sybella Aldersey, who owned the farm to the west of my block, while I planned and then erected a corrugated iron tractor shed with a 10 by 20-foot rectangular room at one end in which I could live. I bought an ancient Ford kerosene tractor with a starting handle that had a kick like a mule and an old four-wheel trailer.

Deciding where the house would be built one day was the greatest fun and having done that I chose a spot for the shed, the sheep yards and the future shearing shed. This determined where the drive would be and the front gate, so I needed a name for the property as I couldn't just go on calling it The Block. The name I chose was Chute Standen, after the farm in England where I had spent so many happy years. I later shortened it to just plain Chute to keep things simple.

The drive ran straight in at right angles from the road over the Black Range and down to a lovely grove of gum trees that one day would shelter the tractor shed and the sheep yards. Just beyond the trees a raised tongue of land pushed out into the pasture and I chose this spot as the site for the homestead. The view was superb, as it looked north up the pasture running along the range. It was high enough to be above the morning fog that sometimes settled over the pasture, leaving the tops of the gums floating like little green islands on a sea of glistening white cotton wool. The sunsets from this spot were amongst the best I have ever seen anywhere in the world.

Noel had fulfilled his promise and arranged for two bores to be drilled. One was near the future house site and the other at the northern end of the property. I had windmills erected to pump the water into large tanks. The water was all right for stock but far too salty for humans to drink.

I soon had the tractor shed built out of corrugated-iron sheets – six ten-foot bays with the last one being entirely enclosed to make a workshop, which would be my living quarters until the house was built. I dislike the normal look of sheet iron with the corrugations running vertically so I used the iron on its side making the ridges run horizontally. I suppose this was the beginning of my becoming artistically pig-headed! The finished shed looked well and much more like a proper building with horizontal courses. As this was the first shed I had ever built I was rather proud of it and couldn't wait to move into my new quarters. Of course everyone asked me why I hadn't built it properly, but I still maintain that it was the best-looking shed in the district!

I had decided that when I built a house, rather than having a wood-burning stove, I would have a bottled-gas oven. I bought one and installed it in my quarters in the shed. The water from the roof was caught in two 2,000-gallon sheet iron tanks so I had everything I needed. I piped bore water to the shed and built a furnace under a 44-gallon oil drum to feed a shower that hung from a gum tree. It worked well enough but it took ages to heat the water so many more quick cold showers were taken than hot ones.

The Ninety Mile Desert was deficient in the small amounts of copper and zinc that are necessary for plant growth, which was why it had not been developed in the past. When it was discovered that the chemicals made the land productive the AMP insurance company decided to develop the area and settle it with farmers. The Government encouraged this sort of thing in those days as Australia was still a primary producing country and, apart from minerals, wool and wheat were its main source of income.

Now came the time to show my father what he had paid for. I hoped he would approve and I looked forward to sharing it all with him the next time he came to Australia. He used to fly to Adelaide quite often on business so on one of these visits he arranged to return to Melbourne by train, disembarking at Keith so he could spend a couple of days with me for his first visit to Chute. The appointed day arrived and I went to meet the train at Keith railway station. The first thing to do was to take my father to meet Noel as he wished to thank him for all he had done for me. Noel very kindly lent us his Land Rover so I could show my father all over Chute, as the VW Beetle couldn't be taken out onto the pasture because of all the rocks and stumps I had yet to clear.

What a day we had together! I made some toast for lunch and warmed up some soup on the new gas stove and we ate sitting at the workbench that I had made in my living quarters in the tin shed. We examined the proposed house site and looked at some plans I had brought from a newspaper advertisement. It was a dear little house and I have yet to find a better design for a bungalow.

The plan showed a lovely big sitting room with an open-plan kitchen off it and three little bedrooms. The whole of the north-facing front of the house was lined with six-foot high windows except for a wooden panel by the front door and the wall of the chimney. The entire sitting-room wall opposite the windows and fireplace was lined with the same timber as the outside wall by the front door. It was a perfectly planned 900-square-foot house and was relatively cheap to construct.

I decided to build the house using white Mt Gambier limestone blocks, the local building material. The stone can be cut with a wood saw and comes in blocks one foot high and two foot long and four inches thick. As the site was still covered with scrub we had to do a bit of guessing as to where exactly the house would be, nevertheless we paced out the approximate area and put in markers for the corners, both getting more excited by the moment. As there was only one camp bed in my shed and no plumbing, I had booked us both into the local motel where we had a brilliant dinner talking together for the first time ever and I fell asleep content, having discovered my father to be a warm friend. Next day we explored other farms around the country and both decided that Chute was the prettiest block we had seen. In all my years at Keith I never saw a block of land that compared with it for beauty.

During his few brief visits to the farm I got to know my father and we had fantastic times together. He loved the property and was interested in everything I was doing and incredibly supportive. There were only three years between his first visit and his premature death aged only 56, but they were some of the happiest years of my life as we built a marvellous father-son relationship. What he did for me was so generous and it made possible everything else that has followed for which I shall be eternally grateful.

The time came for my father to leave after his first visit. He had arranged for Jim to drive up from Melbourne to collect him as he had an aversion to travelling by train. This aversion had started on a superb holiday that my mother had taken us on to Italy when I was aged 12, one in which trains and my father had played an important part. My mother, with Pat and me, had driven down to Forte dei Marmi in our old Humber Snipe on one of her typical exciting holiday adventures.

At the end of the war there were no commercial airlines to Australia so my father created one by buying a Lancaster bomber and fitting it out to carry six passengers. He called it Silver City Airline, after the Broken Hill mines.

The ship voyage to Australia took six weeks, but the Lancaster could do it in six days! The route required going down through Africa and across the Indian Ocean and refuelling on Christmas Island. It was a long journey, but the plane had beds, a kitchen and even a shower! The following year the Lancaster was replaced by a Skymaster, which had a much better range, so they were able to fly via India and do the trip in three days. Within a couple of years airlines had opened up routes between the USA and Australia and he was able to fly commercially, making the plane and pilot no longer necessary.

The pilot, who had been a bomber commander, decided to take over Silver City Airline and start a cross-channel route between Lymph in England and Le Touquet in France. The fleet consisted of two old Bristol Freighters that took two cars at a time.

During the Battle of Britain, Lymph was a Spitfire base situated on top of the White Cliffs of Dover. It was designed for fighters and not for clumsy Bristol freighters. Come the day of our flight we were driven down to Lymph by Studley, one of the farm hands. The poor man had been designated to look after the car and drive us to Italy! The French also had petrol rationing, like the English, and were being very tight about giving coupons to visiting foreigners. To take as much fuel on board as possible, we filled up with petrol before arriving at the terminal that was a converted air-raid shelter.

While the cars were being loaded the Customs men insisted on searching our luggage. Of course they discovered my mother's jewellery and to her fury confiscated it, saying they didn't trust her not to sell it abroad. There were heated words with my mother ending on a gibe about the Nazis having landed in England after all, none of which helped matters in the least!

We boarded the plane and took our places in canvas seats that were only clipped to the floor because they had to be removed to get the two cars on and off. The engines sprang into life when all was ready for the 20-minute flight across the Channel and with the plane vibrating alarmingly, we taxied across the grass field to the furthest point from the cliff edge. The engine roar became louder and louder and when the brakes were released we shot off across the grass taking off just before reaching the edge of the cliff which was fortunate, as the drop was straight into the sea 300 feet below.

We arrived safely after what I thought was a very exciting trip, although I am not sure anyone else agreed. The smell of petrol from the car's over-full fuel tanks didn't add to a feeling of safety. It was on this journey that my mother told me that she hadn't been to Le Touquet since I had been born, at the same time as telling me about her disappointment of my not being a girl! Was she trying to get something off her conscience before it was too late?

That was the beginning of a long trip down to Forte dei Marmi via Paris and Lake Como as there were no dual-carriageways in those days. It had been arranged that my father would travel down by train to Milan and join us at the lake. When he arrived he announced that he was never going in a train again as the trip had been a nightmare. We stayed at the Villa d'Este and the three of us had a very happy time. I shall never forget it because every day we went out in the hotel row boat and I had to do the rowing!

After a week we drove from Lake Como to Forte dei Marmi and stayed in a hotel where many years later, when Margie and I also used it, the manager showed me my father's signature in the old Register. In 1948 the hotel bill was paid in very large Italian notes and by large I mean not only in nomination, but also in length. The Italian 10,000-lira note in those days was over a foot long!

Because of the currency restrictions after the war a barter trade had sprung up whereby the English paid for the school fees of Italian students and their parents paid our hotel bills in Italy. The system worked very well most of the time, but occasionally things went wrong and we were part of such an event. Our student was a very beautiful, bubbly girl named Carlotta who had been to stay with my parents in England. One evening she came to the hotel with her boyfriend for a drink to deliver the money needed to pay the hotel bill. Carlotta said she had forgotten to bring the envelope of money, but would return with it the following day. The fact that the money had been in an envelope turned out to be the problem as she had posted some mail in a letterbox for her mother on the way. Well, you can guess what happened, *but* can you imagine the postman's face when he cleared the mailbox?

When my father came to pay the bill at the hotel he found that he still did not have enough money, even though Carlotta had by then delivered a second envelope. However, fortunately he had the return railway ticket from Pisa to London and luckily, by selling it to the manager at a considerable loss, he was able to make up the difference on the bill. He solved the problem of how to get home by having the Silver City Dove fly down and collect him from Pisa.

My father's favourite story was about a train trip a friend of his made on the Canadian Pacific. During the trip his friend had been eaten alive by bed bugs and when he arrived in Vancouver he wrote a stinging letter to the president of the Rail Company, complaining bitterly. Duly he received a letter back from the president apologising profusely and thanking him for letting him know the carriage number which had enabled the company to withdraw the carriage from service, fumigate the interior and burn the mattresses. The president's letter went on to say that it was only with the help of people reporting faults that the company could maintain the railway at the highest possible standard of cleanliness, so he would sincerely like to thank him for this act of public responsibility. My father's friend was flattered when he read the letter, but then he found his own letter attached to the back and across it was scrawled, *Send this damn fool the bed bug letter!*

My life has been dictated by lucky chances, but the best one of all was about to happen to me. While I was jackerooing in New Zealand my parents had attended a business dinner party in Melbourne where my mother had sat beside Ken Begg, who was then Chairman of ICI, Australia. Ken told my mother during the meal that he and his wife had been touring Europe with their children, Michael and Margaret, and had left them behind to work in London for a year. My mother asked Ken for Margaret's address and promised to invite her down to the farm in Wiltshire for the weekend.

This she duly did and at the same time asked my Australian girlfriend, Margie Edwards, thinking that the girls would be good company for each other in a house full of older people. Margie Edwards was the girl whom I had met after my Tiger Moth experience when I returned to Sydney. We had liked each other and had continued to write ever since that meeting.

I later learnt that when they met in England Miss Edwards showed Miss Begg a photograph of me, which is how the latter came to know of my existence. I distinctly remember receiving a letter from my father in which he mentioned that they had had a beautiful redhead to stay for the weekend, although Miss Begg doesn't believe me!

The Olympic Games were held in Melbourne in 1956. I had been asked to go to one or two events and also to some of the cocktail parties held over that period. It was at one of these that I first met Margie Begg who had just arrived back from England. I had come with a party of friends for a drink before going on somewhere to eat and just as we were leaving I passed a very good-looking redhead talking to a man as they stood by the right of a fireplace. The girl stopped me and said, "I think you are John Robinson. I am Margie Begg and I have just been staying with your parents." I admitted that I was indeed John but said, "I can't talk right now as my friends are waiting for me, but I hope that we shall meet again." Margie's version of that conversation is that I said, "Oh! Give me a ring sometime," to which she replied, "I don't ring men up," but I really don't think I could have been that rude!

The lucky thing was that she had recognised me from a photograph she had seen when staying with my parents. She told me later that she nearly hadn't come to the party as she hadn't been invited. Thank goodness her brother persuaded her that it would be all right.

Margie reported my being in Melbourne to her parents and they insisted that I should be invited to their home as my parents had been so kind to her in England and had her to stay as well as giving her a 21st birthday party. The Begg family lived only a short walk away from the house used by my parents when they were in Melbourne after moving out of Menzies Hotel. I was able to stay at my parents' house when they were away, as there was a permanent caretaker there called Marianna. Soon after meeting Margie at the cocktail party Mrs Begg telephoned and invited me to dinner.

On the morning of the dinner date I had to go into town and collect something from Lorna Hegarty, my father's secretary, at the ZC office in Collins Street. Dear little Lorna was tiny and hardly came up to my father's waist, but he said she was the best secretary he had ever had. She and I were friends and she helped me many times over the years.

After talking to Lorna I crossed over the road and went into the bar of Capers restaurant for a cup of coffee and found an American sailor doing the same thing. The citizens of Melbourne had been asked over the radio to befriend the visiting US servicemen during the Olympic Games, so I started to talk to him and found out that he was from the giant aircraft carrier moored in Williamstown harbour. During our conversation I asked him if he was having a good time in Australia and he said he was but he was a bit disappointed because he had not yet seen a kangaroo.

I was at a loose end so offered to take him out to Healesville Zoo where he would not only see a kangaroo, but also emus and koalas and, as he said he would love to do this, we set out in my little car. The afternoon was a great success and the sailor turned out to be an extremely interesting person to talk to, as at this time of my life I knew nothing about America. When we returned to Melbourne in the afternoon I asked him what he was going to do for the rest of the evening. He answered that he was just going to walk around town until ten o'clock when he was due back on board. I decided to ring Mrs Begg, explain the situation and ask if I could bring him to dinner with me that evening, to which she probably agreed because his presence would make for more conversation since none of the Begg family had met me!

We arrived at the Beggs' house and the American sailor proved to be a great asset to the conversation while we ate a delicious dinner that started with oysters on the shell. Now if you haven't seen oysters before they do come as a bit of a surprise and they certainly were to the poor sailor. When his plate was removed the cook found an oyster carefully parked under each shell, although how he did that without anyone seeing is a mystery. The time came to leave and take him back to his aircraft carrier, but as neither of us had any idea where the harbour was Margie very kindly offered to show us the way to Williamstown, where the ship was berthed.

The three of us got into the little car and set off with the sailor in the back seat. Where Toorak Road meets St Kilda Road there is a set of traffic lights that were red, so I slowed down. Just before we stopped the lights changed to green and we started forward again when suddenly a man ran out from the pavement pulling a woman by the hand. I slammed on the brakes and missed the couple by inches, but by then cars were coming up the other side of the road. The girl panicked, pulled loose from the man, turned back fell and onto the rear mudguard of our car. The sailor and I leapt out and ran around the back of the car to find the poor girl lying in the road.

Fortunately a policeman had seen the whole thing and had immediately rung for an ambulance, which arrived in minutes as a hospital was just around the corner. The ambulance man assured the policeman and us that the girl was only shaken and not injured. As I didn't have my licence on me the policeman said I would have to report to the local police station next morning and show it to the officer in charge, but reassured me by saying that I was not to blame and he would say so in his report. We got back into our car and drove very slowly to the ship, feeling pretty shaken.

We said goodbye to the sailor and returned to Margie's home, where the two of us talked for hours. The accident had made a bond between us and any shyness had disappeared. As she had just been to my home in England she had lots of first-hand news, which was nice for by then I had been away from England for nearly six years and I suddenly found myself missing my childhood home. I am sure that if I hadn't brought the sailor to dinner and the accident hadn't happened I would never have got to know what a wonderful person Margie was. We said goodnight and I left, promising to report what occurred at the police station.

Next morning the police told me that the girl had not even been admitted to the hospital and that I was not to worry about the accident. I called Margie and told her the good news and thanked her mother for the wonderful dinner, which is when I heard about the oysters under the shells!

I saw Margie several times during the Olympic Games at various parties and we became friends. I wanted to see the film that had just been released called *Lady and the Tramp* and I asked her if she would like to come with me. She said she would but unfortunately she was going to a wedding reception at Menzies Hotel on that particular day. I persuaded her that the reception would nearly be over by five o'clock, so if I collected her then we would be able to catch the five thirty show. Luckily she agreed to this plan and I was waiting in the hotel foyer at the appointed hour.

I knew all the staff at Menzies from the days when my father had lived there. The company had used the apartment for years and I remember staying there myself when I was waiting to catch the ship home with Mike and Nana in 1943. I owned two pet lizards that lived in a shoebox and because I wasn't allowed to take them on the ship I had to release them on the roof outside the apartment windows before leaving. I wonder if their offspring are still living under the tiles?

Margie and I both loved the film, but more than that I realised while sitting beside her that I had never felt so comfortable with another person in my whole life. I was also feeling very sorry for myself as I thought that this would be the last time we would have an opportunity to be together. My parents were due to arrive in Melbourne and I would have to go with them for the Christmas holiday as they had rented the house on Mt Macedon again. After the film I took Margie back to her home and we said goodbye. On our parting Margie said that she would always think of me as *Tramp* and I am afraid the name has stuck.

My mother had become very fond of Margie Begg in London and when she found out that she was going to turn 21 she and her friend, Nancy, organised a party for her. It was therefore natural that when my father rented the house for Christmas my mother would invite her to come up for a weekend to stay with us, all unbeknown to me.

After I had met Miss Edwards in Sydney we had continued to write so when she told me that she was going to England for a year I had asked my mother to look after her. My mother had asked her down to Chute Standen for several weekends and it was on one of those visits that the two Margies met. Margie Edwards and I had kept in touch by mail and when she returned to Sydney I had been asked up to stay with her parents, and we had sort of drifted into becoming a couple.

The problem was that I had asked Miss Edwards to come down to Macedon from Sydney for the same weekend that my mother had invited Miss Begg. When I objected about this arrangement my mother said that it would be fun as the two girls knew each other, having met in England the year before. Of course my mother didn't know how I was beginning to feel about Margie Begg and I could foresee problems arising.

I was right! I remember the weekend very clearly as I now thought Miss Begg was a very attractive girl and this fact become obvious to Miss Edwards, who laid into me for paying too much attention to the wrong Margie, who I had taken her for a walk to show her the koalas in the gum forest while she was resting!

It was soon after this difficult weekend that I went to Keith and started working in the Ninety Mile Desert with the idea of looking for land to develop. When I found the block in the Ninety Mile Desert, Margie Edwards and I announced our engagement and Margie Begg went out of my life.

As Chute would be our home it was time that my fiancée came down to have a look at where I expected her to live. This she did, staying with my old boss at Desert Downs for a couple of days as she couldn't stay in my shed. When she came with me to the property she seemed as excited as I was about the future and liked the site I had chosen for the house, even though at this stage it was just a big bare patch of bulldozed limestone.

A month later I drove up to Sydney for our engagement party and on the night I arrived we went out to dinner and she told me that she couldn't marry me. She said that it was nothing to do with me personally, but she could never live in the Ninety Mile Desert. I didn't argue, but of course was terribly hurt. We went to see her parents and both felt very sad and tearful. Next morning I set off for the 500-mile drive back to Chute alone in my little VW beetle. By the time I had reached the Blue Mountains outside Sydney the hurt had gone and I was singing. I shall never be able to thank Margie Edwards enough for releasing me from my promise. When I think of all the things that would not have happened I go quite numb at the knees.

On my return to Keith I threw myself into farm work. My parents were very understanding and my father told me to carry on and build the house. I started looking around for a builder and eventually found one who seemed keen to do the job. He had two workmen to help him, one named Mr Crabtree and the other an Italian, who of course was called Angelo. I took the builder down to Adelaide to sign the contract in front of my newly-acquired solicitor and we ordered all the material and dug out the trenches for the foundations. When the concrete was poured the house looked tiny, being even smaller than the shed I had built. However, everything seemed to be going well and I was very excited by the idea of having my own home, but I should not have counted my chickens before the eggs had hatched!

The builder suddenly announced that he was quitting and was returning to Sydney. What to do? I had some foundations but no house. Fortunately I had only paid for the material used so I was not out of pocket. It was then that Mr Crabtree and Angelo stepped forward and said that they would like to take over the contract and finish the house for me. But there was a problem as they didn't have any transport, the original contractor having left with the truck they had used to get back and forth to Keith where they were camped.

The best way to solve the problem was to give Mr Crabtree an advance on the house so he could buy a small second-hand truck. When he returned to the farm I was horrified to see he had bought a brand new truck! When I asked him how he had been able to afford it he told me that he had bought it on hire purchase. I should have heard warning bells ringing then, but this was my first experience of dealing with builders.

The house slowly took shape with first the timber walls quickly followed by the roof of slate-blue sheeting. Soon plaster board covered the walls and I could walk from room to room on wooden floors! When Mr Crabtree and Angelo finally finished I had a wonderful house to live in. The only problem was they were well over budget.

As time went by I had been getting steadily more worried about costs. I paid for all the materials myself so knew Mr Crabtree and Angelo's profit was disappearing. The final straw arrived when Angelo appeared with a new car as well, again bought on hire purchase. When the time came for settlement there was no profit margin for Mr Crabtree and Angelo after paying all the building supplier's accounts.

I rang my father for his advice and he told me to pay them each a bonus above the agreed price and wish them on their way. He also gave me a piece of advice that I have followed ever since, "As you have to live there, make sure that all the local people are fully paid."

Over the months I had become very friendly with the two men and they had done a wonderful job for me. I could not have been more pleased with my little house and I would like to thank them now, wherever they are. They taught me how to build and when the time came for me to add on a nursery wing with a guest bedroom and bathroom, I was able to do this by myself, but was greatly helped by having the solid little house to lean my timber extension against so it would not blow away.

The next trip that my father made to Chute was with my mother and this became one of the highlights of my life. They flew in on the company's plane as they were on a business trip between Broken Hill and Melbourne and the farm was on the way. The pilot had found a sheep station not far from me with an airstrip long enough for the plane to land on. What the pilot hadn't been told was that very tall gum trees surrounded the field!

The pilot did a couple of passes over the strip to inspect it before he was satisfied that a landing was possible. Luckily there was a good headwind so he was able to come in only a few feet above the tree tops. The moment he touched the ground he slammed on the brakes with full reverse thrust, sending up a typhoon of dust. The plane pulled up and the door opened and out staggered my parents looking rather pale. The plane took off as soon as the cases were out and before the wind could change. We found out later that it was illegal for that size plane to land there! On the drive back to Chute they told me that they were a little nervous as they had just had a very scary experience in Queensland when one of the landing wheels of a commercial aeroplane had collapsed on touchdown, causing the plane to spin around on the runway!

When the three of us sat down to dinner on the first night my parents said that it was the first time that they had been the houseguests of one of their sons, which gave me a great thrill. They marked the event by presenting me with a visitors' book and were the first to sign it. The book stayed in use right up to the end of 1999.

My parents loved my little homestead. To be honest, homestead is rather a big word for such a small house, but it seemed spacious to me after living in a tin shed only 10 by 20 foot square. The three of us had a very happy time, planning what should be done with the interior of the house. Walls were measured for wallpaper, and floors for string mats, while various ideas were discussed about furniture to sit on and eat off.

My mother cooked our meals and my father had brought some tins of his favourite food, *pâté de foie gras*. I had purchased 300 ewes and 6 rams that I needed to separate as hopefully the boys had completed their task. I asked my father to help and it was wonderful to be pushing the sheep up the race and watch him work the drafting gates in the sheep yards, obviously loving it.

The time came for them to leave. My father announced that there was no way he was going to take off from the same strip. He had cancelled the plane and booked seats on the commercial airline from Naracoorte, our nearest official airstrip. I drove them down and waved goodbye. Driving back to Chute I felt very sad, but deep inside extremely happy and content.

My parents' visit was a turning point in my spirits and all sorts of things started to happen. Soon afterwards my father had walked past a second-hand furniture shop and had spotted some superb cane chairs and my mother had made covers for the cushions. She also sent up some floor matting, a dining table and two benches. I had had some bookshelves made, so when all this furniture was added, the sitting room was transformed.

Shortly after this my mother returned to stay with me for a week armed with rolls and rolls of wallpaper. She had taken lessons on how to hang paper after the war, when it was impossible to get house decorators. She assured me that it was easy and it turned out to be just that. Within a week we had the whole house papered and it looked magnificent although the place reeked of glue. Painters came and did the ceilings in the sitting room but otherwise I tackled all the other paint work.

The sitting room with its cane furniture

'Gould' curtain material

I had seen some beautiful chintz material in a friend's house in Adelaide that was covered with birds painted by Gould. I had the material made up in floor to ceiling curtains that went the entire length of the sitting room and the effect was stunning when they were pulled.

It was a wonderfully productive time, for while I worked on the house the pregnant sheep grazed in the paddocks. We had good rains that year and the pasture was blooming. The only eyesore was the lack of a garden as my delightful little house was surrounded by a barren waste of bare white limestone that threw off a blinding glare.

It was time to begin to cut the 600 acres of pasture up into paddocks by first fencing it across the middle into two paddocks. If only I had a dollar for every posthole I dug on the farm! It was not an easy job as the so-called good soil out on the flats was only a foot deep over limestone, the top six inches of which was as tough as flint. To help me I had an auger mounted on the back of the tractor with which I could drill the flint using a one-inch mining bit. Believe it or not, in those days one could buy gelignite in the local store! I rather enjoyed clamping on the detonator, lighting the fuse and waiting for the boom. It was hot work in the scorching sun and one soon learnt not to leave the iron crowbar lying on the ground, as it got red-hot. The worst fright I ever had in my life was when I went to pick up the crowbar and suddenly realised I was reaching for a six foot-long King Brown, one of Australia's nastier snakes. My fright didn't stop me from quickly dispatching the creature. I hate snakes!

Christmas had come around again and I went to Melbourne for a holiday with my parents. When I arrived in the city Margie Begg was very much on my mind, so one day I summoned up courage and left a note with a flower on her doorstep, asking how she was and telling her that my engagement was off. I learnt later that she had a lot of trouble reading my handwriting and had needed the aid of a friend to do so! I waited a day, then rang suggesting that we meet and have a picnic in the Botanical Gardens. Margie agreed telling me that she was working as the receptionist at the Dulux Paint Colour Centre just off Collins Street, but could get off for an hour at lunchtime.

I collected her and as I had promised to have her back by two o'clock on the dot we took a taxi to the gardens so we would have more time to eat our sandwiches before she had to return to work. I told her that we would probably have to hitchhike back, because it would be impossible to find a taxi passing the Gardens in the middle of the day. It was a particularly beautiful sunny day and we found a spot by the lake with a notice that read *Danger Deep Water*. We had a lovely half-hour and thank goodness she hadn't fallen in love with anyone else that year! Come quarter to two we were at the gate of the Gardens with our thumbs in the air looking for a lift. Much to my surprise and our good fortune a car stopped and gave us a ride into town!

Our meeting had been such a success I asked her if we could do it again and as she agreed, we had another happy sunny picnic at *DDW*. We walked back to the road and again stood thumbs up hoping to get a lift back into town. A car approached and pulled up, "Could you take us to Collins Street, please?" The obliging driver said, "Yes, I am going there myself." I kept a straight face for about one minute and then introduced Margie to Jim. What a laugh we all had. Jim and I had set the exact time for the pick-up and I knew he wouldn't let me down. I wasn't going to risk another chance pick-up. They were truly memorable and romantic days.

The Botanical Gardens became our courting spot and we return there whenever we are in Melbourne to give thanks for our joint luck in life of having met all those years ago. We would also sometimes go and have a meal at the fateful Capers restaurant, where I had met the US sailor who had played such a part in our first meeting and the accident that followed. It became our favourite restaurant as it had a sunny courtyard where we could sit outside.

Margie was asked to lots of parties, so when I was in town she would take me with her. This included a black-tie Government House ball where she wore a beautiful long yellow evening dress. Much to her sorrow I never did learn to waltz, but I often think of that evening as being sheer magic.

Margie's parents asked me to their seaside home. They were wonderful people and always so welcoming that I very quickly felt at home. Their house, Rannoch, was at Portsea near Sorrento and had been the holiday home of Ken Begg's mother and father when he was a boy. Ken grew up in Melbourne and went to MGS, but all of his boyhood had been spent at Portsea on the beach barefoot, swimming, sailing or fishing.

Margie's mother, Helen, was descended from an early settler called Thomas Raine, a sea captain who transported convicts to Australia in his brigantine *Surry*. Raine had become a captain at an early age because his skipper died on the voyage out to Australia. He had an illustrious career, found a passage through the Barrier Reef and discovered Raine Island. He also took cuttings from the willows planted around Napoleon's grave on the island of Saint Helena when taking on water during passage to Australia, and then planted them on his property near Bathurst in NSW.

'Helen Begg and Margie' aged two

Helen was one of the best-read people I have ever met and we had many fascinating conversations together. She and Ken both shared an earthy sense of humour so my weekend visits were full of laughter. Ken's favourite story was about the Night Soil collector who used to eat his bread and butter with his cup of tea as he sat up on top of the cans on his horse-drawn cart. One day he dropped one and was heard to say, *How lucky can you be, butter side up*. It became another one of our catch phrases, joining my father's *Bed Bug Letter*.

I was amazed to find that the tiny weatherboard cottage WS had added to Kilmarie for Mike and me in 1940 was still there and only six houses along the cliff from the Beggs' home. When we walked along the cliff I pointed it out to Margie. She was eight when she returned to Australia from New Zealand in 1943, so I must have left for England only a couple of months before she came to live at Portsea! I find the coincidence of our nearly meeting all those years ago quite extraordinary.

On that same path along the cliff I was able to show Margie my Aunt Peg's house, Heron's Pest (the leg of the R had been missing for years). The house was halfway between Rannoch and Kilmarie and I had stayed there aged 17 while on holiday from Roseworthy Agriculture College when Margie was then living just two houses down the cliff!

I remember Kilmarie quite well, but especially the Christmas I arrived aged five as I was given a toy cargo boat that was driven by a clockwork engine. The ship was designed for 'pond use only' and not the 'open sea', but as there was no pond I was allowed to float it in the sea. Of course the engine got flooded and the spring soon rusted up.

Cloudberry, Dodder and Sneezwort loading the 'Jeanie Deans'

My little ship is mixed up in my memory with two of my favourite books, *The Little Grey Men* and *Down the Bright Stream* by BB, which are about the last gnomes to live in England. The gnomes discovered a toy clockwork driven cargo ship named *Jeanie Deans* and used it to navigate the waters of Folly Brook in search of their lost brother. Everyone who loves England should read these two books to their children, as they are utterly enchanting.

WS's house was bordered by big fir-tree hedges cut flat on the sides and top. As children Margie and her brother used to climb up on them and play on the top until they were seen by the gardener and ordered off.

By now I was head-over-heels in love and thankfully Margie was with me, so I asked her to come and visit Chute. Of course she had heard a lot about the farm from me, but before I could ask her to marry me I knew from experience that it was wise that she should see it with her own eyes. She was a city girl and had never lived in the country although she had friends who did and had stayed with them. However, they lived on old well-established properties in the Western District or Gippsland, and the Ninety Mile Desert was a very different kettle of fish.

My brother, Mike and his wife, Bern, also wanted to see Chute, so I made a plan for them to come on the train and bring Margie. In those days young girls didn't stay with bachelors; however, if Mike and Bern arrived a day later no one would know! Margie caught the Melbourne-Adelaide Express to Keith and arrived at midnight. I drove her out to Chute in the little VW, travelling south along the bitumen road until we reached Gum Water Hole, forked right on to the gravel Black Range Road towards Chute.

I don't think I have ever been so excited or anxious in my life. I was taking the most beautiful girl in the world to see my home and prayed she would love it as much as I did. We arrived at my front gate and drove up over the range on the bumpy drive leading to my little white homestead.

Her first reaction to the inside of the house was magic. She loved it and wanted to see everything, but as it was by then two o'clock I tucked her up in the bedroom I used as an office.

At first light we were up and after breakfast I took her for a tour of the farm on my ancient blue Ford tractor. I showed her the shed where I had lived while the house was being built, and the dear girl was enthusiastic about everything she saw. The house was still sitting like a sore thumb on a white rock slab but I told her I planned to bring in some good soil and surround the house with a strawberry clover lawn. In those days she was not the devoted gardener that she now is, so there was no complaint about the lack of flowers. Talking about this time 45 years later I learnt that in fact she was a bit shocked by the barren paddocks, and thinking back I am not surprised!

That night we had a wonderful dinner by candlelight and then drove into Keith to collect Mike and Bern off the midnight train. The tiny house had never had so many people sleeping in it before as on that weekend. I can't remember much more about the visit except that I was walking on air and that the time for Margie's departure came far too quickly. Mike and Bern were going west to Adelaide, so I was able to be alone with Margie while we waited for the later east bound train to take her back to Melbourne. When it arrived I handed her up into the carriage and I felt as though half of me was leaving with her.

A few weeks after Margie's visit to Chute I went down to Portsea and asked her if she would marry me, and, thank goodness she said, "Yes." I then had to pluck up courage to ask her father for his daughter's hand. We went into the sitting room together after dinner and I asked him if I could come and see him in his office the next day. He burst out laughing, sent Margie and her mother out of the room, shut the door and sat me down for a ten-minute grilling. He then went to the door and called the girls in and said, "Well, I had better go and open some champagne!"

Margie and I were engaged and on our return to Melbourne we bought a ring. The date of the wedding was set for December 1st and she and her mother began the hectic business of organising everything to be ready in six months. 1958 was certainly a year to remember.

One of the things I had to do before our wedding was to show Ken and Helen where their daughter was going to live. A visit was arranged and Margie and her parents drove up to stay with me. I could not have asked for kinder parents-in-law. I grew to love them as my own family and when the time came for me to explain to them several years later that I wanted to become a sculptor, they showed remarkable understanding and made no objection to my taking their daughter and grandchildren to England for two years. Both Ken and Helen collected paintings, some of which we now have at Agecroft, and they constantly remind us both of two loving people.

'Tramp and Lady' sharing spaghetti

Margie at her Engagement

WEDDING

December 1st 1958

I was surprised that Margie's parents agreed to their only daughter leaving home and coming to live at Chute with me after their visit, as it was a miracle that their low-slung car hadn't ripped its exhaust pipe off on a rock as they drove up to the house. I was very apprehensive about what their first impressions would be, because although the house was finished and looked wonderful inside, it was still surrounded by a bare white limestone wasteland.

I was so nervous I can't remember anything about the first night's dinner, but everything must have gone well and I presume that Margie must have cooked one of her wonderful meals.

Next morning everyone said that they had slept well and the one bathroom managed to cope with us all! Breakfast was easy as I lived on Ready Mix porridge. Pop Begg smoked baby cigars in those days and caused an outburst of complaint when he left the table and lit up in the sitting room that was also the dining room. He was driven outside where we watched him puff away as he walked up and down the bare limestone wasteland.

When I joined him he asked, "What about building a dry stone wall round the house?" What a brilliant idea and we had millions of rocks on the property so material wasn't a problem, but I had never built a dry stone wall! He then suggested he ask Henry, his Portsea gardener, if he and his wife would like to have a paid holiday in the country and show me what to do. I had met Henry when I had stayed with the Beggs on weekends when we were engaged and had really liked him so was delighted with the idea.

And so it happened. Henry and Joyce came and stayed for a week on their way to see relatives in Adelaide. Together we built the wall around the house from the thousands of stones we collected from the paddocks. Keeping up with Henry was hard work, as he just never stopped.

By the time they were due to leave we had finished the wall and it looked wonderful. The following week I arranged for topsoil to be brought in and soon the house was surrounded by an earth plateau rather than bare rock. What a transformation and all thanks to Pop Begg being made to go outside to smoke his cigar!

As we could only use bore water to irrigate the lawn I planted strawberry clover, it being more salt tolerant, although it was still necessary to water at night to keep the evaporation to a minimum. The seed germinated and after a while there were clumps of clover growing all over the place. You could not call it a swath of green, in fact my father said it looked more like a measles infection! Thankfully over the following years the mild infection turned into a heavy rash by adding coarse buffalo grass Pop Begg gave me from Portsea.

Margie discovered she had green fingers like her father and changed our garden into a riot of colour by planting South African daisies, geraniums and many other plants with blue or orange flowers and grey leaves as they didn't seem to mind the fierce midday sun and blistering summer heat.

Henry's wall and Margie's garden

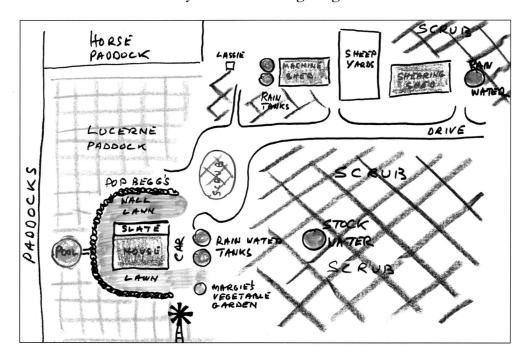

House, first bed and tractor shed, and shearing shed

The days ticked slowly by and our wedding day got closer. I put in a line and installed a telephone so I was at least able to ring Margie up and chat. She even taught me how to make white sauce on-line! As a bachelor I had reduced my evening meal down to a basic menu of grilled chops, carrots, cauliflower with white sauce and ready-mashed potatoes. Breakfast remained pre-cooked porridge and lunch was a raw carrot sandwich.

My raw carrot sandwiches caused a laugh when my father's godson, Bill Govett, was out from England and came to help with my first shearing. I was very pleased to have him as I had not yet built my own shearing shed and had arranged to use my neighbour's across the Range Road. In theory this was all going to be very simple as our front gates were opposite, which meant getting the sheep to his shed should be easy.

Shearers are very particular about the time they start and stop work and insist on the sheep being ready when they want them. The logistics of getting everything done to their liking left very little time for anything else. The two shearers would stop for their lunch but Bill and I would have to keep working, getting sheep penned and pressing up the wool into bales, while praying that it wouldn't rain, as they would not shear damp sheep. There was certainly no time for us to sit down and have lunch.

The quickest thing to make in the world is a carrot sandwich. Slice raw carrots, press between bread and butter and then eat. All very simple! Come the first lunch I rushed home and prepared the sandwiches. The look on Bill's face when he opened the sandwich to inspect the filling caused much merriment with the shearers.

Without Bill's help I would not have been able to get the sheep shorn. Thank goodness there were only 300 that first year. By the following year my shearing shed was finished and things went a lot smoother, especially as Margie was then able to make my sandwich as well as provide the shearers with tea and buns and a two-course hot lunch every day. The week of shearing remained one long slog for us both and we were very glad when it was over. On Tim's arrival Margie put her foot down and told the shearers either to bring their own food, or go hungry!

'Shearing the Rams', Tom Roberts

City folk only see the glamour of shearing because their knowledge is gathered from paintings like *Shearing the Rams* by Tom Roberts. Shearing 100 sheep a day works out at one every five minutes and is the hardest job in the world. Shearers earn every penny of their wages.

At last it was the end of November and time to go to Melbourne. Tim Emanuel arrived by train to stay with me on my last night at Chute as a bachelor. I had asked him to be my best man, just as his father had been my father's and vice versa. Three years later I was his best man when he married Sally Manifold. Sally was a friend of Margie's and was to be one of her bridesmaids, which made Tim happy. We drove down to Melbourne together which gave us a chance to catch up, not having seen each other for years.

Tim and I had not really spent that much time together in England as we had gone to different schools, but we did have some adventures together in London, one of which sticks in my mind very clearly. We were about 12 years old when we arranged to meet in Hyde Park by the Serpentine and hire a rowing boat. There is an island in the middle of the lake that before the last war had been surrounded by a spiked iron fence. All the iron fences in London were cut off, including the one around the island, and turned into tanks. All that remained was a notice saying, *Landing Prohibited.*

We rowed to the island and once out of sight of the boathouse, of course headed towards the notice. The bow touched the bank and we both stood up to jump onto the island. As we moved to the bow there was an awful sound of splintering wood and an iron spike came straight through the bottom of the boat, releasing a fountain of water! Leaping back to the stern meant the spike disappeared but water was still pouring in. We jammed a handkerchief in the hole and rowed for our lives round the island and headed for the shore. Never have two boys rowed so hard or run so fast! I have felt guilty about this ever since and whenever I walk past the island nowadays I remember our panic when the spike appeared through the bottom of the boat.

Margie, Sally, Noel and Sarah

150

Margie, Pop Begg and Helen

It is probably a terrible thing to say, but I really can't remember much about the events that surrounded December 1st 1958. After a family lunch at my parents' house, Tim and I changed into our morning suits and set off for St John's Church. I must have been in some kind of coma and swept along by the events as they happened. It was all very different to the rehearsal the day before, when it had all seemed like a jolly party!

I do remember standing with Tim at the altar waiting for Margie to arrive on Pop's arm and how radiant she looked as she came up the aisle towards me. I do remember being overawed by the dazzling smile she gave me when she stood beside me. I felt that we were alone in the church and completely unaware of everything else around us.

We spoke our vows and I placed a wedding ring on Margie's finger and we were married. What I did know for absolute certain was that it was going to be the best thing I had ever done and so it has turned out to be. Apart from everything else, like years of joy and laughter and the wonderful happening of being parents, without Margie's encouragement there would be no sculpture story to tell.

Ken and Helen gave us a superb reception at the Australia Hotel and Dennis Farrington's Band provided the music. Margie and I led the dancing, although much to her disappointment I still hadn't mastered the Waltz, so we settled for a Fox Trot.

151

Signing the Register

When it was time for us to leave we did a tour of the tables to say goodbye. On arriving at WS's table, Gertrude asked him to give us *one word of advice*. He looked at me for a moment and then in his deep gravelly voice said, "Concentrate." The photograph below was taken at that moment and says it all! How often have I remembered his advice. Concentration is the key to life and all my mistakes have come from the lack of it at critical times.

Gertrude, Margie, 'Concentrate!' WS, and John

Margie threw her bouquet to Sally and Jim drove us to Menzies. What a day for us both! It must be so hard for a girl suddenly to find that instead of being under her father's protection she is the wife of someone whom she really doesn't know, her choice having been based on intuition alone. Our courtship had taken place over a few weekends at Portsea and two visits to Chute to see her future home. I had promised her parents that I would look after her to the best of my ability and this is what I have tried to do for the last 46 years, although in actual fact it is really she who has looked after me.

We awoke to a glorious sunny day and made our way down to the port to catch the ferry across to Tasmania for our honeymoon. My parents had booked a cabin with a little sitting room, so we suddenly felt very grown up and married. We sailed down Port Philip Bay past the two houses at Portsea where we had grown up, but without having met, and out through the Heads into the adventure of a lifetime together.

I had hired a car, which was waiting for us in Launceston and drove down to Hobart to stay for a couple of nights at Wrest Point Hotel. One of the things that I remember most about that week was the fact that we laughed all the time. My parents had very kindly booked us a beautiful suite and filled it with flowers although the bathroom smelt like a public lavatory. I collected the offending green blocks and threw them out of the window, not realising until too late that I should have used paper to protect my hands, as the smell was impossible to wash off. Was this my first lack of concentration? Ever since then Margie and I have laughed whenever we see those terrible green blocks.

The head waiter's name was Charles and he was quite the most pompous man either of us had ever come across. Margie and I only drank red wine in those days, which didn't cause Charles a problem until we ordered half a bottle one night to have with our chicken. "May I point out that Sir has ordered white meat." Our honeymoon catchphrase became, "Charles wouldn't approve", and has remained with us all our lives.

One day we drove out to Port Arthur to see the ruins of the Convict Settlement. The little museum had a display of shackles and other horrible reminders of the cruelty of the times, but also the Prison Register, which we were allowed to look through for family names. We were delighted to find a Robinson who had been deported for drunken and disorderly behaviour, which caused Margie to splutter, "So this is the family I have married into!" We were sure that Charles would not have been surprised. We noticed that quite a few pages had been torn out by families who wished to hide their past!

We drove over the mountains to Zeehan, a mining town on the West Coast, and stayed in the ZC Guest House for a couple of nights. The fumes from the lead smelters had killed every single tree for miles around, leaving the surrounding mountains completely bare, a devastating sight. The manager had arranged for us to ride in one of the ore bins that were pulled up the mountain on a long cable by the bin full of rocks coming down from the mine. We asked what would happen if the cable broke and were assured that they had never had an accident! It was a very unnerving experience, but the view from the top out over the coastline was amazing.

I knew that my father had worked at Zeehan when he was 20 after leaving Cambridge, having been sent there to forget about my mother! At the same time my mother had been sent to stay with her brother Pat in Southern Rhodesia, where he farmed after the Great War. The reason for these drastic removals was that both my mother's mother and father's father were totally opposed to Bill and Nan getting married.

In those days many young men came down from Cambridge University before sitting their final exams, which was probably a good thing, as most had not attended any lectures. May Balls were a very popular pastime and at one of these my father's great friend, Sydney Emanuel, had invited Nan as his partner. She was introduced to Bill and they fell in love. When Nan took Bill home to meet her mother apparently the Colonial Boy did not impress Granny Freeland. This was ridiculous as he had been in England since he was three years old, educated at Harrow for years and then Cambridge.

Bill drove a tiny baby blue Bugatti that Nan told me was not a very good car from a girl's point of view as it was open to the cold and rain. Furthermore my father had to clean the spark plugs often as they used to oil up when driving in traffic. The Bugatti was duly replaced by a Lancia that was the first car ever built with brakes on all four wheels. According to my mother he used to love demonstrating that it could stop quicker than any other make to non-believers by driving at brick walls!

My father told me that he was absolutely terrified of Granny Freeland as she had two very large yellow and blue Macaw parrots tethered to perches either side of the front door of her country house. When guests visited the house they had to run the gauntlet of squeezing between these beasts that screeched and flapped their wings at people they didn't know.

Granny Freeland also had a pet monkey called Jacko that had free range of the house and loved to sneak up on visitors and nip their ankles. Jacko eventually became so aggressive he attacked the postman and my mother was delegated to take him to the London Zoo for adoption. She told me that it was one of the most distressing things she had ever had to do because when she delivered him there he screamed like a child pleading not to be left behind.

WS was equally appalled at Bill's choice, as he was not impressed with the English middle classes, whom he considered to be lazy and effete. The outcome of this expressed horror from both their parents was a year's banishment to either ends of the earth. Luckily there was a proviso. If after a year they still felt the same way about each other they could become engaged, but only if they agreed to wait yet another year before marrying. Thinking about my father's story shows me how lucky Margie and I were to have such fantastic and supportive parents.

I know nothing about Bill's banishment to Tasmania, but having seen Zeehan I don't believe he would have enjoyed his time there, surrounded by some of the ugliest country I have ever seen in my life. The town was originally a convict settlement and the entrance of the harbour was known as *Hell's Gates*. The West Coast of Tasmania has one of the world's highest rainfalls, 120 inches per annum, so he must have always been wet.

Nan fared better as she went to join her bachelor brother Pat on his Soldier Settler's farm. The British Government had a policy of settling the Highlands of Rhodesia with the returned soldiers who had been gassed in the war, so he had been allocated a farm near the town of Bulawayo. Pat had built a primitive bungalow but it was still unfurnished. Granny Freeland decided to send out everything he needed from sheets to plates to a stove all packed into tea chests. I guess that stores like the Army and Navy in London were doing the same thing for people all over the Empire. The tea chests were always of a superior quality so when unpacked they could be made into furniture such as cupboards, tables and square chairs.

Uncle Pat met his little sister at the station with a cart pulled by two mules called *Can't* and *Shan't*. The ride out to the farm took several hours along a bush track, but eventually they reached Pat's mud-brick bungalow. It all sounds a bit like the first tin shed I built to live in at Chute, so I can well imagine what my mother's reaction was on arrival as up to then she had always had breakfast in bed!

Over the next few days the boxes were unpacked and they set about making furniture from them. Included in the shipment were several bolts of cloth and some of this was used for curtains to cover the boxes when they became bedroom cupboards. Nan claimed that she transformed the bungalow into a very pretty house and I am sure she did. The plumbing was primitive. When she banged on the tin wall a native would pour hot water into a basin joined from outside through the wall into the bath inside.

Nan smoked all her life, but as Uncle Pat had damaged lungs he didn't have any cigarettes in the house. This meant he had to send a native into town to collect a new supply each week. My mother told me that she couldn't work out why they tasted so awful until she met the boy running back from the store with them tucked under his armpits!

When the year of exile was over Nan and Bill met again and as their feelings for each other had not changed, a wedding date was set. They went to Devon for their honeymoon, leaving their best man, Syd Emanuel, to deal with the wedding photographs. He ordered one of each, but the photographer wrote a 2 after the 1 on the order form. They returned to their little house in Ovington Square in Kensington and found the front hall stacked to the ceiling with packages of photographs mostly of people they didn't know!

The family soon outgrew the little house and they moved to Cambridge Square near Marble Arch, where I was born in 1935. These pre-war years must have been great fun for my parents. Bill worked beside WS at the ZC office learning the mining business and every year he would be sent to New York, taking Nan with him.

They used to travel over by ocean liner, leaving the children in the care of Nana, cook and the housemaid. My mother told me wonderful stories about the Prohibition Days and how their friends brewed gin in their baths. During the return voyage she used to spend the time sewing the labels from her old clothes onto the new ones she had bought in New York. She did this when Bill was not looking, as he would have been horrified. Without a doubt, he was one of the most honest men the world has known.

As Granny Freeland lived in Madeira for half the year and her chauffeur had nothing to do in London, Bill and Nan used him and the car. The first ten years of their marriage must have been wonderful, but tragedy struck in late 1935 when Bill contracted tuberculosis and had to have a lung collapsed. It was then that Nan bought Chute Standen and moved to Wiltshire. She built a conservatory where he could recover which he did in time to take part in WWII and England's fight for survival. Probably my father getting TB, forcing the family to sell Cambridge Square, actually saved our lives as the square was blitzed by the Germans. Although all the houses were flattened by the bombs the London plane trees survived and are still there!

Margie and I arrived back in Melbourne from our week in Tasmania and after seeing both our parents drove back to the farm in the Ninety Mile Desert to begin our married life in our own home. Because I worked on the farm our honeymoon continued. Margie's parents had asked us down to Portsea for Christmas and as my parents were staying with WS and Gertrude along the cliff we had a wonderful holiday with plenty of sea, sand and family.

The problem I faced on our first Christmas was what possible present could I give my new wife? I walked down Melbourne's main street looking for inspiration in the windows but all I could see were mannequins dressed in elegant dresses staring blindly out at me. One of them was leaning on a mantelpiece and on the shelf was a red china bull, which for me dominated the whole window.

I walked in and asked a shop girl if the window display was for sale. She assured me that it was, presumably thinking I meant the elegant dress because she was very surprised when I asked the price of the bull. "Oh, I will have to ask about that." A senior shop assistant arrived, gave me a funny look and then climbed into the window, my having assured her, "Yes, it was the bull I was asking about." Anyway I bought it and they gift-wrapped it for me and I gave it to Margie for Christmas. It was definitely a surprise! The Red Bull has looked after us ever since and I like to think he was telling me even then that sculpture would be my destiny. All good things come to an end and it was soon time to return to the farm and really start behaving like grown-ups.

Our first summer together was a dream. I don't think we stopped laughing we were so happy. If the temperature got a bit too hot to bear we used to take an icy cold shower under the fire hydrant by the windmill close to the house. I could fill a 200-gallon fire tank in a matter of minutes from the hydrant as it was fed directly from a 10,000-gallon tank and with the valve fully open it was like standing under Niagara Falls. We used to walk down to the windmill stark naked, that is until one day some unannounced visitors arrived at the house, causing us to hide in the bushes until they left. They were halcyon happy carefree days.

'Chute' homestead and fire hydrant windmill

One of the joys of Chute was Friday's mailbag that Cliff Leadham left in a 44-gallon petrol drum down at the gate. He collected everyone's mailbags from the Keith Post Office and stopped at each property along the Black Range Road on his way back to the Willalooka Store and Telephone Exchange which was manned by Mrs Leadham. Years later the Leadhams operated the Willalooka Drive-In cinema that was a delight to our children.

After we had found the key to the padlock, the blue canvas bag would be ceremoniously opened and the contents spilled out onto the floor of the sitting room. It was a very exciting moment and a bit like Christmas every week as we looked for handwritten envelopes and overseas mail. Of course we had our fair share of bills as well, which was always depressing, but usually there would be something exciting. Cliff also brought a *Woman's Weekly* for Margie that was her only source of city gossip as we had no newspaper. When I began subscribing to *Time* it also came in the bag, along with a fresh loaf of bread!

Our little house was beautifully cool in the summer as long as there wasn't a northerly blowing, but because of the sandy soil when winter set in the temperature got decidedly frosty. We had a large open fire in the sitting room, but even so some evenings it was so cold you would only be warm on whichever side you exposed to the flames. Keeping warm was a bit like toasting bread on a fork, one side at a time. Ever since those days I have been very appreciative of central heating.

There was no mains electrical supply in the area, so we generated our own with the same diesel engine that drove the shearing gear. The engine was operated from a remote control button in the kitchen that could not have been further from our bedside. When we couldn't stand the chill of the sitting room another moment we retired to our blankets. Turning the lights out meant one of us rushing to the kitchen and back before freezing to death, so it wasn't long before I had a set of buttons installed beside the bed! By the time the second winter came we had saved up for an electric blanket. This meant that at least we could get into a warm bed.

New rams and new shearing shed

There was always plenty of work to do on the farm. Margie was able to help me in the yards when necessary and soon learnt that bursting into tears while drafting sheep didn't really help if her husband was yelling at her at the same time as screaming blue-murder at the dog. The City girl became a first class Country girl and I was very proud of her.

The house looked out onto a lucerne paddock that gave a small amount of green relief during the long dry summer months. Beyond that was a small horse paddock for my old grey mare that I called Daisy Roots, because she was so hard to pull up when heading for home. On the way out to work and while inspecting the sheep she behaved like an angel, but as soon as I turned her head for home it was a different story and a firm hand was needed. Margie was longing to ride Daisy Roots so I bought another horse for myself and named him Spot after the white blaze on his forehead.

Tim Emanuel had given Margie a beautiful Australian saddle as a wedding present. She had been thrilled by this totally original gift and was dying to try it out. As a teenager she had taken lessons at Sorrento's Tally Ho! riding school and ridden with her country cousins, but that was many years ago. I hoped that if I rode with her on Spot, Daisy Roots would behave. It was great fun inspecting the sheep together, riding around the paddocks either in the early morning or late afternoon, occasionally disturbing a pair of Bronzewing pigeons, who would fly away with a soft whirring of wings.

Occasionally we would ride back to the house through the hidden valley we had christened Glen Gowan, Margie's second name. We felt as though there was not another person on the planet. Years later Glen Gowan became one of our favourite weekend picnic spots with the three little boys.

When Margie became pregnant we would occasionally go out on horseback for a gentle walk around the stock until one day Daisy Roots sensed that her passenger was apprehensive and bolted. Margie did well to stay on board, but it was a worrying moment and horse riding was banned.

Spot was the cause of a very strange happening. Eight years had passed since my visiting the Angas family as a Roseworthy student and sometimes helping their daughter Sarah move stock on horseback. We had only just bought Spot when Sarah came to stay for a night as she was passing through Keith. It was great to see her again and talk about old times and show her around the farm. As we went past the horse paddock Spot trotted over and Sarah nearly fainted. My Spot was her beloved Tankard that she had sold when she left home!

At the beginning of Margie's pregnancy we were asked by Conway Seymour to his wedding to Sue in Sydney. Conway and I had become friends when I had arrived in Keith, but he had known Margie since their school days. He had proposed to Sue at our front gate on their way home after they had been to dinner. Even though it would be a long drive up to Sydney, we decided that we had to go to the wedding as once we had a baby our travelling days would be seriously curtailed and this might be the last chance of the two of us having a trip alone for many years to come.

The wedding was a fun party and much enjoyed. Being in Sydney also meant that we were able to see Margie's brother, David, and his wife, Mitzi, and my cousin, Peter Baillieu and his wife, Edwina. It had been Peter who had taught me to swim, aged six, by tying a halter round me and throwing me in the lagoon from a raft. He had left the land, gone into the banking world and moved to Sydney. After a wonderful dinner with them Peter suggested that we should go to hear a new singer that everyone was talking about.

Peter and Edwina were obviously well known at the club and were shown to a table near the stage. The act was announced soon after we arrived and a girl started to sing. I had never heard such a voice before and we were all enchanted. The voice of Dionne Warwick has since shared our lives. Her partnership with Bacharach has given the world unbounded musical joy. Whenever I hear her sing on the radio I remember the night we saw her perform and sent shivers down my spine.

There is another girl who sends shivers down my spine, Jacqueline du Pré. I have a videotape of her playing Elgar's *Cello Concerto*, which nearly moves me to tears every time I see it. The passion and intensity of her playing is unique. Another piece of music which makes my spine tingle is Beethoven's *Violin Sonata No. 5, Spring*. Sitting in the Agecroft studio with Margie on a summer evening listening to it as we eat our dinner looking out on the floodlit garden is as close to being in Paradise as anyone could desire.

If I were only allowed to choose one piece of classical music by Mozart it would have to be his Concerto for *Harp and Flute*. Alkan's *Barcarolle in G* is another favourite that has given me endless joy as it is without doubt one of the most soothing pieces of music I have listened to.

When Margie was into her eighth month, my parents came to stay for the weekend. We had decided that the baby should be born in Melbourne, so Margie went with them when they left to stay with her parents and await the Big Day. When the time drew near I drove down so I would be able to take her into the hospital. On April 3rd 1960, Timothy William Robinson arrived at St Andrew's hospital with all the church bells ringing because it was Easter Sunday morning.

In those days mothers were encouraged to stay in hospital for ten days after giving birth. When Margie and Tim were discharged we returned to Chute to build a new life around a routine imposed by a seven pound bundle.

'Tim' at four months

Now that Margie and I had a child we began to learn the joys of being a family. Life took on a new format that included feeding him by candlelight in the middle of the night. Tim grew at the required rate and although being a rather fussy eater, he was the perfect baby. He occasionally threw his purée on the floor, which was frustrating as Margie had grown the vegetables and spent hours forcing them through a sieve!

'Four Generations', 1960
JR 25, Tim 0.5, LB 55 and WS 85

Margie, Pop Begg, Tim and Granny 'B'

161

My father came to see us before returning to England. We had a brilliant weekend and I took some great photos of him holding Tim while he and the little boy got to know each other. Tim had developed a strong neck by his visit and it was great to see my father holding the little boy as he studied his gentle giant of a grandfather. We didn't have any idea that it would be the last time we would see him. Three months later he had a fatal heart attack, aged only 56.

'Bill and Tim'

The following year my mother came to stay and told me about my father's death. He had gone to bed early not feeling well and because she was worried about him she had left the door open between their rooms. She woke hearing my father calling for her and found him in a great deal of pain so immediately called the doctor. When he arrived my mother asked him to give Bill an injection to alleviate the pain, but the doctor refused saying that it could kill him. My mother insisted that he do something and the man rounded on her and asked, "Do you want to kill him?" My father was completely lucid and ordered the doctor not to talk to my mother in that way, pointing out that if it were not for her nursing him when he had had tuberculosis he would have died long ago. He then ordered the doctor to give him an injection, as he knew that he was dying and couldn't stand the pain any longer. The doctor did so and went to wait in the sitting room leaving them together. My father died in his wife's arms.

I tell this story, as I believe that it shows what a wonderful marriage my parents had: one of love, trust and companionship, shared over many years. They had lived through many marvellous early years, his illness, WWII, and had seen their children grow and marry and give them grandchildren. What more can anyone ask? I also tell the story because I admire their bravery more than I can say and I pray that when my time comes, or Margie's, that one of us will have as much courage and be as brave in the face of such an ordeal.

My father's death made his visits to Chute my most precious memory of the friendship that had grown up between us over the last four years of his life. By this time Margie was expecting her second baby, but unfortunately my father died before Peter arrived. I treasure the memory of Bill holding Tim, as much as the photo I have of him holding me when I was the same age.

'Gamma and Tim'

"I would like to draw the attention of the Board to the fact that I run this Company and no one should forget it!"

A very happy mother with her son

Tim couldn't be left alone in the house so we used to have him with us when working the sheep in the yards or bumping around on the tractor. He seemed to love everything we did with him and was a very happy little boy.

Margie and Tim drafting sheep

A general rethink was necessary when Peter was getting ready to arrive on the scene. To start with there was no way we were all going to get into the VW, so it was traded in for a Holden that had lime-green plastic seats! Going from a VW to a station wagon was like moving into a bus.

'Peter Lyell', April 1962

Peter was a completely different child to Tim. Apart from eating everything that was put in front of him, he seldom had wind, would sleep anywhere, and never cried. He also was born in Melbourne and as Margie only ever wanted boys he was a very welcome addition to the family.

One day Margie came back from shopping in Keith with an adorable marmalade kitten, which had been found under the school floor! At first it was never allowed in the house, but used to walk up and down the windowsill outside my office that had become the nursery as my desk was under the window and proved to be the perfect height for the baby's bath! We christened the cat Spike Milligan and he provided great amusement at bath time as he paraded back and forth as Peter tried to focus on him and catch him through the glass with squeals of delight.

One of the problems with Australia is that it has more than its fair share of poisonous snakes. Around the house and sheds I had killed several King Browns, some of them a good six foot long. Margie used to put the playpen outside in the shade of the back veranda on hot days so Peter could be as cool as possible. One day, when she peeked through the window to check up, she saw him laughing at the cat who was behaving very strangely beside the pen. On taking a closer look she saw to her horror a snake moving along the edge of the pen and realised that Spike was trying to shoo it away. Luckily I was working close by and was able to dispatch the snake. Spike became our best friend from that day on and was invited into the house, although he never really felt comfortable inside, preferring to hunt in the Bush.

Lassie, my Border collie sheepdog, didn't really like Spike and pretended he didn't exist. Lassie didn't really like anything about my being married and always made sure that I was between her and Margie or the boys.

Spike Milligan and Peter

When Margie and I got engaged I gave her a golden Labrador puppy. We called her Lady to commemorate our first movie date. This name got changed to Heidi during our engagement, mainly because my future mother-in-law thought Lady was 'too awful'. Luckily we both liked the new name and the dog didn't seem to mind the change. Heidi was a beautifully natured dog and was allowed into the house after we were married. When Tim arrived it was Heidi's turn to have her nose put out of joint as she thought he was very bad news and didn't like taking second place. Fortunately Heidi and Pop Begg had fallen in love with each other and when we suggested that he take her, both man and dog were delighted. Pop changed her name again, this time to Heido!

Nan and Bill had a close friend whom we boys all called Uncle Frederick. The three of them had shared many happy times together over the last twenty years and my parents treated his children as their own and his sons, Peter and Henry, often stayed in our country home when they were on leave during the war. He was a tower of strength to Nan when my father died. Uncle Fred's wife had died only months before Bill, so with full approval of all their children my mother became Mrs Frederick Bowring, although to keep matters simple and separate, my mother merely changed her surname by Deed Poll, but kept it a secret from all except the two eldest sons, Pat and Peter. I didn't find out until years later when Peter wrote a book on his family's history! They made a marvellous couple and the partnership brought both of them much happiness.

The first time I was aware of Uncle Fred was when I sat on his knee aged five years old to see the cinema screen. My mother was about to say goodbye to Mike and me as we were to be evacuated to Australia because of the war. It must have been a terrible time for my mother and as Bill couldn't be there, Uncle Fred must have stepped in and taken us to see *Snow White and the Seven Dwarfs*. I have memories of being terrified by the wicked witch, so I am not sure that it was the right film for me, but then my mother never was a good chooser of films.

Pop Begg and Heido

When I was about nine years old she took me to see a Werewolf film in our local cinema in Andover and I spent most of the time hiding under the seat. The outcome of that film was that I became terrified of the dark and afterwards needed a night light in my bedroom for years. I also began to sleep with a dagger under my pillow!

'Peter Lyell and Timothy William'

Uncle Fred was Chairman of C T Bowring and Co, which had become a giant insurance business under his guidance. His great-grandfather, Benjamin Bowring, had founded the company as a shipping firm in Nova Scotia. After the war the company was still building cargo ships and when I was 12 years old Uncle Fred very kindly invited me to join him and his colleagues for the sea trials of their new vessel on the Clyde. The adventure began with my going with him to a London railway station to join the other guests on the night express to Glasgow.

I had never been on a night train before and was thrilled to have my own sleeper. I was packed off to bed as soon as we pulled out of the station, but was much too excited to sleep so lay awake listening to the party that was going on in the cabin next to me. We arrived in Glasgow in the morning and immediately went down to the docks to board the new ship. I was handed over to a foreman who was told to take me all over the ship while Uncle Fred and the ship builders had a meeting. Exploring the ship took me right back to when I was eight years old and had sailed back from Australia with Mike and Nana. Lunch was served on board and at the end of the meal Uncle Fred got up and made a speech, ending with a toast, "To the ship, and all that sail in her." He then called on *Wee John* to say a few words. Dying of embarrassment I was forced to my feet and delivered my first public address!

My mother always said that she was saved by having Uncle Fred as a friend at the time of Bill's death. As chairman of the company he had to travel all over the world to inspect what they were insuring and he took my mother with him. One of these trips was to Australia when they came up to see us for a very happy weekend and I got to know my new father-in-law, as I had not seen him since I was 17 and had sailed for Australia in the *Port Napier*.

During the weekend they told us about some of their funnier experiences, a couple of which I always remember when I think of him. One concerned the Golden Gate Bridge of San Francisco and Uncle Fred's desire to be driven over it. Now the one thing that you are definitely not allowed to do on the bridge is stop, but when they were about halfway over he suddenly ordered the driver to do just that.

The driver thinking that his passenger was going to be sick immediately stopped and Uncle Fred hopped out, touched the iron railing and then hopped back into the car again, saying, "Drive on, my good man." My mother asked him what he thought he was doing. Fred replied, "Bowring's insures this bridge and I thought I should check that the structure was sound." They laughed all the way to the hotel, but I am quite sure that the driver thought that they were both utterly mad.

The other story that I shall never forget was the one they told about their visit to an oil field in Venezuela that Bowring's also insured. The field was several hours' drive from the capital in a very dry area of the country. By the time they got there Fred needed a bathroom. Things were pretty primitive at the site and the loo was just a little shed perched over a deep hole. Fred walked over to the shed, went inside and shut the door. Minutes later there was a yell, the door flew open and Fred came bounding out with his trousers around his ankles, just in time to see the shed burst into a ball of fire and completely disappear in flames.

Fred had gone in, sat down, lit a cigarette and then dropped the match down the hole which was full of very dry paper, so moments later he found he was sitting on an inferno. My mother thought that she was going to die of laughter. I wonder if the little shed was insured and the company made a claim!

Life was treating them both very well and they bought a flat on the south coast of England. Every Friday afternoon they would be driven down in their new Rolls Royce that Uncle Fred had told my mother to go and buy. She said that one of the most fun things she had ever done was to walk into the showrooms in Berkley Square, wander around looking at what was on offer and when the salesman came up to her asking if he could help, say, "Yes, I think I would like that one, please."

Every Sunday they would go for a walk along the promenade and on reaching the end would sit in deckchairs for a spell before returning for lunch. One day Fred fell asleep and never woke up. My poor mother was absolutely shattered by his death. Luckily Peter and Pat were in England at the time to give her support. Years later when I was staying with my mother in London, she began to tell me about Fred's death. She ended by saying, "When I get to Heaven I am going to give Bill and Fred a real rocket for leaving me down here all alone for so many years."

I had always admired my mother's strength of character and I think it is fitting to end this bit of the story by recording her own last days. She had always been a cigarette smoker, as had been Bill, so it was inevitable that Pat, Mike and I were also smokers. You may remember when I was about ten I was arrested by the village policeman because he had caught me smoking in the road!

My mother developed a sore throat, which made swallowing very painful. The doctor told her it was only a constriction and that a small operation would fix the problem. I took her to the hospital and when she was settled in I was very surprised by the strength of her hug as she said goodbye and firmly told me to leave.

During the evening of that day she rang a Healer called Alice, that Margie and I had introduced her to, and asked her to give her strength. My mother died peacefully that night. The doctor told us that the autopsy showed that she had an inoperable cancer of the throat. She had been taking sleeping pills ever since Fred's death and I believe that she had saved a lethal dose and secretly took it that night. I am sure that she knew that she had cancer and she felt it was time to join Bill and Fred. Born in 1904 in the Savoy Hotel with a silver spoon in her mouth, she lived through the horrors of both World Wars; she had lost two husbands whom she dearly loved, but had lived to see her three sons happily married and present her with nine grandchildren. She was content. What more could any of us ask for?

How the world had changed over her lifetime! She and her brother Pat had been two of the first paying passengers to fly from London to Paris after the Great War. The plane was a converted bi-wing bomber and carried only two passengers who sat in front of the pilot wearing leather helmets and goggles in the forward gun turret! They had had to land in a French field to refuel with petrol with a hand pump!

'Peter' getting ready for his christening

But back to life on our farm in the Ninety Mile Desert. Comparing those days with the hectic lives that our boys and their families now live shows me that we also have lived in a Golden Age. In the early Sixties our needs were simple and life's pressures minimal. Peter was born in 1962, two years after Tim.

Peter as a baby seemed to carry the weight of the world on his shoulders and took life very seriously indeed whereas his brother Tim thought the whole thing was a joke. Luckily Peter soon caught on that things were not that bad and by the time he was christened his whole world had become a playground.

In those days we were self-sufficient in most ways. Once a fortnight I would kill a sheep in the shearing shed for meat. My father was always upset by the fact that my sheep dog got to eat the shoulders, as in his opinion that was the sweetest meat. The problem was the sheep would not keep for more than two weeks in our kerosene-burning refrigerator that was temperamental at the best of times as the flame had a tendency to go out unexpectedly. Besides it is hard work to eat a whole sheep in two weeks!

'Tim and Margie with Peter' aged two months

I never liked killing sheep and Margie says that I used to go very quiet on the afternoon of the biblical sacrifice. The deed was done in the shearing shed and the carcass allowed to set over night hanging in a cotton bag made from an old bed sheet to keep the flies away. She used to hate my bringing the still-warm liver to the house after the act, but we both loved the delicious meal she would cook with it the following day.

171

We had the best of all worlds but like everything in life, nothing stays the same. The only thing that is guaranteed in life is Change. Mark arrived in 1964 so Margie had her hands full raising three little boys but also had to help me in the sheep yards.

With three little boys our tiny house began to bulge at the seams so I decided to add a playroom, a guest bedroom and bathroom. The only problem with this plan was that we didn't have any money to employ proper builders, so I had to do the job myself. Margie asked me if I had ever built a house before and I indignantly pointed out that the tractor shed was still standing! She replied that a house was a little different to a shed as it had floors and a ceiling, not to mention proper plumbing!

I took no notice of her acid comment because luckily the west end of our rectangular Mt Gambier house had a solid 22-foot long blank wall. I knew that if I attached a timber frame to the solid wall it would stop the addition falling over. I drew up the plans for a box 22 foot square and ordered the timber for the frame, flooring and sheeting for the walls and roof. I decided that if I could get the outside of the box finished, I could worry about the inside later. Thank goodness we didn't have to get planning permission as it would never have been granted!

The 'West Wing' starting to take shape!

Building the extension was one of the most fun things I have ever done. Because of the white ant problem in Australia everything has to be raised up off the ground on posts capped with tin to stop the termites climbing up to eat the house. The ant posts needed to be three feet apart in each direction and I soon had a forest of stakes ready and level to take the floor. To make sure the floors were going to be exactly the same level on both sides of the wall I drilled a hole through from inside the house.

'Mark Kenneth', March 1964

The only good thing about living in the Ninety Mile Desert with such a low rainfall is that you know that you are very unlikely to be bothered by rain between November and March. This gave me five months to complete the extension in-between looking after the stock, running the farm and helping my neighbours in emergencies, in the same way as they helped me.

Once the posts were in and level I could then build the walls, put on the rafters, making sure the whole skeleton was firmly attached to the existing house before nailing on the wall covering and roof. I bought two windows and a couple of doors and then cut a hole through from the sitting room wall into the new playroom. A plumber gave me a hand to fit the pipes for a lavatory, shower and basin in the tiny bathroom and hey presto we had a bigger house.

Of course the first thing that had to happen was to throw a party. An electrician had helped with the wiring, but without going all the way to Adelaide it was impossible to get light fittings. Margie had five small terracotta flower pots left over from her garden planting, so I drilled out the holes in the bottom of these and fixed them to the centre of the ceiling in a cluster. I hear the West Wing is still standing after 35 years but I am sure the light fitting has been replaced, which is a pity as it was unique.

Having a family is the most fulfilling thing that can happen to anyone.

173

Mark four, Peter six and Tim eight

The years quickly passed. Tim turned five and reached school age so a whole new way of life began for us. The school was in the local town of Keith about 25 miles away and the children got there in a big yellow bus. It travelled a circuit route on a bumpy dirt road around the district, stopping at the front gate of every farm to pick up little its passengers.

Margie had already introduced Tim to the idea of school by leaving him at the Kindergarten while she did the shopping with Peter on her hip and Mark asleep in a pram. Now it was time for Tim to move to the Big School.

He was very excited about going in the yellow bus as his friend Mathew was also starting school. Come the first morning Margie dressed him up in his new uniform and we took him down to the front gate with a tiny suitcase containing a sandwich. The bus appeared with Mathew waving out of the window, the door opened and Tim climbed in. What a milestone for Margie, as she watched her little boy drive away into the next stage of his life!

'Peter' stayed home to help on the farm!

Tim's bus was due back at four o'clock so we all went down to the front gate to meet him. One very tired dishevelled little boy fell out of the door and climbed into the car. "What was it like? How did you get on?" All we could get out of him was, "It was good." The poor boy was shattered. The journey was an hour each way and it had been a long hot day.

Fortunately Gertrude had given me some money to have a 10,000-gallon concrete water tank built beside the house to use as a swimming pool. The tank was set about eight feet out from the stone wall that surrounded the house and I had constructed a drawbridge to enable us to walk across to its lip. It consisted of a couple of planks and served as a barrier to accidents as when they were down, it was impossible for the boys to reach the pool.

'Tim and Peter' with their wheelbarrow tyres

The Keith summers were very hot so the pool changed our lives. I got hold of some wheelbarrow inner tubes from the hardware store and had the valves moved to the outside. The tubes just fitted around the boys' chests so they could jump into the seven-foot deep water and bobbed around like corks. They would stay in for ages, come out and warm up, and then run up the gangplank and jump in again. It was an easier way to teach them to swim compared to what my cousin Peter had inflicted on me in the freezing water of the weedy lagoon when I was five!

The pool became a lifeline and as soon as we reached the house Tim changed, slipped into his tube, leapt into the cold water and quickly came back to life. I am not sure the boys would have survived the long hot summer days without that blessed pool.

Every Christmas we would pack up the station wagon and set off to Portsea for a two-week Christmas holiday with the Begg family. It was a nine-hour drive down to the seaside, but as many of our friends drove to Sydney, which was twice as far, we considered ourselves lucky.

When the families went on holiday the farms were left in the charge of the few who were not going away. Across the road opposite our front gate Glen and Nelda Jones lived on their property, Glenelda. Glen milked a cow and we bought our milk from him for all the years they were at Chute. Only once did we spill the container on the way home, something that taught us to be very careful as after that accident the car smelt of sour milk for weeks. Glen used to check the stock water for us while we were away and when he took his family for a holiday I would do the same for him. It was a very friendly area with everyone helping their neighbour whenever it was needed.

Unfortunately farming in Australia is bedevilled by droughts. In the ten years that we lived on Chute we had three terrible droughts and three near ones. Four good years out of ten is not enough to make ends meet. I shall never forget the anxiety of waiting for the rain when the ewes had already started to lamb. If the rains didn't come I would often be forced to kill the lambs that had been deserted by their mothers because they had no milk. If the sheep got too poor it was impossible to sell them. Once I was forced to get the butcher to come and kill the worst ones so at least I could sell the skins.

Today farmers can collect dead lambs and leave them in a bag at the front gate from where they are collected every evening and then shipped to New Zealand for skinning. The skins are tanned before being sent to China and made into gloves. In my farming days things were a lot less organised.

Our holidays at Portsea were a dream. At first, with only Tim, we would stay with Margie's parents at Rannoch, but as Margie and her brother's wife Mitzi kept producing more children, Pop Begg said, "Enough is enough," and rented a house for us all some way away! Mitzi's Caroline, Kate and Andrew were about the same age as Tim, Peter and Mark and as the cousins all got on very well we had a very happy time together.

Halfway through the morning we would all drive over to Shelley Beach to swim or be taken out by Pop in his fishing boat. Sometimes he would take us out in the middle of Port Philip Bay for picnics on Mud Island, but mainly we would come home to our rented home for lunch and then a siesta before setting out on some kind of adventure in the afternoon.

After Mark's arrival we had so much luggage for the two-week holiday that we had to invest in a trailer for all the baggage so the boys could have the whole of the back of the station wagon to play in. Our holidays by the seaside took some organising and were quite a circus, but they were very happy days, never to be forgotten.

Portsea was the ideal place for a summer holiday for the children but also great fun for the parents. When Pop's boats got steadily bigger and the engines more powerful, he used to take us out water-skiing. It is a fun activity to learn with plenty of spills and laughter.

The old lime-burner's cottage on the cliff had been in Pop's family since 1880 and he and his three brothers had always spent all their summers at Portsea. In those days you could only get from Melbourne across Port Philip Bay to Portsea by paddle steamer. On one famous Christmas Pop's mother proclaimed that as they were all having such a lovely time she thought it unnecessary to return to school so they would stay on until Easter!

Pop liked to fish, had done so all his life so was very good at it and knew all the best places to go. One of these was down at the Rip, the entrance to the Port Philip Bay where the tidal race is very dangerous. It was here that the Yellow Tail liked to hang out and Pop would take us to fish for them. We had to wear leather gloves to protect our hands because otherwise the lines would slice into our flesh as they raced away.

I have never found fishing an enjoyable pastime; however, one day when we were in the Rip I managed to hook a Yellow Tail and get it on board. It was

52 inches long and the most beautiful thing you have ever seen. When we got home Pop sold it to the fish shop after it had been weighed and recorded. It turned out to be the biggest catch of the year and Pop was presented with a gaff as a prize. I have never fished since!

The record 'Yellow Tail' for the year

Tim, Andrew, Caroline, Mark, Peter, and Kate

The farm was no longer a full-time job for me as I had finished building the fences, yards and sheds. The scrub hills had been cleared although they proved to be virtually useless as they were too sandy. I had raked up thousands of tons of stones and mallee roots in an effort to clear the paddocks, so apart from improving the stock there was not a lot left to do. On top of everything else we were having another drought.

Some three years before this time Chooky Newland came into our lives. I was working in the shearing shed one day and heard a car coming down the drive. On stepping outside, I saw a shiny new Land Rover with a neat little man at the wheel, smoking a cigarette. He pulled up, opened the door and jumped out to introduce himself. He was only about five foot tall and looked a bit like a plucked chicken, hence his name.

Mr Newland proceeded to tell me that he had bought a large block of scrub about five miles north of me and he had contracted to have it ploughed and seeded as soon as the rains came. Meanwhile he had nowhere to leave his Land Rover. Would I be interested in housing it in my shed if he allowed me to use it on my own property? I thought this was a great idea as up to then the only way I could take Margie and the boys out to see the farm was on the tractor and trailer, as the pastures were still too stony for a car.

Over the next years we got to know Chooky very well. He would call us from Adelaide to warn us that he was coming to Keith. He always stayed at the hotel, but occasionally Margie would persuade him to have dinner with us. It was during these meals we learnt all about Chooky who, to our surprise, turned out to be a very important man in General Motors and in charge of buying the supplies for the factories.

He had a dry sense of humour and told amazing stories while he chain-smoked Lexingtons cigarettes. He once offered us one each, but we found them so strong that we had to put them out. Chooky always had one hanging between his lips, but this didn't worry us at all because in those days everyone smoked, including ourselves. Pop Begg had once bribed us into giving up for two years so we could buy a car radio, which soon fell to bits because of the rough dirt roads, so we started smoking again!

One day Chooky told us that he had given up smoking himself for five years but had taken it up again during a business trip to Japan. He had intended only to be in there for a couple of days to sign a deal for sheet steel with a Japanese factory, but the Japanese stalled over the deal and then said they wanted to renegotiate the price. At this stage Chooky was so exasperated that he went out and bought a packet of Lexingtons and therefore blamed the Japanese for ruining his health. The sad bit of the story is that it did just that for about four years after we met him he died of lung cancer. I went to see him in hospital and I found him in an oxygen tent looking like an Egyptian mummy. It was awful. I shall always remember him as being one of the gentlest men I have ever met, but somehow a very sad one.

Towards the end of our friendship his property was covered in wonderful pasture, well-fenced and carrying sheep. My responsibility was extended to include doing the rounds of the windmills and checking the troughs to see that the sheep had plenty of water. On one of the days we were out together he turned to me and said, "Are you always going to live here?" The question stopped me in my tracks as I hadn't given it any thought. I answered, "Yes, I love my life here," but the worm had entered the apple and although no thunderbolt struck me, the question never really left me alone.

Looking back to those days and seeing all that has happened to me since, thinking about all the places I have visited and interesting people I have met, puts Chooky's question into perspective. He must have been horrified by my lack of ambition, but then I was living in what I considered to be a Paradise.

One of the problems of living in Paradise is that one is bound to wake up to reality sooner or later. One evening the telephone rang right in the middle of a dinner party. It was my brother Mike to tell me that he had just had a call from Pat to say that our father had died. When everyone had left I told Margie my sad news. A week later I received a letter from my mother. I took it outside and when I had read it I looked out at the paddocks feeling completely at sea and surrounded by totally empty horizons. I cried and then a serene calmness seemed to come over me.

My father had had a heart attack the previous year, but seemed to recover well so the doctors had allowed him to make a trip to Australia. It was then that he had been to stay with us and held Tim on his knee. Now he had gone and would never meet Peter who was about to arrive. My paternal umbilical cord had been cut.

View from Margie's kitchen with cattle grazing

My father died aged 56. Sitting here writing this as I approach 70 makes me extremely conscious of his very short life. I know he had tuberculosis when he was 35 years old and would have died then except for brilliant nursing by my mother, which gave him another 21 years, but 56 is still terribly young. The ironical thing is that in 1936 doctors thought that smoking helped people who had had tuberculosis keep infection at bay. My father had been saved then by having the infected lung collapsed, so his life expectancy could never have been that great, especially as he continued to smoke cigarettes.

The last photograph of 'Bill'

When my brother Pat was next out from England on business he drove up from Melbourne with his wife Ann to visit us for a weekend. I had built a pergola along the front of the house to keep the summer sun off the north-facing windows. This extensive structure needed painting and Pat offered to give me a hand. It was backbreaking work and all up in the air at arm's length. To reach it we had to stand on old tea chests which were not that stable and of course the inevitable happened as Pat got carried away, stepped back into thin air to admire his work and found himself flat on his back covered in white paint. Apart from that we had a wonderful time together and it was the beginning of a close bond between us that had not existed before our father had died.

I decided that we should have a slate terrace under the beautiful white pergola. The truck arrived carrying an enormous load of very large pieces of slate, most of which needed two men to lift. It was a backbreaking job to unload the truck, but that was just the beginning, as I then had to lay it on my own. It took ages to fill the area with sand and lay out the slate like a giant jigsaw puzzle ready to cement the joints; however, when finished it really looked fantastic and was worth the effort. I was so exhausted I decided that the cementing could wait until I recovered from the exertion of laying it, which proved to be a 'bad mistake'.

On the whole we had a kind climate, and if we had a hot day it was usually followed by a cool night. Occasionally we would get a hot night when we would have to take a cold shower and then lie back on the bed wet, but that only happened when the north wind blew. The slate had been down for about a week when the north wind started to blow with a vengeance. The temperature went up and red sand crept through every window crack and under the doors. The howling banshee blew for about 24 hours before peace and quiet returned and we were able to leave the house. The sheep and cattle must have had an awful time. After inspecting the troughs and making sure the stock had water, I looked around the sheds to see if any iron sheets had been ripped off the roofs. Fortunately everything seemed intact, so I returned home to check out the house.

When I went to look at the slate patio, I couldn't believe what I saw. Each piece of slate was balanced on a tiny pillar of sand, making it look like a whole field of flat-topped mushrooms. The rest of the sand was probably at the South Pole! I have never seen anything so heart-breaking in my life. I would have to remove every slate and start all over again. However, once it was down, one of our great treats was to sit out on the slate terrace with a cold beer and watch the sun go down at the end of the day.

The finished patio

Around about this time I read a book on the life of Yogananda, an Indian Yogi and the founder of the Self-Realisation organisation, which now has its headquarters in Los Angeles. It remains one of the most amazing books that I have ever read and it changed my whole perspective of life. Having religion rammed down my throat at Rugby had turned me into an atheist. Chapel twice on Sunday and prayers every day put me right off the life hereafter!

This book recorded the life of Yogananda when he was living in India before he moved to America. There had been a popular book written about a Tibetan monk that had caused a stir, but it later transpired that a retired butcher in England had written it! The Yogananda book was quite different. To cut a long story short, what made it believable was the fact that he left instructions that his body was to be exhumed a year after his death. He prophesied that there would be no sign of decomposition, which his followers were to take as proof that what he taught was a new religion and a way to finding a better life. When his body was exhumed there was no sign of decomposition, or at least that is what the book claimed.

I was impressed and wrote away to the Los Angeles headquarters to enrol in the course. When it arrived I started to follow the instructions and practise the techniques that it promised would change my life. What it boiled down to was a system of controlling one's breathing and learning to still the mind. It was very satisfying and I found that sitting comfortably for half an hour every day, concentrating on a spot on my forehead, made me feel good. The end result of the courses would be to *Know Yourself.*

At this stage in my life I did not know that carved over the doorway of the Treasury at the Temple of Delphi is the same inscription: *Know Yourself.*

I have always thought of the time spent at Chute as my real education. I learnt about being a husband, a father, a farmer, a lover of nature and amateur astronomer. I also discovered classical music and books. I became aware of world politics, subscribed to *Time* magazine and read about the problems of the outside world that surrounded our haven of peace.

Every morning I would get up and make a cup of tea for Margie. As I waited for the kettle to boil I would listen to the news on the radio. This is how in 1963, on a November morning, I heard that President Kennedy had been assassinated. I was dumbfounded. I just could not get my mind around the fact that the man who had founded the Peace Corps had been shot from behind in cold blood. It was just unbelievable. The assassination of Kennedy also killed my innocence.

It took several years for TV to reach as far as Keith, and when it came we had to erect a 60-foot high antennae mast. There was only one station and the reception was appalling, yet we still watched in awe through blizzards of snow. Very occasionally it was crystal clear.

With the arrival of Television News my world changed. *Time* magazine had showed us still photographs of how the rest of the world lived, but it was not until we could see moving pictures of what is always Bad News that we were able to compare our way of life with how people in other countries lived. It was an eye opener and completely shattered my cosy dream-like existence.

Our social life was quite amazingly active as we were surrounded by a group of wonderful farming friends, all of a similar age as ourselves. We partied continually with the Playfairs, Sangsters, Leakes, Gibsons, Birks, Coles, Easts and many others, giving dinners, playing silly games and dancing in each other's houses while the children slept in the cars outside. Occasionally there was a shearing-shed party and we danced until dawn.

All our friends had children, so there was plenty of maternal back-up for Margie. Birthday parties for the little boys and girls were always very well attended. Our boys had plenty of playmates. The mothers arranged weekly tennis parties where toddlers staggered around collecting the balls. Every day was full of activity and the months turned into years with alarming rapidity.

The boys were a joy and all completely different characters. Tim had golden red hair and freckles and was always laughing. Peter had black hair, long eyelashes and loved stomping through puddles and would squat down in the middle of them, seemingly unaware that his bottom was in the water! Mark chose the red genes and was a very contented baby.

Apart from our summer holidays at Portsea, all our time was spent on the farm. Because Margie had been brought up as a city girl she was weekend orientated and this meant the five of us having an adventure on Sunday. We would either go to Glen Gowan, our hidden valley, for a picnic or to places like Gip Gip rocks, which was a perfect hideaway place for children to explore. Sometimes we would take them down to Robe, a fishing village about two hours' drive south of the farm. Most of these adventures were done in the winter as summer temperatures made car travel unpleasant and the flies made picnics a nightmare.

Winter picnics on 'Robe Beach'

In the Robe cliff face are several shallow caves so it was always fun to hide silver coins secretly and then tell the boys stories about Long John Silver hiding his treasure in such places. The searches were followed by great shouts of delight when coins were found. These adventures made for a great family togetherness and I suppose were the beginning of all the exploring we did later with the children when we came to live in England. Camping in Scotland, sailing in the Baltic, walking across the Alps, skiing holidays, or scuba diving. I

184

believe that a sense of adventure is one of the most important lessons parents can give their children.

As the family grew I did as well, because at Chute I was fortunately free to follow any course I wished. Margie and I had been brought up without any knowledge of classical music, so we sent off for a *Reader's Digest* album. It was like entering Aladdin's cave for the first time. The set of long-playing 33 rpm records included popular symphonies by Mozart, Tchaikovsky, Beethoven, Brahms, Handel, Haydn, Grieg, Wagner, Rackmaninov, Liszt, Bach, Chopin, Elgar and Rimsky-Korsakov. Imagine living a lifetime without hearing music composed by such geniuses. Listening to these records for the first time was sheer magic.

The wireless reception was awful in the Ninety Mile Desert and it meant listening with an ear glued to the speaker if you wanted to hear anything, so most evenings Margie and I would read books by the fire. I tried to teach Margie how to play chess but found I didn't have the patience, or she the interest to learn, and as I was never a good speller Scrabble was a non-starter. I learnt to love books and have continued to do so ever since. I don't have a good memory for what I have read but somehow all the information seems to build up into a general understanding of the subject.

Television and the Beatles arrived at the same time. Our black-and-white screen was set into the bookshelf. Now we take no notice of a TV in a room, but in those days it seemed to dominate the room with its Cyclops eye. One of the first things we saw on TV through the snowstorm reception was the heroes' welcome given to the Beatles when they visited Adelaide. We watched the show avidly as their music was all the rage and had been played non-stop when we had danced the night away at the Matron's Ball held in the Keith town hall, under some big red drum lamp shades I had made to liven the place up a bit by turning it into a Red Light District!

I have never been able to read science fiction but love watching it on the screen. The graphics of films like *2001*, *Aliens*, and *Star Wars* I find absolutely riveting. The actual stories usually don't mean much but I find shots of spacecraft orbiting planets send shivers down my spine, as though I am looking into the future. The first science-fiction film I saw on TV was Professor Fred Hoyle's *A for Andromeda*. The story is about a scientist who picks up a signal from outer space that contained a set of instructions on how to build a tank in which the scientists grow an alien eye that wants to take over a body and then rule the world. One day I happened to see a book by Professor Fred Hoyle in a shop and I bought it.

During my life I have been blessed by chance and catching sight of *Frontiers of Astronomy* by Fred Hoyle was one of those special events. I took the book home and discovered the *Universe*.

On my next trip to Melbourne I found a shop that specialised in astronomy and within an hour was the proud owner of a 7½-inch reflector telescope plus a beginner's guide on *How to use it* and *Where to look*. The telescope was a beautiful white enamel tube about three-foot long and stood on a black tripod. I couldn't wait to get back to the farm and set it up. I don't think I have ever been more excited in my life than when I looked through my new telescope for the first time to see Fred Hoyle's universe.

The night skies in the Ninety Mile Desert are among the brightest I have ever seen because there was usually zero pollution in the air. Often at night

Margie and I would take a walk before going to bed and look up at the stars. Then they had meant nothing to me except that they blazed with light, but with my telescope I was now able to look 'in-depth' into the heavens.

Looking through the new telescope at the craters on the moon was breathtaking and I felt that I could almost touch it. I could see the lines of debris radiating out from the impacts that had caused the craters of Copernicus and Tycho. I spent hours gazing at the wonder of the icy cold orb above. It was not the only thing that was icy. After an hour out in the cold desert night air I was also frozen solid.

John Kennedy had promised us that Man would walk on the Moon. Looking at the surface through the telescope it just did not seem possible that this could or would happen. Everyone then felt that if it was achieved it would be Man's greatest triumph when it happened.

I found looking at the Milky Way with binoculars was actually more impressive than through the telescope as there is just so much of it in the Australian sky. It snakes right across the dome of the heavens from side to side like a great white river. No wonder it was so important in Australian Aborigine mythology. By following the twists of the Milky Way it was possible to find my way around the Constellations: Orion's Belt with its giant red sun Betelgeuse; the Pleiades; the Plough; Saturn with its Rings. All the things I had read about in Fred Hoyle's book came alive.

Looking at Betelgeuse is one of the most awe-inspiring things anyone can do because comparing it to our sun is like comparing a 27-foot diameter balloon to a golf ball. It is awesome to think that one day our sun will also be a Red Giant and engulf the Earth.

I found our neighbours, the two small irregular galaxies named the Greater and Lesser Magellanic Clouds. The Aborigines' myth explains them as smoke rising from the campfires of the dead ancestors. They were named in 1520 by Ferdinand Magellan, the first European to circumnavigate the Earth. What a name to conjure with!

By using my beginner's guide, I was able to discover globular clusters made up of 100,000 stars. But my most exciting discovery was when I found Andromeda, the twin of our Milky Way galaxy, the home of Fred Hoyle's *Intelligence* in the TV serial. Andromeda contains 1,000 million stars and is 9,000 million, million miles away. Imagine my excitement at seeing that and thinking about it for the first time.

There are more stars in the universe than grains of sand on the Earth! Astronomers estimated that the number is 70^{22}, or 7 with 22 zeros after it.

70,000,000,000,000,000,000,000

With such a number Scientists say the chances are pretty high of there being other suns with an orbiting planet similar to our Earth and, if so, it could be home to some form of life! I think they are wrong and instead believe that *Homo sapiens* is unique, because if you ran the Earth's history again surely the chances of the climatic sequence that made our evolution possible must also be at least 70^{22} to 1.

We are told that if Jupiter wasn't there to mop up all the asteroids they would bombard Earth instead. We are also told that if the Earth didn't have a Moon exactly the size it is, the climate would be completely different, even

Mars like. Doesn't this mean that we would have to find not only a similar Sun and Solar system with an exactly, but also an Earth with a similar history?

The Earth has suffered five major extinctions over the last 500 million years. The worst catastrophe during the last 200,000 years, the time that Modern Man has existed on Earth, was the super-volcano Mt Toba eruption that vomited such vast amounts of ash into the atmosphere that it caused a six-year winter followed by a 1,000-year Ice Age. The eruption occurred at the north-west end of Sumatra 74,000 years ago and, according to some of our leading scientists, reduced the population of Modern Man to 10,000 adults! I am sure I am not the only person who has noted that the epicentre of the 2004 Boxing Day earthquake that caused the 33-foot high Tsunami is within spitting distance of Mt Toba. The wave that hit northern Chile a hundred years ago was estimated to be 60 foot high! The thickness of crust of the earth is equivalent to the skin of a child's balloon! We are sitting on top of a molten time bomb.

There was a recent TV programme that pointed out that eyes have evolved on earth five times in separate species. But isn't that missing the point because they all evolved on our unique planet. I really do believe we are unique, a mere flash in the pan, but of course a very special one!

Scientists may be convinced that the earth is not the only planet in the universe peopled by intelligent creatures, but I am not. They claim that the odds are just too great for us to be unique, but I think they are looking for a needle in a haystack and if they do find a likely candidate they will find even the space in the needle's eye will be completely different. There may be 70^{22} suns out there, a sum greater than the grains of sand on the earth, but lets not forget that *not one of those grains is precisely similar to another*!

When walking with our dog this Christmas morning it was snowing, the giant flakes gently falling like eider duck feathers. I could see millions at any one moment and suddenly realised that although I could see such a vast number at any split second, each flake was an individual and slightly different to the other, although made of exactly the same material, ice water. Multiply the number by all the flakes falling over the whole of Britain! Everything in the universe is unique, including each of us; it is far more likely that we are the First Intelligence to Evolve, *not Johnnies come lately*.

Of course the universe supports Life, Mankind is the proof, but, although we have a very long evolutionary history that stretches over millions of years back to the original bacteria, *Modern Man* only came into existence 200,000 years ago in Africa! We could be the first intelligence rather than the last and we may be the ones destined to colonise the universe.

In 2003 the Institute of Astronomy at Cambridge University was completed. I had met the Astronomer Royal, Sir Martin Rees, when attending the unveiling of my Symbolic Sculptures outside the Isaac Newton Institute with my friends Damon de Laszlo and Robert Hefner III. Damon suggested that it would be nice if the Institute of Astronomy had an edition of my sculpture *Pulse* to match the one Robert had given to the Aspen Centre for Physics in Colorado and asked me to find out what Martin thought.

I wrote a letter and Martin replied that he liked the idea. Imagine my delight when in Cambridge I was told that the Institute of Astronomy was named after Fred Hoyle, the man who introduced me to the universe.

Unfortunately Fred died in 2002, so I was not able to thank him personally for the wonderful gift he gave me all those years ago in the Bush in Australia when I had read *Frontiers of Astronomy*. Ironically he had lived in a small house near where my sculpture has been placed on the site of the first major telescope in England.

'Pulse', Cambridge Institute of Astronomy

But I am jumping ahead. Because of my Chute telescope I now knew more about Space than conditions on Earth. *Time* magazine was my introduction to the troubled world and reading it made me realise that I had not given much thought to anything outside my own little life.

One of the great legacies of J F Kennedy was the Peace Corps. Nothing like this had ever been suggested before and it was inspiring to read about it in *Time* and to see it working around the world on TV. For the first time in my life I started to think about the fortunate life that we led and the misfortunes of others. What could I do to help? I decided to go to see the organisers of the Australian equivalent of the Peace Corps when next in Melbourne.

I am sure that it was my fault that the meeting between the Director and myself went so badly. I had my own ideas about how I could help without actually going to dig wells in India, but he was only interested in volunteers who were willing to work in the field anywhere he sent them. I left the meeting feeling utterly depressed and set off to walk back into the city, thinking as I went. I have always found that if you want to think something through, the best time to do it is when you are out for a walk. By the time I got back into the city I was feeling better.

As I passed an art shop I happened to see in the window that they were advertising the sale of 50 lb bags of dry clay at half price. I walked in and bought one, some simple wooden modelling tools and a book for beginners. I paid and asked if they would hold them until I came back with a car in the afternoon.

Capers Restaurant was still our favourite restaurant in Melbourne and whenever we came to town we would try to eat there out in the courtyard under an umbrella. After we had ordered our meal and half a bottle of red wine, Margie asked me how my meeting had gone. I told her that there was no chance of our going to India to dig wells, which she must have been very relieved to hear! I then took a deep breath and said, "I have bought a bag of clay and I am going to start sculpting again."

Soon after getting back to the farm I read the book for beginners and started messing about with the clay, modelling little figures. I have seldom felt happier or so totally absorbed in what I was doing. I was completely intoxicated by the feel of the clay as I worked it in with my fingers.

I am sure that learning how to model with clay is one of the most satisfying things anyone can do. By controlling the speed the clay dries you can take a figurine through stages, going from wet, to pliable, to leathery and then bone dry. By doing this you end up with a clay figure that you can carve with a penknife. After a day's work on the farm it was wonderful to sit on the veranda with Margie and carve my little figures while she supervised the boys' tea.

Carving clay at teatime on the slate with 'Peter and Tim'

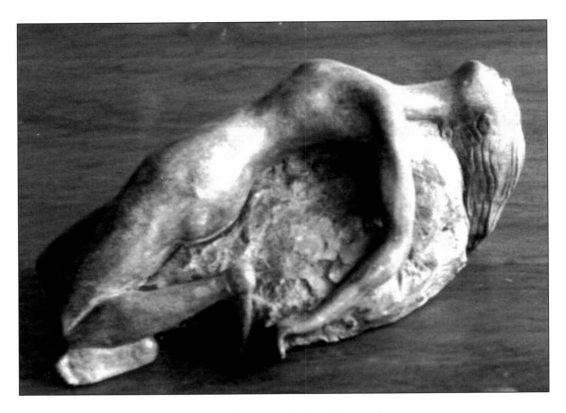

My first small clay figure

The next challenge was to do faces in relief. I took photographs of the boys, modelled their profiles in clay and made a plaster mould. By painting soap lather on the inside of the mould before pouring plaster into it, I could separate the negative from the positive quite easily. When the inner plaster was dry, I chipped away the outer mould. The first time I did this was incredibly exciting and the fact that it worked was a miracle. I remember carrying the first completed head up to the house with great pride to show Margie.

Our friends got to hear of what I was up to and asked me to make relief heads of their children, which I guess you could call my first commissions!

The challenge of doing a head in the round became inevitable. Breaking out the cast of the first head was very satisfying, although I found the ears a problem. Later I learnt to give all my children flat ears, or if that was impossible, fill in the space with plaster and carve it out later.

I decided I would have to tackle a whole figure. Mark was about two years old at the time and became my first model. He had a habit of sitting in a kneeling position as he played with his blocks and this was the ideal pose as it did away with legs and raised arms and needed no armature, something that was way out of my reach at this stage.

I completed the figure in clay and took a plaster mould, which I then filled and let dry. With great care I chiselled away the plaster mould and Mark ended up sitting on the tractor-shed bench. When the plaster was bone dry I painted the figure with bronze paint and added a patination of brown oil paint mixed with lacquer. After the lacquer had dried I was able to lightly rub the surface with methylated spirits which allowed the bronze paint to come through in places, making the sculpture look like an old bronze.

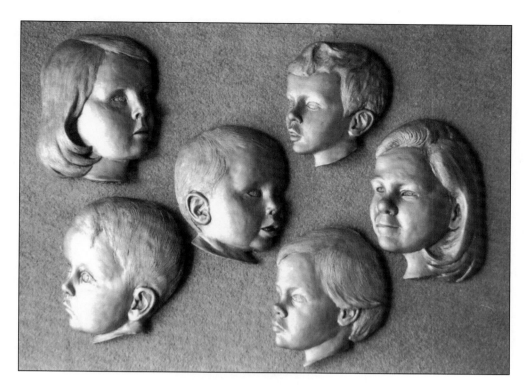

Profile heads of our friends' children

Tim, my mother and a self-portrait

Life on the farm was idyllic. The main benefit of living in a democratic society is the freedom that it bestows on its citizens, which in turn enables them to be creative. Margie and I had total freedom and, being self-employed, we could do what we liked when we liked. On the creative side I had the farm to build and I have no hesitation in saying that my fencing was amongst the neatest in the area, as were the sheep and cattle yards. I built the tractor and shearing sheds by myself and added an extension to the house. I loved every

191

moment of the planning and construction. It had all been quite hard work, but when you are young that is not a problem. The job was finished.

'Mark', my first full plaster cast

The farm had been made possible by a Government policy of allowing people to deduct the cost of land development from their taxes and my father had financed the development of the farm in this way. In theory the farm was now supposed to make money and provide Margie and me with an income to live on. Unfortunately the theory didn't take into account droughts, which are inevitable in Australia, and the farm was not a paying proposition.

But we had three boys to educate. The Keith schools were excellent, but only catered to a certain age. Sooner or later the boys would have to go to a city to finish their education. One of the things we decided was that if we were to continue as farmers, then it would have to be in a greener area so we decided to looked across the Bass Strait to Tasmania as we had been enchanted by the English look of the place on our honeymoon. Again we had the same reaction to the scenery but everyone we met sent their children across the sea to Melbourne to be educated so living there was not going to solve that particular problem. Tasmania was firmly crossed off the list of possibilities.

We returned to Keith thinking that, perhaps, I should stop being a farmer and look for a city job. The more I thought about this the more likely it seemed that it was the only solution to the problem of earning a living. If this was to be the case then before becoming a white-collar worker and committing myself to a lifetime behind a desk, I started to consider taking two years off and indulge myself with sculpture. To justify this choice I thought that perhaps after ten years of continual farming I had earned a break!

One particularly hot north-wind day, fried by the midday sun while working out on a fence line, I suddenly asked myself a question. *Why not move to England, for a couple of years and sculpt?*

The more I thought about the idea the more attractive it became. I drove the tractor home to have lunch in the shade and a break from the heat, having made up my mind to suggest the idea to Margie. When I entered the house I found it was hotter inside than outside. It was a scorcher of a day.

Margie was working in the kitchen and feeling as burnt up as I was. I blurted out, "What about going to England for a couple of years?" Margie replied, "Anything to escape this heat." We talked it over for several days and the more we did so the more excited we both became.

I was 35 years old when we made the decision to sell Chute. I had three wishes. One, I wanted to sculpt; two, I wanted to see the homeland that I had left when I was only 17; three, I wanted to explore Europe. I am sure this last wish was stimulated by a poem called *Letter from Rome* I had just read by an Australian named A D Hope. The poem is about his trip to Italy in search of his roots, having recognised that Europe was the Mother of Western Art.

The poem made me long to see London and Paris again and visit Rome and Athens for the first time. For years I had been reading the history of Europe and books such as Lissner's *The Living Past*. How wonderful it would be to share these places with Margie and also to be able to sculpt full time for two years, maybe even go to an art school and take lessons.

Now that we had made up our minds I decided that the next step should be to tell my mother. From her letters to me I knew that she was worried that since my father's death my two elder brothers, Pat and Mike, both with families to support, had suddenly thrown in their jobs and were looking for new ones. Would a third son doing the same thing be too much for her!

So I sat down to write a letter, spelling out what I wanted to do. I can remember taking a lot of time over the letter, pointing out that the visit would be for two years only and after that we would return to Australia and a job.

I also made clear that we could get a very good price for the farm at the moment so it was the right time to sell even though wool prices were low. But mainly in the letter I stressed that I wanted to find out if I could sculpt. I remember writing, *I feel I have real power in my hands...*

The mail in those days took ten days to reach England. Three weeks after posting my letter we opened the mailbag and out one fell from my mother. I had to read it through twice to take it in, for not only was she in favour of my becoming a sculptor, but said she was not surprised!

She asked me if I had forgotten about the set of chisels she had given me one Christmas. Well, of course I hadn't, but on the other hand I hadn't thought about it for ages. The memory now came flooding back. We always had our Christmas presents in my mother's bedroom while she had her breakfast in bed. I was ten years old and shooting had come into my life. Both my brothers had shotguns and I was longing to have my own. One of the parcels in my pile looked like a gun case being long, wide and flat. *Yes, I thought, it must be a gun*, so I left it to the last. Can you imagine my surprise when on opening the case I found a complete set of very sharp wood-carving chisels? I was very disappointed, I can tell you! The chisels were beautiful, all wrapped in green baize, but what was I meant to do with them?

In her letter my mother went on to explain *why* she had given me the chisels. She and her friend Nancy were then going to fortune-tellers, as a lot of people had started to do during the war. Apparently that Christmas they had gone to one who had told her, "Your youngest son will become a sculptor."

Memories flooded back of my mother taking me to the Victoria and Albert Museum during the holidays and insisting that we spend a lot of time in the sculpture galleries. At the time I thought that this was because of the drawing lessons she was taking at the time. Apparently there had also been another purpose.

The fortune-teller had been the reason behind her giving me the chisels for Christmas. She went on to say not only was she in favour of my trying to become a sculptor, but had been worried that it had taken so long for me to get around to it!

Well, of course I am quite sure fortune-tellers *cannot* see into the future, in the same way that the people who believe what they read in the newspapers about their birth signs must be nuts. But, I am sure you can understand the boost this gave my desire to become a sculptor. I rang the Land Agent saying that I wished to put the farm on the market.

I then had to tell Margie's parents about our decision to go to England for two years to try my hand at sculpting. Again, I was surprised that all I found was encouragement. I also think that Ken knew that the farm would not support our family and that we would have to move sooner or later.

Having decided to sell the farm we started to look for a buyer. As the season had been a good one for once, we soon found several people who were interested especially as we were prepared to leave some money in the farm at a fair interest rate for the period we were in England, so it would provide us with an income to live on for the two years.

Thinking back to those times I have often wondered at Margie's incredible courage and the support she has given me over the past 35 years in what can only be described as a 'hare-brained scheme'. Luckily, fortune has smiled on me and I have been able to share my extraordinary journey with her.

ENGLAND

Having decided to make the trip to England I needed to obtain a passport. I was a bit apprehensive about this because when I arrived in Australia I had 'jumped ship' without a passport, or any sort of entrance documentation. In 1951 no one seemed to care about such things, but this was 1968. I went to the passport office and filled in an application form and without even having to produce a birth certificate they not only gave me a passport, but also issued me with a certificate of Australian Citizenship! All that was required was a photograph of me in my new sports coat, especially bought for the trip.

The passport photo

I don't remember anything about the flight to England. I guess I was too excited after an absence of over 17 years. Looking at my passport photograph it certainly appears as though I was feeling very happy. Margie saw me off and then took the boys down to Portsea, where she planned to stay for the two weeks I would be away. I arrived at Heathrow, caught the bus into London, and then a taxi to my mother's little flat in Cadogan Square. It was a heavenly spot, four floors up, plenty of fresh air and a wonderful view from her roof garden out over Chelsea's roof tops, chimneys and church spires.

What a meeting! My mother was obviously delighted to see me and showed me around her tiny home. There was a minute spare bedroom she called The Slit, where I was to sleep, her bedroom, a dining room, kitchen and then a lovely small sitting room that opened out onto a large roof garden that was her pride and joy. It was the perfect flat for her as it was situated between Harrods and Peter Jones, and only a short walk to Hyde Park.

The purpose of my trip was to look for a furnished house we could rent for two years. My mother had been doing some homework and had found nothing, but my brother Pat, who had just bought a house in Somerset, thought it would be worthwhile having a look around that part of the world, although he said that I had come at exactly the wrong time of the year as everyone was away on holiday in August. I hadn't thought of that possibility!

The first thing to do was hire a car so I could roam around the country looking for houses to rent. Once mobile we set off for Somerset to visit Pat, planning to stay the first night at the Royal Oak in Yattendon so we could call on Uncle Joe.

Dinner with Uncle Joe was sad, as Habby had died several years previously and he now lived alone with his old black dog. We talked about happier days when they had joined us at Reid's in Madeira, and he remembered showing me the cactus that flowered for only one night on the full moon. On that holiday he had also introduced me to the heavens by showing me the Persian Army eye test. The eye test is whether or not you could see a tiny extra star on the arm of what I call The Plough. He was a brilliant man who wrote beautifully and published four large illustrated volumes after the war called *Recording Britain*. A year later I sculpted his head from photographs.

Uncle Joe Palmer

That night I woke to unbelievable pain as my neck had gone into spasm. If I kept looking over my left shoulder I was all right, but move my head a fraction I was in agony. By seven o'clock I couldn't wait a second longer and called on my mother for help. Uncle Joe came around to the hotel in his car and took me to see his doctor. The drive was unbearable, as every time we went round a corner my neck felt as if it was being impaled by a dagger. The doctor sat me down and took my head in both hands from behind and lifted me off the chair, at the same time moving my head back to the front position. *Arrrrrrrr!* but it worked. What a relief and I was extremely glad it had not happened in the aeroplane!

Now that I could move again, we set off to visit Pat and Ann at their new Mill House near Castle Cary. On the way we turned off the road at Andover and drove out along the familiar lanes to the villages of Lower Chute, Upper Chute and Chute Standen. What memories the names and scenery brought back to me, as nothing seemed to have changed since I was a boy. I was so happy to be back in beautiful green rural England. I couldn't believe everywhere was so green. The whole place looked like an enormous garden!

Chute Standen was exactly as I remembered from my childhood. The Farm House we had moved to when the army took over the Big House at the outbreak of the war, hadn't changed in the slightest. I couldn't wait to bring Margie and the boys here one day and show it all to them. The enormous beech trees, famous as being the ones Val had clipped with his plane, as well as the site of the crash of my beautiful balsa wood airplane that my fighter pilot cousin Tony had given me one Christmas, were in full leaf.

The 'Big House' surrounded by high beech trees

We had lunch in the Hatchet Inn and then drove on to see Dorothy who lived in Bottle Cottage. Dorothy had been our maid at Chute all the years of my youth. My parents had given her a little house in the village when they had sold the farm. It was built of flint and brick but set into the walls were diamonds made of bottle ends. Dorothy had two single beds in her only

197

bedroom and to keep the sheets aired she slept in them on alternate nights, which is extremely sensible!

Driving in England was a very different story in 1968, as there was hardly any traffic and no motorways. It was an amazing feeling to be seeing it all again, and the weather was perfect as it was an unusually hot summer. Memories came flooding back as we drove leisurely past Stonehenge on our way to Castle Cary, where Pat had booked us into the George Hotel. Little did I think that one day this old market town would be where we would do our weekly shopping.

Castle Cary

The George is a 500-year-old thatched inn. It was magic for me to be sleeping under thatch for the first time in my life and I could hardly believe it. That evening we went to have dinner with Pat and Ann at their Mill House on the River Brue. Their garden was an island surrounded by the river and the leat which ran under the old mill that Pat had made into a sitting room. The giant paddle wheel under the floor had long ceased to turn, so the grinding stone had become the fire hearth. Pat loved fishing and had caught trout in the mill pool, as well as seeing otters and kingfishers. It was all nearly too much to take in after living in the Ninety Mile Desert for ten years.

Pat told me about an old rectory that was for sale in a village close by, which he thought would be worth looking at and had made an appointment for the following day. When preparing for the trip, Margie and I had looked through hundreds of the *Country Life* magazines that our English-born neighbour, Mike Aldersey, used to receive from his father. He would pass them over to us when he had finished with them and we had spent many fun hours looking at the *For Sale* photographs choosing the type of house we would like to rent. When I saw the old rectory I knew immediately that it was definitely somewhere we would not want to live. It had a run-down haunted feeling and was the worst type of Victorian architecture that you can imagine. It was decidedly not a place that would inspire a budding artist!

My next trip was to see my stepbrother Peter Bowring's coastguard holiday cottage in Norfolk that he had very kindly offered to let us use, but it turned out to be much too small and had nowhere to sculpt. As I drove back from Norfolk I stopped at several estate agents to ask if they had furnished houses to rent. The answer was always "No", so by the time I arrived back in London I was beginning to feel a bit despondent to say the least. Perhaps I really was in England at the wrong time of year as Pat had warned! My time was fast running out and I had only five days left before having to fly home.

My mother cooked me a lovely meal that night, which was really impressive as before the war she didn't even know how to boil an egg. Even after the war on the cook's night off we always went out, as cooking was just not her scene. However, when we boys left home and my parents sold the farm and moved back to London she had decided to take lessons and much to her surprise discovered that she enjoyed cooking. Her great ploy was to say to her guests after tasting her own food, "Now that is delicious," and no one ever dared argue with such enthusiasm.

After dinner my mother told me that my stepsister, Bid, had called and told her about a furnished house for rent near Barnstaple in North Devon and given her a telephone number, so I immediately called and talked to Dr Jimmy Smart. "Could I come down and have a look please?" "Certainly, when?" "Tomorrow?" "Right, come and have dinner with me and I shall show you the house in the morning." In those days North Devon was an eight-hour drive from London, so I was soon in bed prepared for a very early start, having made a plan to meet my mother after my trip in two days' time at Bid's home in Gloucestershire, and bring her home to London.

I set off for Devon at first light having no idea what I was going to see or whom I was going to meet. I felt a bit like Columbus setting sail for China – would I find America? I arrived in Barnstaple and found the hotel where Dr Smart had kindly reserved a room for me. It was the first time in my life that I had been in North Devon and was thrilled to find that it was all beautiful, wild and unspoilt.

After a bath I walked round to meet Jimmy Smart feeling more than a little nervous, never having done anything like this before. The doctor lived in a flat on the second floor overlooking the famous 500-year-old bridge that crosses the Taw River. I rang the bell and a tall man with a kind face opened the door. I immediately relaxed a little. In the sitting room he introduced me to his nephew John who was also a doctor, now working in London but about to move to Australia. This seemed like a good omen as well as providing a topic of conversation.

Jimmy was the perfect host and quickly put me at my ease. After he had poured me a drink and settled me in a comfortable armchair he started to question me about my life in Australia, what I was doing back in England and why I wanted to rent a house in Devon. I explained about my wish to try my hand at sculpting while showing Margie and the boys where I had grown up. I explained how I had been working on the land for 17 years but had decided to sell the farm and take a couple of years off before settling again in Melbourne so the boys could attend a better school. It all sounded terribly sensible and not at all like some madcap scheme where I was going to throw everything to the wind and become an artist. I was not doing a Gauguin and heading off for Tahiti, but looking for a furnished house to rent for two years and ideally a studio to work in. If he had something like that I would be very interested to see it. By the end of the evening he must have thought that I would make a suitable tenant and was prepared to show me his house and barn. He told me that if I liked what I saw I could rent the house for £10 a week!

From my side I discovered very little about Jimmy except that he had never married. He had trained at St Thomas' Hospital in London and spent the war years in the Royal Navy as a doctor.

Months later I learnt that he had twice been sunk by torpedo and had received medals for bravery by swimming around injecting the wounded waiting to be rescued with morphine. After the war he had bought Marwood Hill and set up practice in the house while living there with his widowed father, his sister and her son who was the young man who had dined with us. His sister and father had both been tragically killed in a car accident and rather than live in the house alone he had decided to move into a flat in Barnstaple, give up his practice as a GP and work in the hospital as an anaesthetist. In the time that we were at Marwood I found Jimmy to be one of the most generous and kind-hearted people you could wish to meet. He became our friend and was extremely good fun and very patient with us all. As it turned out, if I had looked for a hundred years, I could not have found a more perfect landlord.

I went to bed feeling very happy, but woke in the middle of the night with terrible stomach cramps. Suddenly the enormity of the step I was about to take hit me like a sledgehammer and I had a violent attack of the jitters. If I took the house it would completely change not only my life but Margie's and the boys' as well. What was I doing? Was it too late to turn back?

I rang Jimmy in the morning and asked him if he and his nephew were all right. He assured me they were and asked why. I told him about my cramps and he laughed. "Well, I am not surprised that you are feeling a little nervous!"

I drove round to Jimmy's flat as arranged and then followed him up the hill out of Barnstable. He drove at speed through the sunken lanes, past the Ring of Bells in Prixford, into the village of Guineaford. All these names were to become very familiar over the next years, but right now they all sounded like magic places in a romantic novel about pirates and smugglers.

We turned left along a tiny lane, past the village hall and the rectory and arrived at Marwood Hill House beside the church. It was the perfect example of a two-storeyed Georgian house, coated with white stucco and south facing. At the drive entrance there was a tiny lodge where a retired schoolteacher called Vera lived. Below ground, in what had once been the kitchens, but now a flat, lived Mrs Mockford.

The driveway that ran past the front-door portico had two entrances, one on either side of the large semicircular lawn that was surrounded by a stone wall. An archway led down to a garage beside the greenhouse. I immediately fell in love with the place and couldn't quite believe what I was seeing.

Inside the front door was a very big hall at the back of which was a grand staircase. On one side of the hall was a large sitting room and on the other a similar-sized dining room. On the ground floor there was a kitchen with a gigantic window facing west and the same facing east that had been Jimmy's surgery.

My first view of 'Marwood Hill House' and church

Upstairs there were three double and three single bedrooms and two bathrooms. The house was completely furnished with chairs, tables and beds, so all we needed were sheets, blankets and towels. Jimmy then showed me the house attics. Here were four large rooms, three of which he said I could have the use of. I was beginning to feel giddy over how wonderful the whole place was and all for only £10 a week!

'Marwood Hill House and 'Studio Barn'

The evening before I had told Jimmy that I was looking for a house with a barn that I could use as a studio and sculpt large figures in clay and not worry about making a mess. He led me out of the drive and across the lane to a wonderful old stone tithe barn. It had enormous wooden doors on either side and was completely empty. The side away from the lane opened into a walled yard waist high in grass. "Would this suit your purpose?" asked Jimmy. Would it what! "It would have to be a separate deal to the house. How about £5 a month?" "Done," I replied and we shook hands.

"There is one condition. You are not allowed to do any gardening. I have a gardener and I don't want you planting anything or mowing the lawns, as I wish to control all that side of things." I have never agreed to anything faster, especially as I had seen roses and flowerbeds blooming everywhere. It looked to me like Eden.

Jimmy then took me across the road that led to the church and showed me a walled garden that contained an enormous glass house where he grew hundreds of camellias. He was very proud of them and the following year he won all the prizes for camellias at the Chelsea Flower Show! Outside the walled garden was the beginning of what is now Marwood Hill Gardens. During the time we lived at Marwood, Jimmy put in dams and created two beautiful lakes, planted hundreds of trees and laid the foundations of the most spectacular gardens in North Devon that have now become famous.

Dr Jimmy Smart

Behind the house was a farmhouse that he had recently sold to a brother and sister who wrote children's books together. From the kitchen window to the west I could see the 14th century stone church. The tall square bell tower was built like a castle lookout and later I was to marvel at the view from the top that reached all the way to the sea.

I spent the afternoon wandering around taking photographs for Margie, hardly able to comprehend my good fortune. Not in my wildest dreams had I thought I would find something so suitable, so beautiful or so cheap. As I clicked away I just could not believe I had been lucky enough to find Marwood Hill House, Jimmy Smart and North Devon. As I drove away from Guineaford I saw a lane leading off to the west that I thought could give me a chance to see the house from across the valley. I drove down between high hedges until I found a gate and there was the house lit by afternoon sunlight on the far side of the valley. It looked stunning and I could not believe the beauty of the whole setting. I took a photograph and turned the car round and headed for Gloucestershire with my news.

▲

'Marwood Church' and our new home from across the valley

I knew that Margie would love it all and that as a family we would be extremely happy living there. I felt a whole new world had opened up for me. Little did I realise then just how different my life would be from that moment on, but I knew I had just made a right-angled turn and was shooting off into uncharted waters. I hadn't felt so excited since falling in love with Margie!

My dealings with Jimmy were of the simplest form possible. No lawyers or paperwork, just a promise to make a standing order with the bank that would start on January 1st 1969 for two years. He seemed very pleased that he had people living in the house to keep it warm over the winter months. He promised to make sure that the oil tank for the central heating was full and that the house would be nice and warm for our arrival in January.

As I drove through Barnstaple I stopped at the railway station where I found a friendly looking taxi driver. I asked him if I could book him to meet the train the following year, as we would need transport from the station to Marwood Hill House when we all arrived. I explained what was happening and he gave me his address and telephone number so I could confirm our arrangement nearer the time. He was the first local I had met, but I later found out that he was typical of the North Devon people. I have never come across a more friendly and obliging people anywhere else in the world. They have a wonderful accent that goes with a warm smile and gentle manner.

I arrived in Gloucester in time for dinner and told everyone about Marwood Hill for which I thanked Bid from the bottom of my heart. Her daughter, Sarah Jane, took me for a walk before dinner past fields of burning stubble. I felt completely at home in England as I talked with this beautifully spoken young English rose. My mother couldn't wait to see Marwood, but she would have to until we returned. Next day we drove back to London and I filled my last day walking around London taking photographs of heroic bronzes. Would I ever be able to produce anything like them? *Oh well*, I thought, *think Big*. I couldn't wait to get into my barn.

'Physical Energy', Hyde Park, London

Margie was in Melbourne to meet my plane. She had left the boys at Portsea with her parents so I had a whole evening and night to tell her all about my adventures. There was so much to tell it was difficult to know where to start. Over the next few hours I tried to describe the house but without the aid of photographs it was hard. I couldn't wait to get the films developed so she would be able to see the beauty of Marwood Hill for herself, but in those days there was no one-hour service and slides took a fortnight.

In the morning we drove down to Portsea and I told Ken and Helen about the house. I still couldn't really believe my fortune at finding something so perfect only hours before having to leave England. Thinking about coming home empty-handed still sends shudders up my spine. Margie's parents seemed to be as excited as we were and incredibly supportive of the whole project. Of course at that stage we all thought that it was only for a short two-year period so I wonder what their reaction would have been if any of us had realised that it would be for life.

At last the slides arrived and I was able to show them to Margie. She was as excited and stunned by the beauty of Marwood Hill as I had been. Back at Keith everyone was asking about how my trip had gone, so one evening after dinner at a friend's house, I put on a slide show. I knew from experience that farmers often go to sleep quite quickly after dinner, especially when the lights are turned down, so I added two or three black and white negatives of nudes as now being classified as a sculptor I was allowed to do this sort of thing! To save embarrassing Margie I put the slides in upside down. The trick worked and the audience stayed awake, although I think they were more interested in the black and white images, even though they were upside down and only flashed on the screen for a second!

Because Marwood was fully furnished we decided to sell all our furniture. This actually only consisted of a set of second-hand cane chairs, a couple of benches, a table and a few beds as all the rest of the fittings were built into the house. All we would take were books, pictures, photograph albums, china, glass, sheets, blankets and towels, which fitted into four large packing cases.

We left the farm on our tenth wedding anniversary and spent Christmas with Margie's family at Portsea, a marvellous way in which to celebrate our leave-taking. It was a hot summer and the boys wallowed in the sea.

Last 'Portsea' swim

Marwood Hill House

MARWOOD HILL

The day came for us to leave for the airport. Destination: London. Our four boxes of treasures had long gone by air and would hopefully be waiting for us at Marwood Hill. We arrived at Heathrow exhausted and took the bus into town and then a taxi to my mother's flat. Margie slept that night in The Slit, I was on the sitting-room floor and the boys camped under the dining-room table. My mother was delighted by our arrival and in hindsight I now see that our coming back to England filled the final years of her life with joy. She loved Margie and the boys and of course I was still her baby. Getting old can be a very lonely and sad affair, so our arrival must have been a blessing in her eyes.

Next morning we went to Paddington and boarded the express to Exeter and changed trains for Barnstaple. I had rung the taxi driver I had met in August and told him the time of arrival and he promised to be there to meet us. England was in the grip of a cold winter that was a far cry from the sun-soaked beach of Portsea we had enjoyed only a couple of days before.

The friendly taxi driver was waiting for us when the train pulled in and we set off up the hill towards Guineaford. The excitement mounted as we turned left down the lane that led to the house, passed the church hall and rectory and drove through the gates of Marwood Hill. It was wonderful for me to feel the tension rising as we got nearer and nearer. We all piled out and burst through the lovely Georgian doorway into the warm hall. The boys ran wild exploring their new domain as I showed Margie around downstairs. I had drawn a plan so the boys knew where they were meant to be sleeping. They quickly found their rooms and took possession while Margie explored the kitchen and wondered how to cook our dinner on an Aga, something she had never used before but soon became expert at. Jimmy had made sure the house was heated and the water was piping hot so straight after tea and a bath the boys fell into bed and we were not far behind, happily exhausted. Next morning we woke to a sunny white world as it had snowed in the night.

It snowed on our first night at 'Marwood Hill'

The boys couldn't believe their eyes as it was the first time that they had ever seen snow! The people who lived in the farmhouse behind Marwood had a toboggan that they lent to the boys. There was a perfect hill for tobogganing across the valley so we had an amazing morning playing in the snow.

The first toboggan ride

When the boxes arrived with our possessions from Australia we unpacked them and hung some of our own paintings on the bare walls so very quickly the house started to become our own. It was wonderful to have so much space, having lived in such a tiny house. Our bedroom was bigger than Chute's sitting room! The boys were meant to use Jimmy's old surgery as a playroom, but soon moved into the vast sitting room with us. The coal fire drew well and the oil-fired central heating was very efficient so we were unbelievably snug in our new and very grand home.

The postman came right to the front door in his little red van bringing letters from Margie's parents in Australia together with a box of quarter bottles of champagne from Uncle Joe to welcome us. I asked the postman if he knew of anyone who did wallpapering, as Jimmy had said we could change the sitting-room walls that were painted a very cold green. The postman told me that he and his mates hung paper and would be willing to do the job on a weekend. He measured up the room and told me how many rolls to buy. I asked our friendly taxi man to collect us so we could spend the whole day in Barnstaple, not only to buy wallpaper, but food and also a little car.

We settled for a funny little NSU car that was made in Germany. It had an engine in the boot, ran on the smell of an oil rag and we could all just fit in with a squeeze. Although it made a noise like a sewing machine, it was incredibly cheap to buy and was perfect for the unbelievably narrow lanes. Passing cars coming the other way was always a challenge and usually meant either finding a gateway to pull into or backing for miles, so we soon became experts at reversing. What a difference to the wide open spaces of Australia!

The boys' first 'Snowman'

I had found out about the local school and met Mr Rochford, the headmaster, when I had first looked at the house in August, so he was expecting Tim and Peter as pupils at Marwood Primary School in a couple of weeks' time when the term started. Mark would have to wait a year before he could begin. It was a brilliant little school with superb staff and we soon made friends with some of the other parents.

As the postmen did such a good job with the wallpapering in the sitting room I asked Jimmy if they could do something to the hall that was also a very gloomy colour. He agreed and the postmen set to and very soon we felt that it was truly our home. The postmen also turned out to be electricians, so I asked them to fit up some lights in the barn. They hung four long strip lights from the rafters that were a great help, but because the grey rock walls absorbed all the light the men suggested that they whitewash the whole place. This made an enormous difference and I now had a magnificent space in which to work.

The only problem remaining was that I had no clay, but when I asked the postmen about local art supplies they told me that Barnstaple was famous for its Barum Pottery. I drove into Barnstaple and found the pottery in the centre of town. The showroom was full of lovely terracotta ware of every conceivable shape and size. The shop assistant asked me if I needed any help and I explained that actually I was hoping to buy some clay and would that be possible. "Of course," she replied, "how much would you like? It comes in 20-lb packs at ten shillings each." I was used to buying it dry and having to mix it with water myself as well as paying a fortune. I bought ten packs, which was the limit that the suspension of the NSU would take. For a mere £5 I had enough clay to last a year! I just couldn't believe my good fortune or wait to get home and tell Margie.

Peter seven, Mark five and Tim nine
Marwood School

I looked around for a suitable subject for my first sculpture and decided that as I had done a sculpture of Mark the next victim would be Tim. I took several photographs of him posing as a marble player and a whole lot of measurements. I bought a developing tank and an enlarger and turned one of the little bedrooms into a darkroom where I made black and white prints. I then built an armature of wooden struts and started to work. The barn was so cold I had to have a bucket of hot water beside me to keep my hands from freezing. Snow boots kept my feet from turning to ice and my excitement kept the rest of my body warm under several jumpers and long underwear.

'Marble Player'

Margie came over to the barn and had a look at the clay when I had finished the sculpture. I have always followed the practice that she is not allowed into the studio until I am satisfied that I have finished the sculpture. She approved of what she saw but being a practical girl asked, "What now?" It was a very good question!

I had read about a process called Cold Casting that used polyester resin and bronze powder. It cost half as much as real bronzes using the Lost Wax process, the traditional way of casting in a foundry. I had seen examples of this method in shops that sold table ornaments and although not having the feel or weight of real bronze, it did look similar from a distance. Not having the money for the real thing, I decided to investigate.

I looked in *Yellow Pages* and found Cold Bronze Casting. Sure enough there were some advertisements for foundries that specialised in the process, one of which was just south of London. I called the telephone number and talked to a Mr Tozer and explained about the clay *Marble Player* and asked if he could help. He said he would be delighted to cast the sculpture for me, if I could deliver a mould to him. I asked, "How am I to get the mould made?" He suggested I contacted a Mr Mancini and gave me a number to call.

I rang Domenico Mancini and had an amazing conversation with a cockney accent who told me to call him Mac. He would be delighted to drive all the way down to Devon, take a plaster waste mould and deliver it to Mr

Tozer on his return. He said he would work out the mileage and ring me back with a price, which he did the following day. He thought the job would take two full days so he would have to stay two nights with us. The price seemed very reasonable to me and I agreed, depending on when he could come. "I shall leave as soon as you send me a map so I know how to find your house when I reach Barnstaple," he announced.

The following Monday evening Mac arrived, and although he had been driving all day, he literally leapt out of his little van. He was an Italian gnome from East London, as cockney as they come and he wore a wonderful cartoon black French beret. We had dinner round the kitchen table and learnt all about Mac's life while he found out all about us. He was a character out of a storybook and we had never met anything quite like him in our lives. He had a twinkle in his eye and asked Margie if we had any female ghosts at Marwood Hill. He loved the girls, even though he was over seventy.

I took Mac to the barn and showed him to the *Marble Player*. I was very apprehensive about what he would say, having listened to all his marvellous stories about all the famous people he had worked for over dinner the previous evening. He walked around the figure humming and hawing for a while and then said, "Not bad." I was thrilled!

Watching Mac over the next two days was an education in how an artisan works. I learnt more in two days than I could have at an art academy in a year. He asked me to help him and taught me how to press the thin brass shims into the clay to form walls that divided the sculpture into sections. When this was finished I helped him mix the plaster and handed it to him when needed. By evening we had the whole figure covered in plaster so that it could set over night and be ready for opening up next day.

After breakfast we commenced stripping the waste mould off the clay. It is called a waste mould because eventually it is chipped off the cold bronze and thrown in a rubbish bin. If I wanted to make a second edition of the sculpture I would have to take a rubber mould from the cold bronze cast that would be backed up by a plaster shell. It was from such a mould that a lost wax model is taken for a molten bronze cast. I was a long way away from such an operation, so I didn't think about it.

When we had turned the lights out the evening before, the plaster was hot to the touch. This is caused by the chemical reaction of the plaster setting. In the morning it was icy cold. Mac had designed the mould to have one large section under the figure so *Tim*'s face, chest, belly and inside of his legs were all one piece. The top was divided into several removable pieces; the back of his head, back, bottom, outside of the legs and front of his arms.

As gently as a brain surgeon, Mac removed the back of *Tim*'s head and revealed the clay inside. We had brought a bucket of very hot water over to the barn and this he started to pour onto the exposed clay. The hot water expanded the icy cold clay and started to force the waste mould apart. Soon water was seeping out along the line of brass shims that divided the mould into pieces and we were able to lift the back off. Next came the outside of his thighs and legs. Soon all we had left was the one large piece of mould under the clay figure. Now we were able to dig the clay out of the mould thus destroying the original sculpture and, without any ceremony, *Tim* was dumped into a plastic rubbish bin!

Mac washed down the inner surface of the waste mould, removing all traces of clay and then carefully put the small pieces back onto the large section, making sure they all fitted perfectly before clamping the whole thing together with hessian wads mixed with plaster. *Tim* ended up looking exactly like someone who had broken every bone in his body and was in a full body cast. Mac explained that this was necessary as otherwise the plaster sections would distort as they dried and wouldn't fit together again properly. At last we shut the doors and went to have a well-earned bath and dinner. Mac, aged over 70, was still chatting away as merry as a cricket while I was utterly exhausted by a simply fascinating day of learning.

Mac set off at the crack of dawn as he had an eight-hour drive back to London ahead of him. When I waved him farewell I was left feeling extremely flat. I have had this feeling every time a mould leaves the studio since that first parting. I have found that the only way of getting over the feeling is to start a new project immediately. *Tim* was out of my hands now and I wouldn't see him again until he was ready to be collected.

The trip to London in those days was a eight-hour drive on a good day and up to twelve on Bank Holidays, as there were no motorways. It was a long drive but we were used to such trips in Australia, besides which it was a chance to get to know the southern counties. It was now spring and the landscape was unbelievably beautiful as England's garden started to bloom. I spent a happy evening with my mother, but couldn't sleep because I was so excited about seeing my first cast sculpture the following day.

I arrived at the foundry mid-morning and was welcomed by Mr Tozer. His workshop was situated in a beautiful old wooden barn about the same size as mine at Marwood. The smell of the resin made the whole place smell like a nail-polish factory, so the large barn doors were kept wide open as much as possible. Inside three men worked on casting cold bronzes.

The process is really very simple and exactly like the one used for making the hulls of plastic boats. The plaster cast is opened up and the inside surface is sealed with a clear varnish. On to this surface is painted a thin layer of polyester resin mixed with bronze powder. When this has dried it is backed up with polyester resin mixed with wads of fibreglass until the skin is nearly a quarter of an inch thick. Once this has set metal rods are wadded on to add extra strength. The body of the mould is done first and then the outside pieces are fixed to it with clamps. It is a bit like a three-dimension jigsaw puzzle.

When all the pieces are in place and stuck together, the plaster is carefully broken off, exposing the bronze skin inside. The next thing is to make good the seams where the pieces meet by filling them with resin mixed with bronze powder. When the job has been completed, acid is brushed on to the bronze powder to give the sculpture the patination of an old penny. The sculpture looks exactly like a real bronze one, but is quarter the weight.

I walked into the barn and there sitting on the bench was *Tim*. I was thrilled. It was the most beautiful colour and shone like a real bronze in a museum. We carried him outside and took a whole roll of film. There were various things I would have liked to have done better, but I have discovered this applied to every figurative sculpture I ever did! It wasn't until years later with the Symbolic Sculptures that I was able to overcome this disappointment and be satisfied by my own work. For now I was more than happy with the finished results. *Tim* looked like *Tim* as though a professional had sculpted him, or at least that is how I saw him, and I was simply thrilled and amazed!

The finished cold-resin bronze of 'Tim'

When Mac had left with *Tim*'s mould, leaving me feeling flat, I had decided the time had come to be brave. With all this clay and such a grand space to work in there was no excuse to put off doing a large sculpture. I decided to leap straight in and tackle something I had wanted to do since reading Françoise Gilot's book, *My Life with Picasso*. I had read the book the previous year on the farm and been fascinated by a photograph of Françoise teaching her son Claude to walk on a beach in the South of France. It was a lovely photograph, slightly ruined by the father!

Having chosen the subject I realised that it would be essential to have a substantial armature to hold up the weight of the clay that would be used in a life-size sculpture of a kneeling woman and a standing child. Using Margie in her swimsuit and a large teddy bear as a model, I took photographs and measurements of limbs and the bear, then cut up stout inch-square lengths of wood and made up a skeleton using plaster to join them together. When I had finished it looked like a stick figure with large white knobbly knees and elbows! I added a few cross pieces of wood as ribs and this made the whole thing look even more bizarre.

I had made a six-foot diameter turntable that rotated on a marble to keep it located in the centre, and used four sofa casters to take the weight. It seemed to work quite well and I was able to turn it around with ease when Margie sat on top of it. I foresaw no problems and put the wooden skeleton on the turntable and started to add the clay, working from the photographs of Margie teaching the bear to walk.

214

Françoise teaching Claude Picasso to walk

The sculpture quickly took form as working with clay of a perfect consistency is a joy. The figures were blocked up within a week and then I started to smooth the surfaces. All of Françoise's body was very accessible except for her bosom and the only way I could work on this was to lie on the floor of the turntable and reach up. It was at this moment that disaster struck! Without any warning Françoise slowly settled down on top of me and trapped me beneath her. With a great effort I extricated myself from the tangled mess of clay, cursing like a cattle drover only knows how.

Staring at the mess of tangled limbs I couldn't believe what had happened, especially as everything seemed to be going so well! Obviously I had to learn more about armatures, as I now realised that even if the wood and plaster one had stayed together, it could not have supported the plaster mould. The armature was going to have to be as strong as a Brunel bridge.

I went into Barnstaple to see what could be found in the Do-It-Yourself store. As I walked around looking for something to use I realised that all the goods for sale were on shelves that were made out of long lengths of angle iron that were bolted together. If these could hold up gallons of paint surely they could hold up Françoise and a plaster mould with ease. I bought several lengths and a bag of nuts and bolts, a set of spanners and a hacksaw, and returned home.

One good thing about having already done the sculpture was that I had learnt a lot, which meant that I was able to avoid the mistakes I had made on the first attempt. I soon had the armature made, and as bore my weight I felt confident it would hold up both clay and plaster. I also realised that if the chest was hollow it would not only lighten the sculpture, but also save clay. I bought some fine wire netting and turned the body into a basket, and stuffed it with wet newspaper. I wrapped netting around the legs and arms and made a ball of it for the two heads.

The new armature worked like a dream and within a week the sculpture was finished. The wet newspaper inside helped keep the clay moist and every night I covered the outside with sheets of the plastic from the bags that come back with the dry-cleaning. Soon it was done and I was really pleased with my first full-sized sculpture. It was time to ring Mac again.

The second attempt remained standing

Mac drove down and this time he had to stay for three nights. We worked away in the barn like slaves mixing plaster and applying it to the figures. At last we had the mould finished, cleaned up and safely in his van that looked decidedly tail heavy as he drove out of the drive.

This exercise had been even more fascinating than taking the mould of *Tim*, as much more planning had gone into the job. Mac had walked around the figures for an hour before deciding where the shims should go so the smaller upper sections could be removed from the large bottom piece. While he worked out what to do he also examined the sculpture, and I was delighted when he at last said to me that he liked it. Then he added, "Maybe her right thigh is a fraction longer than the left one." There was certainly nothing to be done about that at this stage of the proceedings, so I decided to keep that piece of information to myself.

'Mac' with the waste mould nearing completion

Having overcome the problem of armatures perhaps it would be challenging to sculpt a mother kneeling and holding a child up in the air.

Clay 'Mother and Children'

217

Margie and the large teddy bear were again called in for photographs and measuring before beginning work. Sculpture number three soon took shape and with the new armature system the child stayed up in the air, while a second child was crawling on all fours beside her.

I found that the used clay was full of plaster chips and not nearly as easy to work, so went back to the Barnstaple pottery for another load. What a luxury to have new material to work with every time! Years later I visited an art academy in China and was shown the sculpting studio where each student was working on a large nude figure. I picked up a piece of the clay from the bin and tried to model something with it, but found it was impossible as it was full of plaster chips. I thought of my days at Marwood and blessed the Barnstaple pottery, as I couldn't have done any of the sculptures with such awful clay as the students had in China.

Mr Tozer called to say that *Françoise and Claude* were finished. I had not been able to contain my curiosity while they were being cast and made a quick trip up to the foundry to watch the process of resin casting. I had arrived to see the cast with the back off and took a photograph of Roy Wakeford at work. This was the first time that I had met Roy.

'Roy Wakeford' working on 'Françoise'

My brother Pat had decided to buy himself a new car and offered me his old one. We now had two cars in the garage under the house so I could leave Margie with the NSU for the school runs and shopping while I drove up to London to inspect the completed sculpture.

I arrived at Tozer's barn and went inside to find *Françoise and Claude* with a sheet covering them. It was to be my first unveiling and wasn't I excited! The sheet came off. To see my first large sculpture looking like a real bronze was an amazing moment. When I see the sculpture in All Hallows Church by the Tower of London and it makes me think of the barn at Marwood Hill, where I sculpted it, and the day I first saw it at the foundry, and met first Roy. It now hardly seems possible that it all happened so quickly.

Mr Tozer and Roy lifted the sculpture out on to the lawn for another roll of film! In the sunlight the sculpture looked even better than in the barn. I

218

showed him photographs of the kneeling *Mother and Children* in clay and asked if he could do another job for me. If he could then perhaps Mac could down and take the mould as before, and bring *Françoise and Claude* down at the same time. This is how it all worked out and soon Mac was back at Marwood.

'Learning to walk'

Margie and I were worried about Mac when he arrived in his little van. He didn't look well and although over the time it took to take the mould he seemed in good spirits, somehow he had lost his twinkle. We waved him goodbye not knowing that we would never see him again.

When the *Mother and Children* were ready for collection, I drove up to the foundry to hear that Mac had died and was really heartbroken by the news. I had only known him for three working sessions, but during that time we had got on so well I felt we had known him for ever. He taught me an enormous amount, as he was always willing to share his knowledge. He was a true craftsman who had obviously had a tough life, starting to earn his living at 14, but never complaining about anything, which is a pretty rare thing to find in this world.

Domenico Mancini came into my life at just the right moment and was a godsend in those early days when I was learning to sculpt. He was one of the nicest and kindest men I have ever met and a major stepping stone in my becoming a sculptor as he was always encouraging, for which I shall never be able to thank him enough. Domenico Mancini was a gem of a man.

Kneeling 'Mother and Children'
my memorial to Mac now in Marwood Hill Gardens

It was around about this time that Margie and I saw an advertisement on the Barnstaple railway station offering a weekend in Paris for £9 each return, hotel included! That sounds ridiculously cheap but in those days was the same as a week's rent on Marwood Hill. The train would take us to London and then a coach to the Dover-Calais ferry and another coach would take us to our hotel in Paris. Once there we would have two whole days and two nights before returning overnight by the same way. It was so tempting we just had to do it, so we asked our friends Penny and Nigel Spink to see if they would mind looking after the boys for four nights. The friends had two boys who were also at the Marwood School so it would not be too great an imposition.

The train part of the journey to London was simple and the night with my mother fun as it was our first trip to town together since arriving in

England. The early rise to catch the coach was not difficult, but we were a little perturbed by the first sight of our coach because it didn't look very reliable.

Our fears turned out to be well founded as it broke down crossing Waterloo Bridge! A better-looking bus arrived in half an hour and we set off again and reached Dover without further trouble and boarded the ferry. We were relieved to see that the French coach was brand new and we were soon spinning through the countryside heading for Paris. Halfway there we stopped in a town to stretch our legs. It was now about one o'clock and we had been travelling for six hours and were feeling more than a little peckish. Margie and I saw a few tempting restaurants and hoped that we would soon be taken to one.

We couldn't believe our ears when we were all ordered back on board and set off again. Then we noticed that all the other passengers had brought sandwiches with them, which just added to our hunger. All we had was a packet of cigarettes and a duty-free bottle of brandy as a present for my cousin Rachel who lived in Paris. In those days everyone smoked so it was allowed on buses. We lit up and sulked.

We were both feeling so hungry that after a bit of humming and haaing we decided that cousin Rachel would not mind if we sampled her brandy. In those days drinking out of a bottle in public was frowned upon! Luckily Margie carried her hairpins in one of my old tobacco tins so I emptied them out and used it as a cup. Well, of course by the time we reached the hotel in Paris we had drunk nearly a quarter of the bottle and were feeling very happy!

The hotel was in the Place de la République and looked quite respectable from the outside. Inside was a different story. The receptionist could not speak English and just handed each couple a key with a number on it. All the rooms were on the third floor and there was no lift. As we only had a zipper bag this was not a problem, although the winding staircase did trouble some people, especially a black American couple with a large suitcase. We found our room was furnished with a stained washbasin and the rug on the floor was so filthy it would be unwise to walk in bare feet! With some trepidation Margie pulled back the bed to inspect the sheets and to our relief found them to be spotless, crispy white. Then there was a knock on the door.

On opening it I found the black American man. "Could you please help? The receptionist doesn't speak English. Could you ask him if we could like a room with twin beds?" We had already come to the conclusion that the hotel was also a working brothel so I didn't really hold out much hope that a Frenchman would understand the American's request! Using my schoolboy French, unused since I was 16, I tried but was proved correct as all the man did was shrug his shoulders.

The hotel facilities were basic. There was one bath for our whole floor. The one cupboard lavatory on the spiral staircase between floors two and three had a door but no latch. Fortunately the space was so confined that you could hold the door shut with you foot, although as we went up and down the stairs we discovered that men didn't bother to shut the door anyway. The hotel definitely had a laissez-faire air about it, but what did we expect for £9!

None of this mattered, we were in Paris and neither of us had been there since we were teenagers. Our first job was to find cousin Rachel so we hailed a taxi, gave the driver a bit of paper with an address on it and set off for Montmartre. The taxi driver dropped us off and we looked around for Rachel's flat. We asked a couple of people who merely shrugged, but luckily she was on the lookout and heard our English voices, popped her head out of a window and told us to wait. We were soon sitting in her flat apologising that our gift of brandy was somewhat diminished while desperately hoping we could sample what was left. Instead she offered us a cup of tea!

Rachel was our family hero as she had stayed on in Paris during the war and worked with the French Underground. She had married a Frenchman who was known to the family as 'The Chow' because he had a black tongue, like a dog of that breed, from drinking absinthe which eventually killed him. I don't think Rachel was terribly pleased to see us so we soon made our excuses and left, having done our duty by my mother and drunk the tea.

Not having eaten since breakfast we were famished so walked back to the hotel looking for a clean café with a Parisian atmosphere on the way. We found one and, after having a low-cost French meal and a bottle of cheap wine, strolled home feeling very content and very happy to be in 'Gay Paree'.

Our plan was to visit the Musée Rodin in the morning and in the afternoon take the train out to Meudon to visit his suburban studio. I had just read *Naked Came I* by David Weiss, so my mind was full of the great sculptor's life. In fact it was all too much. Not having seen anything larger than a six-inch high Rodin maquette, suddenly to be surrounded by a copy of every sculpture he had ever done including the *Gates of Hell*, was beyond our wildest dreams. We staggered out and fell into a café for a beer. Being very short of money we had decided to skip lunch and save our cash for dinner. One of the nice things about Paris cafés is that they always have hard-boiled eggs on the counter for beer drinkers. We made the most of their generosity and ate two each.

We found the right railway station for Meudon and took the next train out to the suburb. When we arrived a man gave us directions to the studio and we set off up the hill. It was a beautiful day and quite a climb, so by the time we were approaching the top of the hill we were hot and puffing. Suddenly a great jet of water fountained up from the middle of the road as a water main burst right at our feet. It was very spectacular and we took the opportunity to cool down in the spray-filled air.

We arrived at the front gate of Rodin's studio and rang the bell. A very grumpy man stepped out and grudgingly opened up to let us in. He pointed to a notice that said *No Photographs* and then led us round the back of the house to the studio and Rodin's grave with the *Thinker* sitting on top. We had the whole place to ourselves so walked around admired the studio drinking in the atmosphere. Although we found the whole place was very rundown and a bit depressing, one got the feeling that it must have been amazing in the past. We spent an hour taking it all in and then walked out down the drive. As I reached the gates I turned and took a photograph. We heard a great shout of rage and saw the old man begin to run down the drive towards us waving his arms, so we nipped through and shut the gate feeling like naughty school children.

Next morning we went to the Louvre and walked in the Tuileries Gardens, which is always such a pleasure. In those days Maillol's sculptures graced the lawns outside the Louvre making it a much more pleasant place than it is today. The museum was empty of tourists and we were able to inspect the treasures virtually on our own as we wandered through the empty galleries. We even had the *Mona Lisa* all to ourselves.

The trip home was uneventful and, as most of it was overnight, we just dozed in our seats and thought about all we had seen. We arrived back at Marwood happy but exhausted after a wonderful adventure.

'Birth of Adam'

Inspired by all I had seen I went to the barn the next morning and started my Rodin period! The first sculpture needed to be something that I could take a mould of myself now that Mac was not going to be able to help me any more. I decided to do a sculpture called the *Birth of Adam*. I still have it in the Agecroft garden. It is of a baby being born, umbilical cord still attached and being raised by the arm of God from Mother Earth.

Jimmy Smart thought the child was too big and as he was the anaesthetist asked me down to the hospital to see a Caesarian birth. The surgeon asked me if I was all right as he made the incision and I replied, "Yes, it is no different to killing a sheep." He looked at me over his mask and replied, "I jolly well hope it is!" Jimmy continued to listen to the Test Match broadcast!

I took a one-piece mould except for the hand and foot that had a section that could be removed making it possible for me to dig out the clay when it was finished. I took the mould up to the foundry and left it with them to cast.

My next sculpture was the *Lovers*, and that was quickly followed by *Pain*, and then *Christ* that is now in All Hallows Church by the Tower of London. Next was Simeon's Song, *Nunc dimittis*, depicting the Prophet blessing the head of the boy Jesus. This sculpture is now the font cover of Marwood Church. When I saw it recently it brought back many happy memories of our halcyon days at Marwood Hill.

'Lovers'

'Pain'

'Christ', at 'All Hallows' by the 'Tower of London'

'Nunc dimittis', Marwood Church font cover

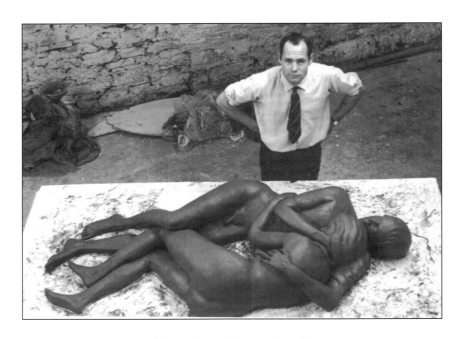

'Peace', sculpture in clay

'Peace', sculpture in cold bronze

My next Rodin sculpture was more ambitious and was called *Peace*. It is of a man and a woman asleep in each other's arms. I was beginning to see that my moulding days were numbered. I could do simple moulds but only if they were lying down! Sculpting figures that are lying down is somewhat restrictive, although I was able to hang *Peace* on the wall when it was cast.

My Rodin period came to an end when I did a life-size sculpture I called *The Awakening*. On finishing the clay sculpture I wrapped plaster it up in plastic ready for the big day when I would take my first multi-piece mould. I went to the barn in the morning, prepared to start work, keyed up and ready to go. The first job was to put the shims in the clay and cut it into sections as Mac had taught me. I started to unwrapped the sculpture and as I removed the plastic from the girl's bottom the whole of the back fell off. I stared at the figure and then decided that it was an omen and scrapped the project. Some years later I was commissioned to do a four-foot high version of the same subject, so all was not lost as I really enjoyed doing it a second time!

'The Awakening'

227

I had first met Roy when I had gone to see *Françoise and Claude* being cast and had realised then that it was only his skill that had produced such a fine finish from my moulds. I was immensely impressed by Roy's craftsmanship as the care he put into the finish of the job had to be seen to be believed.

Roy Wakeford, Master Plasterer and friend

This unassuming man was to make the whole of my sculpting life possible as without his help there would be neither Figurative nor Symbolic Sculptures. I owe everything I have achieved to my partnership with Roy and over the years we have become great friends.

Mac's passing had left me with a dilemma. How was I going to carry on without him. The solution to the problem came when I was dropped at the foundry by my brother Pat, who wanted to see my latest sculpture. He left me there so I needed a lift back to London and when Roy heard this he offered to take me as far as his home in Morden to catch the Underground into town. I was delighted about this as I was dying to talk to him alone.

On the way to London he told me that he was not very happy with his job and as the conversation developed I found myself offering him all my future work if he decided to go solo. When we arrived at his house he showed me his tiny garage workshop and told me that this was all the space he needed and over the years he proved this to be correct. During the next 25 years, single-handed he made every waste mould, positive plaster and resin bronze cast of every one of my sculptures, and all in his garage!

Roy taking a plaster waste mould of the 'Girl on the Cushion'

On the train into town I wondered what I had done! To begin with I had better start working like a Trojan if I was going to keep my word and not let Roy down, so decided to do some more children. Margie had a friend called Sally to help her now and again clean up the enormous house. Sally had a very pretty little daughter called Melanie and they both agreed to my taking some photographs for my next sculptures. I have always liked action and found that this can be achieved by having children interact with each other. I thought of doing a group of three children gossiping on the lawn, calling it *Story Time.*

'Story Time'

The amazing thing about these three sculptures is that they are now being cast by the hundred in Asia and sold in Garden Centres in England, but without my signature! They are beautiful castings and one tenth of the price of what they would cost in Europe so sadly must be done by slave labour.

Before leaving Melbourne I had taken some photographs of the boys playing with a water hose in a garden. Peter had the hose while Tim and Mark tried to avoid getting wet, with little success. Fortunately as it was summer Margie didn't mind. The photographs came out well and I thought that the whole scene would make a great fountain, so I set to with confidence using my new armature skills. Tim running, Peter jumping backwards and Mark holding the hose with his shorts at half-mast as always.

'Peter, Mark and Tim' getting wet

'Water Fight'

When Roy first arrived at Marwood to take the moulds of *Story Time* I introduced him to Margie and the boys who all immediately adopted him as a member of the family. On seeing the three sculptures he knew exactly what to do and set to work. Being younger than Mac he worked twice as fast, which meant that I had, fetching water, cleaning out the moulds and carrying cups of tea back and forth just like in the old shearing shed days on Chute! Roy was a joy to work with and we soon developed a system that lasted for 25 years.

Having committed myself to employing Roy I obviously had to find a market for the sculptures. I decided to write to Derek Crowther of Syon Lodge in London. Margie had seen one of his advertisements in the *Illustrated London News* at the dentist's and thought that there might be a chance of his being interested in selling my type of sculptures. I put together all the photographs that I had, and sent them off, including *Story Time*.

One of the sculptures I had done was called *Water Babies*. The crawling child was the same as the one in the *Kneeling Mother and Children*, so I only had to do the squatting child to complete the fountain. Roy cast a circular platform for the children to play on as a base.

'Water Babies', Harrogate Park

Another of the photographs I sent to Derek was my first life-size animal. The farm behind Marwood had been bought by a woman who owned a Great Dane, and she asked me if I would do a sculpture of her pet. I took masses of photographs and measurements and retired to the barn. The owner would bring the dog to see me and by the time the sculpture was finished both of us were rather pleased with the result, although neither of us asked the dog! Roy took a mould of the Great Dane and when he had finished I asked him to take a rubber mould of it and cast a plaster copy for me. When the plaster arrived I sculpted a little boy to stand beside the great brute with his arm around the dog's neck. It turned out to be a very popular sculpture and eventually we sold twelve copies. Because it was such a good seller I did an edition with a little girl in the same stance, but we only sold two! Why?

231

'Boy with the Great Dane', on 'St Lawrence Waterway', Canada

Several days passed before a letter arrived from Derek Crowther saying that the Chelsea Flower Show was in May and that he would take all the sculptures we could let him have and show them on his stand, *on sale or return*! We packed up *Françoise and Claude* and several of the children sculptures into a hired truck and delivered them to Derek at Syon Lodge.

Margie and I couldn't resist going to the Flower Show to have a look at the Crowther stand. We had a double interest in being there as Jimmy Smart was also taking his camellias for the first time.

As we weren't members we had to wait until the first public day, but that didn't matter as it gave time for something to happen if it was going to. We walked down to the Thames in bright sunshine and eventually found Derek's stand. We hid in the crowd and slowly worked our way forward. The children were displayed on plastic grass and the *Water Babies* fountain was bubbling way. We couldn't believe our eyes when we saw that all of them were wearing red *several stickers*!

232

With a push in the back from Margie, I boldly stepped forward and gave my name, asking if Derek was available. The attendant disappeared and soon returned with Derek wearing a big grin. "We have sold all the children and taken orders for more. When can you deliver them?" He went on to explain that the larger figures were too expensive, but added to the display. Luckily this turned out to my advantage as Jimmy wanted to buy the *Mother and Children* for the island in the middle of his new lake at Marwood Hill to celebrate the fact that he had won all the prizes for his camellias!

What a day it had become, in fact probably the best day of my life. Nothing is more pleasing to an artist than to sell his work. It means he can eat!

'Mother and Children' on 'Jimmy Smart's' island
'Marwood Hill Gardens' in North Devon

After the Chelsea Flower Show not only did Roy have to do my plaster work, he also had to make the resin bronzes Derek had sold. Fortune had certainly smiled on me the day I wrote to Crowther, as Roy now had a full-time job and I had a new career. In the end Roy cast over fifty children for Derek. One of the reasons we went up-market and started to cast in real bronze was because Roy was finding it hard to cope with the volume of work in his garage that Crowther's sales had generated.

Just sculpting children was not much of a challenge and I decided to try something new just in case the market dried up. Another stimulus to this move was the coming of winter. During the first winter at Marwood I had been as mustard keen so working in the barn from dawn to dusk in below freezing temperatures was not a problem. As there was no water supply in the barn I had to carry it over in rubbish bins and every morning the water left there had frozen over night. Only by wrapping the sculpture in plastic and then blankets could I stop the clay freezing, which was a pain, as the ice crystals would swell the clay and destroy all my previous day's work. I kept a bucket of hot water beside me to keep my fingers from going numb on the cold clay. Come the second winter I was beaten and retired to the attic with a hot-air blower, as there was no central heating up in the servants' bedrooms.

My stepbrother, Peter, wanted to buy *Françoise and Claude* and give it to All Hallows Church by the Tower as a memorial to his father, my Uncle Fred. I was very flattered by this proposal as well as being delighted, as it meant that they would be permanently on display in a beautiful church. It is a very historic place as it was from the bell tower that Samuel Pepys watched and recorded the Fire of London. Below in the Crypt they have found mosaics that date back to the Roman city.

'Françoise and Claude'

**Memorial to my stepfather, 'Frederick Bowring',
at All Hallows by the Tower of London**

234

ENZO PLAZZOTTA

My attic studio was a paradise. It had a dormer window with glass on three sides so I had enough daylight to work in. A little staircase led up from the first floor which previously had gone all the way down into the old kitchens in the cellar beneath the house and had been used by the servants so their masters would not have to see them! Now the attic was the home of a pair of barn owls with three chicks!

About six months after we arrived in England and in the middle of my Rodin period, I saw some photographs of bronzes by Enzo Plazzotta in an art magazine. Because I had greatly admired them and envied the skill of the sculptor, I decided to write to him and ask if I could possibly visit and seek his advice. In the letter I enclosed some photographs of the sculptures that I had done so far. Enzo very kindly wrote back agreeing to meet me and on my next trip to London, and for the first time in my life, I entered a real art studio. Northern light, proper stands and even a little changing room for a model! I was overawed. Enzo specialised in ballet dancers and female nudes so all around me were beautiful wax figures.

'Enzo Plazzotta' working in his studio

235

Enzo made me a cup of coffee and looked at some more photographs that I had brought with me. I then asked him if, in his opinion, I should continue to try and earn a living as a sculptor. "Do you want to do anything else?" I replied, "No." He looked me straight in the eyes and said, "Then why are you asking me? Go and do it."

Enzo worked with a medium that he made himself, a mixture of beeswax, resin and a pigment that turned it a beautiful rich red ochre. He advised me to try it, as he found it inspiring to work with, and gave me some to try. The wax had to be kept warm and to do this you needed to have a saucepan of water suspended over a gas flame. When the second winter came I built myself a table with the armature steel and mounted it on rollers so it could be wheeled about the attic. It had a shelf on the bottom to hold the gas cylinder, one pipe going to the burner and another to a hand torch.

So began the era of my maquettes, which was one of the most enjoyable sculpting experiences I have ever had. (A maquette is defined as a small wax model that the artist intends to enlarge.) All that winter I worked upstairs in the warmth of the attic, coming down for lunch and a chance to sit down, before going back to work until it was time for a bath before dinner. Compared to the freezing barn it was like a tropical island.

My first wax maquettes were 'Dancers'

That first winter I did some fifteen different figures. The great thing about wax is that you can make it do anything you wish by using fine copper tubing as an armature. The problem was, what was I going to do with them all? You can't sell wax sculptures, they have to be turned into bronze. Enzo had all his maquettes cast in Italy, something quite out of the question for me.

While I worked in the attic, Margie took care of the boys, driving them to school, shopping and doing all the 101 things busy mothers do when caring for three growing boys and a husband. Because she was so efficient at doing all this I was able to work for as long as I was able to stand up, there being no sitting down for a sculptor as you have to keep moving around to view your work from all sides. It was like being back on the farm with me out in the paddocks all day, only coming in for lunch. It was a routine we were used to and it worked as well now with sculpting as it had then.

Come the spring Enzo advised me to sculpt a small child figure and have it cast in real bronze to test the market so I repeated the small sculpture that I had done of Mark as a two-year-old when working on the farm.

'Mark with Bird', my first bronze sculpture

When I had finished the clay, Roy did a positive plaster cast and it was then that I discovered I could do extra work on the plaster and obtain a smoother surface before handing it over to the foundry. Roy suggested that I have it cast at a place he knew in Chelsea, so I took the plaster to them and left it there. I returned in a month and collected the sculpture.

I was very pleased with the finished product, but found the manager very abrasive. I asked Enzo for advice and he suggested that next time I should try the Meridian Foundry in Peckham that was run by Jack and Peter Crofton. He thought they would also be interested in casting my maquette waxes.

I made an appointment with the Crofton brothers and drove out to meet them. I had never been to that part of London so it was quite an adventure. Eventually I found the foundry after a great deal of searching because it was hidden in the arches of a railway viaduct. If it hadn't been for the fact that they had told me to look out for a railway line I don't think I would ever have found it. Over the following years I used to take clients out there to see their commissions being cast and I always took great delight in watching their faces. They would soon start to ask where we were going and then get really worried when we eventually pulled up in a jumble of arches with steam belching out of pipes sticking through walls. The place looked like a gangster-movie set.

'Leonardo da Vinci's Horse' in wax

Jack Crofton, his wife and Peter, his brother, were three of the nicest people you could wish to meet. The foundry furnaces took up the ground floor of the railway arch while upstairs were the finishing shop and a tiny office. I showed them three of my wax maquettes and asked them if they would be interested in casting them and quote on the cost. "Certainly we will and straight away." Peter showed me around while Jack and his wife worked out the prices.

It was the first time I had watched liquid bronze being poured into a mould. It is one of the most thrilling things to see in the world.

Working in the attic on the maquettes during the second winter at Marwood was a time of great experimenting. By using the hand torch I could stroke the wax with a flame and achieve a polished finish to the surface that appealed to the touch and could be repeated in the bronze.

'Prometheus' in wax...

...and in bronze

'Dancers'

One of the maquettes I left with Meridian was the *Hammer Thrower*. Little did I know at the time that this small figure of a man throwing a hammer while balanced on one foot would play such an important part in my life.

When I went back to collect the maquettes I was thrilled by the job the Croftons had done. Not only were the castings superb, but the patination was amazing and my maquettes looked like antique bronzes. I was delighted and promised to bring more waxes on my next trip. When I got back to Marwood, Margie and I set the bronzes up on the sitting room table and celebrated them with a champagne toast. The *Hammer Thrower* maquette in particular seemed to talk to me, and what he was saying was, "*I want to be BIG.*" I agreed, but the question was, *How BIG?*

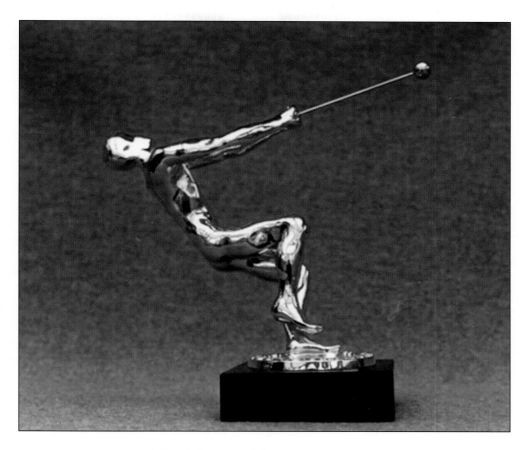

The 'Hammer Thrower' maquette

I have never liked exact life-size adult figures as the finished sculptures always look small, which doesn't apply to children as they come in all sizes. Another problem is that when you hot bronze cools it shrinks, which makes a significant difference. I decided that the *Hammer Thrower* had to be bigger than life, in fact a giant and nine foot high!

The maquette casting had taken place during the spring. Margie and I had watched Jimmy's garden come alive and the buds on the trees turn to leaves. Both of us were enchanted by the Devon countryside. It was a million miles away from the Ninety Mile Desert and we loved every moment of our new life. Jimmy's camellias filled the garden with their pink flowers and the lawns were carpeted with daffodils. In front of the house drifts of crocuses appeared through the grass. With the arrival of the second spring I came down from the attic and moved back into the barn and started to build the armature of my first heroic statue.

Although the *Hammer Thrower* would be nine feet high if he stood up, as he was leaning right back his head would only be six feet off the floor. The angle was dictated by the centrifugal force he was generating as he spun around with the hammer. He was on one foot so I gave him a solid six-inch high thick base to stand on. I hung the armature on wires from the roof beams of the barn to take the weight and climbed up onto the skeleton to test their strength as the last thing needed was for the sculpture to fall on me as *Françoise* had.

I stretched chicken wire over the frame and then filled it with damp newspaper. When all was ready I nearly had a completed figure formed out of metal and wire netting so it would only need an inch of clay to cover it, which would lessen the load on the wires.

241

I bought 15 new packs of clay and was ready to start work. I began to block up the figure that quickly took shape and by the evening had him completely covered. He looked huge! Had I been overambitious? I covered up the figure with plastic to keep him moist and turned out the lights. There was nothing to be done about it if he turned out too big as I certainly wasn't going to start all over again!

I opened the doors of the barn in the morning with trepidation and uncovered the figure. I decided he was the right size and if he had been any smaller he would have been insignificant, so I set to work again. All I had to work from was the little maquette and an anatomical model that Enzo had given me, so there was going to have to be a lot of guesswork about which muscle went where! I wished I knew as much about anatomy as Michelangelo had, but on the other hand I didn't think I could have cut up human corpses, as I hadn't much liked killing sheep!

It was amazing how quickly the *Hammer Thrower* came together. By the end of the week I was able to call Roy to find out when he could come down, as I was beginning to worry about the thin skin of clay drying out and falling off. I called him on Friday evening and he said he would be down on Monday, after collecting some plaster. This suited me as it gave me the weekend to keep working on the clay. One of the troubles with cold bronze is that there is no way you can alter the surface after the waste mould has been taken so it was essential to make the surface as smooth as possible while I had the chance.

Roy arrived on Monday evening and immediately we went to see the *Hammer Thrower*. I thought this was a good idea, as it would give him the whole night to think about how he was going to take the mould! After Margie had given him a good meal we packed him off to bed and I wasn't too far behind. I knew the next day was going to be a tough one, as I would have to lug several large rubbish bins full of water across from the house.

After breakfast we walked over to the barn and stripped off the covering plastic. Overnight Roy had worked out how to take the mould, which in fact he said would be relatively simple as long as the wires from the beams didn't break! He planned to take one large mould off the whole of the back of the figure and have eight small sections covering the front. By lunchtime we had the shims in dividing up the sections and the first layer of plaster all over the back. After lunch Roy bent up metal reinforcing rods that would be incorporated into the thicker second layer of plaster for the back, a job that actually takes longer than the plastering as each rod has to be bent to fit the curve of the area where it is to be used. Roy used to bend all the 3/8-inch diameter metal rods over his knee, which made me wince with pain every time he did it. I tried it once and found it was agony. What his knees looked like at the end of the day I just hated to think.

By the time we knocked off I was exhausted and yet I hadn't done half of what Roy had done. The whole figure was covered in plaster and steaming hot from the chemical reaction of the plaster hardening. We shut the doors of the barn and stumbled into the house ready for a whisky and a bath. I worried all night in case the wires would break and we would find the whole thing lying on the floor in a broken mess of plaster and clay!

We opened the barn doors and much to my relief found that all was intact. The *Hammer Thrower* was still just as we had left him. He hadn't moved a muscle! We started straight in to take him to pieces as Roy wanted to get away early enough to drive back to London. Off came the chest section and then the belly. Next the top of the thighs and the fronts of the lower legs. We dug out the clay and cut away the chicken netting and pulled out the wet paper. I felt like a vulture ripping up a carcass.

Roy had borrowed a trailer, as there was no way we could get the mould into his station wagon. As soon as we cut the wires and freed the back we loaded the giant plaster. Then came the job of sticking all the back pieces on to the front section to stop any warping. The whole thing looked very odd, with the head over the front of the trailer and the feet sticking out of the back with a red danger flag attached. Roy bathed and changed and was ready to go. I said, "Drive carefully, we don't want to have to do that again." He grinned at me and set off for London. I walked back to the house feeling really flat and glad I didn't have an eight-hour drive ahead of me. Derek Crowther had said the big stuff was too expensive for the Chelsea Show, so my next problem was what was I going to do with the sculpture when it was finished.

Roy rang me a month later and said that the sculpture was ready for inspection and asked when could I come and look. "Tomorrow!" I couldn't wait a day. When I arrived at his garage the doors were closed but he had heard me arrive and swung the doors back to reveal the *Hammer Thrower*. It just fitted in under the roof beams! How had he managed to make that in there? To look at the back of the figure I had to squeeze past the sculpture. It was an unbelievable job and I was absolutely over the moon as it was 100 times better than I had hoped. One shouldn't be really pleased with one's own work, but I was! This was the largest thing I had ever done and I was thrilled. Roy and his dear wife Olive were grinning away, waiting for my reaction and asked me if I was pleased. I laughed, "Pleased, I am amazed and delighted. What a job! We need photographs to show Derek."

The husband of a friend from my childhood days called Belinda had bought a mansion not too far from London. It was called Trafalgar and had apparently been built as a gift from the nation to Nelson, although his death at the battle interfered with that plan. I knew she had extensive lawns in front of the house so asked her if I could photograph the sculpture there, to which she kindly agreed. Roy and I hired a van and loaded the *Hammer Thrower*, which was quite a job as even though it was only made of resin, it still weighed an incredible amount because of all the piping Roy had used inside as re-enforcing. To keep it from falling over Roy had left a three-foot length of two-inch pipe sticking out of the bottom to hold it up. I hadn't told my friends that I would have to dig a hole in their lawn, but as I secretly hoped she would buy the sculpture when she saw it in place, perhaps she would never know! My hope of a sale stemmed from the fact that Belinda had bought an edition of the *Hammer Thrower* maquette. Perhaps her husband would like to give her a present of a larger version!

We got the sculpture around to the front of the house, dug the hole, took lots of photographs, and left it sitting there for them to find at the weekend. The photographs came out really well but the husband balked at the price, so we had to go back and collect the sculpture and fill in the hole. Luckily Roy had a friend with an empty shed where we could park the sculpture until I could find a buyer. It was time to take the photographs around to Derek Crowther at Syon Lodge.

As it turned out it was lucky that Belinda hadn't been indulged by her husband as Derek was very enthusiastic about the sculpture and said he would like to show it at the next Chelsea Flower Show. I was really excited by the prospect of the *Hammer Thrower* being seen at such an important venue and couldn't wait for May to arrive.

Again Margie and I went to the show on the first public day and I must say the *Hammer Thrower* looked very imposing on the Crowther stand. Derek told me that he had sold several children but had had no luck with the big fellow, but it had been a great attraction so he was delighted that it was there. I was not really surprised it hadn't sold, as it did look very large outside Derek's stand. However, a miracle happened before the show ended. Derek rang to say he had sold the *Hammer Thrower* to the City of London!

He went on to tell me that it had been brought by Mr Cleary who was in charge of the Gardens of London and it would be placed between All Hallows by the Tower and the Bowring Building. I was delighted by this because *Françoise and Claude* were already in All Hallows and to have another sculpture outside would be simply marvellous. Not only that, the courtyard was the entrance to my stepbrother Peter's office. It all seemed too much of a coincidence to believe.

'Hammer Thrower', London

But I now had a real problem on my hands. If I let the sculpture go to London, which I obviously had to do as it had been sold, it would mean that it would remain unique. Because it was my first large sculpture and because other people seemed to like it, I didn't want to lose the chance of selling it as an edition. I talked this over with Roy and he suggested that he should take a rubber mould from the sculpture between collecting it from Chelsea and delivering it to the City. This would be possible as he had been given the job of adding secure fixing to the base before it was installed on a special plinth. The sculpture arrived back at Roy's garage and he took a rubber mould, added stronger fixings to the sculpture and delivered it for installing.

The *Hammer Thrower* was unveiled on a bitterly cold day. The space had buildings on three sides, but was open to the street on the fourth. I nearly died when I saw the engineers had faced the sculpture so when he let go of the hammer it would go flying straight through the glass of the building on the right and not out into the void!

After the close of the Chelsea Flower Show I received an amazing telephone call from a man who spoke English with an East-European accent. "John Robinson? I am Fred Kobler. I liked your *Hammer Thrower* at the Chelsea Flower show, but I am not paying Crowther's prices! You want to sell me a copy at a special price?" The conversation went on for about 15 minutes, at the end of which he had a deal and I had an invitation for lunch to his apartment in London. Fred told me that he had gone to the Flower Show the previous year and had bought the *Waterfall Children* from Crowther and had installed them in his country-house garden south of London.

I sold the same sculptures to the City of Melbourne and they were installed near the Botanical Gardens and I am glad to be able to say that they have not yet been vandalised.

'Waterfall Children' in Melbourne

Living in North Devon and being invited to have lunch with Fred Kobler in London meant driving up to town and staying a couple of nights. Fred had given me his address in Westminster as Stag Place. On the appointed day I set off in good time to meet my mysterious caller. Stag Place turned out to be a glass skyscraper that looked more like an office than a residence. I told a doorman that I had an appointment with Mr Kobler and was directed to a lift and instructed to press the button marked Penthouse. I stepped out into an enormous grey immense sitting room to be greeted by a handsome young man who introduced himself as Antoine.

Antoine came from Malta and I later discovered he was from an old aristocratic family. He was my age, but tall and slim, with a deeply-tanned skin. He was very elegantly dressed in a dark pinstriped double-breasted suit. I followed him into the grey vastness of the sitting room around which were dotted enormous vases of flowers. One wall of the room was glass that over-looked the gardens of Buckingham Palace. Fred was sitting on a grey leather sofa and, in contrast to Antoine, was casually dressed. He was approaching 70 and in every possible way the opposite to his young friend.

"Would you like a drink?" I can't remember what I had but I do remember that they both drank mineral water and I am sure I didn't, as my nerves needed steadying. After my drink we moved to a glass-topped dining table and Antoine served us a superb meal of cold fresh salmon and salad. The conversation covered a whole range of subjects, but was mainly about how I had become a sculptor having been a sheep farmer in Australia. I personally don't find anything strange about this, but most other people seem to!

After lunch we moved from the grey dining area back to the grey sitting room for coffee, after which Fred took me into an enormous grey bedroom, sat me down on an acre of grey bed and asked me to count the wad of notes he handed me. I had never held that much money before in my life so my counting was not as professional as it should have been, but as I knew Fred would have counted it, I was happy just to pretend. Fred explained that he always paid in notes as he could then just think of it as petty cash, and not have to worry about doing any paper work as accountants cost money!

When I got to know Fred better I learnt that he was very careful with his petty cash. Before the sculpture was ready for delivery he drove me down to his house in the country to show me where he wanted it placed. He owned an enormous 30-year-old Cadillac, which he loved passionately because it never needed repairing, although it did use quite a lot of petrol so we had to fill up on the way. I pointed out a garage soon after he mentioned the need for fuel, but he passed it by telling me that he knew of one further on where the petrol was a penny a gallon cheaper! I hoped that we would not run out before we got there as the car would have been very heavy to push!

It was during this trip that I learnt about Fred's origins. He had escaped from Germany at the outbreak of the Nazi persecution of the Jews, and had lost his whole family to the gas chambers. He had arrived in England without a penny in his pocket. He didn't tell me how he became the silent partner in a hotel chain, only that when he and his colleague sold up he found himself to be a millionaire. Fred's passion was Opera and, as he had no family, he gave his money to Glyndebourne for the production of Mozart operas as a 'thank you' to the country that had given him a home.

His country house was very modern, set in acres of lawn and bordered by giant beech trees. The lawns fell away down the side of a hill, giving a spectacular view out over a valley. It had originally been the site of a Victorian monstrosity, which he had bought and pulled down so he could build a modern home in an old setting. There was a lake at the top of the hill that fed a tumbling stream with rock pools and it was on one of these that Fred had placed his *Waterfall Children*. The extraordinary thing was that when I told my mother where I had been it turned out that Fred's home was only about a mile away from where she had lived as a child.

As soon as Roy told me the *Hammer Thrower* was finished we set it up right in the middle of the front lawn with Fred supervising through the sitting-room window. When the job was completed he invited us into the house to have a look through the glass wall at the sculpture. I must say it looked very spectacular against such a grand vista.

They say that things happen in threes. The Kobler adventure was hardly over when I received a letter from Sir Maurie Mawby, who had taken over as chairman of the Zinc Corporation when my father had suddenly died. He told me that he wanted to commission a sculpture as a tribute to the Miners of Broken Hill for a site outside the office in Melbourne. He envisaged a statue of a miner dressed in working gear holding an ore sample. If I agreed to do the job, he would send me a helmet, light and belt-battery, and a lump of ore!

I of course agreed and set about making a maquette of the sculpture that I thought would be suitable. When finished, I had it cast in bronze and sent him a photograph, which led to him asking me to bring it out to show him so we could discuss its possible enlargement.

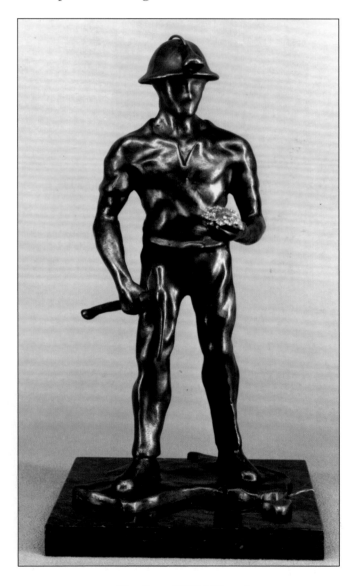

'Broken Hill Miner'

I travelled to Melbourne via New York because I had not been there since the age of five when Mike, Nana and I had been shipped out to Australia. Maurie had given me an introduction to one of his mining associates who asked me if I would like to meet Joseph Hirshhorn, a friend of his who collected sculpture. I had no idea who Hirshhorn was, but said that I would and so he gave me an office telephone number to call. I rang the number and talked to a secretary who made an appointment for me to telephone again next morning. I did as I was told and was put through to Joseph who asked me what I was doing and where I was going. I told him that I was on my way to Australia with a maquette of a miner to show Maurie and that I hoped to do a life-size edition if it met with approval. Joseph said that he would like to see it and would I bring it around to his office on Park Avenue. I agreed and packed up the *Miner* in my canvas bag along with the maquette of the *Hammer Thrower*, which I planned to show Maurie. I threw in the *Shot Put*, which I had brought along with me, just for luck!

'Shot Put'

I arrived at the Park Avenue address, found Hirshhorn's name and took the elevator up to his office and admired the incredible view out over the city. When I was shown in Joseph said, "What have you got to show me?" I

248

unpacked the little *Miner* and then the *Hammer Thrower* and explained that I had been commissioned to do the former, but hoped to persuade Maurie to use the latter, and call it the *Pathfinder*. We chatted about this idea for a while and then he pointed at the bag, "Anything more in there?" I pulled out the *Shot Put* and put it on the desk. Joseph picked it up and turned it around in his hands several times. "I haven't bought anything today, how much do you want for this?" "Two hundred and fifty dollars," I replied, hoping it didn't sound too much. "Done, I'll give it to you in cash when you leave." I had made my first American sale!

Joseph then told me the story of his life and how he had been so poor at one point he had eaten scraps from restaurant rubbish bins! He had somehow made some money and then bankrolled prospectors looking for uranium in Canada. He took half of everything they found and they found a lot, so he was now called Mr Uranium. He told me that he loved sculpture and had the finest collection of Rodin sculptures in the world and asked if I would like to see it? When I said yes, he suggested that as tomorrow was Saturday he would send his car to collect me for lunch at his house in Connecticut. That suited me, as I was not due to fly out until Sunday morning, although it did mean that my visit to the Metropolitan would just have to wait until another time. Hopefully I would return to New York one day!

Joseph's car collected me and we soon arrived at a very large house surrounded by vast lawns crowded with sculpture. I was tickled pink to see the *Shot Put* all by itself on the hall table when Joseph met me at the front door and I thought it looked very good sitting there in such an important place. However, I was soon put back in my box when Joseph took me out into the garden. He had not been joking when he said he had the finest collection of Rodin sculptures in the world as he owned more than were in the Musée Rodin in Paris. It was the most extraordinary display I have ever seen as not only were there Rodins, there were sculptures by Maillol, Giacometti, Brancusi and every other famous sculptor you can think of. I suddenly felt very small.

When Margie and I were in Washington many years later we visited the Joseph Hirshhorn Museum. When I had met him, he had told me that he planned to build a museum next to the Smithsonian and give his entire collection to the nation that had been so kind to him. When we were walking around his museum I wondered if the *Shot Put* was hidden away in a little box in the basements or being used as a door stop! I am sure no one there had a clue what it was, or who did it. Still it is nice to think that I once sold a sculpture to Joseph Hirshhorn and whenever I look at my own copy of the maquette I think of the kind man in Connecticut with fond memories.

I liked the little *Miner* I had done, but while working on the maquette I had had the idea that the *Hammer Thrower* would perhaps capture the *Pathfinder* spirit better. When I went to see Maurie in Melbourne I showed him the *Miner*, which he liked, and then the *Pathfinder* maquette. Maurie immediately chose the *Pathfinder* and thought it would look great outside the offices in Collins Street. I returned home very pleased and immediately rang Jack Crofton and asked him to quote me a price for casting it in bronze. He said he would have a look at the sculpture by the Tower and get back to me.

The casting of the *Pathfinder* was a milestone in my life as it was my first heroic sculpture in bronze. Both the London sculpture and the one for Kobler were in cold bronze and cast by Roy. The one for Melbourne was to be the real thing. I was delighted by this step forward and when I went to see the finished casting I was simply thrilled and couldn't stop grinning.

'Pathfinder' at the Meridian Foundry

By the time the *Pathfinder* reached Melbourne, Maurie had retired. His successor was set on pulling down the offices and building a bigger one where there was no place for sculpture. Maurie decided to lend it to the City of Melbourne and it now stands in the Victoria Gardens between St Kilda Road and the Botanical Gardens. The excitement of Chelsea, All Hallows, Kobler, Hirshhorn and Maurie had opened up a whole new world for me. What a summer it had been and all quite beyond belief!

250

GREECE

After all the excitement of the *Hammer Thrower* and having made a little money, Margie and I decided to take a holiday in the autumn. There was a problem we had to face and a break would give us a chance to think about it. Our two years in England were fast running out and we had to decide what we were going to do. Either I would return to Australia and an unknown future or stay in England and sculpt. Actually there was not really any choice as I just could not imagine giving up after 20 months of excitement with the promise of more to come. As I had been talking about Madeira all of our married life, Margie suggested that I should show her the island.

If we were going to take a trip to Madeira I thought why not see other places on the way. I decided to travel to the island via Madrid so we could see the Prado Museum and visit Toledo, as Margie was a fan of El Greco. After Madeira we would fly to Gibraltar, and then take the ferry across to Morocco, and overnight train to Meknes and Fez, and then fly home from Tangiers. As we were anxious about us both flying in the same plane while leaving three small children alone in England, I worked out a very complicated schedule that had us on separate flights. This turned out to be such a nightmare of logistics that we vowed never to repeat it, so decided that all future holidays abroad without the children were to be by train!

Madrid was as exciting as Paris had been. The Prado was out of this world and seeing Goya's *Naked Maja* in the flesh was thrilling, although I did wonder if Mr Ozane would approve! We took a bus out to Toledo and visited El Greco's house and saw his famous altar painting in S Tomé. It was all excitingly foreign to us Aussies from the Bush. Going back to Madeira was fun and brought back many happy memories for me, especially when we met some of my teenage friends from the past.

In Gibraltar we took a taxi up to the top of the Rock to see the apes before boarding a ferry to cross to Tangiers. It was an amazing feeling to be standing in Africa, a bit like going to the moon. We stayed a night with some of my mother's friends and experienced for the first time the necessity of having a guard sleep across our bedroom door for security.

One of the most exciting places we visited were the caves where Phoenician miners carved the millstones used for pressing olives for oil. Looking up at the ceiling of the cave we could see the circles that had been left when the miners had hacked the wheels out of the mother rock. It was my first experience of the ancient world of Troy, Mycenae, Knossos, Tyre and Sidon.

We visited the market of the old town and for the first time I experienced the unpleasant bartering world of the Arab merchant. We saw the ruined stables of the Sultan that had once housed a thousand horses. Morocco was an interesting experience and I saw things I needed to see, but we were very happy to return to Marwood and the boys.

The trip had allowed us to talk over our future and we had decided to ask Jimmy Smart if we could stay on another year at Marwood so we could see if the *Hammer Thrower* had been just a flash in the pan. If, at the end of a third year things still looked promising and we decided to settle in England, it would mean buying a house and finding a school for the boys. Luckily Jimmy had no plans for Marwood and was happy to extend the lease for one more year, although he then wanted to sell the house to pay for a new one he was planning to build in the garden for his retirement. This meant that we had a year to think of where we wanted to live and in what kind of house. We would never be able to afford a house as large as Marwood, but as we didn't need one that big we started to look at cottages.

Once again the winter had set in and the temperature had dropped to freezing in the barn, driving me up into the attic. Our trip abroad had caused a revival of my interest in the past and led me to search out all I could about Greek mythology. My maquettes started to have titles like *Hera's Cuckoo*, and *Hephaestus modelling Pandora*.

'Hera's Cuckoo'

As I learnt to manipulate the wax my armatures became more daring until eventually I did one of two men, one lifting the other in the air on one arm. I called it the *Acrobats*. I liked the finished bronze so much I decided that it would be my next summer's project. It would be 16 feet tall and be a make or break sculpture, as this would be my last chance to do something really big if the circumstances decreed we had to return to Australia.

Having steeped myself in Greek mythology all winter I decided that we should take a trip to Athens in March before I started on the *Acrobats*. There was no way we were going to fly in separate planes again so chose to take the Orient Express from Paris to Athens instead. Once there we could hire a car and drive around Greece, cross by ferry to Brindisi and from there catch a train to Venice and another to Paris. It all looked very simple on paper so I bought the tickets as soon as we had found some nice girls who would take care of the boys for the three weeks that we needed to do the round trip.

'Acrobats', maquette in bronze

We arrived in Paris in the evening and changed railway stations to catch the Orient Express. In 1971 the train was the original pre-war steam engine with wagon-lit coaches as it had not yet been turned into the luxury joy ride it is today that only goes as far as Venice. This was the real thing, genuine old-fashioned transport and we were really excited by the sight of it when we walked along the platform and looked at the huge steam engine. The wagon-lit coaches looked clean although tired and worn, but this gave them a very romantic air. A uniformed steward, who came straight out of the *Student Prince* opera, welcomed us on board. He showed us our couchette that was set up for the day as a large sofa. In the corner was a little washstand with a potty in a cupboard underneath! Situated by the steward's cubby hole was the one lavatory that catered for the six couchettes in the carriage. As there was no dining car we bought ham and cheese baguettes from a platform trolley, along with a bottle of water and another of red wine. The steward said that he would serve us an Espresso when we had finished our dinner.

Soon we were rolling across France heading for the Alps, eating our picnic dinner and sipping cheap wine. What an adventure and how sad that all this has now gone! The steward brought us our coffee asking if he could make up our beds as we sipped it in the corridor. He quickly changed our compartment into the romantic scene from the film *North by Northwest*. We climbed into our bunks and were soon lulled fast asleep by the sound of the wheels on the track. I woke in the night and looked out of the window at a full moon shining in a clear sky above the snow-covered mountains of Switzerland. It is at moments like these that you just have to hug yourself, you feel so happy and fortunate.

The morning found us rolling across the vast plains of the Po River towards Venice. The steward brought us morning coffee and bread and when we had finished he turned our compartment back into our personal little sitting room. Some way out of Venice we stopped and our carriage was detached, shunted onto the train bound for Athens and we were off again heading for Trieste, about to enter Communist Yugoslavia.

Travelling in our carriage was a young American bound for Trieste. He asked me what I did in life and when I told him that I was a sculptor he said, "Are you going to study the works of Praxiteles?" I am ashamed to say I had forgotten that Praxiteles was the greatest of all the Athenian sculptors. I have never forgotten the withering look he gave me before turning away!

Lunch in Italy had meant another dash across the platform to a trolley when we reached Trieste. The steward announced that there would be a dining car added after we crossed the border, so advised us not to eat too much as we would have a *cordon bleu* meal that evening.

The cabin next to ours was occupied by a rather large and distinguished-looking gentleman. On one of my walks to the end of the corridor he stopped me and asked what we were doing and where we were going. I told him that my wife and I were on our way to Athens to see the wonders of ancient Greece. He informed me that he was a judge and then showed me a copy of *Playboy* magazine! I nearly died laughing inside. He then asked, "Would you do me the honour of joining me for dinner as my guests?" As he couldn't take his eyes off Margie's red hair and had just shown me *Playboy* I realised he was only really interested in one of us! During the afternoon, while waiting for dinner, we watched miles of very unattractive wet muddy Yugoslavian countryside roll past our window.

At eight o'clock the steward walked up and down the corridor beating a gong to announce dinner, so we joined the judge and walked along to the dining car. Margie and I were looking forward to the promised sumptuous meal after eating sandwiches for 24 hours. The dining car had even more atmosphere than the wagon-lit, but of the wrong sort! It was a relic of the Crimean War with wooden seats and practically had straw on the floor, which did not bode well for the *cordon bleu* meal we had been promised. We were handed a very greasy menu that had only three words on it. Soup, Meat, Dessert, with no other explanation whatsoever! The carriage was empty except for two Americans sitting across the aisle from us. Our fellow diners had already ordered and their soup arrived while we were looking at the menu. I heard one man ask the waiter, "What's that in my soup?" I couldn't believe my ears and I saw our dreams of a good meal evaporate before our eyes. However, there was some Yugoslavian wine and the judge was paying. At the end of a quite awful meal we thanked him politely, escaped back into our compartment and collapsed in laughter.

During the night we crossed the border between Macedonia and Greece. On both sides we had to show our passports to heavily-armed policemen. Looking out of the window of our compartment while in no-man's land we found ourselves exactly opposite a steam engine and could see the drivers swigging wine from a large bottle, so we waved at them. A whistle blew and as their train moved off the driver passed the now nearly empty bottle over to me! Believe it or not, we poured the wine into a glass and drank it. It was pretty rough, but we felt a bond of comradeship with the drivers who were heading in the opposite direction. We had arrived in Greece!

Athens and Rhodes

The train steamed on and we eventually reached Athens in the middle of a thunderstorm. We leisurely collected our luggage and climbed out onto the platform to join the back of the longest taxi queue we had ever seen. The other passengers had known about the taxi problem and raced ahead of us so there was nothing to do but wait. As we stood there we saw the judge descend from the train to be met by a ravishing young redhead who gave him a big kiss. We guessed she must have been his daughter! We couldn't help but look with longing at a very large black chauffeur-driven Mercedes that was waiting to whisk him away into town. Due to the heavy rain our queue was nearly static as

255

there was only a dribble of taxis available to collect the large number of passengers.

As the judge was about to get into the car he looked up and spotted us standing at the back of the queue. We waved to him and then to our surprise he walked over to the policeman who was controlling the crowd and prodded him with his umbrella and pointed towards us. The policeman walked down the line to where we were standing and said, "Come, you are the guests of Greece," and led us to the front of the queue and put us in the next taxi that pulled up. We had a Christmas card from the judge the following year so we wrote back and thanked him for saving the day. I hope he survived the Revolution the following year!

'Greek judge' reading 'Playboy'

We had been recommended to stay at a little hotel in the Plaka, the ancient part of the town that nestles under the east cliff of the Acropolis from where we would be able to walk to the entrance of the temple with ease. It is also the part of the town where all the old cafés are situated and the home of Greek music. In the evenings after exploring the ruins we would have our dinner in a café and listen to the unique sound of the balalaika and watch the locals dance. It was all very intoxicating.

Climbing up to the Acropolis for the first time was utter magic. Without realising it we had chosen the Greek Orthodox Easter for our visit and our first day in the city was *Clean Monday*. Apart from the Acropolis everything was closed. When we reached the Temple there was hardly another person in sight! It had poured with rain all night so the white limestone plateau glistened in the soft sunlight. It was awe-inspiring. In those days you could actually walk inside the roofless temple. We wandered around for a couple of hours in a daze watched by a black cat.

As we were about to leave, an old man arrived carrying a camera and tripod. It was the type that can develop a sepia print while you wait. He wanted to take our photograph and we didn't have the heart to refuse as we could possibly be his only customer that day. We agreed to pose for him if he would take one of us with our own camera.

'Clean Monday'

The Caryatides

Because of the rain the three marble caryatides were crying real tears for their missing sister that is in the British Museum that doesn't appear to cry because water doesn't shine on the terracotta as it does on the marble.

The Caryatides' Temple

We descended to the ruined Agora and walked in a field of asphodels, their white flowers and grey-green leaves famous as the garland worn by the Goddess Persephone. It was here that we met another tourist wandering around on her own who she asked if we knew why there were no people about. *Clean Monday*! It was lunchtime so we asked Mary to join us for a meal. She very kindly gave us a book on the Acropolis. Margie and Mary still write!

We passed the Temple of Zeus where some of the columns have fallen. It is not until you see the gigantic drums of marble on their sides that you realise what master builders the ancient Greeks were. The drums leave one breathless with wonder. Margie is standing behind one in the middle!

▲

Temple of Zeus

'My Redhead with Socrates'

One day we visited a small theatre that lies at the southern base of the Acropolis. Although from a ruin point of view it is not very interesting, in the front row of the marble seats there is a wonderful sculpture of Socrates. He looks so wicked and mischievous I asked Margie to give him a hug and took my favourite photograph of my favourite girl. Socrates and Margie have sat on my desk ever since to remind me of that happy day.

Jockey of Artemision

Next morning we went to the museum to see the bronze sculpture of the *Boy Jockey*. We wandered around and couldn't find it anywhere so eventually asked an attendant. *Closed.* What a disappointment! At that moment a nice-looking Englishman walked past and asked if he could help. We explained about our disappointment as we had come all the way from Australia to see this one sculpture. "Come with me." He led us past the guard and into the closed section. There was the *Boy Jockey* and what a delight to see! The sculpture captures such incredible action, which is what I wanted to see, as I believe all sculpture should be active if it is to live.

'Hephaestus modelling Pandora'

We visited the temple of Hephaestus, the god of sculptors. I had just done a maquette of him creating Pandora, his hands modelling the earth's clay into the smooth flesh of woman as she watches, reaching out to touch the miracle of creation. Making ideas come alive is the thrill of sculpting.

In the evening we took a taxi down to the port of Athens and boarded a ferry bound for Crete to visit Knossos. This trip was instigated by a book that we had read in the Ninety Mile Desert entitled *Bull from the Sea*, a story of Theseus and the Minotaur by Mary Renault. I really wanted to see the famous palace

260

that Sir Arthur Evans had excavated, and when we arrived in the morning we immediately hopped into a taxi and were driven out to the ruins.

We spent all morning climbing about on the reconstructed buildings imagining ourselves back in the days of the Minotaur. We had a fabulous time daydreaming and would not have missed the opportunity of seeing it all for anything. We walked along the oldest paved road in the world and sat on the King's Throne, something I am sure you are not allowed to do now!

'Throne Room' of Knossos

'Queen's Chamber', and 'Margie' with her favourite dolphins

The Greek boys and girls somersaulting the 'Minotaur'

262

The magic was completed when across the street we found a restaurant where we drank a sea-dark blood-red wine named 'Minotaur' and ate dolmadies with feta cheese! In the museum after lunch we saw the statue of the Priestess, bare-breasted and holding a snake in each hand, as well as the original paintings of the Madonna-blue dolphins swimming in the waves, and another of the boys and girls jumping over a bull. It was one of those breathtaking days that are full of sunshine and dreams.

Minoan 'Fertility Goddess' with snakes

The ferry was waiting for us at the quay, as was a vendor of sticky Greek pastries. We bought several cakes that looked absolutely mouth-watering for our dinner and climbed the gangway. The ship sailed out of the harbour into a beautiful sunset then turned east for Rhodes. We opened the brown paper bag of cakes as we watched the coast glide by and tried the first of our purchases. It was awful, sickly sweet and impossible to swallow, so over the side it went. Number two was even worse and number three quite appalling. A feast for the fish! As there was no restaurant on the ship we decided that as we were exhausted the best thing to do was collapse onto our bunks. Our cabin was small but had a porthole that I opened with great effort to let in some fresh air.

When we cleared the eastern tip of Crete the ship hit the Aegean swell. It was horrendous and very soon Margie asked me to leave her alone as she lay moaning on her bunk. I have never known such a pitch and roll to occur at the same time. It seemed that most of the other passengers were also feeling the effects of the rough sea as when I arrived in the bar I found it was deserted except for a young couple. The boy turned out to be a native of Rhodes, but his wife came from Scotland, and they were on their way to settle on his island. He was a painter and they planned to open a gallery-café and sell his work as she served coffee to the tourists, which sounded like a good life to me.

As we sipped our drinks and chatted, the motion of the ship got steadily worse, making us hang onto the bar rail with one hand and our glass with the other. It was time to see how Margie was faring. Getting to the cabin was a roller-coaster ride and to my horror, when I opened the cabin door, I saw water sloshing around on the floor, pouring in through the open porthole every time we rolled seaward! No wonder it had been hard to open as we were only feet above the Plimsoll line and was obviously meant to be kept closed! I scrambled over the water using a chair, slammed the porthole shut and fastened the bolts. Luckily I had dumped our bags on the dressing table so only Margie's shoes were afloat. She was fast asleep on the lower bunk and totally unaware of the chaos that surrounded her. I climbed onto the upper bunk and hoped the water would disappear down a plug hole in the corner of the cabin, which it did thank goodness!

Next morning we sailed into Rhodes harbour. What a sight the Colossus must have been as he straddled the entrance to the ancient port! I introduced Margie to my bar friends of the night before and they very kindly asked us to join them for dinner that evening after we had explored the town.

So much happened on the island of Rhodes throughout Mediterranean history. The Crusaders had come and gone, defeated by the Ottomans, but had left their legacy in the form of a mighty castle. We had a wonderful day sightseeing and then met up with our friends and took them out to dinner after which they walked us up to the ancient Greek theatre under a full moon. It was one of those evenings that you never forget and when we said goodnight and wished them both all the luck in the world for their new life, the boy gave Margie a ring set with a beautiful green stone. I wonder if they still run a café and if he is still painting. Hopefully he is.

The following day we hired a taxi and headed out to the temple of Lindos, which must be one of the most romantic spots one can imagine. To get to the temple you have to either walk or ride a donkey up through the whitewashed sugar lump houses of the village that clings to the cliff. The view from the temple to the horizon out over the sea was sublime and you could imagine the Argonauts rowing across it.

While admiring the view we had spotted a little seaside restaurant in the village below us that looked perfect for lunch. As the driver turned out to be so cheerful, we asked him to eat with us and to order, so our meal really was a Greek one instead of being the usual tourist fare.

Our taxi driver buying us oranges

When we had finished we set off to visit the Valley of the Butterflies. Every spring the Monarch butterflies congregate in one valley on the island. They come in their billions and settle on the trees so thickly you can't see a single inch of bark. Walking down the path in the valley is like walking through a glorious yellow tapestry. It is one of those happenings that I would give anything to repeat.

We were sad to leave Rhodes but it was now time to return to Athens and collect our car and explore the mainland: Corinth, Mycenae, Epidaurus, Tirens, Delphi and Meteora, before crossing to the island of Corfu, and then across to Italy to catch our train home to England. We had hired a VW bug for sentimental reasons, as it had been our first car when we were newly married. We collected it and headed south to see Mycenae, the famous city of King Agamemnon, the Conqueror of Troy.

We eventually managed to drive out of the labyrinth of Athens and headed for Corinth. As well as the heavy traffic, all driving at breakneck speed, the signposts were written in Greek, but the names on our map were in English. It was a nightmare! At last we were heading in the right direction and pretty soon left the traffic behind and by the time we crossed the Canal we were able to stop in the middle of the bridge and look down into the water below. It is a very impressive sight and to our delight made more so by a ship passing through just at the right moment, although I failed to photograph it!

Corinth Canal

Lion Gate

We arrived in Mycenae, left the car in the empty car park and walked up to the Lion Gate. One can feel the *Iliad* and the presence of King Agamemnon, captain of the 1,200 strong fleet that sailed to Troy. The names of Clytemnestra, Helen, Cassandra, Hector, Achilles, Paris and King Priam, all rang in our ears. To walk through the Lion Gate that had been used by people of this ancient time is something of a miracle. We passed through into the fortress and looked down on the tombs excavated by Heinrich Schliemann and his young Greek wife. Here they had discovered the golden masks and cups that disappeared from the museum when Berlin fell to the Russians, although luckily not before moulds had been taken. As we passed through the Lion Gate I couldn't resist buying copies of the two cups which now collect dust in the Agecroft inglenook. We climbed up to the Palace ruins to look out over the

267

plains of Argos. It was here that Clytemnestra murdered her husband Agamemnon, while he was taking a bath!

Agamemnon

Capturing the bull with ropes

Up early next day we drove east to visit the mighty walls of Tirens, or at least what is left of them. How they moved the stones in the famous arched tunnel is quite beyond comprehension.

The theatre of Epidaurus is one of the wonders of the world. A great horseshoe of stone seats that reaches to the sky. It is in nearly perfect repair and the acoustics are such that if you drop a coin on the stone in the middle of the theatre floor, people sitting in the top rows can hear its ring. When Margie stood in the middle and recited a poem I could hear every word.

Epidaurus
Margie reciting from 'Ulysses' learnt at school

We returned north and headed for Delphi, spending the night at a hotel in a very unattractive town called Lamia. It was March and when the sun disappeared the temperature dropped to zero. The fact that everything was built out of marble and lit only by fluorescent light makes it seem even colder. We were glad to get up early and continue on our way towards Delphi. The mountains got higher and we could soon see snow-capped Parnassos ahead of us. On up we drove and the sun came out so by the time we arrived it was a glorious day. What a place and what atmosphere! Olive groves surround the ruins that hang on the side of the mountain. The arena for the chariot races is almost in perfect condition; as is the doorway of the Treasury inscribed with the famous words, *Know Yourself.*

Delphi is one of the Earth's magic spots. Years later I did a sculpture entitled, *Know Your Self,* splitting the words into three on purpose to fit a three-sided stainless steel obelisk with a granite base. I had the Delphi inscription *Know Yourself* carved in ancient Greek on one side, Chinese calligraphy on another and Egyptian hieroglyphs on the third.

We walked down to the Tholos having sat awhile at the top of the Theatre gazing out at the fabulous view with not a soul in sight. We had seen the Tholos nestled amongst the olive trees below us, looking like the 'gem in the crown'. No one seems to be absolutely sure what the Tholos was used for, but this little circular temple holds incredible magic. Whatever it was must have been connected to peace and tranquillity, contemplation or meditation. Being there is one of our most treasured memories of Greece.

Tholos of Delphi

After leaving the temple precincts we went to the nearby museum and saw the *Charioteer* that is thought to have been sculpted in 480 BC. He stands, reins in hand, gazing out in front of him, waiting for the starter's signal. Oh what a sculpture! We left the museum totally bemused. In 2004 when Tim ran the pre-Olympic Marathon, I suggested that he should go to the home of the Delphic Oracle and see the Tholos, drink in the atmosphere and then gaze on the *Charioteer.* He had already run the London, Paris and New York Marathons and had decided to retire after this one, which turned out to be the toughest of all, being uphill most of the way. However, he claims that it was a good note to end on! It all sounded like hell to us but we are very proud of his achievement.

Charioteer of Delphi

We left and drove to Itea across a plain full of the oldest and largest olive trees we had ever seen. There were hundreds of them all with gigantic girths at least 15 feet around and must have been thousands of years old. It was an amazing sight and if it hadn't been getting late we would have liked to have stopped and examined one. I have always thought it would be a wonderful place to go for a painting holiday. Van Gogh would have loved it!

Itea is a town on the north coast of the Gulf of Corinth. When we arrived at the guesthouse we had booked into they didn't seem at all pleased to see us. We were shown a bare room with damp walls, damp floor and two damp beds. By now it was well below freezing outside and the temperature inside was not much higher. Putting on every single piece of clothing we possessed, including our overcoats, we wrapped our heads in jumpers and crawled beneath the damp eiderdown and tried to sleep, which was not really possible as the wind kept the shutters banging all night.

We left as early as possible next morning, encasing ourselves in the VW with the heating up full blast, but even so it took a couple of hours for our bodies to stop shivering and thaw out. What a night!

However, we were soon approaching Arta to see the famous Turkish bridge that spanned the river in one gigantic arch. We dutifully marvelled at the grace of the structure, but is not nearly as beautiful as the packhorse bridge outside Lucca in Tuscany.

Having seen photographs of the monasteries of Meteora I was determined to visit them. In the Dark Ages the monks had retreated to the top of these gigantic domes of rock and built their impregnable church fortresses to protect themselves against the marauding bandits that plagued the lands. In those lawless times it was impossible to reach them unless the monks lowered a thousand-foot-long rope attached to a basket down the side of the mountain that must have been quite a hair-raising trip! Talk about having faith!

The church fortress of 'Meteora'

The geology is as amazing as the monasteries. The landscape was carved by a giant river system that scoured out the soft material many millions of years ago, leaving the harder rock as great domes. The truly incredible thing is that the domes are conglomerate rock made of ancient river silt laid down billions of years ago. The geology is awesome as these rocks reach back to the beginning of the Earth's history.

No longer do you have to go up to the monastery in a basket because a stairway has been built. Apart from it being a very steep long climb, it is comparatively easy to reach the tiny church although it left us quite breathless, but I guess not nearly as breathless as the monks were after hauling all the building material up to the top. I am not a great fan of religious Byzantine mosaics so the art in the church did not attract me as much as the scenery did. The monks certainly had a God-like view of the world!

From Meteora we headed for the coast and the town of Igoumenitsa, the port from which the night ferry leaves to cross to the island of Corfu. We arrived to be told that the sea was far too rough so the trip had been cancelled and the ferry would not sail until the morning. The sea didn't look very rough to us, but as there was nothing we could do about it, I walked over to the hotel thinking that it was more likely that the captain was in love with the innkeeper's daughter and wanted to spend the night in port. Ours was the only car waiting to board the ferry and apart from the four people we could see standing on the quay, there seemed to be no other passengers. At the hotel I enquired for a room and found they only had one, but luckily free, so I took it sight unseen. I was also told that the restaurant was closed and there was absolutely no food available until the morning!

Having secured our bed for the night we decided to go for a walk. We still had some of our delicious oranges from Rhodes so we took two to eat as dinner at the end of the quay where we found four very miserable girls from New Zealand. We discovered that they had nowhere to sleep, no money and nothing to eat, as they had depended on getting to Corfu where they had friends to stay with at a campsite.

We went back to the car and they were soon each wolfing down an orange. Greek oranges are quite the best we have ever tasted so pretty quickly the bag was empty. While they were eating I went into the hotel and asked if there was anywhere that the girls could sleep. Very grudgingly they agreed to let them use an empty storeroom, at a price! The girls had sleeping bags and could use our bathroom, so at least they now had somewhere to sleep out of the cold and had full tummies.

The following morning the sun was shining and the sea was as flat as a pancake. The six oranges Margie had hidden for breakfast were soon devoured and then we all walked down to the quay and waited for the captain to appear as surely there was no reason for him not to sail. A couple of trucks arrived and I have a sneaking suspicion they were the cause of our delay and not the innkeeper's daughter. We were soon all on board and set sail.

Apart from the fact it was the only way we could get to Italy, the reason that we were going to Corfu was to see the island that the Durrell brothers had made famous. Gerald Durrell's book *My Family and Other Animals* had enchanted us in our farming days. I was also a great fan of Lawrence Durrell's *Alexandra Quartet*, *Bitter Lemons* and *Reflections on a Marine Venus* as all these books had had an influence on my wanting to return to England and travel in Europe.

We arrived in Corfu harbour and set off to explore the island after saying goodbye to the girls, having made them promise to come and see us in Devon when they reached England. We found the Durrell house, but unfortunately so had the rest of the world. Like many dreams, the reality can be a disappointment, but we could imagine what it must have been like between the wars. The island has been built over and the town has become ugly. Years later the same thing happened to the little hill town of Menerbes after Louis Males wrote *A Summer in Provence*. Such is life. At least we knew Menerbes before it was ruined. Corfu was fascinating and I am really glad we went there 35 years ago, as God only knows what it is like now.

After touring around for a couple of days we regretfully said goodbye to our VW bug and boarded the ferry for Brindisi and Italy. The crossing only took an hour and we were soon settled into our compartment on the train and heading for Milan. Once there we changed for Paris and then again for the Channel crossing and London. A night with my mother and home after what had been for us an Odysseus voyage of discovery. After three weeks of Greece I returned fired up and ready to start sculpting again.

My other exciting discovery had been the ancient Cycladic sculptures from the Aegean island. They are stunningly beautiful and influenced both Modigliani and Brancusi. I bought a sculpture and he sits on my desk obviously meditating on the deep philosophical question of *Know Yourself*.

Cycladic 'Thinker'

As soon as we arrived home I started to build the armature for *The Acrobats* using the 16-inch high maquette to guide me. I was immediately faced with a problem as I planned to make this sculpture 16-foot tall. There was no way I was going to be able to sculpt the two figures in one piece so they would have to be done separately. I decided that I would stop the bottom figure just above the interlocking hands. The maquette gave me the position needed for the join at the wrist, so hopefully it would look right when they were joined together after Roy had cast them. I hung both armatures from the barn's roof beams, as I had done with the *Hammer Thrower*. When the armature was finished the figures looked frighteningly large!

'The Acrobats' maquette – 16 inches high

I started to cover the base armature with clay and soon had the Big Man fleshed out. I decided to think of them as bathers fooling around on the beach as, contrary to what I had seen in Greece, these boys could not be naked! Apart from that I would try to make them look as much as possible like muscular Greek heroes.

As soon as the figures were finished I asked Roy to come down to take a mould. He arrived with a trailer full of plaster and all the other bits and pieces that were needed. We would have to hire a truck to take the mould to London when it was finished, as it certainly wouldn't fit in his trailer. Roy started work

275

immediately and had the two moulds ready for shipping back to his garage in three days! How he was going to get them into a workshop that was intended for a small car was quite beyond my imagination, but he seemed to be completely unfazed by the size of the job and I asked no questions. He promised he would have the job done in time for the next Chelsea Flower show, which I thought would be a miracle.

On saying goodbye to *The Acrobats* I again suffered from serious withdrawal symptoms, so immediately got stuck into doing the *Flute Players*. Having just finished athletic men I decided it was time to do three curvaceous girls. One would be about fifteen, another twelve, and the last three years old. The two elder ones would play flutes and the youngest one a triangle. As sculpting the female forms was so different to doing the male figures, it soon got *The Acrobats* out of my mind.

The 12-year-old 'Flute Player' in clay

The 12-year-old girl was one of the most satisfying children sculptures that I ever did. There is something incredibly endearing about the innocence of that feminine age. I took her pose from a magazine and a friend's daughter sat for a photograph for the 15-year-old.

I am not sure exactly how it happened but at the time that I was working on these figures I was approached by Barnstaple Council, who said they would like to commission me to do some figures for the foyer of their new building. They came out to Marwood to talk to me and I showed them the finished clay figures of the *Flute Players*. They liked what they saw and bought them on the spot. When Roy had cast them they installed them around a pool just inside the entrance to the Barnstaple Council Offices, where presumably they still are.

The left-handed 'Flute Players'

The troubles began when an article appeared in the local paper saying that no one played the flute left-handed, claiming that all flutes were made to be played by right-handed people. The paper said that I had made the Council out to be an ignorant *bunch of yokels* and the sculptures should be removed immediately! Thank goodness a flautist from the Manchester Orchestra who lived in Barnstaple happened to read the article and wrote to the paper and told them that he was a left-handed flute player!

Roy rang up and told me that *The Acrobats* were finished and ready to be assembled. To do this we would have to move the bottom figure out onto his driveway and then add the top man. Could I please come up and help.

By the time I arrived the following day Roy already had the Big Man out of the garage, lying on his side. We carried the top man out and slipped his arm over a pipe that joined the two figures and together we heaved *The Acrobats* upright. The first time we saw them standing there as one piece was quite a moment for us both. The wrists fitted perfectly and although I say it myself, *The Acrobats* looked pretty good and we were both absolutely thrilled. Roy had done another amazing job and every time I look at them in our garden, I am staggered that he was able to complete such a feat, but then he was a truly great craftsman and I should not be surprised. The man's a wonder!

I drove into town and went to see Enzo. I was dying to show him the finished sculpture and asked him if he would be able to come and have a look the following day. We drove out together in the morning and I shall always remember his face when we arrived outside Roy's house and saw *The Acrobats*

277

standing in the driveway. The whole street was also amazed and Roy's neighbours all came to gawk at the sculpture. The next problem was what to do with it! Crowther didn't want to show *The Acrobats* at the Flower Show beside the children sculptures, which was disappointing. I needed a setting to take some photographs so I asked my godmother, Angela, (who had saved my life by giving me the money to buy a typewriter in New Zealand), if I could put the figures up on her enormous lawn. When she agreed Roy hired a truck and we took *The Acrobats* for their first ride.

As we were able to drive out onto the lawn we placed the sculpture right in the middle! We were becoming experts at the job and could have the sculpture up and down again in a trice.

'The Acrobats'

278

We thought they looked all right standing out in the middle of the lawn but Angela didn't want to keep them, so again Roy had to ask his friend if we could borrow his shed while I had another think about what to do next.

At the beginning of the year we had all been shaken by the tragic road accident in which the young wife of Jeremy Thorpe, our local MP, had been killed in a car crash. The tragedy was made even worse by the fact that the couple had a one-year-old son who fortunately was not in the car at the time of the accident. One evening I was surprised to have a call from Jeremy asking if he could come and see me. He arrived a couple of days later and said he had seen the font cover in Marwood Church and liked it. He then asked me if I would be able to do a memorial sculpture of his wife from photographs. As we talked it came to me that perhaps the sculpture could be a Madonna and Child, so I suggested the idea to him. He agreed immediately and asked if I would start work as soon as I received the photographs.

'Caroline and Rupert', Jeremy Thorpe's wife and son

The sculpture was fairly simple, involving only a bust of the mother holding her son, so did not take long to do. Roy did his usual superb casting job and Jeremy said he was extremely pleased with the result. Soon afterwards he arranged a memorial piano recital by Moya Lympany in the Barnstaple Town Hall with the sculpture on the piano. It was quite an evening and very moving. The Council named the new Barnstaple hospital after Caroline Thorpe and the sculpture was placed in the foyer when the building was opened.

Jeremy told me that he had been asked to open the Summer Exhibition at the Royal Academy of Arts that year. He had shown the President my sculpture and asked if the bust could be included in the exhibition.

The President told me later that if it hadn't been for the circumstances he would not have agreed to show Caroline at the Exhibition! I was not surprised by his comment, but confess I was a bit miffed and thought the man very rude to say so. I decided then and there that I would submit an entry and hopefully have it accepted on its own merit the following summer.

It was around about this time that I was rung up by Swartz and Sackin Fine Arts Gallery. Mr Sackin told me that he rented space on the third floor of Harrods in the antique furniture department. He then told me that his assistant, Joanna Harding, had been to the Chelsea Flower Show and had seen my children sculptures on the Crowther stand. He asked if I would be interested in showing some of my sculptures in his gallery if they were cast in bronze. I told him that I thought that sounded a good idea and agreed to meet him and Joanna and discuss what would be possible.

When we met the three of us got on very well and I agreed to show a bronze on a 'sale or return' basis, sharing the profit 50/50 after casting costs had been deducted. It was a good deal for them, but also for me as being in Harrods was a step up the market ladder for the sculptures. I lent them the bronze sculpture of Mark as a child and Joanna made up a catalogue of children sculptures to show to perspective clients. Included in the catalogue were the photographs of *The Acrobats* so at least now the public could see the sculpture. Meanwhile I had my first real commission to attend to down in Devon, *Mr Banbury*.

I had of course been disappointed that my godmother, Angela, had not wanted to keep *The Acrobats*, however, one day she rang and said that her husband, Kit, would like to commission me to do a sculpture of their gamekeeper, as he was about to retire. They wanted to put the finished sculpture in the woods where they buried their Labrador gundogs! I immediately agreed to do the job as it sounded fun.

Margie and I were asked for the weekend so I could meet Mr Banbury, take photographs and measure the old man. Mr Banbury was less than five feet tall, a little wizened gnome of a man with a wicked twinkle in his eye and everyone loved him. When we went to see him he was dressed in gaiters and plus fours, woodcock feather in his hat and a tall fork stick in his hand, just as though he was about to go out on a pheasant shoot. He was magnificent and I couldn't wait to sculpt him.

Mr Banbury was soon completed and with my usual trepidation I asked Kit and Angela to come down to Marwood and have a look. They arrived one beautiful sunny day in an enormous Bentley and I walked them over to the barn and stripped the plastic off *their gamekeeper*. Luckily they were overjoyed and couldn't wait to get him into the woods.

'Mr Banbury' in clay

The film *West Side Story* was playing in the local Barnstaple cinema. I have always loved Bernstein's music, so to get over my usual depression that followed the completion of a sculpture I decided to go into town and see the afternoon show. Margie had to collect the boys from school, but agreed to drop me off if I could find my own way home.

We set off in the little NSU car with me driving. As we crested the rise out of our village I saw a large car bearing down on us right in the middle of the road where two small cars could barely pass. The driver was looking at a map that the passenger was holding up. I slammed my foot down on the brake but it was impossible to stop and *wham*, they drove right into us. What a terrible noise a car crash makes! In those days seat belts had not been invented so Margie shot forward and crashed her head on the window and her knee on the dashboard, while the shock of the impact went straight up my right leg into my hip socket. The doors had sprung open so we were able to get out of the car without any trouble, but the poor NSU was a complete wreck.

The other people were fine as they were in a heavier car. Margie sat on the grass verge dazed from the bump on her head while I was hopping around on one leg with a lot of pain in my right hip. Luckily there was a telephone kiosk a few yards down the road and someone had rung for the police. An ambulance soon arrived and we were driven to the hospital with both of us strapped to stretchers. On arrival we were taken to the x-ray department, Margie for the bump on her head and me for my hip.

The next thing I knew was a doctor telling me that I had fractured the socket in my right pelvis and that I would have to spend six weeks in traction. Margie was diagnosed with concussion and would have to spend a night in hospital for observation. It was as though the whole world had crashed in on us both. One moment happy and free, the next imprisoned. It was almost impossible to believe. A hole was drilled through my leg bone below the knee and a steel rod screwed through it. Margie was wheeled away to a women's ward and me to a men's one. Ropes and pulleys were arranged and a weight added to the end to stretch my leg away from the fractured hip socket. I was trapped and felt as though I was in one of Roy's plaster moulds!

The news of the crash spread and our friends the Spinks immediately stepped in and collected the boys from school and took them to Marwood. Sally, the mother of Melanie the little girl who had modelled *Story Time*, gave the boys tea when they got home and then spent the night in our house to look after them. Jimmy Smart rang my mother in London who said that she would be down on the first train the following day to help. The nurses told me that Margie was sleeping well and advised me to have a knockout pill, as it would help get over the shock.

Waking up the following morning in a 30-bed ward was the most depressing thing that has ever happened to me. I still could not believe what had taken place, and all so quickly. I was very depressed until a nurse came and told me that Margie had woken up was feeling fine. I have never been more relieved in my life.

The arrival of my mother in the afternoon was a complete surprise. She had been to see Margie and reassured me that she was all right. She was appalled by the hospital, which was not surprising as it was about to be pulled down. My mother immediately took charge and booked two rooms in the Imperial Hotel saying that she wouldn't allow Margie to stay in a place as awful as the Infirmary a moment longer! There was nothing to be done about me as unfortunately I was tied to a ton of lead hanging off the end of my bed. When Margie was ready to leave she came to reassure me that she was fine apart from a bad headache and a whopping bruise on her knee. She also pointed out things could have been a lot worse! That thought cheered me up, but watching her leave the ward reduced me to tears. It was not a good day.

Luckily we had two cars by then so she was still able to carry on with school runs and every day she came to see me in the hospital. If it hadn't been for these visits I would have gone raving mad. Being 38, in traction and trapped in a bed flat on your back was absolute hell because of the utter boredom. Although surrounded by 29 other ill men I felt as though I was in solitary confinement, but at the same time chained to a galley oar. It was a very sobering situation. Margie kept me supplied with books to fill the hours, but you can only do so much reading. As each day dragged by one after another my situation seemed increasingly like a prison sentence and ever since those days I have felt profoundly sorry for anyone confined and admired them for their courage and stoicism.

The nurses were always jolly and caring and without their constant bustling around as they went about their duties the days would have seemed even longer. My respect for the nursing profession has been unbounded since then. The worst time was during the long hours of night when I couldn't sleep and was unable to read. It is during the night that the black fears come to haunt you. What made these dark hours bearable was one particular nurse who seemed to be on nearly every night. She would make her inspection on the hour and when she came past my bed would always check if I was awake. Usually I was and so she would stop and have a whispered conversation with me. She was about my age and had just been through a messy divorce. She lived in a tiny caravan parked in a farmer's field way out of town so that she could be on her own during the day. I have forgotten her name but I can still see her in my mind's eye as clear as though it was yesterday. When she had to leave me to go about her other duties she used to kiss my forehead and tell me to go to sleep, which I immediately used to do. She was about to leave the hospital and move to Southampton and remarry. I hope that everything worked out for her and she has a wonderful life. She deserved it for she was a true Nightingale.

The other thing that kept me going was the memory of the Yogananda Self-Realisation course that I had done when on the farm. If you remember I had become very interested in Yogananda's teachings and had my Third Eye opened in a rather weird ceremony! One of the things that Self-Realisation had taught me was to exercise my body mentally without actually moving a muscle. What you do is think of a particular muscle, say your right biceps, and then mentally flex it. The muscle doesn't move but you can feel the nerves tingling in the muscle. I was able to go right through my whole body from toe to scalp flexing the nerves without actually moving. I used to do the exercises two or three times a day and also if I woke during the night. The whole process took about an hour so it helped fill the time as well as do me a lot of good both mentally and physically.

One of the books Margie brought in for me to read was a slim volume of Pushkin poems. I found his poems enchanting and incredibly wise. The little book included a very brief history of his exile in Paris. It was this exile that provided the inspiration for one of his poems that I came to love and read time and time again. It is based on the Russian Orthodox Church Easter

283

tradition where the youngest daughter of the household releases a caged bird after the service. The verses captivated me and go as follows:

The Bird

From home an exile, still preserving
The custom of a bygone day,
The Festival of Spring observing,
A captive bird I loose away.

Consoled at one with Nature living
How could I now to God complain
Who gave to me the joy of giving
Its freedom to this bird again.

I knew that the first thing I would do when I got out of hospital was try and capture the poem in a sculpture. Some months later when I was back in the attic again for the winter, I sculpted the *Bird of Spring*. We had met an army couple called Tim and Dinny Green when they were having their summer holidays in our village. We became great friends and I asked them if I could use the hands of their eight-year-old daughter, Della, as a model.

'Bird of Spring'

After four weeks in hospital I was going berserk. All semblance of pain had long since disappeared and I was beginning to feel like a convict with a ball and chain attached to my ankle. I had Margie ask a farmer friend of ours if he would come and visit me, as I had thought of a plan of escape. When he kindly came I asked him if he would build a frame with lengths of the same shelving steel that I used for armatures over a single bed at Marwood on which I could suspend a weight. I planned to attach the weighted cord to an eye screwed into the heel of a shoe. I had done a sketch of the frame and he agreed to do it. I then consulted the doctor and much to my relief he agreed to my leaving as long as I stayed in bed for another two weeks, so I discharged myself.

As soon as the frame was completed I was carried out to an ambulance and driven back to Marwood. Oh what joy to be home! It was wonderful when the boys arrived from school and came to see me. That evening Margie cooked a welcome-home meal for us to have on my bed. What an evening and what bliss to be out of that awful ward. However, there was a problem. The idea of having the weight attached to my shoe didn't work as I woke up in agony feeling as though my foot was going to snap off at the ankle. I sat up, undid the laces and got rid of the shoe, which never went on again except when the doctor came.

I couldn't wait to get back to sculpting so Margie brought me some plasticine in bed and I modelled a pair of otter cubs at play. When I had been incarcerated I had read Williamson's book *Tarka the Otter* that is set on the River Taw, which runs through Barnstaple.

'Otter Cubs'

The doctor finally agreed for me to get up as long as I remained on crutches for another six weeks. He also suggested that it would be very good for me to go bicycling, as this would exercise my legs. Margie borrowed a bike and I rode around and around the circular drive for an hour every morning and again in the afternoon. I am not sure what the neighbours thought but it didn't matter, I was up and mobile again. Margie's mother had suggested that I put a rose behind my ear and quote poetry to really get the locals talking. Freedom!

Two hours of bicycling every day!

My main concern while I was incarcerated had been about *Mr Banbury*. I had rung Roy before the accident and he said he would be down in a couple of days to take the mould. My mother had booked him into the Imperial Hotel and after work he would have dinner with her. Later Roy told me how after the meal they would go to the bar and sip green Chartreuse and tell yarns. When he had finished he somehow got the mould in the trailer on his own and took it back to London.

Sitting in a car also didn't put weight on my hip so when I got a call from Roy telling me he had finished the sculpture I immediately set off to London to inspect it. One day while I had been lying flat on my back in hospital Margie had come in with a message from Roy saying something awful had happened when he was chipping out *Mr Banbury* from the plaster mould. Somehow or other he seemed to have knocked off a little finger from his left hand! He had been through all the rubbish twice and had not been able to find it. Would I be able to model a new little finger?

I think that caused my one moment of amusement in the hospital. I was able to tell Margie that she could tell Roy not to worry because there was not a problem. The finger wasn't in the rubbish because it didn't exist! He had lost it in a shooting accident many years previously. I arrived at the garage and found *Mr Banbury* looking absolutely magnificent, missing finger and all. We loaded him into Roy's station wagon and drove down to Fosbury in convoy for an

286

unveiling. Angela and Kit were delighted with the sculpture and with the aid of a couple of gardeners and a little tractor we moved *Mr Banbury* into the woods so he would stand guard over the graves of the gundogs for ever.

'Mr Banbury' the gamekeeper
standing guard at the gun dogs' cemetery

The following day Angela and Kit took the real Mr Banbury to see his statue and they told me that he had burst into tears and that his dogs had jumped up on the sculpture to have a good look. Gundogs are not meant to jump up, but there was apparently something about the sculpture that broke all the rules. It is probably the best compliment I have ever had!

Many stories in life have sad endings and Mr Banbury's statue is one of them. Aunt Angela died and Kit was lonely in the big house, so he decided to move and give it to one of her sons. One weekend Kit visited the house and in the evening walked up to see *Mr Banbury*, but found that he had disappeared. Thinking that it had been stolen he returned to the house to raise the alarm. His stepson then told him that they had not liked the sculpture so they had stored it in a shed. Kit was furious and immediately had it put into his car and drove away. He had decided to end his days by living in a small bungalow with his butler in a Yorkshire village near where he had been born. *Mr Banbury* was placed in the middle of the lawn and as far as I know he is still there.

On our first Christmas at Marwood we asked my old nanny, Nana, to come and stay so she could get to know our three boys. Obviously her caring for me for the first eight years of my life had played an enormous part in her life as a woman. To now laugh and play with my children must have made her feel like a grandmother. It was wonderful that this happened when it did as the following year she developed cancer and died soon afterwards. What a remarkable woman and what an amazing life she had led! She and her sister were born in a Glasgow slum and orphaned as children. She had looked after me and my two brothers, travelled to Australia during the war, and on her return become a matron at a preparatory school. She always had a smile on her face and never said an unkind word.

**'Nana' having Christmas at Marwood
with Margie, my mother and Peter**

The one thing I did a lot while in hospital was *think*. Firstly, lying on my back I gave thanks that I hadn't been crippled in the accident. I also now knew that all I wanted to do in life was to be a sculptor. I had had some success and had proved that I could earn my bread and butter as an artist. This was exceedingly lucky as the people who had bought the farm had gone bankrupt and I had found the farm back on my hands, worth half of its former value. None of that seemed to matter as I now had a wonderful life and a new income. Our main problem was that Jimmy wanted to sell Marwood Hill and we had to move. This was not a bad thing because it again forced us to face the problem of finding a suitable school for the boys. It also had become abundantly clear that North Devon was too far from London and my clients. We needed to move nearer the capital, the foundries and Roy.

The first thing was to find a school that would take the three boys. On my trips up and down to London I had often passed the gates of Hazlegrove Preparatory School, so I decided to call in and take a look. The school had a long drive up to it through a park that reminded me of my days at Sandroyd. The main building was a converted stately home, but when I met the headmaster, Paddy Heazell, I knew immediately that he was nothing like Sandroyd's Mr Ozane. Luckily he agreed to take three young Australians as day-boys, there being no beds available, which suited us. Over the following years Paddy and his wife, Julyan, became our very good friends.

The next thing was to find a house not too far away from the school, so I set about looking around the district. Margie had once seen a beautiful thatched house on our way up to London and had said, "Wouldn't it be fun to live in a house like that." I made enquiries in all the towns and villages around Hazlegrove. I found forty possibilities and set off for a three-day tour of inspection. On the first day I had found nothing that I liked and the following day I again drew a blank, so began to feel worried. Many of the houses didn't even look like the photographs in the brochures, while others were beside a main road or a railway track. Towards the end of the third day I still had found nothing and began to think I was on a Mission Impossible. The last house on my list before heading for home was in the village of Galhampton and had only just come onto the market the previous day.

I turned off the main road into Long Street and took a right into Middle Street and thought how mundane after all the quaint names in Devon. Middle Street did change to March Lane, which sounded a better! The address I had was for a thatched cottage behind a large green box hedge opposite a red telephone box. I found an open gate and drove in. I was so enchanted with what I saw I made up my mind to buy the house before I had stepped out of the car! The cottage was to the right and opposite was a barn. Could this be real I thought, it's all too perfect! What was it like inside?

Major Thurston greeted me and showed me around the house. I liked everything I saw, even down to the colour of the walls, which were all painted off-white. We wouldn't have to change a single thing. It was perfect.

"Could I see the barn please?" One end of the barn had been an old cider press and the other a pair of horseboxes. It had an upstairs floor that had been an apple store. It was incredible, even better than my barn at Marwood. We stepped outside and shook hands. He had a buyer and we had a home.

I think I probably floated all the way home as I couldn't wait to tell Margie all about Agecroft. I had told the Thurstons that I would bring my wife to see the house the next day but not to worry, I knew she would love it as much as I did. I assured him that we had a firm deal and nothing would change my mind about the purchase. I would telephone my lawyer in the morning and asked him to do the same straightaway. To hell with surveyors, if the house had just been refurbished, it must be all right.

I was right about Margie loving the house as much as I did. Agecroft had the same magic as our home on the farm in Australia, something that I have never found anywhere else in the world. It almost seemed that the house had been waiting for us and over the last 35 years it has become our best friend. Coming back to Agecroft from a trip is like crawling into a warm comfortable bed after a hard day's work.

When everything was signed and sealed and the Thurstons had gone, we brought the boys to Agecroft for a camping weekend to show them the house and introduce them to their new school. They were as excited as we were and couldn't wait for the big day, January 1st 1972. We had been at Marwood for three years and what wonderful years they had been! Now it was as though we were setting out on yet another journey, but in our own home and at the start of a new life. On top of all that I had a new gallery in Harrods. Could life get any better?

Agecroft on my first visit

The news of our purchase of Agecroft must have been a disappointment to Margie's parents, but their letters remained full of encouragement plus they had a plan. Would we all come out as their guests for a holiday at their new beach cottage called Araganui on the wild coast of NSW.

We arrived in Melbourne and drove straight down to Portsea. Pop Begg had hired a car for us so that we would be independent. The boys of course remembered Portsea from our summer holidays spent on the beach. It still amazes me that Margie and I had both grown up on the cliff only a few houses apart. We had become engaged here and walked Shelly Beach together. It was breathtaking to be back standing on the same sands again.

We had heard so much about Araganui in their letters we couldn't wait to see it. A long day's drive across Gippsland and through the Rain Forests got us there on time, but only to find that the dirt track through the wild bush was flooded and impassable. Margie's brother turned up in a jeep and we bumped through the bush to the bungalow that overlooked the beach. As the cottage only had two bedrooms and there were ten of us, Pop had hired a caravan for the overflow of children. So began an enchanted holiday and family reunion for us all Down Under.

'Araganui', Easter 1972
John – Tim – David – Andrew – Pop – Mitzi – Kate
Heido – Mark – Margie – Helen – Judy – Michael – Peter – Caroline

The sun shone and dried the track out, but the stream that usually just trickled across the beach was still in flood and had washed away tons of sand.

Peter – Kate – Mark – Caroline – Tim – Andrew
Young sculptors at work

In the morning we fed the goannas on fresh eggs and in the evening we played Charades. During the day the children played on the sand and as the sea was warm and the beach was covered with spume it provided the perfect material for mock battles between cousins. What a holiday!

Cousins fighting in the spume

All good things come to an end and I was dying to get back to my new studio at Agecroft. It was time to say goodbye to Margie's parents and Australia and start work on the *Leapfrog Children*. We all helped tidy up the cottage and then sent the cousins down to the beach to dig a very deep hole in the sand and bury the organic rubbish. They came back giggling and asked us to come down for the Burial Service.

Burial Service followed by Prayers

I never saw Pop or Helen again, but I remember them both as two of the kindest and most warm-hearted people I have ever had the privilege to know and I shall always be grateful for the way they supported my new career.

I had done a maquette of the *Leapfrog Children* in the attic of Marwood during the winter and was dying to enlarge it into a life-size sculpture. As soon as we were all settled back into Agecroft and the boys had returned to school after our Australian holiday, I started to build the armature for the sculpture. It was by far the hardest one that I had done, as it had to be assembled with mild steel rods and welded together. Thank goodness I had taken a course in welding all those years ago in Melbourne so was able to ask our village garage man if I could hire his electric welder for a couple of days and luckily found I still had the knack of using it. It wasn't very professional but was strong enough for the job. I attached the whole structure to the ceiling of my new studio although this would mean that I would have to stand on a box to sculpt the top figure. However, the jumping up and down would be very good for my still very skinny legs from the accident!

'Leapfrog Children' maquette

When the sculpture was ready Roy drove down to Agecroft for his first visit to our new home. I had warned him that the mould was going to be tricky so he should bring plenty of steel rods and plaster as the top child was only attached to the bottom one by her two wrists. He examined the clay sculpture and announced, as always, that he foresaw no problems! Thank goodness for Roy and his skill as a master-plasterer. Apart from being one of the nicest people I have ever met he was always a joy to work with.

293

When he had finished I collected the positive plasters and brought them back to Agecroft. I had developed a technique of working on the plasters with fine sandpaper before sending them to the foundry for casting. Before, when we were casting in resin bronze, the finished surface could only be as good as the surface of the original clay sculpture. Now I was able to have a second go at working on the surface before a rubber mould was taken for the lost-wax casting. It made a world of difference to the finish as I was able to get it as smooth as skin, which made it much more life-like.

I had found a new foundry in the Midlands and I decided to give them the job of casting the *Leapfrog Children*. The foundry was run by Lloyd Le Blanc and it turned out to be a good choice. He has continued to handle my children sculptures and has produced many wonderful bronzes.

'Leapfrog Children' life-size in Agecroft garden

I was thrilled with the sculpture and submitted it to the Royal Academy for their Summer Exhibition, which is a bore, as you have to take the sculpture physically to the Academy in Piccadilly for judging. However, once again Roy kindly gave me a hand with both the transport and carrying it into the building. Then came the month of waiting to see if it would be accepted or not. I had so enjoyed doing the interactive children sculpture I decided to start on another action pair straightaway. When I was working on the *Leapfrog* I thought of the children as a typical brother and sister at play. Siblings also occasionally war against each other so I did a maquette of a *Pillow Fight*, and decided that would be my next sculpture.

'Pillow Fight' maquette

I set to work again on an armature with the borrowed welder. This was going to be an even more ambitious one than the last. To get the action right I would have to do both figures at the same time and have the pillows in mid-air. By the time I had it finished the armature looked like a Heath Robinson contraption! I thought Roy would have a fit when he saw it, but of course when he came down he just hummed and hawed a bit and then made the usual announcement, "No problem."

Eventually the letter arrived from the Royal Academy. Had the *Leapfrog* been accepted or rejected? What a moment! Opening the letter set my nerves jumping. I read the letter with disbelief as the *Leapfrog Children* had been accepted and enclosed was a ticket for Varnishing Day. This day is so named because in the times of Turner and the like, the day before the Exhibition opened to the public, the artists were allowed to give their oil paintings a last touch of varnish.

With great excitement I went along to the Royal Academy with my duster to give the sculpture a final polish and see where it had been placed. I arrived feeling extremely nervous and climbed up the grand staircase to the galleries on the second floor. How would the *Leapfrog* look with all the other sculpture exhibits and would it seem terribly amateurish? At the head of the grand stairway there is a large foyer from which you can go left into a painting gallery, right into the shop, or straight ahead into a circular room, which also has exits to the left and right into other galleries. The circular gallery is probably the best place to have an exhibit so I was bowled over when I saw the *Leapfrog Children* straight ahead in a prime position.

The Opening Day is for Members only but the artists are invited and allowed to bring a guest. Margie and I trooped along to mingle with the great and famous. I had not told Margie where the sculpture was placed so she could enjoy the surprise of seeing it in such a prime position.

When visiting a gallery like the Louvre or Tate we have always played the game of choosing one sculpture and one painting that we would like to take home. Unashamedly we both decided that we would take the *Leapfrog Children*, as they really did look well and the Committee had been very kind to me.

'Pillow Fight' on my mother's roof garden

296

When the *Pillow Fight* was finished, Lloyd brought it to London and together we erected it on my mother's garden roof in Cadogan Square so I could show Joanna Harding, as it was a bit big for the Harrods Gallery. If a client was interested in the photograph she would be able to bring them around to the flat which was only just round the corner.

Fortunately the public liked the *Leapfrog Children* and the Summer Exhibition brought me many commissions. It also led directly to Damon de Laszlo getting in touch with me and asking if I would be able to visit him to discuss my sculpting his three children, Lucy, Robert and William.

I consider myself to be one of the luckiest men alive, not only because I am fortunate enough to live the life of an artist and enjoy the freedom that it brings, but because I have two Patrons who are also my closest friends. One of these friends is Damon de Laszlo.

I first met him when he had an office in Montague Square. I was really excited as it was the first time that I had ever been approached by the father and not the mother of the children. I felt something special was about to happen and I wasn't wrong. Damon met me at the door, introduced himself and then led me through to his sitting room. He asked me if I would like a cup of coffee and we sat down in comfortable armchairs and started to talk. The coffee arrived and I was introduced to Chris, Damon's secretary. Little did I know at that moment how great a part Damon would come to play in my life and what friends he and Chris would become over the following years.

Damon showed me some paintings by his grandfather, the famous portrait painter, Philip de Laszlo. This was my first introduction to the incredible works of this painter and, looking at them, I knew that I was going to have to do the best I could with his great-grandchildren if I got the commission. The outcome of our conversation was positive and Damon said he would like me to sculpt his eight-year-old daughter Lucy, and his son Robert, nearly seven, and young William just five. He asked Margie and me to come and meet the children and their mother at his country house in Hampshire so we could take the photographs and measurements.

I can't remember when Damon told me his grandfather's story, but here is probably as good a time to record what I have since learnt about this remarkable man, who in his day was recognised as being one of Europe's leading portrait painters. From a very humble beginning Philip went on to paint many of the Crowned Heads and their Consorts. His fame spread and during his lifetime he painted four American Presidents.

Philip was born in Hungary and from childhood he had loved to draw and because of his skill he was awarded a place at the Budapest Art Academy. When he moved away from home to earn enough money to keep himself he began teaching foreign students as they made the Grand Tour of Europe.

It so happened that two young Irish girls arrived in Budapest and decided to take a painting course. The young man they chose to teach them was Philip. One of the girls was Lucy Guinness. Well, of course the student and teacher fell in love and on returning home she told her parents that she wished to marry a poor Hungarian artist, which did not go down very well with her father! His answer was an emphatic "No!" In those days children did what their parents told them to do so no doubt Lucy must have been broken-hearted. However, she and Philip stayed in touch and he worked hard at his profession until his natural talent made him famous. Philip became well known in Budapest, but soon his fame spread across Europe to England and he became the painter of the hour.

To soften the blow of his outright refusal to the marriage, Lucy's father had added one condition. If Philip became successful and could support her in the manner to which she was accustomed, he would agree to the marriage. The King of Hungary rewarded Philip with a title in appreciation of his artistic skill and father Guinness gave his consent to the marriage. In Damon's house there is a black and white photograph of the wedding group at the ceremony in which Philip is wearing his full Hungarian Court dress of cloak, sword and a hat sporting long peacock feathers in it. The seven-year courtship ended and a blissful marriage began. Several sons were born, one of whom was named Patrick, Damon's father.

Damon inherited Patrick's elegant chambers in Piccadilly that had once been occupied by Lord Byron, and very kindly allows us to use the bedroom when we are in London. The sitting room is hung with Philip de Laszlo's paintings, one of which is a wonderful self-portrait.

Philip de Laszlo

298

'Le Corsair'

While all this was happening I had started another large figure to match the *Acrobats* and the *Hammer Thrower*. The sculpture was based on the famous Russian dancer, Rudolf Nureyev, partner of Margot Fonteyn. Margie and I had seen them dance together in Melbourne the night before Peter had been born, and I wanted to try and capture the incredible performance we had seen. Again the armature would have to be attached to the ceiling, as I wanted the dancer to be supported only on his left toes.

While I was working on *Le Corsair* the telephone rang and a very broad Australian voice asked, "Is this John Robinson? Are you the artist that shows work in Harrods? I like your *Acrobats*, but I am not buying them from Harrods. Give me a good price." *My God*, I thought, *it is another Fred Kobler!*

The voice belonged to a man called Lindsay Fox and the explanation he gave for calling turned out to be the beginning of an amazing story and one of the greatest adventures of our lives. Lindsay had been in Harrods that afternoon with his friend, Chris Hemmeter. They had been looking for old furniture and had stumbled across the fine arts gallery. They had seen some of my bronze children and at the same time had looked through the catalogue of other works and seen the *Acrobats*, and the prices. They had really liked the sculpture but thought the price was ridiculous, but as Harrods doubled my price he wasn't wrong about that. For fun, over a drink before dinner, the two men had tried and found my telephone number and decided to give me a call.

When we had moved to Agecroft I had rung British Telecom and asked to have my name and profession added to the local book. The operator had agreed to do this and then asked if I would also like my name included in the London book. I thought, *Why not!* Lindsay had picked up the book and found a whole page of John Robinson but only one had sculptor after his name. I silently blessed the BT operator for making the suggestion.

"The very best price I can do is half of the Harrods price." "Done," he said. "Give me your address and you will receive a letter of confirmation in about two weeks when Chris returns to Hawaii." Hawaii not Australia! I was becoming more and more bewildered and wondered if I would receive the promised letter or was this just a hoax. I do have a friend in Sydney called Philip Gibson who plays those kinds of pranks. I once had a call from him pretending to be an Arabian Sultan wanting a sculpture!

I returned to *Le Corsair* to keep me from thinking about the *Acrobats*. It was soon finished and Roy came down to take the mould. How we were going to keep the sculpture from falling over was quite beyond me, but Roy said he would insert a steel shaft in his leg and out through his foot down into a heavy concrete plinth to act as a counterweight. It worked!

'Le Corsair'

One day a very smart looking envelope arrived from Hawaii heavily embossed with the words Hemmeter Center. With a great amount of trembling I opened it and took out a letter ordering the *Acrobats* and a cheque! I was completely overcome, as now the *Acrobats* could be cast in real bronze. I don't think I have ever been so excited. It was all way beyond my wildest dreams.

Such a large job could only be done by a really big foundry. I had already visited Morris Singer Foundry, famous for doing large pieces by Henry Moore. The foundry was on the road to London so I had called in to get a casting cost for the *Acrobats* on the off chance of a Harrods sale. It had been quite an experience to see Moore's sculptures being worked on in the enormous sand-casting workshop when the manager, Dave Vallance, showed me around. Having received the order I rang Dave and asked him to come and inspect Roy's cold-bronze edition I had set up in the Agecroft garden. Dave confirmed the price he had given me from the photograph and sent a truck to collect the *Acrobats* the following day. Watching them leave was like waving goodbye to old friends setting off on a voyage around the world.

Agecroft

When we arrived at Agecroft in 1972, the first thing we did was to plant some trees in the old apple orchard. The property was about two acres, one of orchard to the west and one of garden around the house and studio to the east. The thatched cottage runs along the road but was protected from it by a box hedge. The house used to be the village bakery and the bow window in the sitting room was the shop front for displaying the loaves. Previous owners had closed off the shop door and replaced it with a front door in from the garden on the opposite side away from the road.

The orchard was fenced off from the garden and used for grazing cows. The apple trees were old so we decided to plant some new specimen trees amongst them and create an arboretum and ban the cows. We went to a garden centre and met Mr Kean, a truly remarkable old man. When he came to see us we staked out positions for the many trees he advised us to plant. Several weeks after his first visit, when he considered the ground was warm enough, he returned with two workmen and the planting began. All the trees grew, except out of the 40 eucalyptus trees we planted only one survives today, a snow gum! One day in Sydney I could not resist buying two toy koalas to climb in it during the summer. They are very happy and have had a baby!

Our one surviving gum tree and wildlife

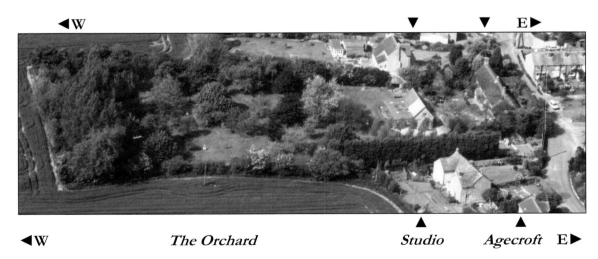

◄W   *The Orchard*   *Studio*   *Agecroft*   E►

Peter told us that all he wanted for his tenth birthday was a puppy in a box. Margie found a Border collie Springer spaniel cross and gave her to him in a cardboard box, as requested. She paid the grand sum of £1 for Lassie. It was the best pound we have ever spent as she turned into a marvellous companion, loved by all for 16 years.

Peter and Lassie

Lassie grew into the most intelligent dog I have ever come across as she could not only open the back door, using her paw to push down the lever handle, she would also close it on command by standing on her hind legs to push it shut! When we went camping she would happily come along and sleep in the boys' tent. She loved travelling in the car so came on trips to London and once we even took her to Ireland. When she died we were all heartbroken.

We had the 12 giant 100-foot high elms that grew along our western border felled as they had the dreaded Dutch virus. We were very upset about this, but Mr Kean said that we should do it as there was no way of saving them. He was right and within five years millions of elms had died and needed to be felled, changing the English countryside for ever. The removal of our trees made the orchard even barer, so planting our seven-foot high saplings turned out to be a blessing.

For the summer holidays we invested in two tents as we planned to introduce the boys to camping. We put them up in the orchard to try them out for a night. It was a great success and later led to many happy camping trips into Wales and Scotland. The tall tree between the tents in the photograph below is an elm and the year after we camped on this spot it came crashing down during a storm right where the tents had been!

Camping in the "Agecroft' orchard 1973

Lassie

Over the last 35 years we have had the enormous pleasure of watching our trees grow from saplings to monsters so that now we have a forest. The poplars that we planted to replace the felled elms, are now 100 foot tall.

Actually, I think they might be even taller than that, but I might be accused of exaggerating if I said so. Unfortunately the Electricity Board has told us that they are so tall they are a danger to the power line that passes nearby and have to come down!

When we arrived Margie planted acorns for each of the boys and these have already become 25-foot high trees. Unfortunately over the last 35 years the American Grey squirrel has driven the English Red ones almost to extinction. However, the grey squirrels hide acorns in the ground for the winter so we have several free young oaks and even a walnut tree. Margie has planted climbing roses in the old apple trees making a stroll in the orchard on a summer evening a delight as the blooms cascade down in their hundreds.

Agecroft garden

To begin with I used to mow the whole area so the boys would have a football ground. They also used it for their engine-driven go-kart I built from a kit. Racing around the lawns trying to avoid being hit by apples that are thrown by one's brothers was a good way to learn how to drive a car. When the need for acres of lawn has gone and we are travelling a lot I allowed the wilderness to return under the trees to encourage the birds. We mowed a network of paths though the jungle so we could still enjoy walking the orchard.

The bird life includes a resident buzzard, woodpeckers, flycatchers, blackbird and a robin who feeds from Margie's hand. The orchard has become an animals' haven as well as an arboretum of specimen trees. Walking beneath the canopy in the summer it is hard to believe that all the growth has happened in so short a time. England is a very green and pleasant land if you can escape from the traffic noise and cities.

Several of the wilderness areas have reverted into large stinging nettle beds that we explain away to tidy gardeners as designated butterfly areas. I had been told that Red Admirals bred on nettles although I had never seen any in our wilderness, as they seem to prefer feeding around the house on Margie's buddleia. I decided to rectify this situation and purchased ten caterpillars that were guaranteed to turn into Red Admirals. I fed them on nettles in a special cage where they soon changed into chrysalises. Eventually one beautiful Red Admiral hatched and with great excitement I took it up to the back of the orchard so I could release it in the middle of the largest patch of nettles.

I gingerly opened the netted cage and the beautiful creature walked out onto my hand and did some wing exercises, but refused to fly. Getting impatient I made an upward flip of my hand, which forced it to take off.

SNAP. I couldn't believe my eyes when I saw the four beautiful wings flutter to the ground. The poor thing had only flown about a foot when a flycatcher grabbed him and zipped away to feed it to one of her babies. None of the other chrysalises hatched so I didn't have to worry about other butterflies surviving in the big cruel world. Lesson – never interfere with nature!

Our flycatchers are so precious I couldn't be cross. Every year we wait for the tiny birds to arrive from Africa, which they usually obligingly do around May 4th for my birthday. To think that they have come all the way from the Sahara and have returned to nest within a couple of feet of where they were hatched is truly amazing. Our pair have two broods every year, always building a new nest for the second family on the opposite side of the house!

While the trees were growing I was sculpting. Every morning of the first 20 years of our life at Agecroft I used to walk across to the studio and sculpt. Lunch was a fast-food affair around one o'clock and then I would work through to a good stopping place, which sometimes meant not shutting up shop until nine in the evening. I would often come in cold and tired and find the boys ready for bed. Thankfully Margie understood about the need for me to press on when things were going well and kept my dinner hot waiting while I had a hot bath.

'Fred'

306

Fred is now a grown man and lives in Seattle with his wife and children. The *Squirrel Children* were two of Mr Taylor's grandchildren and were commissioned by his wife to place over her husband's grave in the cemetery of a beautiful old Somerset Church at Cricket St Thomas, famous as the setting of the TV programme called *To the Manor Born*. The *Squirrel Children* were so popular at the Safari Park John Taylor purchased several bronze children.

'Squirrel Children'

'Jigsaw Puzzle'

The *Jigsaw Puzzle* boy's name was Kerr and he came from America wearing OshKosh dungarees. Kerr was one of the bronzes bought by John Taylor. I welded the last piece of the puzzle into his right hand but it didn't stop people taking it for a souvenir. The problem was solved when a souvenir hunter decided to take the whole sculpture instead of the puzzle piece!

'Girl with Puppy'

Nearly all of the 100 or so children that I sculpted were original commissions. The child's parent had Number One of the edition and I had the right to sell a further eight, making a total of nine. Of course I didn't sell the full edition of all the children, but by the time I gave up my figurative work there must have been children all over the world! The *Girl with Puppy* was one of several bronzes that ended up in a Disneyland hotel in Orlando. She was the first who had an Elastoplast on her knee, but after that I put one on all the children's knees and it became a trademark.

'Flute Player II'

Margie and I were asked to fly over to Florida and see the sculptures as there was talk of building another hotel and buying more bronzes. The hotel never happened but we did have a marvellous trip, and visiting Epcot was an incredible experience, as was eating alligator, which tasted a lot better than crocodile had in Kimberley way back in 1955!

The *Flute Player* was the daughter of the couple who bought Marwood Hill House from Jimmy Smart after we had moved to Agecroft. I wish we had kept a copy, but the edition sold out within a year.

'Genevieve'

Genevieve is the granddaughter of Geo and Pam who live in Geneva. I did a head of Genevieve and a life-size sleeping child for their garden. She was their first grandchild and is now nearly 20 years old. She also sleeps in the Agecroft garden giving us enormous pleasure.

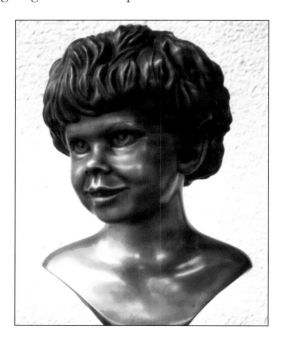

'James'

'Umbrella Children'

311

The *Umbrella Children* began with my finding a photograph in which my father was spraying water from a hose over my elder brothers, Pat and Michael, as they sheltered under an umbrella. I thought it was a charming idea and would make a great fountain. I sculpted a couple of new children and used Mark again as the aggressor with the hose. When we put the whole thing together it worked well, the water dripped off in all the right places. It was fun and makes people laugh.

One day I had a call from an Irish surgeon asking if we could meet in London as they were looking for a fountain to go in a clinic he was building in Dublin. I met him at my mother's flat and showed him a photograph of the *Umbrella Children*. He said it was just what he wanted and immediately bought them without even seeing the bronzes.

During the Irish Troubles one of the punishments the IRA would inflict was to shoot off their victim's kneecap. This had so appalled the surgeon that he went back to university to study engineering and then applied the knowledge to inventing a mechanical knee that became so successful he decided to build the Black Rock Clinic in Dublin. The clinic was built around an atrium with a pond in the middle and it was here that he decided he needed a fountain.

Some time after the clinic was finished and the sculptures installed, Margie and I made a trip to Ireland to deliver a bronze and went to see what the fountain looked like. A café reception area for the patients was on one side of the pond and the consulting rooms were across on the far side. The surgeon said that it all worked very well as by the time a patient had drunk a cup of coffee and listened to the fountain there was never any trouble in obtaining a urine specimen!

'Roller Skaters'

The *Roller Skaters* was a private commission for a charming Dutch family who lived in a suburb of Rotterdam. The house was on a bend in the road and they told me that it became known as Roller Skater corner.

Some parents would know the position they would like, usually because they had seen one of my other sculptures. This became a problem as it meant that I did the same sculpture time and time again with only the size, sex and face being difference. I soon learnt that it paid to suggest a visit to the site chosen for the sculpture and a meeting with the children, as this left me free to suggest poses that I wished to do, but which also suited the landscape.

Taking photographs of children in Sussex before sculpting them

Finished bronzes on show at Crowthers of Syon Lodge

I would talk to the parents and quickly learn what their interests were, and then suggest a pose for the sculpture. I have always tried to make my children sculptures active as it makes the subject come alive. The action creates a story, and we all love stories. One of the fun commissions was to create a water fight in a ravine that the parents had built in their garden. Getting the water pressure exactly right so that it hit the boy's shield was a real challenge.

'Boys playing in a ravine'

There are as many positions as there are children. Varying the positions kept my job challenging, like standing a boy on a stool to feed parrots!

Occasionally I would be asked to sculpt only the head, which I enjoyed doing but found it a time-consuming and non-commercial exercise.

'Jill'

315

In trying to work out when it was that I began to see the limitations of only doing figurative sculpture, I keep thinking about Watts Towers. I had read about them in *Time* so when passing through Los Angeles on our way to Hawaii to see the *Acrobats*, I grabbed the moment and a cab and asked the driver to take us out to see them, and wait, it being a problematical area.

Watts Towers

Simon Rodia built the three towers single-handedly between 1921 and 1955. One of the towers has the longest concrete column in the world, standing 90 foot high. Truly they are a tour de force. Rodia used scrap metal, broken pottery and bottle bottoms, just like Dorothy's Bottle Cottage!

I am sure that seeing the Watts Towers challenged me to do my own unique thing and sowed the seed that eventually germinated and grew into my Symbolic Sculptures. If Simon Rodia could do it, so could I.

316

One day I received a call from a woman asking me if I would be able to sculpt her son and how much it would cost. As the price I quoted seemed to be acceptable I suggested that she and her husband visit us at Agecroft with the boy. The appointed day arrived and a big silver Mercedes drove into our courtyard. Erica, her husband John and two children got out, a boy of four and a little girl of two.

Erica was a very attractive young woman, and she soon told us that she had been a leading model in London before marrying and had also acted in several minor films. She did indeed move with the grace of a model. After showing them around the garden, looking at children bronzes on the way, we sat down to one of Margie's special studio lunches and started to talk about the possible sculpture.

Imagine my surprise when Erica announced that actually John wanted a sculpture of her and the two children. *Fine*, I thought, looking at Erica, *I would love to try and capture her face.*

They told us that they had bought a large Victorian mansion in the Midlands and were creating a garden for the house. They had purchased a classical water feature for the centre of the lawn to match the Roman Temple they had already built against a backdrop of old beech trees. They would like me to visit the garden and suggest poses for the three sculptures.

My son Peter had started sculpting in the studio at about this time so I suggested that he should come with me. We fixed a date and drove north armed with a camera, tape measure, pencil and paper, and our clubs because I was going through a golf phase. Our appointment was not until after lunch so I thought Peter and I could steal time for a few holes beforehand, as I had noticed on the map there was a course near the house.

As we unpacked our clubs from the back of the car a pucker English colonel-type walked past and said, "Players are not allowed to wear blue jeans!" Peter was wearing jeans so we had to buy a pair of trousers in the pro-shop before hitting off. Peter tells me that he still wears the trousers, so it was worth buying them, but I am still laughing at the snobbery.

I have never been able to master the driver or cure my slice. I allow for this by aiming to the left of the fairway knowing my ball will land on the right. I hit off and watched the ball swing away in its usual arc before hearing an almighty crash. I walked off to see what I had hit, cursing because it probably meant I had lost the ball. We arrived at a tractor to find the driver sitting on the front wheel rolling a cigarette and looking rather white. "Seen a ball?" I asked. He pointed at the shattered windscreen of his cabin. "First time that has happened," he said, holding up a golf ball. I apologised, hurried away and after playing a couple more holes went to a pub for lunch!

After lunch we found the house and it was as enormous as Erica had warned. In its heyday it must have been amazing, but now it was a rundown Victorian mansion and gone were the dreams of grandeur. If Erica and John planned to return it to its past glory, they had a gigantic task ahead of them.

They had started by walling in a vast area of lawn in front of the house. Right in the middle of this expanse was a rectangular stone pond. Erica had decided that she should be sitting on the back wall of the billiard-table sized pool, so I suggested that her son could be fishing on one side, and the little girl standing beside her mother. Having agreed on a plan we were led into the dead house, past workmen fixing a leaking roof, and followed Erica into an immense room that had been the library to take the photographs.

I had brought a large sheet of brown paper that I put down on the floor in order to pencil round Erica when she took up her pose. When everything was ready I asked her to do just that and in a flash off came all her clothes! I took a quick look at Peter and then started to fiddle with the camera. Erica's body matched her face. She was a very well put together young lady. Having regained our composure, as they say in the novels, we began discussing the position of the legs, arms and angle of the head. Being an ex-model and having no sense of shyness, she soon found a pose she felt comfortable with and we went to work.

I took the job of using the tape and Peter had to put up with jotting down the measurements! One of the most important measurements for a female nude is of course the separation. Get that wrong and you are really in trouble! As I stretched the tape between Erica's nipples I could not but help think of a wonderful cartoon by Peter Arno from the *New Yorker* magazine. When I was a boy my parents subscribed to the magazine each month just to see their favourite cartoonist.

Have you tried an oculist?

Outlining the body onto the paper was intoxicating and then I took far too many photographs, as I couldn't see there being a repeat performance. As you can imagine Peter and I had plenty to talk about on the way home!

I worked away at the three clay figures and pretty soon was ready for the first sitting. Erica arrived and I spent the morning working on the children. After lunch they were put down for a rest in the house with Margie while Erica and I went back to the studio. Off came all the clothes again and I set to work. She really did have a very good figure! It is surprising how detached one becomes when working with a live nude. The eyes and hands work together concentrating on the edge of the model, going round and round, while slowly the clay figure takes shape.

'Erica' taking shape!

A final visit was arranged when I had gone as far as possible without another live sitting. Erica and John arrived to inspect the children who were finished and they approved what I had done, but Erica thought I needed to do some more work done on her as she wasn't satisfied with her bosom!

The husband sat reading the paper while we worked. Suddenly she said, "Would it help if you felt?" A very loud, "Erica, that will do," came from behind the paper. Erica winked at me and we continued to work as before!

'Erica and the Children' in place

The sculptures turned out pretty well and when I set them up on the water's edge, everyone was pleased. So ended my only live female nude modelling class! It had been an enlightening experience and I really got to know Erica and liked her immensely. The story of her life that unfolded as I worked was fascinating. I often wonder what has happened to all the children I have sculpted, but most of all I wonder what happened to Erica. She was a really nice girl.

Margie and I have met some incredibly kind people and had many fantastic adventures with them. I would go and take photographs and measurements of children all over the world and then do the sculptures at home. Sometimes the child would not be able to come to the final sitting, so I would have to take the head to them. I remember one child with great affection, as she was one of the sparkiest little girls I have ever met. I took the photographs of Lilly in Florida, sculpted her in England, had the final sitting in Toronto and shipped the sculpture back to Florida.

There was no way the whole of the clay sculpture could go over to Toronto for the final sitting so I only took her head. I found that the best way to transport heads was in Pop Begg's top-hat case! I don't know how I came into possession of the case but it was just the thing for carrying the clay head through Customs and on to the aeroplane. I should have taken a photograph of the officer's faces at Toronto Airport because it was a treat to watch them when they opened the lid, and tasted the clay!

Lilly in Florida and finished in bronze

Lilly insisted on helping me sculpt her own head. It was a joy to watch the little fingers and her utter concentration. She now drives a car!

Lilly helped to sculpt her head

Another wonderful commission was for my old friend, Michael Ball, who had bought a sheep station near Bowral. The property is on the road from Sydney to Canberra and situated in beautiful gum country. Michael has had an eventful life, ending up with four sons by two wives. He asked me if I would sculpt his two youngest boys, and their dog. Tim I did climbing a tree while Nick chased after the King Charles spaniel.

Michael then asked me to sculpt his two older sons and his horse! I had never really been interested in sculpting animals, but the challenge of a horse was too much to resist. I asked the foundry if I could sculpt the horse in one of their studios and asked a young friend of mine called Willie Newton to help me. I had met Willie when Julyan, the Hazlegrove headmaster's wife, asked me to give sculpting lessons to his art class.

At the time Willie had two ambitions in life, one was to become a jockey and the other was to sculpt horses. He was very successful as a jockey but eventually gave up riding to become an even more successful sculptor. Michael had taken some photographs of his horse and when I showed them to Willie he took me to see a similar horse to take correct measurements.

We then set about making the horse out of foam on a steel armature, and when we had the basic shape right, we gave the foam a coat of chestnut plasticine. I couldn't have done the job without Willie's help. I was getting pretty good at human anatomy, but horses were a whole new world.

Michael's stock horse in plasticine

I finished Michael's two older boys and Roy came to take the moulds at Agecroft. One of Michael's boys was called Joshua, and as he was working at the time as a cowboy, I decided he should sit beside the horse on a real fence.

On my last visit to check the sculpture at the foundry I shaped the horse's tail as a ladder so children could climb up on its back. When I had finished the tail I left Willie to clear up the foundry and headed for home. I was really very satisfied with our joint efforts and thought that Michael would be pleased.

Joshua and the Stock Horse

As I was quietly driving home thinking about the next project I came upon two tractors going the other way. Because they were travelling very slowly a queue of cars had built up behind them and unfortunately the last car was exactly on a blind corner. As I came level with the end of the queue a small car shot round the corner and the driver, seeing a blocked road in front, swung right and drove straight into the front of my car. The joint impact must have been well over 100 mph so the small car hurtled right over my bonnet and roof with a horrendous noise. There was no time to think of anything except that I was going to die!

My car came to a standstill and I was still alive. I couldn't believe that I had survived such a fearful head-on crash. I had swung to the left immediately I saw what was going to happen and watched the accident as though it was in a slow-motion movie. When my car stopped I looked over my shoulder at the other car and was just in time to see it land on its roof and then bounce back onto its wheels!

Surrounded by a mess of junk from the glove box I sat there silently thanking the inventor of seat belts. An ambulance arrived and I walked over to it, thanking God I was in no pain and wouldn't have to spend another six weeks in traction. The other driver was a girl and talking, so was obviously all right as well. We arrived at the hospital and I was taken into Outpatients. By now I had recovered from the shock and when the sister told me, "All you need is a brandy." I said, "Yes please, I would love one." "Not here, when you get home," was her answer. So much for the sympathetic National Health Service!

I rang the foundry and asked if Willie had left. Luckily he hadn't so was able to collect me and drive me to Agecroft, where I did have a brandy. Now, when I look at the photograph of the finished horse, I think it could very easily have been my last sculpture. I could have been killed or ever worse crippled, which was a terrifying thought as Margie and I had just seen a play in London called, *Whose life is it anyway?* in which a young sculptor had lost both his hands!

The following year Margie and I were able to go and see Michael and I must say I thought the sculptures looked very original. On arriving at the property we found that since our previous visit the front gate had been moved. This was a pity as originally the house had been approached down a lovely avenue of mature silver poplar trees. The gate had been moved because the Highway Authorities had decided to upgrade the main road by raising it 20 foot. Michael was very upset about this as he was left with a beautiful avenue that ended with a colossal embankment.

While I was listening to Michael's tale of woe my mind started to think about another problem I had concerning an enormous Carrara marble sculpture sitting in Italy. On one of our trips my interpreter, Pam Launari, asked me if I could come with her and look at a sculpture belonging to one of her students as she wished to sell it and needed advice. Pam was my right arm when it came to checking up on the Italians at the Mariani Foundry in Pietrasanta, but earned her living by giving English lessons. Her student had told her that the sculpture was a Rodin, which was doubtful, but I agreed to have a look to please Pam.

The Chini 'Danaide' by Rodin

We arrived at the house and were taken into the sitting room by a middle-aged woman. As soon as I saw the sculpture I exclaimed, because it definitely was by Rodin and called the *Danaide*. We had seen an edition of the sculpture in the Musée Rodin in Paris. I examined the sculpture and found it to be a signed plaster cast that had been painted to look like terracotta.

We sat down to listen to the extraordinary story behind the sculpture. The woman's grandfather, Galileo Chini, had been born in Florence in 1873 and made his living as an avant-garde potter and painter. In 1901 one of his vases had won the *Grand Prix della Ceramica* in the Brussels Exhibition and he had gone there to accept the award. On the journey he had passed through Paris, called on Rodin, and done a pen and ink drawing of the famous man.

'Rodin' by Chini, 1901

In return Rodin gave him a plaster of the *Danaide* that Chini took back to Florence where, as a potter would, he coloured it with oil paint to look like terracotta. Rodin's method of working often involved experimenting with the original clay on different bases. Obviously the plaster cast he gave Chini must have been one of these experiments that he had rejected. Rodin was 43 when he worked on the *Danaide* and he used his mistress, Camille Claudel, as the model. She was 33 at the time and also a sculptress.

We took the sculpture outside and photographed it from several angles. The woman then asked me if it would be possible to sell it for her as one of her sons wanted to buy a bookshop and the other to rent a strip of beach and hire out umbrellas to the summer tourists. I pointed out that she would not get very much for the one plaster and suggested that instead, because the family owned the copyright and it was unique, she should have a mould taken and an edition of eight cast in bronze. In this way she would be able to keep her grandfather's original, give copies to her sons, and make much more money. I offered to ask my friends if they would be interested in buying an edition of the bronze before she did anything. To cut a long story short I managed to place several editions for her, so I presume the bookshop was bought and the beach rented.

Damon de Laszlo took an edition and then asked me if I could arrange to have a copy carved out of marble one and a half times life-size as he wanted a fountain for his garden in Hampshire. When the carving was finished we flew down to Pietrasanta to inspect it. I shall never forget his words when they unwrapped the white Carrara figure for us, "It's too big!" I reeled back saying, "No, this is the size you ordered." His reply was, "No, I mean it is too big for the pond in my garden. I need a smaller one." "What are we going to do with this one?" I asked. Damon said, "Sell it. Can you find a buyer?"

So here I was walking down Michael's Australian avenue that went nowhere but which was the perfect site for a copy of a large white sculpture by Rodin. I explained about the *Danaide* to Michael and luckily he thought it sounded a wonderful idea. Soon the marble was on a ship bound for Australia and it now looks incredible in its new surroundings with the 20-foot high bank behind it planted with daffodils. It has become a landmark for the truckers as they drive down to Sydney from Canberra, because from their high cabins they can look down on the backside of a beautiful naked woman!

Michael's 'Danaide', one and a half times life-size

The last sculpture I made for Michael was a boot puller. He said I could do anything I liked, so I did. The heel of a boot fits in the last curve of the goanna's tail as he tries to reach the frog on the handle!

Goanna and frog boot puller

Having survived the crash I continued to sculpt for the rest of the Seventies and would moan and groan when it was necessary to take time off once a month to handle the necessary office paper work.

During the school holidays I was able to stop work and organise adventures for the boys so it was not all work and no play. We took the boys to Scotland, camping in the Lake District on the way. We climbed over the Welsh mountains and rode terrible horses up the Brecon Beacons. In the summer we played family tennis and croquet on the lawn at Agecroft and in the spring took the boys by car to Venice and Florence via Paris. In the winter holidays we introduced them to skiing in Switzerland and in the autumn made trips to London and the theatre. They were very happy, carefree days.

One of the holidays in Scotland with the boys led me back to Kincardine Castle. It was here that I again met the sister of my mother's closest friend, Nané Brennen, the woman who had organised my first ever exhibition in Seattle. She wanted to present a trophy to the Canadian Shorthorn Society in Toronto. The idea was that I should visit hers friends who farmed near Edinburgh, take photographs of their best Shorthorn bull and sculpt it. When we arrived at the farm I was shown two bulls; one apparently had a superb front half while the other had a better rump. I personally couldn't see the difference, but dutifully took photographs of both animals, promising to join the two good halves together in a one-foot long bronze.

I sculpted the creature in red wax as Enzo had taught me which enabled me to give the surface plenty of texture. When I had finished it we went up to Scotland to show the wax to the farmers and as they approved how the front of one bull had been successfully added to the backside of the other, I gave it to the Meridian Foundry to cast.

On the way back from Scotland we decided to go and have a look at Hadrian's Wall, which we had heard about all our lives but never seen. Living in a 500-year-old house had made us very aware of English history, besides which we could see Camelot from our orchard and often walked around the earthworks of the Iron Age fort that the Romans had occupied during Hadrian's time. From Camelot you can see across to Avalon and the Mendip Hills where the Romans had vineyards and shipped the wine back to Rome.

Romans re-occupy Hadrian's Wall

328

We arrived at the Wall on a cold bleak day, climbed up through the remains of the soldiers' barracks and nearly dropped dead as walking towards us was a Roman Centurion talking to a Senator. Thank goodness I had my camera and could take a photograph. They were well wrapped up in furs and as we approached we saw that they were fortifying themselves from what looked suspiciously like a small bottle of whisky!

When I reported that the Bull had passed inspection and I had taken it to the foundry for casting, Nané ordered an edition of six, four of which she wanted for herself, giving me two to sell. I had no idea where I would be able to place my two copies but thank goodness I did take them as one was sold through Malletts in Berkley Square, which opened an amazing door to another adventure and a friendship that reached from New York to Miami. The other was bought by friends in our village so I often see it, which brings back many happy memories.

The 'Canadian Shorthorn' trophy for Best Bull

Nané asked me to take two editions of the sculpture over to Toronto and give them to the President of the Canadian Shorthorn Society, one for him and one for the Society. I did this and took the opportunity to visit Fred and Marg Helson as they had purchased a child sculpture and were thinking of buying another so had kindly asked me to stay. As it turned out they lived only a few miles from the cattle breeder and knew him well. They very kindly suggested that I couldn't go home without seeing Niagara Falls. I was thrilled about this as of course I had seen photographs of the famous scene and read all about people going over the Falls in a barrel.

This all took place in February when the countryside was covered in snow a foot deep and the temperature was well below freezing. The edges of the pavements in Toronto were piled with three-foot high walls of frozen snow and the gutters were full of slush. As we drove down to Niagara through a snowstorm in a well-heated car, I could not help but admire Fred's driving skill as the roads looked lethal to me. Being totally out of season we were able to park right beside the viewing terrace, which meant only a ten-yard walk to the rail and the 167-foot drop.

Niagara Falls

The mist rising from way below us was like dry ice. Within seconds my ears were frozen solid and, by the time Fred had taken the mandatory photograph, the rest of my body was as well. The noise of the water cascading over the edge of the cliff only feet from where we were standing made speech impossible. I had a movie camera and tried to capture the scene between shivers so I could share the experience with Margie. I have never seen anything so awesome in my life and could feel the force of nature tearing at me as I stood by the edge of the Falls.

The reason that some of my bronze maquettes were being shown in Malletts was due to my childhood friend Belinda, the girl who had allowed me to photograph the *Hammer Thrower* in front of her house. Belinda had shown her collection of maquettes to one of the Directors of Malletts and he kindly agreed to my leaving a few dotted around on his incredibly expensive furniture. One of the sculptures I left with him was the *Shorthorn Bull*.

One day a young American couple went into Malletts to buy furniture for their apartment in New York and the *Bull* caught the husband's eye as he thought it would look good on his desk on their horse farm in Florida. He bought it and asked Malletts for my name, address and telephone number.

When Dr John Weber read that I lived in Somerset he rang me, told me he had bought the *Bull* and said that he and his wife Charlotte were going to be visiting an orchid farm near Castle Cary and staying at the George Hotel. He asked if we happened to live anywhere nearby, and if so, could they possibly call in and visit the studio.

The Studio

I of course agreed and asked him if they would like to have dinner with us as we lived only a couple of miles from Castle Cary. He said that they would be delighted to after they had visited the orchid farm. John and Charlotte arrived around six with the biggest bunch of orchids for Margie that you have ever seen in your life. After I had showed them around the studio we settled down to one of Margie's famous meat stews. By sheer coincidence she had made some vichyssoise soup as a first course and when serving it apologised for it not being as white as the one Campbell's soup made. This caused Charlotte to laugh and then tell us that she and her brother owned Campbell's! We had a very happy meal and they asked us to come and see them in New York when we were next passing through.

A few months later I was again summoned by Ron Beaver in Canberra so decided to go via New York and try to see the Webers. I wrote warning them that I was on my way and John replied that he would be delighted to see me, although unfortunately Charlotte would be in Florida with the children.

I arrived in New York and after booking into a hotel near his apartment on Fifth Avenue I walked around to the hospital where he had asked me to meet him. He took me into the Common Room for a cup of tea as by now it was late afternoon. In those days my entire portfolio fitted into a small black plastic photograph album. As John thumbed through the pages I confess I hoped that he would be tempted by the *Acrobats*! Instead he stopped at *Le Corsair* and asked the price!

For some reason I was really surprised by his choice but I certainly wasn't going to try to change his mind. I was absolutely thrilled and totally amazed as he had given no indication that he was actually interested in buying a sculpture. John invited me to come to the apartment around eight that evening and join him for dinner. I walked back to my hotel along Madison Avenue on cloud nine.

In an effort to pull myself together I had a long hot bath before walking around to the Fifth Avenue apartment. A doorman let me in and guided me to the smartest elevator I have ever been in. John met me at the door and after pouring me a drink took me for a tour of their fabulous collection of paintings that included a beautiful Van Gogh, two stunning Corots and over the fireplace in the dining room the most impressive Modigliani that I have ever seen. I was dumbfounded by the collection and the beautiful antique furniture. I don't think I have ever seen such a display of superb taste.

We had a very good meal at a local restaurant and although I learnt a little about John, he found out much more about me. We got on very well and when the meal was over he kindly walked me back to my hotel as in those days New York was a pretty risky place at night, especially Central Park. What a day it had been. There was something about selling a sculpture to a couple with such taste in a city like New York that made the day miraculous.

Le Corsair was cast by Morris Singer and shipped to Live Oaks Plantation in Florida. John wrote when it had arrived and suggested that I should fly over at his expense and help him install it in the garden. This suited me as I was due in Sydney for an exhibition of my maquettes. I flew to New York to join him and then we flew down to Orlando together. I shall never forget the trip as when the pilot switched on the speakers he said, "Welcome aboard folk. Take off seems to have gone okay, but I now have to read the manual so we can land, so don't expect any more chat for the next couple of hours!" Can you imagine a pilot saying that today!

The pilot made a perfect landing and we set off by car to the farm arriving in time for dinner. We were joined by the horse vet's wife for a beautiful meal and a quite superb wine. John took me down into his cellar to choose a bottle and I have never seen such a treasure of red wine. The following morning we did a tour of the gardens and he showed me where he had decided to plant *Le Corsair*. There were several strong men ready to bury the steel supports that kept the sculpture from falling over, and the job was soon completed. It was a great change to have an ample supply of muscle available rather than just Roy and myself struggling alone.

Having finished our work, John took me for a tour of the estate that was beautiful, like an English parkland planted with fine specimens of Live Oaks, all dripping with Spanish moss, that grew in profusion around the rolling countryside. The Homestead and Stables were based on the English architecture of Newmarket Race Course. Everything and everywhere was 'high maintenance' and a joy to look at. When he took me to the farm office I was delighted to see the *Shorthorn Bull* sitting on his desk.

The vet's wife returned after lunch and the three of us set off for Hobe Sound Island, arriving in time for dinner after an easy four hours' drive through very flat country. The island is a private club with its own police force and golf course. The Webers' home was big and airy and right beside the pounding surf. It was a paradise peopled by Charlotte's children.

Next day I spent the morning taking photographs of the children and swimming in the pool. In one of my conversations with John we had talked about Mexico City and the Pyramids. I told him that I had studied the Aztecs at school, had written a paper on their history and ever since then had dreamt of names like Montezuma, Tehuantepec and Popocatapetl.

"Why don't you change your ticket and fly to Australia via Mexico City so you can spend a couple of days there at my expense?" Being with someone like John gives one confidence, so I picked up the telephone and within minutes had changed my ticket. I said goodbye to John and Charlotte, climbed into a taxi and headed for Miami Airport and within hours I had landed in Mexico City all due to John's generosity.

On arrival I checked into a hotel near the cathedral and the following day took a tourist bus out to Tenochtitlan. I climbed the Pyramids of the Sun and the Moon and marvelled at the scale of the whole complex. I had to buy an Aztec terracotta god on the way out of the grounds as a souvenir. The god now sits at the back of the Agecroft inglenook where the soot of many winter fires has made it look very old indeed!

I spent an incredible afternoon in the National Museum and admired many amazing sculptures. One in particular was a quite incredible carving that had left me breathless with admiration. It was called the *Wrestler* and was labelled as being Olmec, but looked incredibly Chinese.

The Olmec Wrestler

Before going out to the airport to catch the flight to Sydney I went for a walk around the Cathedral Square and happened to pass a little shop that sold Olmec sculptures. I found several little three-inch high terracotta figures similar to the ones that I had seen in the museum and couldn't resist buying four to celebrate John Weber's purchase of *Le Corsair*. The *Supplicant* is my favourite and is a superb sculpture. Although it looks in proportion, the arms are of different lengths, as are the legs. The imagination behind this sculpture belongs to a genius. Years later when I visited the cave called Trois Frères in France to see the painting of the *Sorcerer* I stole a tiny bit of clay from the trampled floor and rolled it into a ball and keep it in the *Supplicant's* bowl. I like to think there is a link between the Mexican sculpture and the French painting.

Drummer   *Teacher*

Oracle   *Supplicant*

I still have these figures in my study and although they are probably fakes, it doesn't bother me. I find them remarkable. It had been a breathtaking experience to visit Mexico City and one for which I shall always thank John.

On the 14-hour flight to Sydney I found myself sitting next to a teenage girl. I learnt through her tears that she was emigrating from Brazil, having won an Australian Government lottery passport. She had left behind her family and was quite alone and adrift in the world. She had already been travelling for 36 hours and was absolutely exhausted and near collapse.

We arrived in Sydney late at night. Because I was travelling on my Australian passport I was quickly through the barriers, but while waiting for my luggage, I saw the tiny girl being escorted away between a couple of very large Customs officers. I followed them and asked if I could be of any help. The men told me that the girl had no money and no address, so she would have to spend the night in police custody. I explained that I had sat next to her on the flight and asked if it would be all right to give her a lift into town and leave her at the Young Woman's Club. "Fine, sign here!" We collected her luggage and walked through the Exit to be met by Margie's brother, David. We drove into town and, as David knew where the YWCA was, we soon had her inside. The episode made a deep impression on me and since that experience I have often thought of the plight of migrants. I never heard from her, but I hope she found happiness and a friend to share life with.

I had returned to Sydney for the opening of an exhibition of my figurative sculptures that was being held at a gallery in the suburb of Woollahra. I had shipped out a dozen or so maquettes for this show and hoped that I wouldn't have to ship too many home! Fortunately this wish came true as the gallery sold most of them. The one sale that made the whole thing worthwhile was a two-foot long bronze I had done of a *Mother and Child*.

'Mother and Child'

335

The Mother and Child theme is a universal one that fascinates me. When I was in New York with John Weber I had happened to pass a gallery and saw a Picasso print that I couldn't resist and still enjoy.

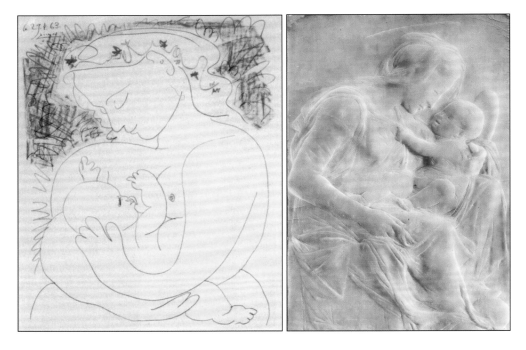

Picasso   *Desiderio da Settignano*

When I first got to know Margie's mother in Melbourne she showed me a postcard of Desiderio da Settignano's *Madonna and Child*. This beautiful carving is in the Victoria and Albert Museum in London. When I went to England to look for Marwood, I visited the V&A to look for it, eventually finding it tucked away in a corner. The postcard-size white marble low relief dominates the room. I copied it recently in clay and had it cast in rose glass.

When I tell the story of how we took a mould and made an aluminium cast of the *Dabous Giraffe* in the Sahara, you will find out why my son, Peter, and I were in a tiny mud town south-west of the Aïr Mountains. Suffice to say, before leaving the town to return to England we had to visit the local souvenir market. The shop was tiny and stuffed full of objects and people. I quickly backed out leaving Peter to bargain as he tried to exchange a battery-driven CD player we had brought with us for a Tuareg sword!

I escaped outside but was immediately surrounded by another group of vendors trying to sell me a mass of things that I definitely didn't want. Suddenly I saw a man holding up a wooden sculpture of a mother and child. Again I couldn't resist it and am glad I didn't. She sits feeding her child on my windowsill watching me very intently as I type.

Our next encounter with John and Charlotte was a night to remember as they gave the party to end all parties in the Metropolitan Museum in New York. They had just donated the Chinese Room to the museum and they asked Margie and me to the inauguration. What an evening we had as much of the museum was open to their many guests to wander through at will on their way to the Greek Temple for a private dinner dance. The Temple is surrounded by a water-filled moat that Charlotte had filled with floating pink candles. It was quite the most elegant and unforgettable evening we have ever experienced.

Tuareg 'Mother and Child' from Agadez

When we went to Orlando to talk about sculptures for a new hotel, we wrote to Charlotte to ask if she was going to be at Hobe Sound at the same time. Luckily she was there with her friend, Gloria Garfunkel, and asked us to stay for a couple of days to make up a golf foursome. Margie and I had taken to playing nine holes each week to get me out of the studio. Margie always managed to beat me but then she had been Captain of Hockey at Clyde School and in the tennis team!

Gloria, Charlotte, John and Margie

The private golf course on Hobe Sound has to be seen to be believed and the fun we had playing on it was amazing. This may be due to the fact that being a very hot day every time we went past the Golf House we would pick up another round of Margueritas on crushed ice! There are a lot of water hazards on the course, which I suppose is to be expected, as it is jammed between the sea and the inland canal that runs the length of the east coast of Florida, and I think we visited all of them. When it rains in Florida it pours, but luckily only for a few minutes although long enough to soak one to the skin. We didn't take our game very seriously that day! I don't think any of us have ever laughed so much.

Playing golf in Florida reminds me of one other game that we had on an island near the city of Mobile, Alabama. This happened when I was working for the President of the United States Sports Academy, Tom Rosandich. He had lent us his holiday house on Dauphin Island for the weekend, so we hired some golf clubs and buggies and set off around the course, which also had many water hazards. The fairways were flattened sand dunes and running parallel to them were lagoons that had a tiresome habit of collecting our balls. On about the third hole my ball stopped just short of the water so I walked down to hack it back towards the green. Staring at me from the lagoon's edge was the largest alligator I have ever seen! When we had left the Club House we had seen a notice, *Please do not feed the Alligators*, but had ignored the warning thinking that it was a joke. We later discovered that they had learnt to follow the players on the off chance of collecting a sandwich!

Tom is a dynamo of energy. He founded the USSA to teach sports coaches around the world. He wrote to me saying that he was looking for someone to do some relief heads of Sporting Heroes and asked if I would be interested. To cut a long story short I did several of these heads, including actor Ronald Reagan. Each plaque had a large edition for the Academy wall and a smaller version as an award. I did the heads in clay and then had the foundry cast them in bronze. It was fun working for Tom and we had several great times going to his award ceremonies. Margie was thrilled at one dinner because she was seated next to Perry Mason in his wheelchair.

'Ronald Reagan', President of the USA

339

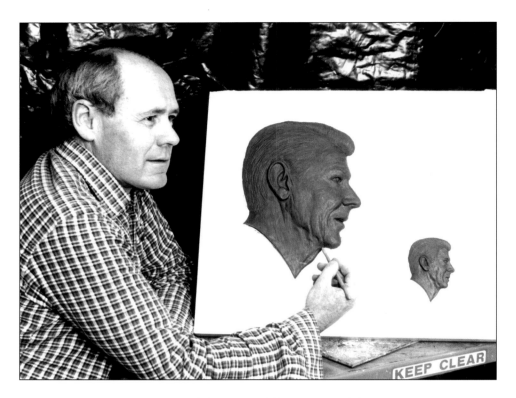

'Ronald Reagan' Sports Medal

One weekend when we were staying with Tom and his lovely wife, Sally, on Dauphin Island, he suddenly said to me that he would like to buy an edition of the *Pathfinder* for the quadrangle of the building he had just bought. Tom was a tough negotiator and said, "Give me a price that I can get excited about!" The following year we went out for the unveiling ceremony.

The 'Pathfinder', United States Sports Academy

340

I made Tom some gold-plated maquettes of the *Pathfinder,* but I don't think anyone really appreciated what they were getting when they received their awards. I keet one in our sitting room, where it still gives me a thrill every time I look at it.

Once again back in England I was rung by a woman with an amazing request. She told me she lived in a large house near Bristol that, until a recent storm when one had blown over, had been graced by two beautiful beech trees. She went on to say that she had seen the *Acrobats* when I had showed them at Wells Cathedral and wondered if I had one available as she thought it would replace the fallen tree and be a nice present for her husband's 70th birthday and at the same time!

I told her that we had the original in our garden and asked if she would like to see it. The following day a bright yellow sports Jaguar swept into the drive and a tall blonde woman in a leopard skin coat climbed out. In a total state of disbelief I walked her up the garden to look at the *Acrobats*. She made several circumnavigations and then turned to me and said, "That will be fine."

The *Acrobats* left again for Basingstoke to be cast by Morris Singer and when they were finished I let the owner of the yellow sports Jaguar know so we could arrange a date for the delivery, having warned them that they would need to hire a very large crane to reach the spot where the tree had been.

'Acrobats' filling in for a tree

341

At the very first exhibition of my figurative maquettes in Seattle when I had sold Margie's head as *Joan of Arc*, I had also sold sculptures to Peg Newman and she commissioned me to sculpt her two grandchildren. Over the following years Peg became a great friend. Because she loved the theatre she would come every year to London and then stay with us for a weekend. She was a wonderful character and one of the kindest people we have ever met.

If Peg was in town and I was going to the Meridian Foundry under the railway arch to inspect a sculpture, she would ask if she could come along for the ride. She was fascinated by the casting process and loved to see the molten bronze being poured into the moulds, especially when one day they had a breakout that caused a flood of molten bronze across the floor! One of these trips out to the foundry was to inspect John Weber's *Le Corsair* that was going to Florida. While I talked to Jack Crofton about packing and delivery I saw Peg walking round and round the sculpture so I presumed she must have liked it, but when on the way into town she said, "I think we should have one of those outside the Seattle Opera House," I was completely taken aback!

I rang Jack and asked him to please cast another edition straight away, which he did, and we shipped it out to America. Peg organised an unveiling and asked us to come for an opera night. Margie couldn't go but I did and had a grand evening with Peg and her aunt watching a superb ballet performance before the unveiling. The tragedy was that the sculpture was unprotected and only lasted a week before vandals had ripped it from its base. I think the mindless action broke Peg's heart, for over the next ten years she didn't mentioned the vandalism and the sculpture was never repaired.

'Le Corsair', Seattle Opera House

Seeing the Webers' Modigliani was the motivation to read about the artist and study his paintings more closely by trying to copy them. All through my years in England I have now and then dabbled with brushes, as without doubt the best way to understand a painting is by copying it.

Tim, Mark and Peter being teenagers

The 'Swiss Family Robinson' crossing the Alps!

The story of how we came to do the Grand Traverse started during our last summer at Marwood Hill. Margie's brother, Michael, came to stay with us for a weekend and announced that he was off to live on a Greek island for a month or two! Michael is a couple of years older than Margie, an inveterate traveller and was then a confirmed bachelor, who at that time made his living by selling Aborigine bark paintings in the USA. He was happiest when travelling fourth class on a ferry, village hopping up the Amazon!

At the time there was a very popular book about an Australian couple who had opted out of the rat race and gone to live on an Aegean island. We all read the book and found it incredibly romantic. Unfortunately the story ended in tragedy when the freezing winter set in and one of them became ill so they had to return to the rat race for medical attention. However, reading about the halcyon summer period had really set all our hearts aflutter.

Michael had some American friends in Melbourne, who also decided to take an extended holiday on a Greek island with their three young children decided they would all meet in Samos and rent two cottages for June.

Michael came to see us at Marwood on the way and about a month later we had a call from Margie's father to tell us that he had persuaded his girlfriend Judy to join him and they had decided to get married. The problem was that this was to happen in Athens so would we please all go to the wedding and represent the family at his expense, and at the same time take out some money to pay for the Wedding Breakfast!

Our house in Kokari

We arrived in Samos and after spending a night in an awful hotel I decided that we would also look for a little house in the village. I found a fisherman's cottage, owned by a widow, who was happy to move in with her daughter for two weeks and let us rent her home. The front of the house opened directly onto the pebbled beach and azure sea so we were able to swim across the bay to the two-room cottage Michael had rented.

The boys loved the sea, the village and the sun. Michael and Judy were obviously very happy and their friends could not have been nicer. Their three children were delightful and I was thrilled when their parents asked me to sculpt them. The eldest was a girl of seven, the youngest a boy of four, and between the two another girl. When I got home to England I sculpted the two girls watching their brother building with blocks. The sculpture was very popular and Crowther sold the entire edition of nine, twenty-seven children in all, so it turned out to be a working holiday, which are always the best!

Michael and Judy's house

Every morning we would go to the village bakery and buy delicious loaves. More organised families would bring a leg of lamb or a chicken and pay to have the baker put them in his bread oven. While standing in the queue one day waiting to buy bread, I heard an American voice behind me, and on turning, found another family of four seeking the romance of the Greek islands. We got talking and they invited us to their cottage at Little Lemon Tree bay for a swim and a meal. Harvey Edwards turned out to be a documentary film producer. Suzy, the mother of the two small boys, was French and they all lived in Chamonix in the French Alps.

I had hired an old bright-blue army jeep to enable us to explore the island so drove the short distance to their secluded cove. We found their cottage was even more primitive than our humble abode being a one-storey building that was really just a garden shed surrounded by grape vines and fig trees. The drinking water was at the bottom of a well in the middle of a vineyard. Van Gogh would have loved the place and could have done some beautiful painting of the cove! Harvey told us all about his life as a filmmaker and how fantastic it was to work in Chamonix, walking in the mountains in the summer and skiing in the winter. It sounded like a very good life.

346

One evening Harvey suggested that we all drive along the coast to the next village for dinner at the Swallows. We arrived to find the taverna was a circular concrete dance floor about the size of two tennis courts set amongst plane trees full of fireflies. Some lights were strung amongst the trees, a band sat on one side and tables were set up around the floor. Waiters brought wine and bread, the band played and people danced. Balalaika music filled the air, turning the night into one of sheer magic.

Swallows Taverna

A young girl in her early teens was dancing with a man who was obviously an expert and we watched entranced. The floor cleared and they gave a wonderful exhibition of sublime joy. We could have watched them all night. When they were exhausted and sat down a middle-aged man took to the floor on his own and did a Zorba dance with a handkerchief. The young couple had been magnificent to watch but seeing the Zorba dance was to experience pure Greek emotion being enacted to passionate music. It was a night to remember.

Samos is within sight of the Turkish coast and a ferry took tourists from the island across to Ephesus on day excursions, so I decided that we should definitely see this famous place. I bought large straw hats for us all as the ferry was open to the sun. We had a smooth crossing to Ephesus and walked up to the temple, had a good look around the ruins and then returned to the harbour to wait for the ferry to depart while eating our picnic. We bought a beautiful alabaster vase from the tourist stall, which Margie fills with flowers bringing back many happy memories of an incredible day.

The ferry left on time and although the day was still beautifully sunny, the wind had changed and was now blowing against the current. By the time we were halfway back to the island the waves had become frighteningly large. The small ferry was plunging straight into them as the wind was head on causing the boys to hang on to the wooden seats to stop sliding overboard! The new hats were soon in use and then thrown over the side. I have never been gladder to reach port.

Our island holiday was over and the wedding was on. Michael, Judy, the Melbourne friends and children, and all the Robinsons, climbed into a plane and set off for Athens. We set up camp in the hotel Margie and I had used on our train trip to Greece and to show the boys some of the wonders of ancient Greece hired a van for a day's excursion to Mycenae and Epidaurus.

The wedding day arrived and the service was held in a little Presbyterian church. It was a moving ceremony and Judy looked angelic. Afterwards we walked up to the Acropolis to take some photographs of the newly weds. Being summer the tourists were in their thousands, so getting a shot without people in the background was a problem.

Judy and Michael

348

Michael wanted a photograph taken in the Temple of Athena in front of the altar. In those days we were allowed inside the temple although the altar was roped off and an armed guard made sure you didn't step over it. The couple stood by the rope and I tried to get back far enough to take a photograph without including a host of tourists. It was impossible. The guard saw my predicament, lifted the rope and took Judy by the hand and led her over to the altar. I got my photograph and so did hundreds of other people. There must be photographs of Michael and Judy in albums all over the world! That evening we joined the Bride and Groom for their Wedding Breakfast on the roof terrace of a hotel. The wedding cake was the restaurant dessert trolley. It was the best reception we have ever been to!

That winter Margie and I took the boys skiing in Chamonix, staying in a little house that Harvey, the film producer, had rented for us. We went by train so were able to stop in Paris and show the boys some of the wonders of that city on the way. We had a superb holiday and were taught to ski by André, the Chamonix postmaster. Harvey and Suzy often asked us to eat with them and we got to know each other very well.

What, you are asking, has this to do with the Grand Traverse? Well, one evening a couple of months later, Harvey rang me and asked if the Robinson family would be interested in walking from Geneva to Nice? He went on to explain that he had been commissioned to make a film for the French Tourist Bureau about an English family walking in the Alps on one of the official trails. The film script told how we would meet up with two American girls during the walk, and that the seven of us would finish the journey on the Promenade des Anglais in Nice. He would be the producer and an American friend would be the cameraman. The journey would take four weeks, but a truck would carry us between panoramic locations, so we would actually not be walking the whole 500 miles! I said I was certainly interested but would have to talk it over with Margie and call him back.

That evening Margie and I decided that it was just too good an offer to pass up, especially as we had no other plans for the summer holidays. Harvey had promised us that he would provide all the equipment; tents, backpacks, sleeping bags, boots, all from a firm called 'North Face'. He would also pay for our trip out to Chamonix and back and our food for the whole month, but he would not be able to pay us wages!

Having decided we would do it I rang him and then worried for months if we had made the right decision. The day arrived for our departure and we set off again by train for Chamonix. Harvey met us and introduced us to the American girls, one of whom, Martha, was his niece, and the other, Janet, was the girlfriend of the cameraman named Duke. Harvey had sent our boots to England so we could break them in. We had done a couple of walks but nothing serious, so we were definitely not prepared for what lay ahead.

The first night under canvas was spent in the Geneva municipal campsite! It was not a grand start as we were surrounded by happy campers who had no intention of going to bed. Next morning we followed Harvey onto the Geneva-Lausanne paddle steamer and we set sail feeling a bit like David Niven in *Around the World in Eighty Days*.

Thankfully we were not quite amateurs at the art of camping. The tents that I had bought and first tried out in the Agecroft orchard had been used once in Wales and again in Scotland when we had taken a tour right up to the top and experienced millions of midges, or as the Scots call them, *wee beasties*. Only once, when it had poured, were we forced to retire to a motel!

Camping beside Loch Hourn

Harvey had provided us with knee-length walking breeches and bright red socks, so we looked the part when we landed at St Gingolph on the south side of Lac Léman and started off up the mountain. We were soon wondering what we had let ourselves in for, the main problem being the weight of our packs. Mine was 60 pounds, Margie's 40 and the boys were carrying 30 each!

The view from 'Col de Bise' of Lac Léman and Lausanne

The climb to the top of Col de Bise was murder. Thank goodness on the first night we camped halfway up so we could put our packs down. The

Robinson team were obviously not in good shape! We all slept like logs and could have stayed asleep all day but for Harvey getting us up at the crack of dawn to reach the top in time for good filming light!

The view was magnificent from 6,000 feet!

From this point on, the path got steadily rougher and the packs seemed to get increasingly heavier. Obviously something had to be done about it before we all died of exhaustion! The solution came to me during the night when luckily we met up with Suzy and our back-up truck. I emptied most of our gear into boxes, keeping only bare essentials, and filled the space with scrunched up newspaper. I saw no point in our carrying two sets of spare clothes and all those other last-minute things one tends to pack, just in case. The packs became manageable and our trip became enjoyable.

With a new spring in our step we were now prepared to follow Harvey anywhere he wished to go, and go he did, even over places that goats would avoid. We happily followed our leader, usually repeatedly, so Duke could film us from every conceivable angle.

The night at *Le Lac des Neuf Couleurs* was the highlight of our misery. None of us has ever been colder and the wind was blowing a gale and rain was pelting down in stair rods. Going outside for a pee reminded us of poor Captain Oates on the way back from the South Pole with Scott.

But all things come to an end and as each day was ticked off and we got nearer and nearer to the Mediterranean, we all got into the rhythm of the march and really started to enjoy the beauty of the Alps. We would stride down the track greeting those coming up with a smile and, "Courage, mon ami." On the way up, they would do the same to us. We were told that a million people are marching around the Alps every day throughout the summer as it is one of France's national sports.

Tim, Peter , performing for Duke

Mark studying the terrain ahead

*Peter and Tim asking Harvey if he really wants them
to wade through the torrent*

The girls had difficulty in finding privacy

Demonstrating the new super lightweight pack
stuffed with 'Le Monde' newspaper

At last we reached the outskirts of Nice and climbed into our bus and headed for the 'Promenade des Anglais'. Harvey had worked out a final scene for us when we hit the beach. Martha and Peter were to hang back as the rest of us walked down onto the pebbles, and then they would rush past us straight into the sea, fully clothed! We would then let out a yell and follow them in still booted, take them off in the sea and throw them back onto the beach!

We over-acted our parts with gusto. As I raced for the waves I heard a bikini clad beauty say, "From their clothes I think they must be Austrian." We were filmed from behind running into the Mediterranean, then Harvey wanted Duke in the water with us running towards him! This of course meant getting our boots on again and doing the whole thing over again in wet clothes! As it was to be the *Final Wrap*, as we film people say, we didn't mind as it was a gloriously hot day. The beach audience enjoyed the performance, but I think we enjoyed showing off more!

We retired to the hotel Harvey had booked us into and had one of the best baths we have ever had in our lives. Putting on clean clothes was a joy and after meeting in the lobby, Margie and I took everyone out to dinner. It turned into quite a celebration as halfway through the meal Duke and Janet announced that they had decided to get married! We ordered a bottle of champagne and a large bowl of rainbow ice cream to act as an engagement cake. The French Tourist Bureau was very happy with Harvey's epic and when he showed it at the New York Documentary Film Festival he won a medal. No Oscars came our way; our reward was a unique journey. Thank you Harvey!

SAILING

I am not sure why, but at the age of 40 I became interested in learning how to handle a yacht. Maybe something brought back the magnificent adventure I had with some friends from Rugby when I was in my mid-teens and four of us had chartered a yacht on the Norfolk Broads. None of us had any experience of how to handle a sail and although we had a couple of very hairy moments, we managed to stay afloat and not run into anything.

Whatever the cause, the urge suddenly descended upon me so I bought a yachting magazine and looked for someone who could teach me how to sail. I found an advertisement offering lessons on a 36-foot long sloop on the Solent waters between Southampton and the Isle of Wight.

I rang the number and asked a nice sounding man if I could arrange for some lessons. He suggested that I should take a one-day course to start with, so one afternoon I packed a bag and drove down to meet Captain Tony, a gentle man about ten years older than myself. There were four other students and none of us had been on a yacht before. A young lad aged 20 named Mark acted as Tony's Mate. They behaved like father and son and obviously had a very close relationship. Mark turned out to be extremely competent and ran the boat while Tony gave the lessons.

When the introductions were over we climbed into a rubber dinghy and rowed out to the *Fair Endeavour*, that was moored midstream on the river Hamble. Tony cooked us a simple meal, showed us our bunks, and left us to sleep onboard with Mark, while he went back to his warm bed. The boat was a single mast sloop, had very pretty lines and had been built before the swing to resin fibreglass hulls, so had a lot of traditional character.

It was an interesting night as I had never stayed with strangers in such cramped quarters before in my life. The loo on the *Fair Endeavour* was the standard pump-action type and housed in a tiny cupboard, so incredibly awkward to use. It was a good introduction to the confines inflicted on the crew of a yacht. The night finally passed and we were all up at first light and had finished our breakfast by the time Tony arrived.

We started right from scratch, which meant that the first hour or so was spent learning the names of ropes, sails, and of course which sides were Port and Starboard. By the time we cast off from the mooring my mind was reeling with names and I had begun to wonder if I was doing the right thing; however, it was too late to change my mind. When we cleared the river and headed out into the grey choppy waters of the Solent we were put to work hauling up sails. There was a brisk wind and soon we were buzzing along at a fair lick, heeled over, with spray coming over us and I was delighted to be there.

It was a great day and I learnt an enormous amount and being at sea all day meant each student had several turns at the helm. We moored for a sandwich lunch in a small harbour on the Isle of Wight. In the afternoon we sailed back to port using the Genoa sail, which was fun. The whole day had been a breathtaking experience and I was hooked. Before leaving to drive home I signed up for another four days over the summer.

This is all boring but necessary information to introduce the next Robinson Family adventure. I was so hooked by the sailing experience I decided that it would be educational for the boys also to learn to sail a yacht. Margie was in favour of the plan as she had spent all her youth by the sea, sailing with her brothers and boyfriends.

I decided that I should put all my newly gained knowledge to the test. I looked through the yachting magazines and found a small 30-foot long sloop named *Shedo* for charter. It was moored just up the river from Falmouth in Devon so was easy to reach from Agecroft. We would take it for a week and sail in the bay at the mouth of the Fal River. There was a first-class hotel in the area so perhaps my mother would agree to stay there and give us the occasional meal and allow us to use her bathroom now and then! This sounded like a good idea to Margie, especially the bath bit, so I chartered the yacht. We had an amazing holiday, and the weather was very kind to us. The hotel idea worked out well as my mother had the boys to dinner one at a time and Margie and I got to have the occasional wash. When we were out sailing I tried to teach the boys all that I had learned from Tony. Sailing is certainly a marvellous way to share time as a family.

We would hold *Man Over Board* practice while tacking back and forth across the bay. I had a large four-gallon plastic container that we blew up, and, when everyone was relaxed, I would throw it into the sea and yell "Man Over Board", causing the crew to spring into action.

The exercise taught us all to handle the boat very efficiently. One day, when it was Peter's turn on the boat hook we used to recover the container, he fell in! I shall never forget the look on his face as he held his arm high out of the water being more concerned about keeping his watch dry than getting wet. We always wore life jackets and thank goodness there are no man-eating sharks in English waters. The holiday was a great success and we were getting pretty good at handling a yacht as a family, so I decided that the following year we would have to try and do something a little more adventurous.

I am not sure when I read *The Riddle of the Sands*. Without doubt it is one of the best adventure books ever written, and as exciting to non-sailors as it is to sailors. It was one of Churchill's favourite books and the story goes that when he was Lord of the Admiralty he made all his staff read it. The reason for this was that it is about the planned invasion of England by German troops being pulled across the Channel in barges during the Great War.

I started to think that it would be wonderful to have an adventure like *The Riddle* and then suddenly thought of Captain Tony and *Fair Endeavour*. Would he take us on such a trip? I rang him up and asked if we could charter his boat for a fortnight during the school holidays with him as Captain. He said that we could and suggested crossing over to France and back. "No, I want to sail across to Holland, up through the Kiel Canal, across to Sweden, back round Denmark and down the North Sea to London."

There was complete silence at the other end of the telephone. "I shall have to think about that and work out a price." Several days later Tony rang up and agreed to do the trip. We set a date to meet at the Tower of London marina and I went off to buy five bright-red waterproof suits.

The best laid plans of mice and men sometimes go astray. One day Tony rang me and said that he had been offered a job in Nigeria to teach navigation and the pay was so good that he could not refuse it. But he had a suggestion: "Would I be happy if young Mark was Captain instead?"

I immediately agreed, knowing Mark as I did from my courses with him as Mate, and in fact was very pleased, as I thought that he would be much more fun for the boys, besides making me the oldest person on the boat and therefore theoretically in charge!

Roy and Olive gave us a hand to get all our gear to the marina and my mother came down to wave us off although I am sure she thought that I was quite mad to take the whole family to sea with an 18-year-old captain. It was pouring with rain when we motored through the marina lock out into the Thames. Suddenly the 36-foot long *Fair Endeavour* felt very small indeed beside Tower Bridge!

It was cold and wet but we were warm in our bright red suits, and I thought we looked rather smart. The wind was against us so we had to motor down the Thames but when we reached the English Channel we were able to hoist the sails. After a superb hot dinner prepared by Margie from packets of ready-cooked food, Mark split us into Watches. Margie and Tim were to have First Watch and Peter and I the Second. Captain Mark would be on standby all the time and we were to call him immediately if we saw another ship or there was a change of wind. Our Mark was designated to be a standby pair of hands when needed. I guess Tim was 16, Peter 14 and our Mark 12, the youngest member of the crew.

The sky darkened and we sailed on across the Channel through the night. I was thrilled to be out in the swell of the sea ploughing along on the first night of our family adventure. We changed watches every four hours so the time sped by. The wind was constant and no sail changes were needed and no shipping interfered with our crossing. Dawn came and then breakfast and before we could believe it we had arrived off the coast of Holland and were sailing into The Hague marina. We had arrived in Europe and I was ecstatic as I think was everyone else. Our adventure had really begun!

The next leg of the trip took us through the canals of Holland past stately windmills, up to Amsterdam, and then across the Zuider Zee, under sail most of the way, although we had to motor through more canals before passing out into the North Sea again. We sailed between the islands and the coast of Holland during the night. The phosphorescence that bubbled along in our wake was an astounding sight. We pulled a bucket of seawater onboard and stirred it up with our hands, making the water glow with light. We were sailing in the waters of *The Riddle of the Sands*.

The following day we reached the entrance to the Kiel Canal. We motored through and out into the Baltic Sea. Once more under sail we headed north up the Kattegat and arrived at the Danish port of Frederikshavn, where we had arranged to meet Margie's cousin who lived in Sweden but could cross over on the ferry. Before the meeting we decided that we all needed a bath so booked into the local hotel for a few hours. What a luxurious feeling it is to put on clean clothes after a hot bath, especially if you have been at sea and become salt-encrusted!

We were extremely fortunate with the weather. Since leaving London in the rain we had had sunny days and clear nights. The wind had been kind to us and we had made good headway but were behind schedule. We decided to cut our trip short. Originally I had hoped to sail across to Sweden and then around the top of Denmark. Instead we decided to cut across Denmark through the Limfiord Canal, a series of lakes that link the Baltic to the North Sea, thereby cutting miles off our return journey. It was a lucky decision as halfway through the canal our engine packed up! An excellent mechanic from a nearby town soon had it fixed, but we were fortunate the engine misbehaved when it did and not in the North Sea. Hopefully we wouldn't need the engine on our trip south, but as we would be travelling through one of the world's busiest waterways, an engine would be needed if we had to get out of the way of a super tanker.

The Limfiord is shallow and full of mud banks, which we continually got stuck on. The only way to get free was to row out in the dingy with the anchor and then pull ourselves off on the sail winches. We nearly pulled them off their mountings by doing this, but fortunately we didn't as it would have made our trip home very difficult!

The two days we spent in the Limfiord were our last days of sunshine. By the time we headed out into the North Sea the weather had changed and a gale was forecast. Should we go, or should we stay? If we were to arrive back in London on time we had to leave immediately. If we stayed we could be trapped in an awful industrial harbour for a week! We decided to leave as the wind was from the north-east and would be in our favour for some hours. We prayed that the gale would not arrive for 24 hours, the time it would take us to reach London.

We sailed out into the North Sea in the evening light with a brisk wind pushing us south. Skipping along we were pleased that we had decided to leave. *Faint heart never won fair lady.* Peter and I took the First Watch. We sailed until midnight and made wonderful progress. The wind had increased and we had reefed the mainsail twice and changed to a storm jib. We had passed by several of the massive gas rigs that dot the North Sea, but had no need to take any avoiding action from shipping. The rigs were an extraordinary sight as they were lit up like Christmas trees and you could see them for miles.

When Margie and Tim took over, the trouble began. Peter and I were pretty tired so were soon strapped into our bunks and fast asleep. Captain Mark was about and helping Margie and Tim with their Night Watch. They had been sailing for an hour when the storm hit and the wind steadily increased until it was blowing Gale Force 8. Tim was at the helm when a rogue wave crashed into the cockpit. Margie looked up to see Tim standing up to his chest in water, luckily well strapped in and hanging on to the helm, laughing! Then the mainsail split, top to bottom. Margie took the helm while Mark and Tim got the sail down with some difficulty and stored it away. We sailed on with only a storm jib, but even so we were still creaming through the water as we headed south before the storm surfing on the wave tops.

At four in the morning Peter and I took over the watch. By then the storm had passed and the weather had settled. The sea remained extremely angry but we were able to get the spare main up, well reefed, and a larger jib as well. Tim and Margie retired to their bunks exhausted. Captain Mark said he reckoned that we were somewhere off the coast of East Anglia, or at least that is where the 'dead reckoning' should have us, so we still had quite a long sail to reach the mouth of the Thames and London.

With Peter at the helm we continued to sail for an hour, not sighting anything, neither gas rig nor ship. We felt completely alone, running with the giant swell that was left after the gale had passed. The wind held in our favour and we seemed to be making astonishing progress. Suddenly I spotted a buoy bobbing away on the port side. "Sail over to it, Peter, so we can get a fix from the name on its side." We certainly did get a fix as we sped past! In large red letters we clearly read one word, *Calais.*

We were off the harbour of Calais for God's sake, nowhere near East Anglia! In fact we had passed London and were heading towards Cherbourg!

I woke Captain Mark to report the discovery. As there was no way that we could return to London against the wind the only thing we could do was turn sharp right and head for Brighton on the south coast of England.

Before long we saw the White Cliffs of Dover and then the wind died. The sea turned to a glassy soup and if we had not been able to fix the engine in Denmark we would have been becalmed. As we chugged west along the coast, Mark was able to make contact with the Brighton marina on his antiquated ship-to-shore telephone. We had arrived back in England on schedule, but in the wrong port!

I then had a brilliant idea. When we had left 14 days earlier my mother had told me that she was going to stay at her favourite hotel near Brighton for a few days. I knew the name of the hotel and wondered if she was still there. I called Enquiries, got a number, and rang the hotel. "Yes, Mrs Bowring is staying. Hold the line, please." My mother came on the line and I told her where we were and explained that we needed a hotel to clean up in, as we were pretty smelly. I asked her to make the arrangements, which she said she would do, but added there was no way that she was going to meet us. She would return to London and wait until we were respectable!

We docked, said goodbye to Mark, giddily walked ashore looking like a mob of gypsies and climbed into a taxi, deserting our poor captain like rats scampering off a sinking ship! However, I think he was delighted to have a moment to himself and be able to get *Fair Endeavour* shipshape again. Fourteen days of confinement with the Robinson family is asking a lot of anyone! Captain Mark was a really nice young man and we all often wonder what happened to him.

The hotel greeted us warmly and seemed to be not in the least fazed by our appearance. They showed us to a couple of rooms where we luxuriated in hot baths and scraped off the salt. An hour later we were having a gourmet lunch of fresh food, none of us missing the packaged food that Margie had heated on a tiny swinging gas stove for two weeks.

After our superb meal we took the train to London, thanked my mother for making the arrangements that had saved us, and headed home. We were glad to be back after our exciting family adventure. It had all worked really well and everyone had so enjoyed it that I decided we would do something similar the next year, and began to look for another adventure.

As a little aside I must tell you that the packet food Margie had cooked so impressed us we gave a whole box of it to a bachelor friend who has a house on a tiny island off the west coast of Scotland. We thought it would be handy for him to have ready-made food in such an out-of-the-way part of the world! He was very grateful and enjoyed the few packets he tried before storing the remainder in his larder in a box for his next visit. The only trouble was the rats also found the food very enjoyable and dug a hole from one end of the box to the other, right through the middle of every packet. They had then proceeded to run all over the larder wiping the food off their fur! Our friend was not pleased and asked us never to give him any more ready-to-eat food unless it was in tins!

This same man usually found some form of trouble when he returned to his lonely island farm home. On one occasion he had not shut the back door properly, allowing a number of lambs to take shelter in the house. The lambs became thirsty but eventually discovered a source of drinking water in the lavatory. Of course they managed to push the door shut as they milled around inside the bathroom. They were in there for a whole day before they were discovered, so you can imagine the state of the room.

'Hoshi' sailing off the coast of Ireland

One day I came across an article in a yachting magazine about the Salcombe Island Cruising Club in Devon and read that they owned a 65-foot long wooden schooner named *Hoshi*.

In the photograph she looked absolutely stunning when under full sail. The Club used it to train nine students at a time, sailing over to Ireland via the Isles of Scilly, round the Fastnet Lighthouse near Cork, and then home. The trip took ten days and sounded a very exciting experience for young people.

I thought, *would they charter the whole schooner to me if we could fill all the berths*? It would certainly be a wonderful adventure if they would. If each boy took a friend, we would add up to eight people with Margie and myself. I rang the Club and made an appointment to come and inspect the schooner. The Club was having some financial trouble and finding it hard to fill *Hoshi*'s berths, so they were delighted for me to charter the schooner, as long as I paid them in advance. Everyone seemed to be happy so I told the boys to find a friend they would like to take sailing. Tim asked Bella, his first girlfriend. Peter asked his skiing friend, Jean Pierre, from Chamonix, the son of our postmaster ski instructor, and Mark asked his best friend at school, Piers Le Marchant.

Margie told her great friend, Sue, about our coming adventure, and asked if her son Simon would like to fill the free berth. Simon said, "Yes please." We now had our crew of nine so I went out and bought more red suits.

The day for embarking arrived and we climbed on board *Hoshi*. The Captain was a short nuggety 40-year-old Cornishman. He was unsmiling and didn't appear to be very happy about taking on the Robinson crew. The Mate was a tall lanky Viking type with long blond hair tied in a pigtail. The cook was a really nice girl who loved sailing and was much friendlier.

We sailed at first light and soon the Captain and Mate had the young gang working. It was a big job handling all the ropes, so there was always something to do. The Mate turned out to be just a big kid so was friendly with the gang as he was. The Captain remained aloof, but I guess all captains cut themselves off so they can keep things in order.

Jean Pierre had never been to sea before and unfortunately was prone to seasickness as soon as we hit the Atlantic swell so it took the poor boy a couple of days to find his sea legs. *Hoshi* sailed like a dream and we spun along with fair winds reaching the Scilly Islands in two days, by which time our gang were a pretty efficient crew.

We anchored off the main island of St Mary's, which I knew well from my school holidays after the end of WWII. We looked for a hotel that would allow us to bath, but they were not nearly as friendly as the Danes had been the previous year and directed us to some awful showers down by the jetty. Beggars can't be choosers, so we made do and then retired to the local café for a big English fry-up.

We reached Ireland by sailing through a moonlit night. Again we were lucky with the wind and the weather. Sunny days and moonlit nights with fair winds, what more can you ask for? We passed the Fastnet Lighthouse, dropped anchor in a beautiful little harbour and rowed ashore to the local pub.

Piers Le Marchant may have had a little too much Murphy's but the Captain certainly did! We had all been asleep for hours when he arrived back, *all sails to the wind*. He did not appear next day so we happily lay at anchor and took walks ashore, which was probably a good thing anyway, especially for Jean Pierre, who was still looking a little green about the gills. Next morning the Captain was on deck behaving as though nothing had happened, and we prepared to set sail.

Margie with Peter at the helm of 'Hoshi'

It was such a beautiful day when we left the harbour that I asked the Captain to set me adrift in the tender so I could film the *Hoshi* under sail. It did cross my mind that he might not return to pick me up as I had asked him what all the noise was about when he came back on board the night before. He had

361

ignored the question and me ever since! Watching *Hoshi* sail past me, go about and return was sheer joy, in more senses than one!

The trip home was again by moonlight. Sailing at night is a glorious experience. We arrived safely at Salcombe and said our goodbyes, especially thanking the fun girl who had been such a good cook. I think Jean Pierre was particularly glad to be back on terra firma, although his parents later told us he said that he had loved every moment of the trip. He went on to become a top snowboard champion.

Hoshi was the last sailing holiday we had as a family. I hankered for a boat of my own and toyed with the idea of buying a large catamaran so we could sail to Australia, but common sense prevailed and I settled for a 14-foot long dinghy with a Thames barge rig! She was so unusual and beautiful to look at under sail that people used to cheer us as we sailed by. She had tan sails, a white hull, and could spin along when broadside to the wind or when we were goose winging, Margie's favourite run.

The Brigantine 'Surry'

Margie's great, great, great-grandfather, Thomas Raine, was the Captain of a brigantine. He carried both free settlers and convicts out to Australia and once brought the Governor of New South Wales back to England. His ship was the *Surry*, so we named our little beauty after her.

Margie and I used to drive up to the Lake District with *Surry* on a trailer and sail her on Coniston Water. We found a little hotel on the water's edge and used to spend all day out on the lake sailing down to Rat Island, made famous in *Swallows and Amazons*. The island is tiny and remains as it is described in the adventure and just as romantic. We would tie up in the little harbour that we recognised from the illustration in the book and have our picnic on the rocks while our dog, Lassie, explored the island.

'Surry' moored in the Rat Island harbour

If you are ever lucky enough to sail Coniston Water one of the things you have to do is visit Ruskin's house where he wrote *The Stones of Venice*. Behind the house there is a wood full of bluebells, so it is best to be there in early May. In the woods there is a ravine carrying a stream that tumbles down in little waterfalls from pool to pool. A truly romantic and beautiful spot.

Ruskin must have liked the ravine as he chose it as the background for his portrait by Millais. The painting clearly shows the stream and cascades behind Ruskin as he contemplates the beauty of nature. Or might he have been contemplating the problem he was having with his new wife? He had recently married, but the wedding had not been consummated because, so the story goes, he was horrified when he saw his bride undressed only having seen naked women as marble statues!

While Millais was painting Ruskin he fell in love with the poor rejected girl and she, not surprisingly, with Millais. Ruskin divorced her and she married the painter. Perhaps the young couple met secretly in the wood and enjoyed the beauty of the ravine while prudish Ruskin was back at the house writing his book about 'Venetian stones'!

We rented a mooring at Wareham in Dorset and sailed *Surry* on Poole Harbour. We could drive down in an hour and sail all day, but we decided to sell the boat when we found we had no time for sailing on a regular basis. There was no way I could give up wind and water so instead I bought an inflatable yacht and christened it *The Rubber Duck*. When collapsed the whole thing could fit in the back of the station wagon so we could drive up to the

Lake District and pop it in the water at the drop of a hat. It was not elegant but it allowed us to retain the freedom of setting sail for a picnic to explore hidden and untrodden shores and trespass in secluded private bays.

'The Rubber Duck' and First Mate on Ullswater

The Lake District is without doubt one of the most beautiful places we have ever been in the world, when it isn't raining, which it often is. One of our favourite views is from the shore of Crummock Water at Buttermere. To stand on the shore of the lake is like being in a private paradise. You can touch the silence, absorb the colour and scent of the bracken that covers the hills which are reflected in the mirror-still crystal clear waters, while watching the mist rise.

Crummock Water

When we were enjoying the celebrations that marked Queen Elizabeth II's Golden Jubilee, it amazed me to think that this great lady came to the throne when I was only 17 years old, 50 years ago. What incredible changes we have all witnessed during that time while the world's population has doubled!

While watching the pageantry with Margie on TV, I saw shots of Buckingham Palace which instantly reminded me of my time in the Yellow Chinese room on the first floor, arranged as an artist's studio. The windows of the room are the last three on the left as you look at the building from Pall Mall and face out over St James's Park. The room gets its name from the imperial yellow wallpaper of picturesque oriental gardens and several large Chinese vases. In the middle of the room is a raised chair used by the sitter.

Whoever is reading this must be asking, "How did you ever get into the Palace?" Well, it is a convoluted story but certainly one of the most thrilling and extraordinary moments of my life. It all began with Roy being asked to mend Dr William Harvey's nose. Harvey was born near the White Cliffs of Dover in a town called Folkestone on April 1st 1578. As a young man he had walked over the Alps to Padua to study medicine, wearing out several pairs of shoes on the way, and he went on to become the famous physician who discovered how blood circulates through our bodies.

The town was very proud of their illustrious son and erected a large stone statue of him on their waterfront promenade. The problem was that vandals had knocked off his nose. Someone in the Council offices knew Roy and asked him if he could replace the nose with a new one. Roy said he could and asked me to model a replacement, which he cast in resin stone and then glued back on so William could breathe again!

Folkestone Council offices are located in the adjacent town of Hythe, which is one of King Henry VIII's ancient Cinque Ports. The Council was so impressed with Roy's work they asked him if he could do a head of the Lord Warden of the Five Ports who happened to be the Queen Mother. Roy asked me if I was interested and I told him to tell the Council that I would of course be delighted to accept the job and do it for free!

I received a letter from the Council telling me that the Queen Mother had agreed and could I please contact her secretary and tell him what I would require in the way of sittings. A date was set for the first of two sittings and I turned up at Clarence House with my tape measure and camera and a large bouquet of primroses specially picked by Margie as a gift for the sitter. I was shown into the Queen Mother's study and while waiting took the opportunity to look at her paintings. One was the famous *Eve of St Agnes* by John Millais, painted in 1865, and another the portrait of the Queen Mother by Augustus John painted soon after her husband King George VI's coronation. What a privilege to be able to have such a close look at these two paintings!

Suddenly the door opened and I was caught red-handed in front of the Millais. "Isn't it beautiful? I really love that painting." That broke the ice and we shook hands as I introduced myself. She then sat down in a chair in the middle of the room and put her left leg up on a stool. "I am afraid I have given my leg a bit of a biff. I have taken some arnica so it should be all right soon, but I have been told to keep my weight off it."

By this stage I was so won over and totally relaxed that I had enough courage to pull out the primroses and give them to her saying that Margie had picked them that morning in Somerset. "Oh how lovely, one of my favourite flowers. Reminds me of playing in the woods with my brothers. I shall take them to Scotland this afternoon."

The conversation then turned to arnica and homeopathy and I told her how wonderful I thought Ainsworth the Chemist was. "Dear Mr Ainsworth, what would we do without him?" At that stage a corgi bounced into the room and sniffed my ankle. "Don't put your hand down, he bites strangers!"

It was time to go to work, so with my hands well above corgi height I explained that on the first sitting all I did was take measurements and photographs. I clicked away from all sides and then pulled out my tape measure. It amazes me when I think back that I was actually allowed to put a tape measure around the Queen Mother's head, neck, and with callipers, measure from her ear to the tip of her nose and between her eye pupils, but this is what I did. I felt awful when I saw that the eye measurement, which I find is the most critical one of all, had made them water.

We then discussed what the head should look like. "Please no hat," she said, "and I would really like to be remembered as how I looked in the war years, so make me a lot younger." This meant doing a 40-year-old woman from the photographs of an 80-year-old one! I decided that I would have to go and buy some books of photographs of the Queen Mother taken during the war.

Her Majesty the Queen Mother

A month later I took the clay head to Clarence House for the second sitting. I only had one real problem as the best photograph I had found of her in the war years showed that she had her hair parting on the other side. When I queried this she told me that she had always worn her hair as now, so we decided that they must have printed the photograph back to front. Luckily I had used the parting from my photographs so no major changes were required!

The finished clay head with the Queen Mother

The most memorable thing about this visit was our conversation about the engagement that had just been announced between Charles and Diana. I congratulated the Queen Mother on the engagement of her grandson and she replied, "Yes, isn't it wonderful. A Royal Wedding is just what the people need." If only she could have foreseen what heartbreak the wedding would bring to everyone involved, but thankfully none of us can look into the future!

I handed over the clay head to Roy and he cast a plaster for me to take to the foundry. I ordered two heads as I thought it would be fun to have one for myself because nothing like that would ever happen to me again. I had been asked to leave the bust at Clarence House so Her Majesty could have a look at it before it went to Hythe. I had serious doubts about how successful the head really was as taking away 40 years means that the head you sculpt is not the head you see. When I collected the head I was told that the Queen Mother had found it 'interesting', which basically means that she must also have had her doubts. Still it was what she asked for and who was I to argue.

There was an unveiling ceremony in the Hythe Council Chambers and everyone seemed happy, except one old councillor, who came up to me and said that she didn't like it. I have always wondered why, when people don't like something, they feel impelled to tell you. No one is interested in negative reactions and I personally believe it is much better to keep them to oneself. I told the woman that the Queen Mother had asked for the head to be as she was in the war years, but I might as well have been talking to a brick wall!

Some months later my friend, Tim Green, called into Agecroft on his way to Devon. It was his daughter's hands that I had used for the *Birth of Spring* based on Pushkin's poem. He saw the Queen Mother's head in the studio while we were having lunch and asked me about it. "What about doing one of the Queen?" and went on to tell me that Her Majesty was Colonel in Chief of the Royal Tank Corps of his Regiment. He was sure they would like to have a head at their Headquarters.

"You get permission and I shall do the job at cost," I said, and immediately put the idea out of my head as it is easy to have such ideas, but usually they don't come to anything. I hadn't allowed for Tim's persuasiveness so when one evening he rang up and said the job was mine, I couldn't believe it. He went on to explain that the Queen had agreed, but as there are three Royal Tank regiments, each would like a head! He also thought it would be nice if he had a copy and as I would certainly want to keep one myself, it meant casting five. What would it cost, he asked, reminding me that I had said I would do the job at cost price if I got the job! I had been talking about one cast, not five! Why hadn't I kept my mouth shut?

A letter arrived from the Queen's secretary at Buckingham Palace setting the time for an appointment. At least this time primroses were not in bloom so I wouldn't have to take a bouquet!

I arrived at the front gate of the Palace and showed the secretary's letter to the policeman, who then checked a list before directing me to a parking spot near the right-hand entrance door. I walked up the steps between uniformed porters and was directed by them to the secretary's office.

At that time the secretary was an Australian called Bill so we got along famously. He led me across the enormous entrance hall to an old-fashioned iron cage lift and we slowly rose to the first floor. We turned left and walked all the way down the length of the palace along miles of red carpet and past the drawing room that leads out onto the 'Waving Balcony'. I took a quick peek in as we passed and couldn't believe what I was actually doing. When we arrived at the end of the corridor he showed me into the Chinese Room, telling me that this is where I would be working. He pointed out where there was a loo across the corridor before saying that the Queen would be with me soon.

The first thing to do was to visit the loo as perhaps that would stop my knees knocking together! I unpacked the camera and the trusty tape-measure, and checked the flash several times as I couldn't think of anything more embarrassing than it failing to go off. Having set everything up I looked around the room. It was hard to believe I was standing where Anagoni had stood when he painted the Queen. It was all just too much!

The door opened and Her Majesty walked in with Bill. I was introduced and then she asked what I wanted her to do. I explained about taking the photographs and then the measurements and suggested that the best place for that would be if she sat in the chair. She sat down and looked out of the window at St James's Park. "Isn't it amazing how long the willows keep their leaves compared to other trees?" I felt all my tension drain away as she went on to chatter about the park while I happily clicked away.

Suddenly she leant forward and waved at a car that was trying to come in through the gate in front of us. "No, no, go to the other end, we're keeping that one shut now." She turned to me and said, "It doesn't feel like a home any more now we have to keep the gates locked." I knew immediately what she was talking about as only the week before a man had crept into the Palace and somehow found his way to her room and sat on her bed while he talked to her! The outcome of that event had led to a severe tightening of security and the locking of the gates.

My photographs of Her Majesty Queen Elizabeth II

I told her that my wife and I had been very distressed by the reports of the bedroom intrusion and that we hoped that she had recovered from the shock. "Yes, it did give me a bit of a fright, especially when he started waving a glass ashtray around. I felt very sorry for him, as I knew he wanted me to help him, but I just can't interfere."

By this time I understood why everyone around the Queen adores her. If she had asked me right then to lie down in front of one of Tim's tanks I think I would have. Then came the moment for taking the measurements. Out came the tape and around the Royal Head it went, followed by the callipers to measure the distance between her pupils warning her that I wouldn't come too close as I had made her mother's eyes water. I took the measurement and jotted it down. "I think you should do that again and check that you have got it right." I did what I was told although by then I had so much adrenaline running through my eyeballs I could hardly read the numbers on the tape!

Bill arrived back and the session was over. Before the Queen left she shook my hand saying, "I look forward to seeing the head." The two of them left the room and I walked over to the window and took a deep breath. What a half-hour that had been!

As soon as I got home I started work on the head as I had a fixed date for the next sitting because Bill had told me that there could be no delays as she was about to leave for a Commonwealth tour.

This was to be a Symbolic Head as well as a likeness I decided, having learnt from the Queen Mother's head that a portrait was not what was required. What the Royal Tank Corps would get was a symbol, more like the head that appears on the coins. I decided to give the Queen a polished gold crown like the one she had worn as a Princess at her father's coronation. I also

369

decided that I would make the top of her dress polished bronze so the Royal Tank badge would stand out as a brooch. All this meant that the head would have to be cast in Italy.

The morning came for the clay to be carried into the Palace for the second sitting, but as it was very heavy it was impossible for me to do so on my own. I thought it would be fun if Margie could give me a hand so she could come in as my assistant and share this incredible experience with me. We drove to the door and between us we carried the head through the door.

A footman rushed forward and asked if he could help, but Margie hung on to her side and I told them that she was used to carrying heavy weights! I explained that we would rather do the job ourselves, but if they wouldn't mind carrying the stand and my tools it would help! Up we went in the lift and down the passage following the footman until we arrived at the Chinese Room and put the head on the stand. Margie had a quick look round and then left with the footman while I waited for the Queen to arrive.

The second sitting was even more wonderful than the first. We chatted away for a while and then Bill came in to talk over details of the coming events of the day with his boss while I got on with my work. Actually there was not very much to do as I felt that I had already taken the sculpture as far as I could. When the secretary looked at his watch and asked me how I was doing, I said I had finished. We all shook hands and they left. I wrapped up the head in plastic and waited for a couple of footmen to come and give me a hand to get everything back to the car.

So ended what must be one of the most bizarre things I have ever done. I drove back to my mother's flat to have lunch with her and Margie and report on how it had gone. Margie told me that she had walked out of the Palace and along the railings until she was opposite the Chinese Room window where she could see my back as I worked at the stand on the head. I wish I had known she was there and given her a royal wave!

Roy took a mould of the clay and I took his plaster down to the foundry in Italy for casting. Some months later Margie and I collected the five heads and smuggled them back across the border, nearly getting caught as we passed through the Saint Bernard tunnel. I delivered four bronzes to Tim Green, three of which he took to the Barracks.

After finishing the Queen and the Queen Mother I framed the tape measure that I had used and now have it hanging in my study above Hans Holbein the Younger's portrait of *Sir Thomas More*, painted when he was Chancellor to Henry VIII. Thomas is on our family tree and as his head had been removed by a monarch I thought it was an appropriate place to hang the tape that had been around both queens' necks!

Margie and I prefer the Grand Saint Bernard to all the passes that cross the Alps. We have used the Chamonix Tunnel several times, but the terrible fire several years ago had confirmed our own mistrust of the ten-mile long tunnel, so we had decided to avoid using it again. Another pass between Italy and Switzerland that requires driving your car onto a train and sitting in it for half an hour while you slowly chug through! It is very dark, low, claustrophobic and spooky, necessitating a glass of vino and very loud music on the cassette player. We have only used that particular tunnel once!

Three heads of the Colonel in Chief of the Royal Tank Regiments

The Grand Saint Bernard is different as it is composed of a long open gallery for most of the way and only a short tunnel section at the top. If you are lucky enough to travel in the summer you can use the old high pass. It is well worth the extra hour's drive to go via the monastery to enjoy the views. It amazes me to think of all the people who have passed that way. First to cross the mountains were people like the Iceman who was found frozen, murdered by an arrow in his back 5,300 years ago. The Roman armies marched over the pass on their way to invade England and later Napoleon with his armies did the same to invade Italy. Grand Tour dandies, like Lord Byron, headed towards Rome, walking behind their coaches as the horses strained to drag them over the pass. It is a very romantic route.

On top of the 'Grand Saint Bernard' pass

However, the high pass is usually closed so we are mainly forced to use the tunnel. I always feel sorry for the Customs officers who have to work in the fumy atmosphere so I wasn't surprised to hear my friend, Geo Urban, tell me that the Swiss had done an in-depth study of Border Custom officers who work inside tunnels. The results had shown that there were two kinds of men who took the job: Manual and Intellectual. It turned out that the Manual officer sees you coming and waves his hand in front of his belly indicating that you are to pass through the barrier without stopping. The Intellectual officer sees you coming and flips his head left and right to indicate the same thing!

Usually this is exactly what happens and fortunately we have never been stopped. Actually that is not quite true as we were once stopped at a German border because we didn't have a GB sticker on the back of the car! In those days we were travelling on Australian passports so I explained to the German that as we had an AUS sticker we didn't need a GB one. I could see his brain struggling with this information until he said, "No, the car has a GB number plate so you must have a GB sticker. You will have to buy one from me before you can proceed." He charged us an outrageous amount that made me wonder how much he earned this way every year. The officer didn't even get out of his cubicle to take a look at the back of the car so he must have had a mirror set up on the side of the road. I guess he has now retired and is living in comfort on the Spanish coast at 'Costa-a-Lot'.

As we were constantly taking plasters down in the car and bringing back bronzes and were not breaking any laws, we had become a bit careless. Of course it had to be when we were bringing back the heads of the Queen that we had a heart-thumping experience. We had loaded the bronzes into the back of the car at the foundry and covered them over with a blanket.

We arrived at the checkpoint inside the tunnel and found ourselves stuck behind a stalled campervan. Rather than help push it out of the way the officer started to walk towards us. Because we were in a British car and had the steering wheel on the right side instead of the left, it was Margie who lowered the window and handed over our passports when asked if we had anything illegal to declare, which we didn't, only having *works of art*.

We had discussed being searched on the way up the mountain and had dismissed the possibility as it had never happened. "No, nothing to declare." My heart practically stopped when the bored officer walked towards the back of the car and peered through the windows at our load.

Bang, the campervan in front of us backfired and jumped forward. I held my breath and let the clutch in and slowly rolled forward as I could see in my rear-view mirror an irate Italian in the car behind waving his fist at the officer. I prayed that the two of them would get into a shouting match and the officer forget about us. Luckily that is just what happened and we crawled away.

We rolled out of the tunnel into Switzerland and pulled off onto a narrow farm track. We fell out of the car and found our legs had turned to jelly, but soon relaxed, started to laugh and then fantasised about the newspapers headlines, *Smugglers apprehended at the border with Queen of England's Head*. We decided to celebrate straightaway with a glass of wine and share a Mars bar. We continued the trip with our hearts in our mouths and were very happy to arrive home without any more scares.

On the Last Night of the Proms, *Land of Hope and Glory* makes my eyes water, an emotion I have inherited from my father. I think Queen Elizabeth II is one of the most remarkable women who has ever lived. After only a short apprenticeship she has reigned for 50 years without putting a foot wrong. It is quite remarkable and I don't believe that we shall ever see the like of her again.

I am also a fan of Princess Anne. She holds herself superbly and appears to be quite tall, which to my surprise she isn't. I discovered this when Margie and I were invited to a dinner at the Victoria and Albert Museum by the Royal Geographical Society in 2000. Our invitation was one of those fortunate happenings that came about because I had lent the RGS some of my Symbolic Sculptures for an exhibition. The dinner marked the end of Princess Anne's tenure as Honorary President of the RGS. After the meal she spoke with wit and we were very impressed with her style and assurance She is lucky to be a wonderful mixture of her mother and her remarkable father.

I have always admired Prince Philip as he is completely his own man, says what he thinks. A wise and witty man who has done marvellous things for young people throughout the Commonwealth. My one brush with the Duke came about at the unveiling of the *Bonds of Friendship* in Portsmouth.

The story of the *Bonds of Friendship* started with my receiving a letter from Admiral Scotland, the President of the British Australian Society, in which he asked me for my ideas on how to mark the 200th birthday of the departure of the First Settlers from Portsmouth and their landing in Sydney Australia. I can't remember how he found out about me, but when he invited me to come and see him in London, I took along a maquette of the *Bonds of Friendship* in Pop Begg's old leather top-hat case.

'Bonds of Friendship' maquette

When the admiral asked me if I had had any ideas I opened up the case and pulled out the polished bronze of the *Bonds of Friendship*. I already knew from the admiral's letter that the Society wanted a memorial to be placed in

Portsmouth where the convicts had embarked on the ships bound for Australia and another memorial was to be placed where they disembarked at Sydney Cove on arrival.

I suggested that the English edition should be patinated to represent the Old Country and the Australian one should be polished gold to represent the New Country. I explained that I saw the symbolism of the sculpture as representing the inseparable link between Britain and Australia. Scotland liked the idea and asked me to find out how much two eight-foot long versions of the sculpture would cost. I left the meeting full of hope for the commission but, knowing that we were talking about a vast amount of money, I was not very confident that it would happen, thinking that it would all be too good to be true, in fact, unbelievable!

The admiral also asked me to explain my ideas to Austen Spragges, the Head of the Portsmouth branch of the British Australian Society. So began an extraordinary encounter with a larger-than-life character. Austen asked if he could come and see me in Somerset and on the appointed day a large car arrived and a large man got out. We welcomed Austen with open arms as this would be the biggest job any artist could hope for, if it came off. Margie had made a special lunch and a lot of it, which was lucky as Austen also turned out to be a large eater!

It was a very successful lunch and by the time Austen left, plans had been made for a granite stone to be quarried on Dartmoor as a base for the Sydney sculpture. I personally thought getting a plinth from Dartmoor, home of the famous prison, was rather rubbing salt in the wound but kept my mouth shut! Portsmouth already had a plinth at the Sallyport, as a granite slab had been quarried in the Blue Mountains in NSW and sent over by the Lord Mayor of Sydney. It had been erected on the exact spot from where the First Settlers had embarked 200 years previously and would be the perfect plinth for a giant *Bonds of Friendship*. The only problem was that all this had to be completed in nine months so the Queen could unveil it on the anniversary of the Fleet's departure from England, and the Australian edition was to be completed in time for the Governor General to unveil it on the anniversary of the Fleet's arrival a year later in Australia!

I rang Roy and asked him if he could make me a plaster ring six foot diameter and two foot wide. There was a moments silence at the other end of the telephone and then he said, "It will take a couple of weeks." Nothing ever fazed Roy Wakeford! True to his word he had a plaster ready for Jack Crofton's Meridian Foundry under the Peckham railway arch, where the sand casting would be poured for the Portsmouth sculpture. Jack did a wonderful job of casting the two rings and joining them together to make the *Bonds of Friendship*. When I went to see the finished sculpture with Austen we were absolutely delighted.

While Meridian were sand casting the Portsmouth sculpture that would be patinated dark brown for the Old Country, I ordered the Australian edition from the Mariani Foundry in Pietrasanta, as it had to be a lost-wax casting and polished bright gold for the New Country.

To cut a long story short, both sculptures were miraculously completed and delivered on time, one to Portsmouth and the other to Sydney. There had been a problem about paying for the Australian edition, but it was solved by Peter, the cousin who taught me to swim by throwing me in the lagoon full of weeds. Peter was now a Director of the Bank of New South Wales and he persuaded the Board that this would be a very good thing for the Bank to support. Perhaps he was still feeling guilty about how rough he been with me at the end of a rope!

Events moved steadily forward and the day of the Portsmouth unveiling arrived and what a day it was! It started with the Lord Mayor of Portsmouth asking Austen, Margie and myself to an official lunch at the Town Hall. At the end of the meal we all boarded a bus and were driven down to the Sallyport, where the sculpture was hiding under a Union Jack and Australia's national flag. We filed out of the bus and walked over to two rows of chairs on one side of a square of spectators with John Slim, the son of Lord Slim of Burma, who had taken over as President of the British Australian Society from Admiral Scotland. I had met him a couple of times and really liked him and, as he was standing in our row, we at least had one friend close by, which stopped me feeling quite so nervous.

As we passed the benches of spectators we saw Roy, his wife Olive, our three boys and Admiral David Martin and his wife, Susie, Margie's closest friend from her days at Clyde School near Melbourne. They had all met for lunch in a fish and chip shop and had a much jollier party than we had had in the Town Hall.

"What's hiding under the flags? An elephant!"

While we waited for the Queen, who was busy commissioning the Royal Navy's new Aircraft Carrier *Invincible*, a troop of soldiers dressed in period uniforms marched into the square and took up a position along the ancient city wall while the band of the Royal Marines played stirring marches. The Queen arrived and mounted the rostrum, and with a yank on a string she pulled the flags off the sculpture. Everyone clapped and I gave a sigh of relief.

No one had told us that we would be introduced to the Royal couple. They walked around the sculpture and came across to our row of chairs. The Lord Mayor introducing everyone as he went and it soon came to our turn. After the Queen came Prince Philip and when he arrived in front of Slim he joked, "I thought you were hiding an elephant under the flags." Come to think about it that's exactly what it had looked like.

The unveiling of the 'Bonds of Friendship' by the Queen

It was then my turn to be cross-examined with the inevitable question. "What are you doing here?" When I confessed that I was the sculptor all I got back was a big grin!

A year would have to pass before the *Bonds of Friendship* would be unveiled in Sydney by Sir Zelman Cohen, the then Governor General of Australia. If the ceremony turned out to be anything like the one at Portsmouth it was something to look forward to!

My first trip to Italy with Enzo Plazzotta in 1974 was a *Coming of Age* adventure for me because I was leaving behind the world of cold bronze, which I had used up to then. All my first children and heroic sculptures were cast by Roy using a mixture of bronze powder and polyester resin. Harrods had asked me to upgrade to casting in real bronze so they could charge more for my sculptures, which made sense, as it would also lighten the work Roy had to do when we had multiple orders.

With great excitement I set off by train with Enzo from London bound for Italy. His car went with us and when we got to Milan we headed south in it down the Autostrada heading for Pietrasanta and Fonderia Mariani. I hadn't been in Italy since I was 14 years old, so it was wonderful to be back.

Enzo's house was just up the coast from Forte dei Marmi, the seaside resort where I had stayed with my parents on the famous holiday when the money was put into the mailbox by accident. Just inland was the ancient 11th century fortified town of Pietrasanta, for a time home to Michelangelo. He was mining marble in the famous Monte Altissimo quarries behind the town of Carrara in the Apennines. The quarries are so high they can only be worked in the summer months, snow closing them throughout the winter.

We arrived at Enzo's home on the side of a hill looking out to sea to be met by his wife Gillie after an exciting journey across the Po Valley, over the Apennines to Genoa and the Mediterranean, then down to La Spezia. My eyes were exhausted from taking in all the magnificent scenery and although I have now driven that road many times I have never ceased to be thrilled by what I see along the way.

Next morning we drove to the foundry in Pietrasanta to deliver the wax sculptures that Enzo had brought out for casting in the car. After he had finished at the foundry he took me to see the studio he kept in the town so he could work in peace when his family were staying and used to live in when he was down on his own. I couldn't believe his generosity when he said that I could use it whenever I liked. It was a magic place full of his old plasters.

The first time I used the studio was about six months after this trip. Fred Kobler had commissioned me to sculpt a life-size figure of Papageno, the comedy hero of the *Magic Flute*, which he wanted to give to Glyndebourne. I had done a maquette in plasticine of Papageno wearing the original feather suit designed by Mozart so I asked Roy if he would drive down with me and help enlarge it in Pietrasanta, take a waste mould and then produce a positive plaster for the Italian foundry to use for a bronze casting. This was a tall order as we would only have a week and meant working at top speed, but I knew with Roy's help we could do it.

It was February, the mountains were covered in snow and it was freezing in the studio as the only heating was a tiny hot-air blower. The warmest spot around was in the next-door café, so when we weren't working, we lived there. The enlargement was straightforward as I had already done the clay head in England, using one of the boys' teachers at school as a model. The Customs man had been very suspicious of the head when we arrived at Calais and insisted on poking it, much to my annoyance.

We soon had *Papageno* finished dressed in a simple suit of feathers. All that was left to do were the hands and feet. Roy had no complaint about my using his hands as a model, but when it came to having to bare his feet to the cold there had been a considerable amount of grumbling! However, with the hot-air blower directed straight at his toes he was able to survive the ordeal and, with his constant urging from above, I finished the feet in record time!

Three maquettes of 'Papageno'

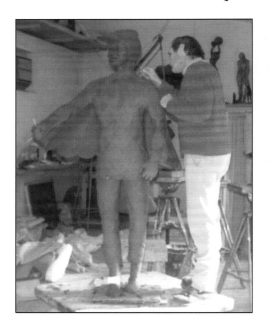 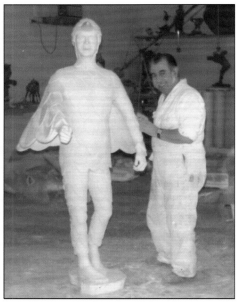

From clay to plaster in record time

As it was Roy's first time in Italy I had promised to take him to see Florence before going home. Roy called it the 'Umbrella Tour' as I used mine to point out all the famous sites as we hurried past them. We managed to visit the Uffizi, Cathedral museum, Baptistery, Pazzi Chapel, Ponte Vecchio,

Loggia, statue of *David*, and have lunch, all in record time. We got home in the dark and packed up for an early start in the morning. Up at three o'clock we drove all day, arriving at Calais in time to catch the night ferry!

Papageno came up from Italy and was placed in the gardens of Glyndebourne. The sculpture was to be a memorial to Fred Kobler in recognition of his generosity for all the money he had given to finance the Mozart productions at Glyndebourne.

The sculpture was erected that summer and we were invited to a performance of the *Magic Flute*. George Christie kindly lent us his box for the evening and as Margie's brother Michael and his wife Judy were in England at the time, we took them with us. The four of us had a wonderful evening absorbing the magic of Mozart. It was also the hottest and stuffiest night I have ever experienced, but luckily we could take off our coats, ties and shoe as we were in George's private box. The new theatre I am told is air-conditioned!

'Papageno' at Glyndebourne

379

I did an edition of the maquettes for Glyndebourne to sell to Mozart fans and they all sold. The sculpture was fun to do and people said they liked it. However, I am afraid it didn't please everybody and when Fred Kobler died it was sold at an auction house in London, and *Papageno* disappeared taking Roy's feet with him.

Thankfully the story has a happy ending as some of our friends happened to visit the Petto Gardens near Bath and reported that they had seen him in the woods! The owners had bought *Papageno* and had taken him home, so Fred's memorial with the plaque still exists and is well cared for, but I am glad he doesn't know it is no longer at Glyndebourne!

The only other sculpture I sold to Fred was a five-foot long version of the Chinese Flying Horse. When the first Chinese exhibition came to the Royal Academy in London I had fallen in love with the Flying Horse. The models that they were selling as souvenirs did not do the sculpture justice so I decided to make my own. I still have it and it continues to send shivers up my spine.

'Flying Horse' maquette

The Chinese used to believe that when they died their souls were carried to Heaven on the back of a horse that could fly. As the horse races past a swallow, one of its hooves grazes a feather, causing it to look round in surprise as it believed that it was the fastest creature in the sky! Having done the maquette I decided that if I did a five-foot long version perhaps someone would buy it, so I made the sculpture and Roy cast it in cold bronze.

I showed it to Fred and thank goodness he liked it and said he would buy one, but only if it was in the middle of his lake! If we put my *Flying Horse* in the lake the swallow would have to be only inches above the water and therein lay the problem. The first difficulty was to find out how deep the lake was! Fred had a little boat so I was able to row out into the middle and measure down to the concrete bottom. Having found out that the water level was maintained at exactly four feet, Roy welded up a pipe stand that would keep the sculpture upright and the swallow above the surface.

When everything was ready we took the sculpture down to Fred's country house. Can you imagine two men in a tiny boat with a five-foot long horse, struggling to get a one-inch diameter spigot onto a pipe stand? With a great deal of cursing and a lot of laughter, but without anyone falling in, we eventually managed it. We rowed back to the shore after tying a string to the horse's tail so we could turn the sculpture into the best viewing position. When we had finished late in the evening my *Flying Horse* looked very much at home with the swallow skimming over the water.

The 'Flying Horse' in Fred's lake

Fred died soon after we had placed the sculpture and I like to think that my *Flying Horse* took his soul straight to Heaven. By supporting Glyndebourne he gave countless thousands of opera fans an opportunity to enjoy the wonderful music of his beloved Mozart. He was a unique man and it was an honour to have known him.

As I am talking about Amadeus Mozart I think it would be right to include another story here about the composer before returning again to Italy. We were on our way home from the foundry and as I had just made a very good sale I decided we would treat ourselves to a night in Monte Carlo as neither of us had been since we were teenagers with our parents. Margie had actually won at the tables in the casino with her father, but I had been too young to be allowed in! We arrived as the sun was setting, drove into the main square and parked outside the Hôtel de Paris. We took the cheapest room available and relaxed in a hot bath before going down to dinner. The dining room of the hotel is one of the great extravaganzas in the world, a bit like the Hall of Mirrors at Versailles, with masses of marble columns and golden statues. The room was a wonder to behold, although completely empty except for a table of Americans who were obviously celebrating.

We had a superb meal made doubly so by the attendance of two gifted violinists who were both well past retirement age. They played superbly and as we were the only people in the room who seemed to be listening, the two old men gave us their full attention.

If there is one piece of music that Margie and I associate with our life together it is *Fascination*. We asked the men if they knew it? "Yes, of course." They played beautifully and we thanked them with a glass of champagne each, which of course led to several more renderings of the song throughout the meal. We began to feel like Gary Cooper and Audrey Hepburn in *Love in the Afternoon*, the theme music of the film being *Fascination*.

We were within earshot of the Americans' table so couldn't help but hear some of the rowdier parts of their conversation. Suddenly they started to toast each other and the signing of a contract for a new film, *Amadeus*. Actually I didn't like the film much as it made Mozart out to be a course person and I just don't believe that someone who could write such divine music could be.

One day when I was on my way to London in the car I happened to tune in to *Desert Island Discs*, a programme where the interviewer asks a famous guest to name his ten favourite records that he would like to have if shipwrecked on a desert island. I can't remember who was being interviewed, but I shall always remember that one of their choices was the adagio movement of Mozart's *Bassoon Concerto*. The interviewer asked him why he had chosen this particular piece and was told by the man that the first time that he heard the music was one sunny day when he was driving along the Corniche towards Monte Carlo. He said he had been so overcome by the melody that he had to stop the car and listen to it as he gazed out over the Mediterranean. On hearing that I of course had to buy the tape. One concerto led to another and eventually Mozart's *Violin Concertos* and my falling in love with the adagio movement of the *Third*, the opening bars of which float in the air like a gossamer thread on a zephyr breeze.

After a day in the studio I always like to relax in a hot bath before having dinner as standing all day on concrete turns my feet into blocks of ice for which there is no better cure than to lie in a hot tub. One evening I was doing just this while listening to the *adagio* from Mozart's *Third Violin Concerto*, when suddenly in my mind's eye I saw the form of the opening bars of the movement as a sculpture. Next day I made what I had envisaged on a copper tube armature coated with plaster. It was my first abstract sculpture and I called it *Adagio*.

'Adagio', my first Symbolic Sculpture

I loved what I had done and immediately understood that if I could get inspiration from music I would be able to do the same thing for all the values of life. So began my *Symbolic Sculptures*, which now number over a hundred, all thanks to *Desert Island Discs* and Mozart for starting me along such a rewarding path of creativity.

But to return to our evening in Monte Carlo at the Hôtel de Paris. It had been quite a dinner and as we had both overeaten we decided to go for a walk along the casino's terrace. As we walked I told Margie the story of my maternal grandmother Nell and her engagement to Alex Freeland. Nell, then aged sixteen, and her recently widowed mother, were on holiday in Monte Carlo. My mother told me how when the two of them were waiting for the lift in the casino a 30-year-old gentleman had joined them and, during the trip between floors, he had fallen in love with her mother. Nell, loving the attention, naturally fell in love with Alex and they were married the following year. They had four children spaced over a period of 18 years, my mother, Nancy, being the last child.

There is one other story about Monte Carlo, not the one in Monaco, but a village of the same name in the hills above Lucca. When Enzo became ill he could not continue to use the studio in Pietrasanta so to keep it occupied he lent it to an American sculptress named Laura. Enzo still allowed us to use the studio bedroom so we got to know Laura, who was married to a conductor on a scholarship to study music at Lucca University. During his research the husband had discovered a previously unknown overture to Rossini's opera, *The Silken Ladder*, and was going to give the first performance of it in the little village of Monte Carlo. Laura asked us if we would like to attend the premiere.

We found the village on the map and drove up on the appointed evening which turned out to be one of the most enchanting we have ever had. The village opera house was on one side of the square and was tiny. The auditorium was horseshoe shaped with five rows of seats, six chairs to a row, while the first and second tiers were divided into tiny boxes with just two seats. The theatre could hold about 50 people at a pinch and every seat was taken. The theatre's acoustics are so famous that La Scala artists begged to sing there. The stage was minuscule and the orchestra consisted of just six musicians. Laura's husband arrived, the opera started and we were spellbound. The performance in the doll's-house theatre was sheer magic.

When the opera ended the encores went on and on and on! Eventually the curtain came down for the last time and we all filed out into the warm evening air. Laura had kindly asked us to join their party for supper with the cast at the local restaurant. Neither of us had ever been to such a noisy party. Margie sat next to an elderly pear-shaped retired opera singer, who immediately fell in love with her red hair, but as he could speak not a word of English he failed miserably with his seduction!

Enzo died much too young. He had exhausted his body by living a very full life. During the war he had been a member of the Italian anti-Fascist guerrilla army and had been captured twice by the Germans. The second time he was arrested was outside the castle in Milan dressed as a nun! He was sentenced to a German labour camp but managed to escape by jumping off the train while it was moving. Unfortunately the bumps and bashes had taken their toll. Enzo was a gifted and generous man. He not only taught me about sculpture, he introduced me to his accountant Allan Russell, without whose help I could never have coped with the business side of my life, and Mario Benbassat in Geneva, who became the principal backer of Edition Limitée.

However, Enzo did *not* approve of my Symbolic Sculptures. One evening he grinned at me and said, "Why are you making all these shitty shapes?" This made me laugh as it reminded me of when we were living at Marwood and Mark as a little boy had been asked by his schoolteacher what his father did for a living. His reply was, "He makes *rudies* in the barn."

Enzo's sculptural aim was to capture the woman of the Sixties and he just did not understand my attraction to symmetrical mathematical forms.

I visited Enzo when he was very ill in a London hospital before he died. It was time to say farewell and he did so with a big smile and a joke, in exactly the same way as he had greeted me when I first sought his advice. He was a great man and a marvellous friend to whom I owe an enormous debt.

Sculpture by Enzo Plazzotta

Around about this time some friends bought a farmhouse called Puccetti in the olive groves above Lucca, about 30 minutes' drive away from Pietrasanta. The farmhouse dated back to the 15th century and not much had been done to the plumbing since that time, so bathrooms had to be added and electric lights installed before they could use it for summer holidays. They needed someone to oversee the alterations and I suggested that they should use my interpreter, Pam Launari. Pam, the sister of the boys' teacher at school who had posed for *Papageno*, had married an Italian who would be very useful in dealing with the men working on the house. To cut a long story short they gave Pam the job and a little second-hand car so she could journey between her house in Forte dei Marmi and the farmhouse in the hill village of San Stephano.

When the time came for our next visit to the foundry our friends suggested that we use the farmhouse. To get to the house we had to drive over a steep hill and through beautiful chestnut woods. The views from the sitting room balcony on the second floor were breathtaking, looking out over a valley of olive trees and vines, a view to record on canvas.

As soon as our friends found out that we would be at Puccetti they would just happen to be in the area and come to call! Margie's brother Michael and his family liked the farmhouse so much that they rented it for a month. It really was a special place. Pam and her husband also loved the house and in the winter, when there was no chance of the owners arriving unannounced, they would throw 'bring your own bottle' parties for all their friends. The old house must have enjoyed coming to life again.

Olive trees above Pietrasanta

Puccetti owned some vine terraces that were cared for by the local farmer who harvested them on a share basis. The wine was stored in enormous glass bottles that measured a good four feet around the girth. I discovered that instead of a cork the locals sealed the wine by adding an inch of olive oil in the neck of the giant flasks to stop the air turning the wine sour. The mice knew about this custom and would lower their tails down into the oil for a free meal! Beatrix Potter would have loved the idea!

A tiny mountain village store supplied us with basic food for breakfast and dotted around the hills were several restaurants we could use in the evening. I shall always remember one particularly glorious summer evening when we had Margie's niece, Kate, staying with us. On the way home after a very good dinner we saw that the woods were alive with Fire Flies, all signalling with their little flashing lights. We stopped the car and got out to see if we could catch one, and found we could do so with ease. When Kate lay down in the middle of the road they came and buzzed all around her making it a truly magical scene.

Our Puccetti days came to an end and we moved back to Forte dei Marmi and found a marvellous hotel so we could walk up and down one of the best beaches in Europe, much to Margie's joy. It amazes me to think that we had walked the same beach with our parents, me aged 12 and Margie when 20.

*The beach at Forte dei Marmi with Monte Altissimo
on Margie's left shoulder*

Michelangelo's Monte Altissimo quarry

Whenever I think of the Puccetti wine I remember a little story I was once told about an Englishman who bought a house in Tuscany that had two terraces of vines, an upper one and a lower one. He made his own wine from the crop and became rather boring about the quality of the product, bringing it out for his friends to try when they came to stay. A wine expert called one day and was subjected to the homemade vintage. "What do you think of that, eh? This one comes from the lower terrace." The expert sniffed and sipped and replied, "I don't think it travelled very well." Well, I think it's funny!

Over the last few years we have made the journey to Italy our annual holiday. We have found a delightfully easy route that just happens to pass by some of our favourite restaurants at lunchtime and quiet hotels where we could stay a night or two to break the journey!

Portofino
Our windows are above the big white boat

Once we left Pietrasanta in the morning and as it was my birthday we decided to stay in Portofino. I rang our favourite hotel and booked a room that overlooked the harbour. As we drove along the narrow road that hugs the coast from Santa Marguerita to Portofino it began to rain. For some reason a policeman was stopping cars from entering the port, which meant that the tourists had a half-hour walk into the village. As we were staying in the hotel they allowed us through and on the way passed a young couple getting very wet so stopped and offered them a lift.

They were Americans on their honeymoon and by the time we arrived at the hotel we had discovered that they lived in Fort Worth, Texas. I told them that we knew the town as I had sold some children sculptures to a man called Bill Davis. They couldn't believe this because their house was directly below Bill's home, as he lived on top of the cliff behind them. Of course they had to join us for lunch and at the end of the meal very kindly bought me an ice-cream birthday cake!

Our room looked out on the wide fishermen's quay and down the tiny harbour. The quay had been cleared for a carnival that evening and the main attraction were some acrobats. We watched them rehearse in the afternoon from our balcony and then after dinner performing to a packed crowd. It was a birthday to remember and I shall never be able to work out how Margie was able to organise the carnival especially for me, and keep it a secret!

Acrobats practising in Portofino

One day I found a little Penguin book of Goethe's *Letters from Italy*, and read the following, which I think worth quoting as it sums up the country architectural heritage so well.

> *When I indulge in self-reflection, I discover in myself a feeling of great joy. Let me put it like this. In this place, whoever looks seriously about him and has eyes to see is bound to become a stronger character. He acquires a sense of strength hitherto unknown to himself. So let me seize things one by one as they come; they will sort themselves out later. I am not here simply to have a good time, but to devote myself to the noble objects about me, to educate myself before I reach forty.*

Over the last 30 years I have loved visiting the 'noble objects' of Italy. It is an enchanted country and without doubt it is one of the most uplifting places in the world. I suppose the place took off when the Etruscans arrived around 3,000 years ago, so that is probably a good place to begin.

ETRUSCANS

They were the first Italians of note, but amazingly no one is absolutely sure where they came from! The most likely explanation is that they arrived by sea from south-west Turkey. There is an ancient story about a terrible drought that happened in that area and it is said that the king solved the problem of feeding his subjects by putting half of them into ships and packing them off to found a colony, thus leaving enough food for those who stayed behind. That story rings true to me because its how the world was peopled.

The Etruscans arrived and settled along the coast between Rome and Genoa. Perhaps because they brought useful skills with them the indigenous natives welcomed them and the two peoples seemed to have lived in harmony. The Etruscans certainly appear to have been a peaceful party-loving lot if their tomb paintings are anything to go by! Most of these scenes depict feasts with the diners drinking from raised cups as they toast each other. It is an experience to visit the tombs as the precision of the cut stone walls is masterly.

The Etruscans prospered and spread up through the Apennines and founded cities like Florence and Voltera. I believe they are the ancestors of the present day artisans of Tuscany, because if you look at the eyes in their sculptures and compare them to the eyes of the people of Florence today, you will find that they are very similar. Despite the fact that the Romans tried to obliterate completely the Etruscan culture after defeating them in a bloody war, their genes are still very much alive in Tuscany.

One of the skills the colonisers brought was the casting of bronze. A visit to the Etruscan Museum in Florence is well worthwhile, as there you can find many examples of their exquisite bronzes and terracotta sculptures and tomb paintings that show their way of life.

The Etruscans used to go to the island of Elba to collect iron-ore pebbles from the rivers to ship back to the mainland for smelting. It is a very quick crossing to the island nowadays by catamaran ferry, but it must have been quite a trip 3,000 years ago. This indicates to me that these people were not only good artisans, they were also very good sailors which supports the story of their originally coming from southern Turkey by sea.

One of the finest examples of the skill of the Etruscans can be found in their polished bronze mirrors but to see the best collections of these you have to go to the Metropolitan Museum in New York. One side is highly polished to act as a mirror while the other is engraved with fantastic scenes of the gods and goddesses. The line drawings are beautiful and tell us most of what we know about the people themselves, even though we are still unable to read the text engraved on the mirrors.

In Voltera city there is an original Etruscan arch in the ancient defence wall through which is still used by motor traffic. However, it is not the gateway you have to see, but the Museum of Etruscan bronzes, because here lives, in my opinion, one of the most elegant and exciting sculptures ever created. It is called *The Shadow of the Evening* or *Ombra della Sera*. The Etruscans apparently believed that their shadows were their souls. I like this idea because I have always been fascinated by my own shadow. I find looking at one's own shadow on a bare expanse of beach, as the sun is setting, is quite enthralling!

Ombra della Sera really is an exquisite 18-inch high bronze sculpture. The young man's head is of normal proportion but his body, arms and legs are immensely elongated. He is truly beautiful and full of spirit. I bought a bronze copy from the museum shop and it now stands in my study and fills me with awe. The sculpture was ploughed up by a farmer who for years used it as a fire poker! I find it very hard to believe that Giacometti didn't know of the sculpture. I personally have no problem with artists using ideas from the great masters of the past, in fact, I see it as paying a compliment to the original artist's concept and the adaptation as another act of creativity.

Ombra della Sera   ***Detail***   ***Giacometti***

The same ideas have been popping into artists' heads from time immemorial. I have recently been introduced to a 10,000-year-old sculpture found in a Judea wadi by a Bedouin that is in the British Museum's superb collection of man's artistic skill. When I saw it I immediately thought of Brancusi's *Kiss*.

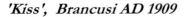

'Kiss', Brancusi AD 1909   ***'Kiss', Judea 8,000 BC***

Did Matisse see *The Age of Gold* by Zucchi that was on exhibition in Paris when he was painting *Joy of Life*?

Zucchi : The Age of Gold, 1540–1609

I can see four scenes in Zucchi's painting used by Matisse. *The Dancers*, marked number 4, is the most obvious. I admire him for being able to gain so much inspiration from the one painting. Don't miss the Brussels sculpture of the little boy peeing in the river by number 1.

Matisse : Joy of Life

GREEKS

The Greeks were the next to arrive in Italy. They came to trade with the Etruscans who taught them how to cast sculptures in bronze using the lost-wax process. They in turn taught the Etruscans how to paint pottery. It must have been a lively trade as Greek settlements soon sprang up along the coast of Tuscany and the finest of these was the port of Paestum south of Rome.

Temple of Neptune at Paestum

The Temples of Paestum are some of the best preserved Greek temples and are a wonder to behold. Three of them, the Basilica, Poseidon and Ceres, stand beside each other on a slight rise of ground. It must have been a very important port to have three such unbelievable architectural gems. It is a magical spot where you can still capture the spirit of the place.

Paestum ended in tragedy, which is why it has been preserved for us today. Malaria was unknown in the area when the port was built, but of course it was inevitable that one day a sailor would arrive on a trading vessel carrying malaria in his blood. Over time the mosquitoes breeding in the marshes around the port became carriers of the deadly disease, which caused the population to abandon the city leaving the temples to stand as a memorial to the Grecian architects and builders for us to admire today.

ROMANS

After defeating the Etruscans in war the Romans enslaved the people, burnt all their books and outlawed the language. So complete was the ethnic cleansing that linguists still can't decipher the majority of the Etruscan script that has been found in their tombs or on the mirror backs. The Romans were not nice people when it came to dealing with their enemies. When Crassus defeated Spartacus he crucified 6,000 slaves along the entire length of the Appian Way between Rome and Brindisi on the heel of Italy, and left the bodies to rot!

However, the Romans were quick to learn and set about constructing the greatest buildings ever created by man. It is hard to fathom how the Romans were able to construct such buildings and it fills one admiration for the architects. After Goethe visited the Coliseum he wrote:

> *...which made me realise for the first time what solid masonry means. These people built for eternity; they omitted nothing from their calculations except the insane fury of the destroyers to whom nothing was sacred. We came to the Coliseum at twilight. Once one has seen it, everything else seems small. It is so huge that the mind*

cannot retain its image; one remembers it as smaller than it is, so that every time one returns to it, one is again astounded by its size. In a letter on the Pantheon he wrote: *...so great within and without, has overwhelmed me with admiration.*

What an incredible structure it is! Margie and I stayed in the Albergo del Senato beside the Pantheon on our last visit. I chose the hotel because I wanted to be able to see the temple roof from our bedroom. When I had rung up and made the booking, I had asked if we could have such a room. "Si si," was the reply, but I wondered if that was just another Italian answer!

We had took the train down to Rome from Pietrasanta and arrived on a wet afternoon. The pink walls of the buildings were reflected in the puddles on the empty streets. We registered and with the porter and our cases squeezed into the smallest lift in existence. Up we went to the top floor, down a passage to room 666. We walked out onto an ivy-covered balcony where, right in front of our eyes, was the temple's great domed roof.

Pantheon
The fuzzy green growth top left was our balcony

After exploring the city we would return to our room and sit gazing at the temple, in fact we gazed for so long we got to know by sight each of the cats that live in the walls. I always carry binoculars with me when travelling, so we were able to study closely these feline citizens of Imperial Rome as they climbed up onto the dome. A narrow cornice runs around the building eight foot down from the eaves, a veritable catwalk! The tabbies would appear out of tiny slots in the gigantic walls and jump down onto this narrow ledge and use it to reach the portico roof, jumping over places that had broken away. It was amazing to watch, as we were six floors up! Once on the roof they would walk all over it, right up to the skylight in the dome. It was the greatest entertainment to watch them stalk across the roof.

Pantheon

Entering through the colossal bronze doors of the Pantheon is one of the world's greatest thrills. Nothing prepares you for the shock of what you see before you. The portico of the temple is of a size and structure that is familiar to the eye because it is similar to St Paul's in London or the Madeleine in Paris, but step inside and a whole new world floods your senses.

The interior is one vast circular space that soars up to the sky. An enormous round hole in the centre of the roof lets in the sunlight. There are no windows around the walls, only this great orb of light above one's head. Clouds drift across the space as though there is a painted canopy moving above you. We walked into the centre across the beautiful inlaid wet marble floor that glistened with the morning's rain. The architect was a genius.

The circular wall is divided by great pillars that support the massive roof. Between these pillars are alcoves, occupied by Roman Catholic altars, as the Pantheon is now a functioning church. You can imagine yourself back in the glorious times of the Roman Empire. Senators in their white togas attended by priestesses wearing diaphanous tunics! Nothing brings back the feeling of ancient Rome more than a visit to the Pantheon. We looked up at the hole in the roof to see if a cat was looking down at me, but couldn't see a little head peaking over the edge, although would not be surprised if one could see us.

Pompeii has to be visited, but it is a place that I personally find very depressing. The art from Pompeii is mainly housed in the museum of Naples and it is worth going to that lawless city to see the wonderful mosaic of Alexander the Great defeating Darius. Alexander looks like a wild-eyed gangster, so the horror on the face of Darius is not surprising to see. I felt the same horror myself when we got a puncture driving through a very poor area of Naples. I have never changed a tyre faster in my life!

RENAISSANCE

Leaving the Romans behind, a visit to St Peter's Basilica takes you into the Renaissance. The façade with its colonnades on either side is as impressive as any building could be, but for me it is all just too much. We stood under the dome and wondered at Michelangelo's ingenuity of being able to span such a width, but there is nothing here to compare to the power of the Pantheon.

Michelangelo's Pietà is of course a *tour de force* and is rightly known around the world as such, but it is not my favourite sculpture although it is without doubt one of the great masterpieces of the Age.

My main fascination was to see the spot where Charlemagne had knelt to be crowned in the year AD 800 as the Holy Roman Emperor. We once made a pilgrimage to Aachen in Germany to see the chapel that Charlemagne built a year before the Pope crowned him.

Emperor Charlemagne's throne in Aachen

396

Aachen is a gem that should be visited by anyone interested in architecture. Napoleon stole the Roman marble pillars from the church, but after Waterloo they were restored thank goodness.

The story of our visit to see Michelangelo's Sistine Chapel rounds off my memories of Rome. To get to the Sistine we had to walk through the Vatican Museum where we saw the *Apollo Belvedere*. I wondered if it was so named because Apollo was the God of Imagination and Creativity?
The Vatican Museum is also the home of Raphael's *School of Athens*. Although this is an astonishing painting I am afraid it just doesn't grab me. For me the interesting thing about the seated figure, which is thought to be of Michelangelo, was I believe used by Rodin as the model for his *Thinker*.

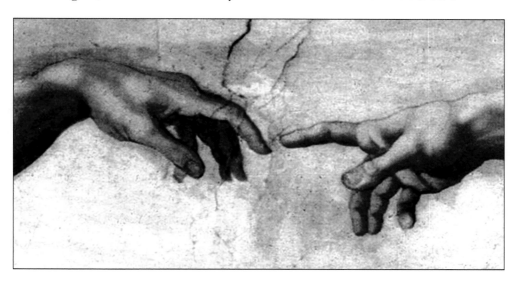

The Sistine Chapel on the other hand is quite out of this world! I sculpted the *Hands* in clay and had two casts done, one in blue glass and one in white. I altered the angle to add strength. How cheeky can one be!

Walking into Michelangelo's Chapel is best summed up by Goethe:

The self-assurance, the virility, the grandeur of conception of this master defies expression. If only there was some means of fixing such images in one's memory!

How right he is! All one can do is lie on the floor and gaze up in wonder. It is in places like this that the value of binoculars really becomes apparent, as the ceiling is so far above you that it is impossible to see any detail with the naked eye. I have been lucky enough to visit the Chapel before and after the cleaning that has been done over the last decade. The colours now glow with their original life and personally I like that. We were very lucky on our second visit as there were no more than 20 visitors in our group. Each group is only allowed to stay in the chapel for only 15 minutes, so every moment is precious and how time flies in such places!

We lingered until everyone had been herded out by the guards except ourselves and a young mother with her baby. She was sitting on a side bench and had started to breastfeed her child, and in a typical Italian way, the guards signalled her to continue. I am sure the young girl was performing what was for her a sacred right in the most holy place that she knew. She was not there to look at Michelangelo's masterpieces, but as some kind of religious act for the benefit of the child. It was a bonus for us as we stayed on as well and because the baby seemed to be in no hurry to finish suckling, we managed to have another five minutes to enjoy the magic of the paintings!

I confess to stealing three ideas during my lifetime from the Sistine Chapel. Just before we had moved to Agecroft our local church in the village of North Cadbury had been attacked by vandals. They had pulled the four stone saints from their niches above the altar and smashed them on the floor.

The vicar decided that as a sculptor had moved into one of the villages that make up the Camelot Group of Parishes he should ask him if he would consider replacing the saints for them! The Reverend Tony rang me and asked if he could come and see me, explained the problem and invited me to visit the church with him and talk about a possible replacement.

The unfortunate thing about the North Cadbury church in my opinion is that the Victorians ruined the original centuries old reredos. I looked at the altar and the brown granite cross and, with the arrogance of a sculptor of three years' standing, suggested that instead of replacing the saints, a job that didn't excite me in the least, I should do something different. "Why don't I do something and you can either accept or reject it?" The thing that did excite my imagination was the possibility of filling the tall medieval niches on either side of the reredos by stealing some ideas from the Sistine to fill the side panels.

Michelangelo painted the wall above the Sistine altar with the Righteous rising to Heaven on the left, and the Damned being cast into Hell on the right. Amongst the Damned there is a young woman falling towards Hell peeking through her fingers as she goes, not being able to resist having a look at what lay below her.

I did the sculptures flat on a table in the same way as I had done *Peace* at Marwood, but when the clay figures were completed and it was time for the vicar and his committee to inspect them, I propped them up so the group could get an idea of how they would look on the wall. Although I had enjoyed doing the figures, I was very nervous about what everyones reaction would be.

The committee arrived and hummed and hawed over the figures while I chatted on about the Sistine Chapel and Michelangelo's genius! There was no outright condemnation, just a stunned silence. After a while they announced that they would go away and discuss the sculptures, as they were not quite what they had expected. *Fair enough*, I thought at the time, but looking back some 30 years I am surprised at my cheek of even suggesting such a radical concept when all they really wanted were four little saints!

When Margie asked how the meeting had gone I told her that I didn't expect the committee to be returning, but I certainly hadn't regretted doing the figures. I believe that artists should always be allowed complete Freedom of Expression as that is how Imagination is released and Creativity born, but I was probably pushing the boundaries in this case. The vicar rang me a few days later and much to my surprise said that they had decided to accept the figures. I could hardly believe it. As they were to be cast in cold bronze, I decided to have a second copy done for myself. Roy came down and collected the figures to take back to London as he would have to take a gelatine impression off the clay to be able to do a second edition.

When Roy brought the figures back we went down to the church and with the vicar's help hung them up. By now I think there were a few cold feet in the committee, so it was decided to hang the figures temporarily on wires in the appropriate places, and allow the congregation to hold a *Keep or Reject* vote in a couple of months' time. I thought that this was a good idea, because by then I was getting cold feet myself!

North Cadbury church reredos with figures

The Parish committee eventually did make a decision and asked if I would be offended if they moved the figures out onto a beautiful old stone wall that is beside the path that leads up to the church through the graveyard. This was done and I must admit they certainly looked much better outside.

The 'Heaven' and 'Hell' figures in the churchyard

While the Parish jury had been deliberating the Headmaster of a large boys' school near Bristol asked me if it was possible to have another set cast for his chapel. This was a blessing as by then Roy had delivered the second set of figures and I didn't have enough money to pay him. I quickly agreed to a sale saying I would deliver them straightaway, just in case he changed his mind.

A few years later I received a call from the new Headmaster of the school, saying he was appalled by the nude women above the altar in a chapel used by young men! To add insult to injury he asked me take them away and give him back the money! I replied that if he returned them to me I would try and sell the figures and if successful would of course return the money. He agreed to this and sent the figures back and I hung them up in my studio.

They only stayed there for a year because the vandals attacked the churchyard yet again, this time stealing both *Heaven* and *Hell* although leaving *Christ*. A very distressed vicar rang me and asked if it was possible to have the figures repeated as they were sorely missed and they had the insurance money to pay for them to be replaced!

I assured him that would be no problem and next day pulled the figures down from the studio wall and delivered them to the church before they also changed their minds and decided to keep the insurance money to fix the church roof. I sent the Headmaster the sale price I had agreed to and kept what was left over as I thought by then I had earned it!

Heaven and *Hell* are now firmly fixed to the wall with gigantic bolts so to steal them you would also have to take the barn! Walking past them one Christmas Day Margie turned to me and said, "I think that would be a nice place for our ashes," pointing to a spot under the figures. I agreed, as I think Margie is a saint for putting up with me and is definitely going to *Heaven*, and no doubt I shall go to *Hell* for all the sins I have committed!

You would think that this story ends with a lonely Christ hanging on my studio wall, but it doesn't. The last twist in this convoluted tale is that within weeks I received yet another telephone call, this time from a Brotherhood of Christian monks who ran a retreat in Dorset. They had visited North Cadbury church, which by the way is one of the loveliest churches I have ever been in, and had fallen in love with the Christ figure. Would it be possible to buy a copy for their chapel? "No," I said, "you can have one for free." So ends the story of the first idea I stole from the Sistine.

The second idea I stole was a subconscious one. Lying on the floor of the chapel looking up through binoculars at God reaching out to Adam is without doubt one of the great moments of my life. It is an amazing image and leaves one gasping with admiration.

My subconscious robbery happened in this way. As I continued trying to capture the values of life with the Symbolic Sculptures, I arrived at the point of wanting to express the magic of being alive and made the *Spark of Life*. One day I was taking a group of young students around Damon's garden explaining how I gave the sculptures names to act as doorways for the viewer to go through so they could then interpret them as they wished. When I came to the *Spark of Life* a young girl turned to me and said, "I see that as Michelangelo's painting of Adam and God on the ceiling of the Sistine." I am sure you can imagine how pleased I was!

'Spark of Life'

On our first visit to Rome we had visited the Villa Borghese Museum to see the Canova sculptures. In those days, because I envied these masterpieces, I would gaze at sculptures like *Daphne and Apollo* and groan with agony recognising my own lack of talent. Canova was probably the most gifted marble-carver who has ever lived, but to me they now appear almost dead.

There are so many wonderful things to see in Rome that the list is endless. While walking around the forum ruins, being stalked by the innumerable cats, one absorbs the atmosphere of the grandeur of this ancient city: Trojan's column, triumphal arches and ruined palaces and the spooky castle. Rome has to be absorbed.

I talked earlier about A D Hope's poem *Letter from Rome* as being one of the first things that got me thinking of selling the farm and coming back to Europe to try my hand at sculpting. Then I could only feel the magic of the city through his words. Being there allowed me to feel the magic in my mind.

MICHELANGELO

When you go to Florence and visit the Accademia to see the original *David*, you are overawed by the scale. The marble sculpture is in the setting to reflect the light on the polished surface, unlike the copy outside the castle that is so badly weathered and unreflective. The Medici Chapel figures of *Night and Day* are also utterly overpowering. All these sculptures are 'highly finished' like the famous St Peter's *Pietà*, but for me they are too perfect.

Awakening Slave

402

It is the 'roughly finished' carvings that appeals to me, as the technique captures movement making the sculptures come to life. When I look at the *Awakening Slave* I can feel the slave straining to free himself from the marble block, symbolising Man's struggling to obtain Freedom.

Many people have asked me, "How did Michelangelo see the figure in the block of marble?" Here is an explanation of how I think he worked.

If you are working from a positive plaster it is easy to copy the original in marble with a pointing machine that uses three fixed points on the plaster, which are repeated on the marble. The machine has a moveable fourth arm so you can measure one point on the original plaster and copy the same point on the marble. This is a long process, but makes it relatively simple for a skilled carver to copy a plaster sculpture. Michelangelo was a master carver so he was able to bypass this whole process that took time and required a middle man.

So how did Michelangelo enlarge the little wax models that he must have made into heroic statues like *David*? First of all he measured the height of the block of marble and divided it into units. In this example we shall use units of 'one foot'. Now think of the statue of *David* and then think of the marble block that he carved it from. It must have looked like a giant loaf of bread standing on its end. Suppose the block was ten foot tall and he divided it by ten, he would have ten units each measuring one foot high.

I think he made a ten-inch high vase out of beeswax with the inside of the vessel the exact shape of the block of marble he had quarried. Next he placed his ten-inch high wax model of *David* in the vase.

So how did he transfer the measurements from the maquette to the marble? Actually it is surprisingly simple. First of all you drill nine holes down all sides of the ten-inch high vase all precisely one inch apart, starting with the first holes one inch from the bottom. The last hole is one inch from the top. Next put the model into the vase, plug the holes with matchsticks and fill it with olive oil to the top.

The first thing Michelangelo would have wanted to do was find out exactly where the top of *David*'s head would be at the top of the block of marble. The top of the model would be level with the surface of the oil so he could measure in from the lip, multiply the distance by ten and transfer the measurement to the marble. Next he would want to know exactly where the left hand and shoulder were. To do this he removed the top match from the vase and let the oil run out, thus exposing that part of the model. He could measure from the four sides of the vase through the holes, and then chisel away the marble around the area.

Suppose he then wanted to find out where the left elbow came. By removing the match near the left elbow of the maquette and letting the oil run out, then taking that measurement and multiplying by ten, he could work out where the left elbow would be in the marble. And so on until he had roughed out the whole figure. I don't believe this takes anything from the wonder of his carving, but increases it, because it adds to the man's genius.

When you have seen all of Michelangelo's sculptures in Florence, it is time to go to Milan to see his *Pietà Rondanini*. The experts say this is his greatest carving as it shows more of the sculptor's genius than any other of his works. He was still working on the *Pietà Rondanini* six days before he died, aged 89!

Pietà Rondanini

The sculpture has a room all to itself and is set slightly back to one corner to catch the best light from the windows. The opposite corner is filled with rows of seats that curve around the two walls like a theatre, so you can view the sculpture from every angle at different heights.

The wonderment of the sculpture is that Christ, who is being lifted by Mary, has two positions. It seems that Michelangelo nearly completed Christ and then changed his mind and started to carve a second Christ. The first right arm of Christ is finished to a polished stage, while the second right arm is roughly hewn and unfinished. The effect is that Christ seems to be disappearing back into the unfinished body of Mary, thereby giving the impression that he is passing from flesh to spirit.

Goethe wrote: *The self-assurance, the virility, the grandeur of conception of this master defies expression.*

I like to think back to the vessel and model stage of the carving of the *Pietà Rondanini*. Were his ideas fixed when he began the sculpture and then at some stage, when nearing completion, did he have another vision? Or was the image already in his mind when he began?

Florence is a truly magical place. The Ponte Vecchio is so special that even the Germans desisted from blowing it up as the Allies approached at the end of WWII. Later the General was so ashamed of his action that he claimed he didn't blow it up because he thought it was too weak to carry tanks! Years ago I bought Margie a wonderful necklace of amazonite on the bridge and every time she wears it I take a little trip to the Ponte Vecchio. Whenever we are in Florence we cross the bridge because on the far bank a little upstream is a café with the best view of the bridge. It also serves excellent food! What more could anyone ask for after a morning in the museum.

The museums of Florence have the greatest collection of Renaissance art in the world. I find it impossible to spend more than an hour or so in the Uffizi because my senses just can't take in any more and I have to escape to open space. We bless the Uffizi Museum authorities because they never move paintings around. Year after year they have remained in the same place enabling us to go directly to each of our old friends without distraction.

After climbing the grand staircase that seems to go on forever, the first person we visit is the Duke of Urbino. What an ugly profile, but what a face! The Botticelli paintings are the next stop, but only if you are there before the tourists arrive. The crowd around the *Four Seasons* and the *Birth of Venus* can be 20 deep! Next stop has to be out on to the Loggia to pause to gaze at the Arno. One of our favourite little rooms in the world is to the left as you step out into the Loggia. It was decorated by a Medici for his wife, the daughter of the King of France. The ceiling is painted as though it is a domed lattice arbour covered with flowering vines. Hundreds of birds are depicted amongst the leaves and we feel that the French bride must have been very happy here, far away from her native country. I had a plan to paint this scene on the ceiling of the entrance hall of a penthouse I Houston, but never got around to it, probably fortunately as it would have been a mammoth job. I did lie on the floor and take the photographs much to the other visitors' amazement!

After a long lingering look at the river and the Ponte Vecchio you pass on to Michelangelo's painting of the *Holy Family*, followed by Titian's *Venus of*

Urbino and the *Bacchus* by Cararvaggio. Next to the end of the gallery to admire the carving of the *Laocoon* and don't forget to use the excellent Rest Rooms before staggering back out into the street, your mind reeling!

Painted ceiling

The Baptristy and the Cathedral are superb buildings and Brunelleschi's Dome is one of the greatest examples of architecture ever achieved. Ghiberti's bronze doors are incredible works of art and will never be surpassed as examples of perspective or of casting.

A quick visit to the Bargello for a lingering look at Donatello's *David* and then to the Michelangelo room to gaze on the round white marble Pitti Tondo. Next a short walk to the Loggia to admire Cellini's *Rape of the Sabines*. Whether you like the sculpture or not, every artist should read Cellini's autobiography in which he explains how he cast this colossal bronze in one piece, at the same time setting fire to his house! It is an amazing story.

The next and last stop has to be the Duomo Museum behind the east end of the Cathedral where, in my humble opinion, is a collection of some of the most breathtaking sculptures in the world. You climb the stairs to the galleries, passing on your way Michelangelo's *Nicodemus Pietà*, which is said to be a self-portrait of the master. The museum has recently been refurbished and Donatello's *Mary Magdalene*, one of the most moving woodcarvings I have ever seen, has rightly been given its own room. Moved and saddened by this elegant sculpture you arrive in a gallery full of happy dancing children.

One panel is by Luca della Robbia and the other by Donatello. Moving from one to the other and then back again is one of the great joys of life. Although it is hard to choose between the panels, before leaving I always seem to end up looking at Luca's *Dancing Children*. It is quite superb. I love it so much I made a small tile copy in clay and had it cast in crystal glass in Prague.

'*Dancing Children*' in marble by Luca della Robbia

Before leaving Florence I have to mention Brunelleschi's Pazzi Chapel, because the Renaissance was as much about Architecture as Painting and Sculpture. The Chapel is without doubt a perfection of design, every inch of it being in harmony with the rest, beautifully simple and sophisticated.

'Dancing Children' in crystal glass

Sketch of the Arno at night from our hotel balcony

The cathedral in Ravenna is full of gold and white figures and is one of the finest examples of the art of mosaic anywhere in the world, but behind one of the churches you will find a tiny cell-like chapel of cerulean blue dotted with gold stars. It has the gem quality of smallness and is a joy to see.

In contrast to the tiny chapel is the Barbarian Emperor Theodoric's mausoleum. He conquered Italy by taking Ravenna in 493 and gave the country peace for 33 years! He is remembered for three things: lowering taxes, being tolerant of all religions and, because he was terrified of being struck by lightning. The capping stone of his mausoleum is claimed to be the largest stone ever quarried in Italy. How it was ever moved from the quarry to the mausoleum is hard to imagine. But it was, and the dead Emperor has been well protected from lightning ever since!

I have mentioned the portrait of the Duke of Urbino in the Uffizi, so I must tell you about our visit to his castle. The Duke was a mercenary soldier who commanded the best army in Italy, which he hired out for exorbitant fees making him an extremely rich man. He was also a patron of the arts and an example of how the 16th-century art critic, Sperone Speroni, defined Civilisation: *The creation of wealth and the patronage of art.*

When you arrive at the gates of Urbino the enormous walls of the Duke's palace overshadow you. The massive façade of pink brick that towers above is set with white marble window frames.

The palace within the castle may be very impressive but it must have also been bitterly cold in the winter, that is, for everyone except the Duke, who worked in a tiny study, one of the treasures of Italy. The study is lined with the finest example of inlaid wooden panels that exist. Some panels depict cupboards of books, other are full of musical instruments. The pictures are so three-dimensional that they make the room feel twice as large as it really is. What a snug study to keep warm in while everyone else froze to death while waiting to see you!

The people of Urbino are very proud of their cuisine. The hotel dining room was closed but the concierge recommended a restaurant, which he said had the finest food in town. As it was a cold wet evening we wrapped up well in our raincoats and set off to find this gourmet's paradise. On arrival we discovered the place was empty, that no one spoke a word of English and the menu was in Italian. We overcame this problem by ordering the *Specialità della Casa*, feeling pleased with ourselves for having solved the problem so simply.

Bread and red wine appeared and we started to nibble and sip while we waited with bated breath, our hunger mounting. The meal arrived in an earthenware dish, but when the lid was lifted a nauseating smell invaded our nostrils and the sight was equally as horrifying. With a big smile the host announced with triumph the name of the dish and left us to help ourselves.

After looking at each other while trying to control our laughter there was nothing else to do but try it. Perhaps it tasted better than it looked or smelt. Bravely we helped ourselves and took a taste. No, the meat component didn't taste better than it looked and the white mush was disgusting. Was it horsemeat? Luckily we had a big basket of bread and a bottle of wine, so we didn't starve, but this still left the problem of what to do with the food so as not to offend our host!

Very luckily we had been given a large number of thick paper napkins. Stealthily we began to wrap up some of the meat in the paper napkins and secrete the little packages into the poacher's pocket of my raincoat, which was the type that detectives wear in the movies. I had inherited it from Margie's father and had never really liked it, but tonight I blessed him as the poacher's pockets were enormous.

We called for the bill. As the restaurant was empty and the host was longing to close, we were soon out on the street and fit to bust our sides. The problem now was to find somewhere to dump the parcels as they were already beginning to feel soggy, so we began to walk around the old town looking for a rubbish bin. We walked for at least half an hour before we found a bin and, would you believe it, yes, it was right outside our restaurant, which luckily was in complete darkness and locked up for the night. I emptied my pockets and we hurried away.

Finally I must write about Venice. What a wonderful place! Goethe wrote:

> *It was written on my page in the Book of Fate that five in the afternoon of the 28th day of September in the year 1786, I should see Venice for the first time. I entered the lagoons from the Brenta, and set foot in this beautiful island-city, this beaver-republic.*

In some cases the streets are only wide enough for two people to pass and this intensifies the bustle of the citizens going about their normal business. It is a bit like watching a trail of Leaf Cutter ants. Only on entering the Piazza San Marco do you find any internal space, all else being canals.

Goethe arrived at the very end of September. Italians call the first week of June and the first week of October the Golden Weeks, when the weather is exceptionally good, so I guess he had good weather!

Venice is to be avoided during the crowded tourist season, July and August. The first time I visited Venice was in 1948 when just 13 years old. I can only really remember it because of riding in a gondola with my mother and brother Pat. The city was still recovering from WWII and completely deserted, which was lucky as we were there in August! The place was bright with sunshine and the palaces along the Grand Canal glowed in the warmth.

The Grand Canal, Venice

The reason for our first trip to Venice together was to meet the Reverend Frederick McDonald of Seattle. He had booked Margie and me into a hotel opposite S Giorgio Maggiore. Our room was brilliant because it looked out across the water to the church. One of the amazing features of the mixture of the Venetian sunlight and sea mist is that the view seems to change with the varying light. Sometimes we would look out of our window and swear that we could touch the church, while at other times it seemed to be floating on the horizon in a mist. The view was like a Turner's watercolour!

'Venice and Salute', Turner 1775–1851

The Reverend Frederick had asked us to meet him at Harry's Bar for a Dry Martini before lunch! I had first met Frederick in Seattle when I had gone for my first exhibition of the figurative bronze maquettes that included a head of Margie, which I called *Joan of Arc*. Frederick turned out to be a collector of anything related to the heroine and bought Margie's head.

We arrived at Harry's Bar and as he was well known in the establishment, we had a very jolly lunch. He then asked us if we would like to cross the canal and see the English church before having tea with his friends.

We climbed on the waterbus with a crowd of other Venetians going about their daily business. It was just like hopping on to a London bus, but it floated. The skill with which the crew handled their craft is amazing to watch as they zigzagged back and forth across the Grand Canal, each stop taking no more than three or four minutes to dock, speedily disgorge passengers, gobble up others, and then off again, all the time avoiding the gondolas and barges that were plying up and down the canal. The whole thing reminded me of old prints that show the chaotic muddle of traffic around Piccadilly Circus in the days of horse-drawn carriages.

I am afraid I don't remember anything about the little church except that it was very cold and dark inside and smelt of incense. It must have been a private chapel before being converted to Church of England for the fashionable colony that had sprung up in Venice at the end of the last century.

It was time for tea so we followed Frederick and entered what was once the home of a Prince bordering the Grand Canal, but had long since been converted into apartments. We climbed a palatial staircase and arrived at the door of a majestic apartment.

Margie as 'Joan of Arc'

Frederick knocked and a servant let us in and showed us into the most incredible and immensely long blue-carpeted room. Perhaps it wasn't as large as the impression it gave but at the time it seemed to go on forever. The reason for this was because there was only one enormous window that filled the far end of the room that looked out on the Grand Canal. The rest of the room was dark, so it was a bit like looking down a tunnel.

Tea came and went while Frederick talked with our hosts. I don't remember anything that happened because I was so overcome with the eerie feeling of the place and wondering how anybody could want to live there. Perhaps in the morning the sun poured in and it was more cheerful. I certainly hoped so for their sakes as it gave me the shudders.

Being in Venice is very different to being in Florence. In Venice one tends to wander around soaking up the atmosphere of the city rather than visiting museums. Apart from the splendid bronze horses that the Venetians stole from Constantinople and which now grace the portico of the Bascilica, for me Venice is not so much a place of Art but of Architecture, where all the buildings live in harmony with each other, like Ruskin's *The Stones of Venice*.

Canal San Guiseppe

Many years before this I had seen a painting of the *Canal San Guiseppe* in a London art gallery. I thought it was a really beautiful scene and I would have liked to have taken the painting home, but fortunately it was far too expensive. Instead for years I carried a photograph of it around in my briefcase. I showed the photograph to the driver of a water taxi and asked if he knew where the canal was and, if so, could he take us there. He said he did know the spot but was afraid I would find that things had changed since the painting was done.

Still it was a beautiful day and we decided to have a look. I am afraid the boatman was right, it had changed beyond recognition, but I still like to look at the photograph of the painting and think that it showed Venice as Goethe would have seen it in 1786, with girls washing clothes in the canal!

We climbed the clock tower to watch the bronze giants strike their great bell with their bent hammer handles, which is something that has always worried me, even when I was 13 years old. It has never ceased to amaze me that the Melbourne *Hammer Thrower* has had its hammer replaced at the wrong angle and no one has noticed. The hammer droops down at an angle of about ten degrees and looks very odd. One year the Lord Mayor of the city used the *Hammer Thrower* on his Christmas card! If he had asked my permission I would have pointed out the fault and he could have corrected it!

I must admit that the Melbourne sculpture has had a rough time. The hammer originally was a bronze ball on a twisted shaft to resemble the wire cable as used in the Olympic Games. The sculpture had only been unveiled for one day before vandals stole the hammer causing an urgent request for a replacement to be cast in England and flown out to Melbourne. Meanwhile the authorities replaced it with a broom handle and the float from a lavatory cistern! Before the replacement arrived in Melbourne the broomstick and float had disappeared three more times.

413

There was obviously no point in putting back the new bronze hammer so each time it is stolen the custodians of the park have replaced it with another broomstick and float. I am told the last count is approaching an unbelievable 100 times!

In January 2002, Margie and I made a trip to Melbourne on Bradshaw Foundation business. While we were there one of the things we wanted to do was visit the Botanical Gardens because it was where we had spent many happy hours when we were courting 46 years ago! After breakfast we drove over the river and out along St Kilda Road towards the Gardens. The road passes the *Hammer Thrower* and I could see he was empty handed! "Let's go and have a look," Margie suggested. I replied, "No, the hammer's missing and I don't want to see it like that." Well, of course, like all well-trained husbands, I gave in and we parked nearby so we could walk over to the sculpture.

The *Hammer Thrower* is set on a tiny island in a small pond. He really looked very sad without his hammer and a bit lost as to why he was there leaning back with no centrifugal force to hold him up. We walked around the pond with me muttering about 'the way people behaved nowadays' so by the time we headed back towards the car I was not in a good mood. As we arrived at the roadside a car pulled up and a Park Warden got out, walked round to the trunk of his car and opened it just as we passed by. "He's got the hammer!" Margie exclaimed, and sure enough, he did.

Of course Margie asked him what he was doing and had to tell him that I was the sculptor! The Warden then explained that every evening he came to remove the hammer and returned in the morning to replace it every single day of the year. We couldn't believe it! This is when I learnt that they had lost 100 hammers. The only way that they could solve the problem was by removing it over night, so he had been doing it for the last ten years. All quite incredible!

We walked back to the sculpture with him and helped replace the hammer. He had a Polaroid camera with him so Margie took a photo of us both replacing the broomstick with the copper float on the end so he could show his mates. We walked away marvelling at the coincidental timing of the whole event. It was worth going all that way to Australia to have such an extraordinary experience.

The *Hammer Thrower* suffered another indignity in Melbourne. One day I received a letter from a friend reporting that it had appeared on a billboard in the heart of the city. The sculpture is of a nine-foot high nude man, but on the billboard he was shown as twice that size, *but wearing underpants*!

I wrote to my cousin Michael of Arthur Robinson and Co, (a company started by WS's elder brother and now the leading firm of solicitors in Melbourne) hoping that we possibly could squeeze the manufacturer for a charity, as they had not asked my permission to use the image. Michael wrote to the firm, who blamed the advertising firm, who eventually handed over a cheque for a miserable amount for our chosen charity.

The last trip we made to Venice was by accident as we were meant to be in the Dolomites visiting some of the famous Palladio houses. We were on our way to the foundry, but instead of taking our usual route over the Grand Saint Bernard Pass we had decided to take the Brenner Pass instead. We reached Cortina in the evening and booked into a hotel.

All the way through the Alps we had been driving in golden autumnal sunshine, but that night it snowed and we woke to a very different-looking world. We even had trouble getting out of the car park, but as the main road seemed to have been gritted we decided to head up towards the next pass, as there were no signs out to say that it was closed.

After driving for about 15 minutes it started to snow and soon there were no wheel tracks on the road. That was enough for me so we found a place to turn and retreated back down the mountain in first gear for by now the slightest touch on the brakes turned the car into a toboggan! We reached the Autostrada and headed south thinking about what to do with our spare day. It was Margie's birthday, so we decided to go to Venice.

When we had been there with our parents as children we had both used the same hotel, the famous Luna. We wondered if we just turned up whether they would have a vacant room. They did have a room, of course it was one of their grandest, but what can you do on your wife's birthday? What a room, but even more so, what a bathroom! And the towels! We settled in with ease and prepared to go out to dinner.

While Margie was taking a bath I arranged with the concierge for a surprise to be waiting for her when we came downstairs. The *Michelin Guide* recommended a restaurant by the Opera House so I asked him to book a table.

We arrived at the front desk and talked to the concierge who told us that he had been working in the hotel for 40 years, starting as a bellboy. That meant he had been there when we had both stayed, which for me was 38 years ago. This led to much laughter and a photograph of the three of us at the front door of the hotel the following morning before we left.

By now our transport had arrived and the old man handed Margie into a gondola. The surprise on Margie's face was a delight to see. Off we set into the night gliding up the Grand Canal towards the Rialto Bridge. The night was black and still with only intermittent lights glowing in the odd palace window. The canal was completely empty of traffic, it being late October. It was a moment of pure magic.

Much too quickly we arrived at the side canal that led to the Opera House. The only sound was the creak of the oar and plop of the water drips as they fell back into the canal. When we glided under the tiny arched bridges the sound was magnified almost to music by the pitch-black surroundings.

On approaching a corner on the canal our gondolier would call out just in case another craft was coming, his cries echoing between the walls of the dark canyon. Suddenly we burst out into the Opera House Plaza ablaze with lights. What a journey! Out we hopped and into the warmth of the restaurant for our dinner, which luckily turned out to be nothing like the one in Urbino, as the meal being delicious. Two weeks later the Opera was burnt down!

We walked back to the hotel after dinner, crossing over the same little bridges we had floated under, zigzagging our way back to San Marco for one last look, and then to the Luna to sleep, two very contented people. What a city and what an evening, all totally unplanned and unexpected, brought on by snow in the mountains.

For a change one year we had crossed the English Channel from Southampton to Cherbourg, then had driven up to Paris and down to Italy, but the traffic had been so bad we decided that we would take a different route home. When we reached Lyon we headed west over the Massif Central and then north up through Poitiers to Cherbourg and avoided Paris.

We planned our route by using the *Michelin Guide*'s list for three-star hotels. The road happened to pass through Aubusson where the guide said there was an old hotel with a good restaurant, so we decided to stay there the night and see the town's famous Tapestry Museum the next morning.

We arrived in the late afternoon and fortunately the Hôtel de France had room for us. Everything was well over a hundred years old, including the bathroom. The floorboards creaked magnificently and the enormous bed had a valley in the middle. It was all perfect and once settled in we went for a walk around the ancient town perched on the banks of a gushing river.

I can't remember how I became intrigued by tapestries in the first place, but I think it was probably from a visit we had made to The Cloisters in New York to see the fabulous Unicorn, woven in the Netherlands in 1500.

The Unicorn in Captivity

416

Aubusson became a centre for tapestries in the 17th century when a Flemish Princess married the owner of the town's castle and, as part of her dowry, she had brought a retinue of weavers with her and set up a workshop. Very soon the town became famous for its tapestries, which presumably she had woven to hang on her damp castle walls.

The Hôtel de France was owned by a family, the father being the chef. He was a wonderful old character and could he cook! His 'lamb's brains in black butter' was a dish to be dreamt about for ever. Dinner was so good it required another walk around the old town before turning in.

Next morning we went to the museum and found it shut! We discovered several shops that sold printed copies of tapestries but nothing done on Aubusson looms. Disappointed we returned to the hotel to pay the bill and leave. When I went to the desk I found the chef behind the counter and he asked if I had enjoyed the museum. I explained that in fact we were really disappointed, because it was closed. He picked up the telephone, spoke, and said, "My friends would be delighted to show you their atelier."

The chef drew a map and we drove to Madame Suzanne Goubley's atelier. We were greeted at the door by a very stylishly dressed woman in her late seventies, who took us on one of the most intriguing tours we have ever made. The three-storeyed mill in which the Goubleys lived was also the workshop, the top floor being where the looms were housed. The south wall of the loft was all glass, allowing sunlight to flood the enormous room.

Tapestry by the monk Dom Robert

417

The looms were the same design as those that had been brought to Aubusson by the Princess 300 years before, being horizontal rather than vertical as is usual. A bench was fixed to the front of the loom and the wood was as smooth as satin from hundreds of years of weavers' bottoms sliding up and down them. The room smelt of wool and Madame Suzanne told us that they only used the finest merino wool from Australia, which pleased us greatly.

The paper cartoon of the tapestry is spread under the warp so the weaver can follow the pattern exactly. It was a joy to watch the women working as their fingers moved like lightning. The fascinating thing was that they work looking at the reverse of the tapestry because they have to tie off the threads at the back, which means they never see the front until it is finished. The tapestry is a mirror image of the cartoon so the signature has to be written in reverse!

After our tour Madame Suzanne and her husband asked us to their apartment for coffee and gâteaux. What a sitting room! It was one of those mixtures that the French are so good at, the very old and very modern. One wall was completely covered with a gigantic tapestry, some 15 feet across by 12 feet high. It was an original work by Dom Robert, a famous monk who had only just died. Madame Suzanne's atelier had woven all his tapestries.

I was so excited by everything I asked Madame if she would consider weaving a tapestry for me. "*Certainement!*" We drove away having had an enthralling morning with the woman whose father had been employed by Queen Victoria to mend her tapestries at Windsor Castle!

On the trip home I began to think about symbolic subjects that I had rejected as being impossible as sculptures and wondered if perhaps some of them could be adapted to a two-dimensional form.

Perhaps what followed was because of my concentrating on my new challenge! Margie and I were still both in our early forties so to save money when we made trips to Italy we used to take the tent that we had used on our Grand Traverse over the Alps with the boys. It was an incredible thing that looked like an upturned boat, was easy to erect, completely watertight and weighed nothing. Our policy was to sleep alternate nights in hotels and the tent. Having spent the previous night at the Hôtel de France we were due a night under canvas on the drive up to Cherbourg.

As the light began to fail we found a lovely spot off the main road soon after passing through a little town where we had noticed a promising restaurant. After a fine dinner we returned and erected the tent in a jiffy in the car's headlights and I set the alarm clock for six o'clock. As we dropped off to sleep it started to pour with rain.

When the alarm went off it was still pitch black being winter and the rain had turned to a torrential downpour. We struggled out of our bags and I made our usual breakfast by mixing orange juice with ready-cooked porridge. When we were dressed we bolted outside and collapsed the tent, pushed it into the back of the station wagon and drove away. After we had been going for a couple of hours we both started to wonder why it was still pitch dark outside, so I turned on the interior light to look at my wristwatch and, to my horror, saw that it was only four o'clock! We both started to laugh as we realised what had happened. I hadn't used the clock since our last trip to Australia and I had set the alarm without checking the time it was due to go off! I pulled over into the first lay-by we came to and within seconds we were both asleep. Needless to say we did not have another breakfast on waking!

On arriving home I started to think seriously about a tapestry design. I had had some ideas about *Spring, Summer, Autumn* and *Winter*, but had rejected them as not being possible. I then thought of *Water Planet* based on the 'I Ching'. Once I started, all sorts of subjects popped into my mind, such as, *Galaxies, Time, Love Union, Trust Bonds, Tribe*, and *Beyond Light*. The problem was which one would I choose? I sat by our pond looking at the water lilies as the goldfish swam beneath them. *Tranquillity*. It was impossible. I would do all the designs on graph paper with Golden Mean proportions of 36 inches by 58 inches and then make up my mind as to which ones should be woven as tapestries.

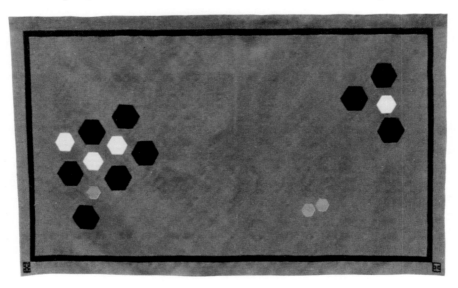

'Tranquillity'

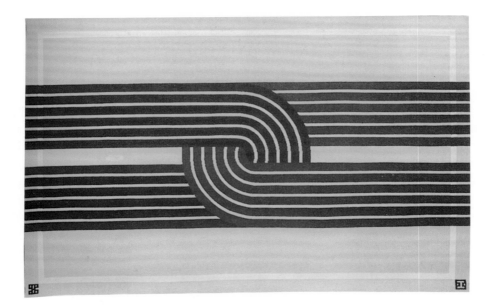

'Trust'

While I was working on the tapestries a letter arrived from Australia asking me if I would be interested in entering a competition to do a sculpture for the marble foyer of the newly built Bank of New South Wales in Melbourne. I

419

accepted the challenge and to my utter surprise won the commission to do the 15-foot high sculpture I called *The Universe*.

This meant that I now had money to spend on the tapestries, so maybe I could have three or four done if the price was right. In fact this commission also allowed me to have several of the Symbolic maquettes enlarged as well, so *The Universe* completely changed my life in all sorts of ways. I drew the spiral on the floor of Enzo's studio in Pietrasanta using a paint tin and a length of string attached to a pencil.

Margie and I drove down to Italy to see the sculpture before it was polished. We took our friend Sue with us and laughed all the way, some nights all crowding into the tent, but mainly finding wonderful small hotels.

Seeing the sculpture propped against the foundry wall for inspection was one of the most exciting things that has ever happened to me and something I shall never forget. The circle is the Chinese symbol for the Universe, the spiral symbolises Consciousness and the stick figure is Man.

'The Universe', Fonderia Mariani

Things were looking pretty good and it was time for a new adventure so we went to see Madame Suzanne in Aubusson. We had made a booking at the Hôtel de France and were already looking forward to eating 'lamb's brains in black butter' again!

'The Universe'
Bank of New South Wales

Madame Suzanne gave us a great welcome the next morning. I was feeling very nervous as I unrolled the paper cartoons of not one, but 12 tapestries! What would she say? Would they be possible to weave? How much would one cost and how many could I afford to do? We spent all of that day in the jewel box of a room choosing colours. Yes, she would like to do them and would work out a price that evening. It was a wonderful day and whatever happened it had been an incredible experience watching Madame use her expertise to match my choice of colours to her wool samples.

'Love Union', Parliament House, Canberra

'Spring'   *'Autumn'*
Centre for Computational Biology, Montana State University

Next morning we returned to hear the verdict on how many could be done before having to make the choice of which ones to leave out. Yet more coffee and gâteaux, but this time with pencil and paper. Madame Suzanne announced that she thought the cartoons would make a fine series so I should have them all woven and she could then give me a special price! We accepted her offer and she told us to go away and come back in one year's time.

We returned a year later to collect the tapestries. What an exciting moment! We went into her storeroom and there on the table was a stack of tapestries. As each tapestry was revealed I saw for the first time the vibrant colours that had been added to my designs.

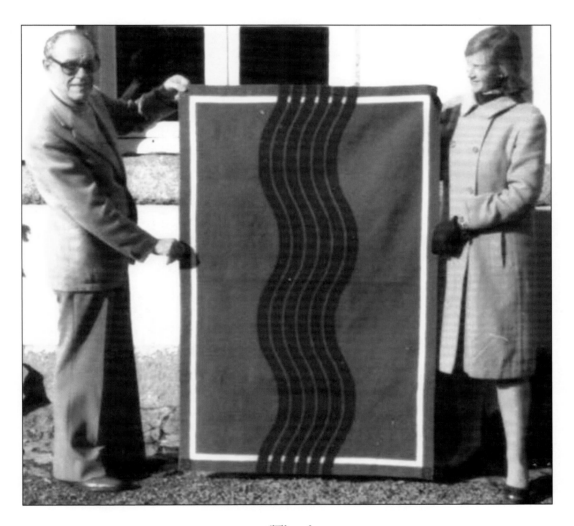

'Time'
As a stream running through a meadow

It was all a bit overwhelming. Running my hands over the finely woven wool was an amazing feeling. Because many of the designs are made up of straight lines and circles, the weavers had found the cartoons very hard to follow, but they had done a fantastic job and not one stitch was out of place. I couldn't wait to take some photographs so Margie and Monsieur Goubley took them outside for me, one at a time, into the winter sunlight. Unfortunately Madame Suzanne refused to be photographed so I only have my memory of this marvellous old lady.

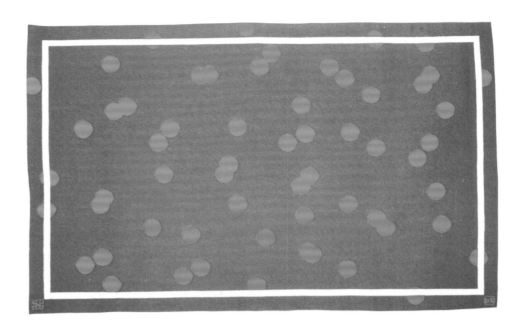

'Summer'
Poppies in a wheat field

I was thrilled by the results and relished the thought that I must surely be the only Australian sheep farmer who had ever had tapestries woven at the famous Goubley Atelier in Aubusson out of wool from my own country. It is sad to think, when writing this, that the elegant Madame Suzanne and her charming husband have both died, that the atelier has closed and another ancient skill has disappeared for ever.

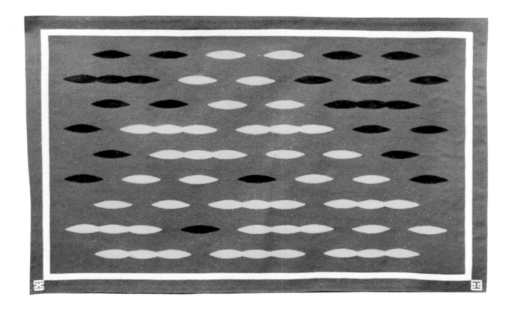

'Water Planet'
Using 'I Ching' symbols as 'sunlight on water'

I had been asked to give an exhibition of my Symbolic Sculpture maquettes in the Wells Cathedral Chapter House, built in 1306. I was delighted by this request as it meant that I would show the tapestries for the first time in the most glorious medieval cathedral in England. The maquettes would sit on the vicars' seats and I could hang the tapestries above them.

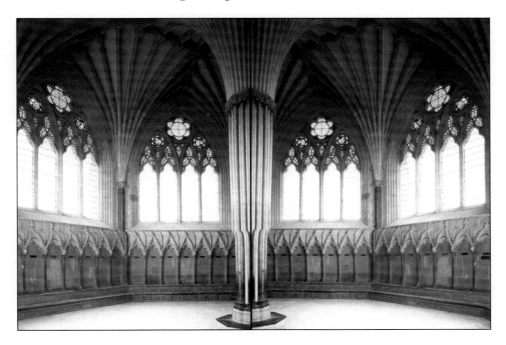

Wells Cathedral Chapter House

Every day I would drive over to Wells and sit on duty with the tapestries and gaze in awe at the colours of the wool. The tapestries turned the room into a colourful jewel box. What an experience and what a privilege!

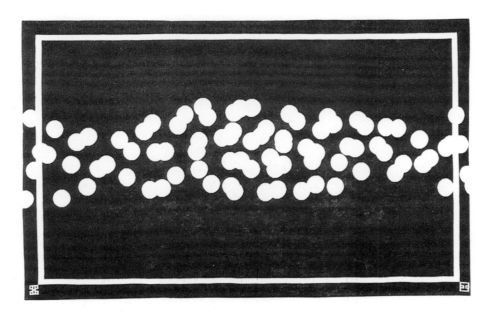

'Winter'
Milky Way

425

This was the second time that I had had an exhibition in the Cathedral. Four years earlier Dean Patrick Mitchell had asked me if I would show my figurative maquettes in the Chapter House and the *Acrobats* in the Cloisters, in an attempt to raise money for the restoration work that was being done. I had agreed and it was because of this that Patrick had then asked me if I would do some work on the 14th century sculptures on the West Front.

Wells Cathedral
The West Front of England's finest medieval building –
the Twelve Apostles are above the central windows

My job was to copy in plasticine four of the heads of the Twelve Apostles that stand in a row below the top centre statue of Christ. The whole of the West Front was covered in scaffolding as the entire face was being cleaned. Some of the finest 14th century sculpture remaining in England is on this wall, as fortunately Cromwell and his Puritan Army did not use the Saints for target practice as they had done on many other cathedrals.

In Victorian times the authorities realised that some of the sculptures were loose so they had decided to cement them to the stone wall behind them. The problem now was that the stone used for the sculptures was softer than the cement making it impossible to remove them and put them in a museum. The only thing left to do was to put lime soaked cotton wool poultices on the stone and try to strengthen it against the pollution caused by the traffic's exhaust fumes and acid rain.

Before this was done Patrick wanted me to copy four of the heads in plasticine so they had a record of what they looked like before the lime treatment took place, which was a good idea as it turned out that the treatment altered the carvings quite considerably.

It happened to be the hottest June that we have ever had and working on the West Front was like working under the Australian sun again. The mornings were fine but by midday the temperature was up in the 90s and continued to steadily climb so that by four o'clock in the afternoon it had reached 100 degrees, which caused the plasticine to melt! To cut a long story short, I did eventually get the job done and the heads down off the scaffolding with Roy's help so he could take waste moulds and cast them in plaster.

I enjoyed doing the job and was mesmerised by the old stone carvings that had not been studied that closely, literally face to face, since the original sculptor had carved them 700 years before! I asked Roy to do a set of heads for me in stone resin from the moulds and they made a handsome foursome. They now guard the ruins of an ancient chapel in a wood in Wales.

Four of the 'Apostles' cast in stone resin

I had grown to know many of the Cathedral wardens very well during the work and had been given a free run under the roof of the Cathedral. Walking though this space along giant oak beams that had been put in place all those years ago was a simply amazing experience.

When Patrick had asked me if I would do another exhibition, this time of my Symbolic Sculpture maquettes and the tapestries, I was of two minds about agreeing. It was the first time that I had shown any of my Symbolic work to anyone outside the family so it would be their debut onto the world stage! What would the public think? *Oh well, in for a penny in for a pound.* Patrick had seen the sculptures and had suggested the idea of exhibiting them so I presumed that he liked them, although I nearly had second thoughts when he told me that the Bishop of Bath and Wells was to open the exhibition! However, it all went off very well and everyone seemed pleased and the Cathedral did manage to make a little money.

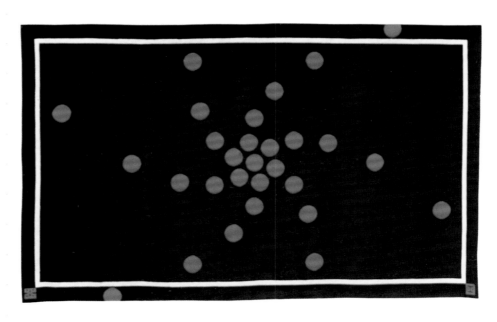

'Galaxies'

Thank goodness I had agreed because on the very last day of the exhibition just before closing time as I was about to leave, a couple arrived in the Chapter House who changed my life. After walking around the exhibition they started to question me and soon found out that I was an Australian. They introduced themselves as Ron and Betty Beaver and told me that they came from Canberra where they ran the Beaver Gallery. Ron asked me if I would like to show my Symbolic Exhibition in Australia. I replied, "If you can arrange a suitable venue I would be delighted to ship everything out to you." So began an unbelievable adventure and my friendships with a marvellous man.

'Beyond Light'

Before branching off into the Beaver story I must finish the Cathedral episode by mentioning Dea and Bernard Sterner's visit. Most of my visitors were casually-dressed sightseeing holidaymakers, so I was taken aback when an amazingly elegant woman swept in followed by a small thick-set man. They turned out to be a couple who lived near the town of Menerbe, not far from Aix-en-Provence. He was a South African and she was an Italian, but had grown up in Luxembourg.

In the war Bernard had worked for the Secret Service as a locksmith, and this had led him to designing a foolproof lock for sealing the dispatch cases carried by British couriers. The outcome of the Sterners' visit to the cathedral was that they asked us to call in on them and stay a night when we were returning from our next trip to the foundry in Italy. I agreed as we were due to do a trip a few weeks later to collect some new sculptures.

We were still using the tent and so a night in a bed with a bath on the way was always very welcome not to mention a free dinner! The little town of Menerbe is on the north side of the mountains that shelter Aix-en-Provence from the Mistral wind. The map showed a road over the mountain and the *Michelin Guide* said that there was a good restaurant just before you started to climb up into the foothills. I knew that the mountains were actually just a long limestone escarpment as we had driven past them several times. My map also said that it was a national park, so I thought that we would be able to find a place to pitch our tent without much trouble after dinner without anyone knowing for the night before we were meant to arrive at the Sterners'.

We found the restaurant and after a very good meal we set off under a full moon into the park to look for a tent site. Feeling very happy we soon discovered a sidetrack and some way down it we found a flat space for the tent. However, we had not taken into account the Mistral or that it was impossible to get the steel pegs into the rocky ground to keep the tent from blowing away! We gave up the unequal struggle and returned to the road that led down to the town of Apt to the north. Just outside the town we saw a sign pointing to a campsite that we decided to investigate because it was getting very late although the sign said it was closed.

We found the gate was unlocked so we crept in and soon had the tent up as there was not a breath of wind and the ground was soft. We crawled into our sleeping bags very ready for a well-earned sleep, but it was not to be as the night was full of the song of nightingales. We had never heard anything so beautiful and lay awake for half an hour listening to them singing.

Next morning we were up and away before anyone discovered us and headed into Apt for breakfast. We weren't due to reach the Sterners' home until mid-afternoon, so we spent the day exploring the little fortified medieval town of Menerbe that was in those days still undiscovered. I had read about the town in the book by my heroine Françoise Gilot, the model for the life-size *Mother and Child* figure that I had done at Marwood on arrival in England. Picasso had owned a house in Menerbe when he was married to Françoise, but like many French towns, during the day all the shutters were locked tight and the streets completely deserted so we found no one to ask which was his house, but it was fun to walk around trying to imagine where they had lived.

After the war Bernard had been very clever and bought a little wood-covered hill. The valley has several of these hills dotted along it and he had obtained permission to bulldoze the top off one and build a house amongst the scrub oaks. It was a lovely spot with incredible views, but thankfully when it was completed the authorities realised that if any more such houses were built it would ruin the look of the countryside so banned anyone else doing the same thing to the other hills. It was too late to do anything about Bernard's house; so he and Dea kept their fabulous view. There was one drawback to the house, it was in the eye of the Mistral, which of course was the reason that nobody had ever built on the hilltops in the first place!

The woods around the house were laced with narrow paths that wandered this way and that between the scrub oaks. It was fun to explore these paths and one day we chanced upon a salamander. It was the fire variety with beautiful egg-yolk-yellow spots on its pitch-black eight inch long body. We had never seen one before and were fascinated. To think that they have the ability of being able to grow a whole new leg if it is bitten off is quite incredible and must be one of the miracles of nature.

We stayed several times with the Sterners on our way back from the foundry and every time we arrived they would insist on my showing them what I had in the back of the car. They ended up buying four maquettes and two museum-size sculptures over the next few years.

'Creation' floating over Menerbe

So ended the wonderful adventure of my working with the finest Tapestry Atelier in Aubusson. Meeting Madame Suzanne and her husband had been an incredible chance experience and their kindness to me was beyond comprehension. They were two of the gentlest people I have ever met. I was fortunate to have known them and I shall never be able to thank the chef of the Hôtel de France enough for arranging for us to visit the atelier. It had been another lucky day for me leading to another great friendship.

430

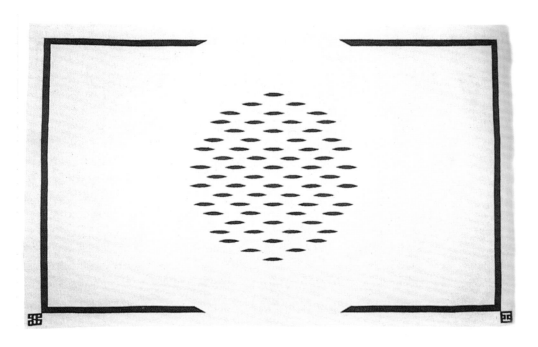

'Tribe'
As a shoal of fish

The Aubusson Tapestries now hang in the Houses of Parliament in Canberra and the offices of both Peat Marwick and North Broken Hill in Melbourne. A complete set hangs in Dr John Miller's Centre for Computational Biology, a department of the Montana State University.

A set was bought by C T Bowring and Co and hung in their new offices by the Tower of London. This was an in-house purchase by my step-brother, Peter Bowring, who was then chairman of the company!

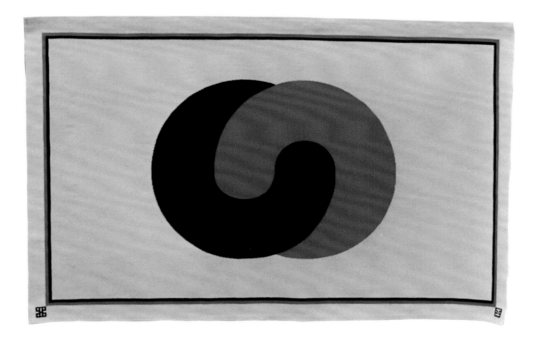

'Bonds of Friendship'

431

But now I must write about my friend, Ron Beaver. Our chance meeting in Wells Cathedral played such an important part in my life it is fitting that I should start *Volume II* with his story, *because he changed my life from top to bottom.*

'The Acrobats', Canberra

THUMBNAIL IMAGE INDEX

3	Yellow Roses	109	Crocodile lunch	196	*Uncle Joe Palmer*
5	*Hula Hula Girl*	110	Andreas and Katharina	197	Big House, Chute
7	Shearing shed	111	Katharina painting	198	Castle Cary prison
8	*Tim* clay UK	111	Munich Museum	201	Marwood Hill House
9	*Mother and Children*	112	Unambal Aborigines	201	Marwood Barn
13	Nan Robinson	115	Cattle mustering	202	Dr Jimmy Smart
14	John and Father	116	Drover Clancy	203	North Devon
15	Nan and John	117	Drover John	204	'Energy', Hyde Park
17	John, aged three	118	Cattle droving	205	Last swim, Portsea
19	WS, *The Age*	119	Derby prison	206	First snow, Devon
21	Bill, Peg and Charlotte	121	John, aged 20	206	Marwood roses
22	Peg and Bill	130	Ninety Mile Desert	206	Marwood Hill
23	Gertrude	140	Chute	207	Snow-blocked lanes
24	Nana, Mike and John	142	Helen, Margie, aged two	208	Sledging
25	*Captain Marvel*	143	Little Grey Men	209	Snowman
26	Mike, John and Pat	145	Tramp and Lady	210	Peter, Mark and Tim
27	John in kilt	146	Margie engagement	211	The *Marble Player*
30	Portsea cottage	148	Chute wall and garden	214	*Tim*, cold bronze
30	Shelly Beach	148	Chute Homestead	215	Françoise Picasso
31	John, aged six	149	*Shearing the Rams*	216	*Françoise and Claude*
32	Certificate of Discharge	150	Bride and bridesmaids	217	Mac Mancini
34	Account of Wages	151	Margie, Ken, Helen	217	*Mother and Children*
34	Dorothy, Bottle Cottage	152	Signing the Register	218	Roy Wakeford
37	Chute Farm House	152	Married	219	*Françoise and Claude*
38	Hatchet Inn	153	"Concentrate!"	220	*Mother and Children*
38	Nan's mobile canteen	156	Red Bull, Xmas	223	*Birth of Adam*
41	*Harvest*	157	Aerial view of Chute	224	*Lovers*
42	*Threshing*	158	First rams	224	*Pain*
43	Bluebell wood	160	Tim at four months	225	*Christ*
44	Milking time	161	Four generations	225	*Nunc dimittis*
48	WS	161	Tim, Ken, Helen, Margie	226	*Peace* clay
49	Laura Knight	162	Bill and Tim	226	*Peace* cold bronze
50	Nan and Bill skiing	163	Gamma and Tim	227	*The Awakening*
51	Nan and Bill	163	The Boss	228	Roy Wakeford
52	*Gare Saint-Lazare*, Monet	164	Tim and Margie	229	Roy moulding
58	Michell House	164	Margie drafting sheep	229	*Story Time*
60	Dormitory	165	Peter at two months	230	Water fight
61	Rugby School	166	Spike Milligan and Peter	230	*Water Fight* bronze
63	*Hula Hula Girl*	167	Heido and Ken	231	*Water Babies*
67	Michell Reunion	168	Peter, Tim and John	232	*Great Dane and Boy*
70	*Santa Maria*, Madeira	170	Peter's bath	233	Marwood Gardens
71	Sunderland Flying Boat	171	Margie with boys	234	*Françoise and Claude*
72	Jacko and Nan	172	Building extension	235	Enzo Plazzotta
74	Reid's, Madeira	173	Mark at two months	236	*Dancers I* first wax
77	*Port Napier*	174	Three boys	237	*Mark* first bronze
78	Cadet officers and John	175	John and Peter	238	*Leonardo's Horse*
80	SS *Gt Britain*	176	Chute pool	239	*Prometheus* wax
81	Gt-grandfather and WS	178	Yellow Tail	239	*Prometheus* bronze
83	John, gold miner	178	Portsea cousins	240	*Dancers II*
86	Roseworthy College	180	Kitchen window	241	*Hammer Thrower*
91	Professor Hedley Marston	181	Last photo of Bill	244	*H-T*, London
99	GoGo Station	182	Slate patio	245	*Waterfall Children*
100	John, Police Patrol	184	Robe Beach	247	*Miner* maquette
102	Kimberley Trek	188	*Pulse*	248	*Shot Put*
103	Waterhole	189	Carving at teatime	250	*Pathfinder*
104	Jump Ups	190	First clay sculpture	252	*Hera's Cuckoo*
105	Gibb River Station	191	First commissions	253	*Acrobats* maquette
106	Wandjina Site	191	First plaster heads	255	Greek tile
107	Katharina Lommel	192	*Mark*, first figure	256	Greek judge
107	Wandjina serpent and girl	195	Passport photo	257	Parthenon

257 Acropolis
258 Acropolis
258 Temple of Zeus
259 Margie and Socrates
259 *Boy Jockey*
260 Pandora
261 Knossos Throne
262 Knossos Dolphins
262 Minotaur Bull
263 Priestess
265 Lindos oranges
266 Corinth Canal
267 Lion Gate, Mycenae
268 Agamemnon Mask
268 Gold Grave Cup
269 Epidaurus
270 Delphi
271 *Charioteer of Delphi*
272 Meteora
274 Cycladic Thinker
275 *Acrobats*
276 *Flute Player*
277 Barnstaple Trio
278 *Acrobats*, 16 foot
279 *Caroline Thorpe*
281 *Mr Banbury* clay
284 *Bird of Spring*
285 *Otter Cubs*
286 Exercise
287 *Mr Banbury* bronze
288 Nana first Xmas
290 Agecroft
291 Araganui, 1972
291 Beach sculpture
292 Araganui spume
292 Rubbish burial
293 *Leapfrog* maquette
294 *Leapfrog* bronze RA
295 *Pillow Fight* maquette
296 *Pillow Fight* bronze
298 Philip de Laszlo
299 *Le Corsair* maquette
300 *Le Corsair* bronze
301 Agecroft
302 Koalas in orchard
302 Aerial view of Agecroft
303 Peter and Lassie
304 Orchard camping
304 Lassie
305 Summertime
306 *Fred with Bird*
307 *Squirrel Children*
307 *Jigsaw Puzzle*
308 *Girl with Puppy*
309 *Flute Player II*
310 *Genevieve*
310 *Genevieve* head
311 *James and Puppy*
311 *Umbrella Children*
312 *Roller Skaters*
313 Posing for camera

313 Crowthers, Syon Lodge
314 *Ravine Children*
315 *Boy with parrots*
315 *Jill*
316 Watts Towers, LA
316 Watts Towers, LA
318 Peter Arno cartoon
319 *Erica* clay
320 *Erica and Children*
321 Lilly
321 *Lilly*
321 John and Lilly
322 *Horse* plasticine
323 *Horse and Joshua*
325 *Rodin* by Chini
326 Danaide marble
327 *Goanna boot puller*
328 Hadrian's Wall
329 *Shorthorn Bull*
330 Niagara Falls
331 Studio, Agecroft
333 Olmec Wrestler
334 The Drummer
334 The Teacher
334 The Oracle
334 The Supplicant
335 *Mother and Child*
336 Picasso
336 *Settignano* glass
337 Tuareg Mother and Child
338 Hobe Sound, Miami
339 *Ronald Reagan*
341 *President Reagan*
340 *Pathfinder*
341 *Acrobats*, Bath
342 *Le Corsair*, Seattle
343 *Modigliani* paintings
344 Swiss Family Robinson
345 Samos
346 Kokari village
347 Swallows Taverna
348 Judy and Michael
350 Scotland tents
350 Grand Traverse
351 Margie on GTA
352 Duke filming
352 Mark in the Alps
353 Peter and Tim
353 Margie and Judith
354 Lightweight sack
360 *Hoshi*, 63-foot schooner
361 Margie and Peter
362 Brigantine *Surry*
363 *Surry*, Rat Island
364 *Rubber Duck* and crew
364 Crummock Water
366 HM the Queen Mother
367 HM the QM and *clay bust*
369 HM Elizabeth II
371 *HM EII* bronzes
371 Grand Saint Bernard Pass

373 *Bonds of Friendship*
375 Unveiling, Portsmouth
376 Sallyport unveiling
378 *Papageno* maquettes
378 *Papageno* clay
378 *Papageno* and Roy
379 Glyndebourne
380 *Flying Horse* maquette
381 *Flying Horse* bronze
383 *Adagio* maquette
385 Enzo Plazzotta nude
386 Pietrasanta olive grove
387 Forte dei Marmi Beach
387 Monte Altissimo quarry
388 Portofino
389 Birthday acrobats
391 *Ombra della Sera*
391 Brancusi *Kiss*
391 Judea *Kiss*
392 Zucchi, 1540
392 Matisse, *Joy of Life*
393 Paestum Temple
394 Pantheon, Rome
395 Pantheon inside
396 Charlemagne's throne
397 Sistine Chapel
397 *Spark of Life* glass
399 North Cadbury church
400 *Heaven* and *Hell* with *Christ*
401 *Spark of Life* painted steel
402 Michelangelo *Slave*
404 *Pietà Rondanini*, Milan
406 Uffizi Museum ceiling
4 07 Luca della Robbia
408 *Luca della Robbia* glass tile
408 *River Arno at night* paper
410 Venice, Grand Canal
411 Turner: *Santa Maggiore*
412 *Joan of Arc* bronze
413 Venice painting
416 *The Unicorn*, New York
417 Dom Robert, Aubusson
419 *Tranquillity* tapestry
419 *Trust* tapestry
420 *The Universe*, Mariani
421 *The Universe*, Melbourne
422 *Love Union* tapestry
422 *Spring* tapestry
422 *Autumn* tapestry
423 *Time* tapestry
424 *Summer* tapestry
424 *Water Planet* tapestry
425 Chapter House, Wells
425 *Winter* tapestry
426 Wells Cathedral
427 *Apostles' Heads* stone
428 *Galaxies* tapestry
428 *Beyond Light* tapestry
430 *Creation* bronze
431 *Tribe* tapestry
431 *Bonds of Friendship* tapestry
432 *Acrobats* bronze, Canberra

434

THUMBNAIL PHOTOGRAPHS with PAGE NUMBERS

3   5   7   8   9

13   14   15   17   19

20   21   22   23

24   25   26   27   30

30   31   32   33

34   37   38   39

41   42   43   44

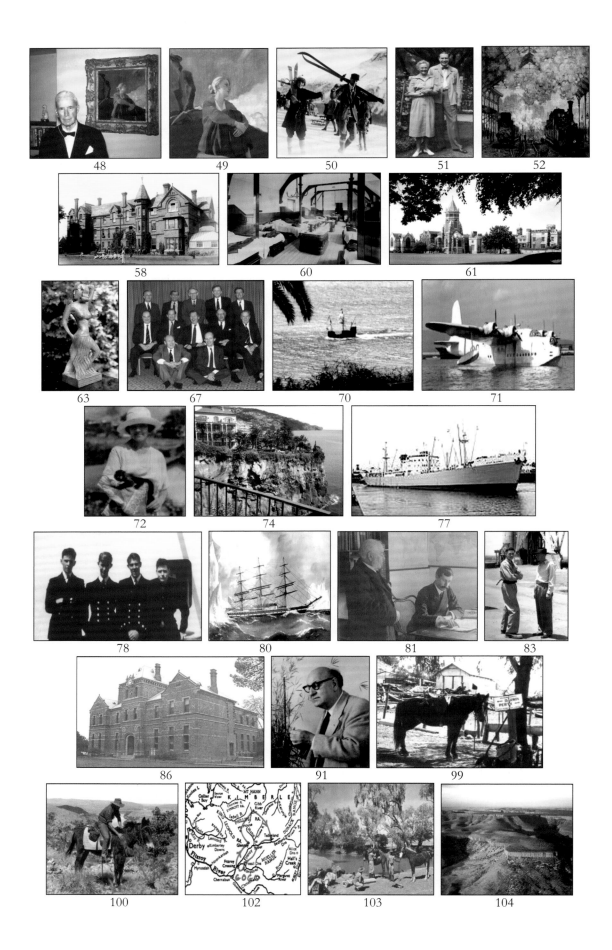

48

49

50

51

52

58

60

61

63

67

70

71

72

74

77

78

80

81

83

86

91

99

100

102

103

104

105   106   107   107   109

110   111   111   112

115   116   117   118

119   121   131   140

142   143   145   146

148   148   149

150   151   152   152

153

156

157

158

160

161

161

162

163

163

164

164

165

166

167

168

170

171

172

173

174

175

176

178

178

438

180   181   182   184

187   189   189

190   190   191

195 196   197   198

201   201   202

203   204   205

206   206   206

207

208

209

210

211

214

215

216

217

217

218

219

220

223

224

224

225

225

226

226

227

228

229

229

230

230

231

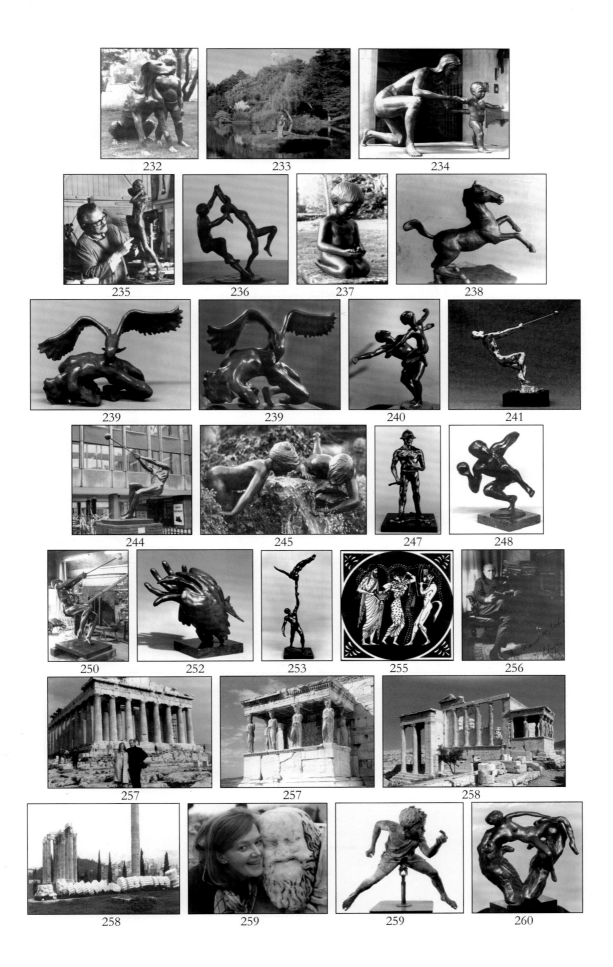

232

233

234

235

236

237

238

239

239

240

241

244

245

247

248

250

252

253

255

256

257

257

258

258

259

259

260

441

261   262   262   263   265

266   267   268   268   269

270   271   272   274   275

276   277   278   279   281

287   285   286   287

288   290   291

291   292   292

293

294

295

296

398

299

300

301

302

302

303

304

304

305

306

307

307

308

309

310

310

311

311

312

313

313

314

443

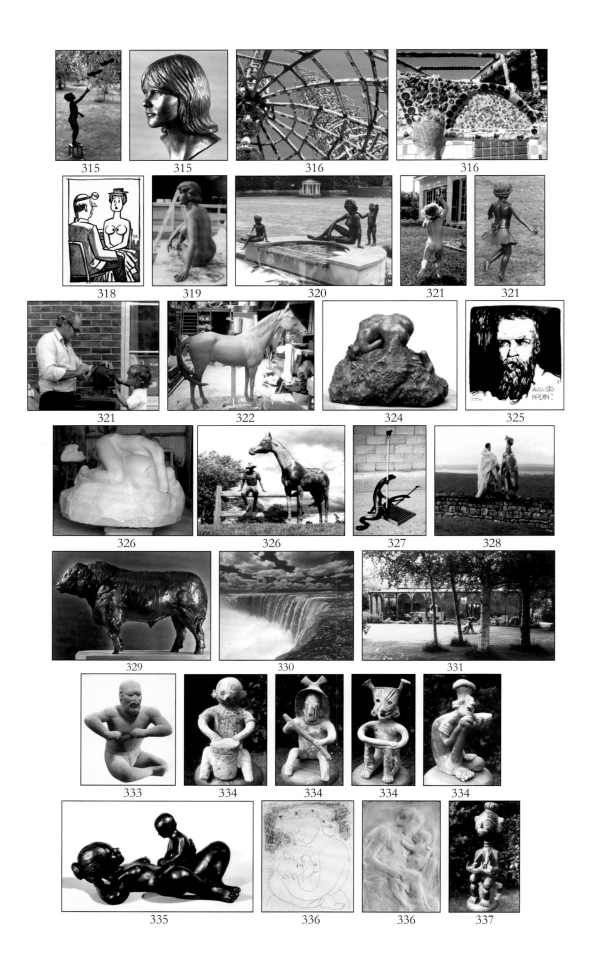

315   315   316   316

318   319   320   321   321

321   322   324   325

326   326   327   328

329   330   331

333   334   334   334   334

335   336   336   337

338   339   341   341

341   341   343   344

345   346   347   348

350   350   351   352

352   353   353   354

360   361   362

363   364   364

366

367

369

371

371

373

375

379

378

378

378

379

380

381

383

385

386

387

387

388

389

391

392

392

391

391

393

394

395

396 397 397

399 400 401

402 404 406 407 408 408

410 411 412

413 416 417

419 419 420 421

422 422 422 423

447

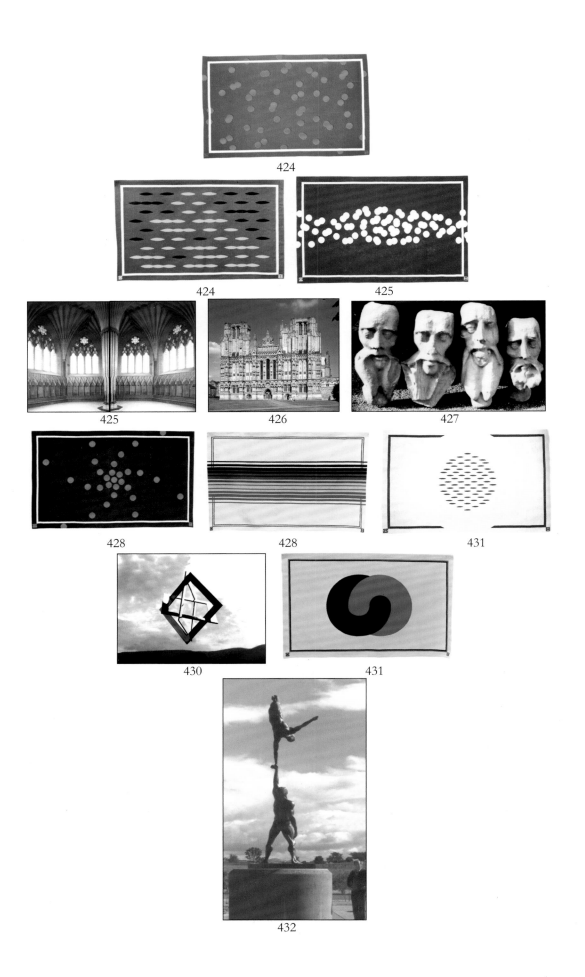

424

424 425

425 426 427

428 428 431

430 431

432

448